THE SHORT
PROSE READER

THE SHORT PROSE READER

SEVENTH EDITION

Gilbert H. Muller
The City University of New York
LaGuardia

Harvey S. Wiener
Adelphi University

McGraw-Hill, Inc.
New York   St. Louis   San Francisco   Auckland   Bogotá
Caracas   Lisbon   London   Madrid   Mexico City
Milan   Montreal   New Delhi   San Juan   Singapore
Sydney   Tokyo   Toronto

This book was set in Century Schoolbook by The Clarinda Company.
The editors were Alison Husting Zetterquist, Laurie PiSierra,
and David Dunham; the production supervisor was Paula Keller.
The cover was designed by A Good Thing, Inc.
R..R. Donnelley & Sons Company was printer and binder.

THE SHORT PROSE READER

Acknowledgments appear on pages 457–461, and on this page by reference.

 This book is printed on recycled, acid-free paper containing
10% postconsumer waste.

2   3   4   5   6   7   8   9   0   DOC   DOC   9   0   9   8   7   6   5   4

ISBN 0-07-044249-5

Library of Congress Cataloging-in-Publication Data

The Short prose reader / {compiled by} Gilbert H. Muller, Harvey S.
    Wiener,—7th ed.
        p.   cm.
    ISBN 0-07-044249-5
    1. College readers.   2. English language—Rhetoric.   I. Muller,
Gilbert H., (date).   II. Wiener, Harvey S.
PE1417.S446   1994
808' .0427—dc20   93-29710

ABOUT THE AUTHORS

Gilbert H. Muller, who received a Ph.D. in English and American Literature from Stanford University, is currently professor of English and Special Assistant to the President at LaGuardia Community College of the City University of New York and adjunct professor at the Graduate Center. He has also taught at Stanford, Vassar, and several universities overseas. Dr. Muller is the author of the award-winning study *Nightmares and Visions: Flannery O'Connor and the Catholic Grotesque, Chester Himes,* and other critical texts. His essays and reviews have appeared in *The New York Times, The New Republic, The Nation, The Sewanee Review, The Georgia Review,* and elsewhere. He is also a noted author and editor of textbooks in English and composition, including *The McGraw-Hill Reader* and, with John Williams, *The McGraw-Hill Introduction to Literature.* Among Dr. Muller's awards are National Endowment for the Humanities Fellowships, a Fulbright Fellowship, and a Mellon Fellowship.

Harvey S. Wiener, Vice President for Academic Affairs at Adelphi University, codirects the National Testing Network in Writing (NTNW). Previously University Associate Dean for Academic Affairs, the City University of New York, he was founding president of the Council of Writing Program Administrators. Dr. Wiener is the author of many books on reading and writing for college students and their teachers, including *The Writing Room* (Oxford, 1981). He is coauthor of *The McGraw-Hill College Handbook,* a reference grammar and rhetoric text. Dr. Wiener is a member of the Standing Committee on Assessment for the National Council of Teachers of

English, and has chaired the Teaching of Writing Division of the Modern Language Association (1987). He has taught writing at every level of education from elementary school to graduate school. A Phi Beta Kappa graduate of Brooklyn College, he holds a Ph.D. in Renaissance literature. He currently teaches as an adjunct in the doctoral program at Columbia Teachers College. Dr. Wiener has won grants from the National Endowment for the Humanities, the Fund for the Improvement of Postsecondary Education, and the Exxon Education Foundation.

To the memory of George Groman

CONTENTS

CHAPTER 1

On Writing   1

William Saroyan   *Why I Write*   6

A Pulitzer Prize–winning author explains how his determination "to understand the meaning of his own life" led him to live "in a special way" since the age of nine.

Amy Tan   *Mother Tongue*   13

Chinese-American novelist Amy Tan explains how her writing style achieved both passion and simplicity when she learned to value the criticism of her mother, who said after reading her daughter's novel, "So easy to read."

William Stafford   *Writing*   24

William Stafford offers his "process-rather-than-substance view of writing," in which we must be willing to fail, cannot bother to insist on high standards, and will often be baffled about what "skill" has to do with it.

William Zinsser   *Simplicity*   32

According to this writer-teacher, "clutter is the disease of American writing." We must simplify. In this essay, Zinsser connects clear writing to clear thinking, which, he declares, doesn't appear nearly enough these days.

Summing Up: Chapter 1   **41**

CHAPTER 2

CHAPTER 3

before me," writes an environmentalist of her often spiritual journey to find the source of a river.

CHAPTER 4

In a narrative of her youth, a writer remembers her efforts to obtain "a cultural divorce" from the heritage into which she was born.

One of America's foremost poets tells of his childhood disillusionment as he struggled desperately to see Jesus.

The perils and discoveries of being a modern father are humorously narrated by Native American writer Michael Dorris as he travels through a New England winter storm to get his daughters a special present.

The renowned author of 1984 discovers how precious human life is as he tells of witnessing an execution in Burma. "It is curious," he recalls, "but 'til that moment, I had never realized what it meant to destroy a healthy, conscious man."

CHAPTER 5

Here from the noted science fiction writer is the wonder of Halloween, 1928, with all its gorilla fangs, pumpkin pies, creaking stairs, black confetti, banshee trains, and much more.

An "avid night walker" explains how his seemingly innocent habit has turned him into "an accomplice in tyranny."

Through an accumulation of comic inventions, highlighted by the "too-

CHAPTER 8

CHAPTER 9

CHAPTER 10

CHAPTER 11

CHAPTER 12

ALTERNATE THEMATIC CONTENTS

Childhood and Family

Social Problems and Issues

Men and Women Today

The Minority Experience

City and Country

Sports, Travel, and Leisure

Psychology and Behavior

Science, Technology, and Medicine

Language and Thought

Humor and Satire

PREFACE

The seventh edition of *The Short Prose Reader* maintains the best features of the earlier editions: lively reading selections supported by helpful apparatus to integrate reading and writing in college composition and reading courses. Each of the twelve chapters presents an essential pattern of writing. The student progresses from basic description and narration through the more rigorous forms of analysis and argument by means of diverse and lively prose models suited for discussion, analysis, and imitation.

While maintaining the organization of previous editions, this new version of *The Short Prose Reader* features many new reading selections by women, African Americans, and writers with immigrant backgrounds. Students will find engaging essays on issues of gender, race, and class by such women as Gloria Naylor, Alice Walker, Mary Mebane, Amy Tan, Anna Quindlen, and Maxine Hong Kingston. Patricia Volk and Ellen Tashie Frisinia recall the perils and inspirations of immigrant ancestry. Also new are essays by Robert Ragaini and Michael Dorris exploring the nature of manhood and fatherhood in the nineties, as well as explorations of our changing culture, such as Pico Iyer's meditation on California and Jeannine Stein's piece on punk.

These new readings on multiculturalism are balanced with some favorites from the earlier editions of *The Short Prose Reader.* Russell Baker returns with a new selection instructing us how to carve a turkey, while Malcolm X's "Prison Studies," William Least Heat Moon's "Arizona 87," Jonathon Kozol's "Are The Homeless Crazy?", and Judy Brady's "I Want a Wife" continue to offer timely and controversial subjects for reading and writing.

The organization of *The Short Prose Reader* is one of its major strengths. Chapter 1, "On Writing," is followed by a chapter offering four unique views on the craft of reading by well-known authors.

Each of the following nine chapters contains four short essays that illustrate clearly a specific pattern or technique—description, narration, illustration, comparison and contrast, definition, classification, process analysis, causal analysis, or argumentation. Students learn to build upon earlier techniques and patterns as they progress through the book. The last chapter, consisting of eleven essays, offers students the opportunity to read and discuss short prose pieces that reflect the various rhetorical strategies.

This is a readable text, and one that has ample representation by many different types of writers. Moreover, the essays, which range typically between 300 and 1,200 words, achieve their goals succinctly and clearly and are easy to read and to understand. The essays will alert students both to the types of college writing expected of them and to the length of an essay required frequently by teachers. The detailed questions that follow each essay can be used in reading as well as writing classes, since they ask the student to analyze both the content and the form of the prose selections.

Finally, the exercises we have included for each essay are comprehensive and integrated—designed to develop and reinforce the key skills required in college writing. Each section includes two vocabulary exercises. "Words to Watch" alerts students to words they will read in context, and "Building Vocabulary" uses other effective methods (prefix/suffix, context clues, synonym/antonym, abstract/concrete) of teaching vocabulary. A section called "Understanding the Writer's Ideas" reinforces reading comprehension. Sections entitled "Understanding the Writer's Techniques" and "Exploring the Writer's Ideas" provide excellent bases for class discussion and independent reading and analysis. The last exercise for each essay involves a dynamic approach to writing projects. Guided writing activities—a novel feature of *The Short Prose Reader*—tie the writing project to the reading selections. Instead of simply being told to write an essay on a certain topic, students through "Guided Writing" will be able to move from step to step in the process of composition. At the end of each chapter we provide a Summing Up section, a means for students to focus their attention on comparative issues and more writing topics.

The Short Prose Reader can be used flexibly and effectively by students and teachers alike. An alternate table of contents suggests thematic groupings of readings. The text is simple yet sophisticated, inviting students to engage in a multiplicity of cultural and traditional topics through essays and exercises that are easy to follow but never condescending. Weighing the needs and expectations of today's college freshmen, we have designed a rhetoric reader that can serve as the major text for the composition course.

We wish to thank our colleagues across the country for their support and are especially grateful to those who read the manuscript for this and previous editions: Judith Branzburg, Pasadena City College; Dan Gallagher, Laredo Junior College; Joyce Jenkins, Fort Valley State College; William Knox, Northern Michigan College; Valden Madsen, Brooklyn College; Inez Martinez, Kingsborough Community College; Billie Theriot, Southeastern Louisiana State University; and Barbara Truesdell, Purdue University.

Gilbert H. Muller

Harvey S. Wiener

THE SHORT
PROSE READER

CHAPTER 1

On Writing

WHAT IS WRITING?

Writing helps us to record and communicate ideas. It is a definitive and essential part of daily human experience. Whether we write a shopping list or a great novel, we use a tool without which we would find ourselves isolated. Without writing we cut ourselves off from vital processes like the expression of political opinions, the description of medical emergencies, the examination of our feelings in diaries and letters.

Writing crosses many cultures. Whether we consider historic cave drawings or the transmission of fax messages during the Chinese rebellion in Tienamen Square, we find evidence of the human instinct to communicate ideas to other people.

In the past, writing brought about change. African-American slaves were frequently forbidden to learn to read or write, but some managed to find ways to gain literacy anyway. Their narratives of slave life helped fire the abolition movement. Women in the nineteenth century used writing to advance the cause of suffrage, winning votes with passionate speeches and articles in newspapers. Immigrants struggled to learn English in order to find a better life in the New World.

Writing celebrates human achievement. In religion, in love, in wartime and in peace, in astronomy and medicine and archaeology, in the arts and humanities, writing reminds us of our shared human identity. From the Song of Solomon in the Bible to the words of Martin Luther King, Jr.'s "I Have a Dream," from the Declaration of Independence to song lyrics by Bruce

Springsteen or Ice-T, writing helps us come to terms with who we are and what we want.

What is writing, exactly? For most of us, writing is so familiar that the question seems silly. We all know what writing is. Yet when we try to write ourselves, we may find that asking and answering the question is vital.

Writing is both a product and a process. Writing is, of course, *what* we write: a letter, a law brief, a term paper, an inaugural address. Since it is a product, we must think of writing as having a public as well as a private purpose. While some writing, like shopping lists or a diary, may be meant only for our own eyes, most writing is intended for an audience. In learning what writing is, we need to think about who the audience is, and what the purpose of the writing is.

Writing is also a process; it is *how* we write. In learning to write well, we examine the process of transferring ideas from head to hand. We realize that the actual, mechanical practice of writing out ideas helps us to think more carefully, to plan and arrange ideas, to analyze our vague thoughts into solid words on a page.

HOW DO WE WRITE?

The process of writing is not absolute; there is no one sure way to learn to write well. However, there are some common elements in this process that will help anyone getting started as a writer.

Warming Up: Prewriting

Like an athlete, the writer benefits from warm-up exercises. Usually called prewriting, these steps help a writer prepare gradually and thoughtfully for the event of writing a long essay. Writers stretch their intellectual muscles by thinking about a topic before they write about it. They talk to friends and colleagues. They visit a library and flip through reference books, newspapers, magazines, and books. Sometimes, they make notes and lists as a way of putting pen to paper for the first time. Some writers brainstorm: they use free association to jot down ideas as thoroughly as possible in an unedited form. After these preliminary warm-ups, many writers try to group or classify ideas by making a rough outline or drawing boxes or making lists to try to bring some plan or order to their rough ideas.

Once the writer has a rough topic area outlined, he or she may return to the audience and purpose for the essay. Who will read the essay? How will the writer aim the essay sharply at the audience by selecting the best material from the rough notes? How will the writer choose the most appropriate language for the intended audience? What is the purpose of the essay? How can the writer help make writing the essay easier by carving out a clear intent? Often the purpose or intent becomes clearer as the writer continues to think and write. Choosing the audience and purpose carefully makes the writer's as well as the reader's task easier.

First Draft

Prewriting leads to a first draft. Drafts are usually meant for the writer's eyes only; they are messy with rethinking, rewriting, and revision. Drafts help the writer figure out what to write by giving him or her a place to think on paper before having to make a public presentation of the writing. Everyone develops his or her own style of draft writing, but many writers find that double-spacing, leaving wide margins, and writing on only one side of the paper are steps that make rewriting easier. If you can write on a word processor, you'll find you can easily revise and produce several drafts without discarding earlier versions of the essay.

In a first draft, a writer begins to shape paragraphs, to plan where to put each piece of the essay for maximum effect. Sometimes, a first draft doesn't have an introduction. The introduction can be written after the writer has finished the draft and has a better sense of what the essay is about. The audience will see only the final draft, after all, and will never know when the writer wrote the introduction.

Having finished the first draft, the writer tries to become the audience. How will the essay sound to someone else? Does it make sense? Are the ideas and expression clear? Is there a main point? Do all the ideas in the essay relate to this main point? Is there a coherent plan to the essay? Do ideas follow logically one from the next? Would someone unfamiliar with the topic be able to follow the ideas? Would more information be added? What should be left out?

In attempting to answer these questions, writers often try to find a friendly reader to look over the draft and give advice. Whatever else they may look for at this stage, they do not pay too much attention to spelling or grammar. A helpful reader will enable the writer to see the essay as the audience will see it, and suggest ways to reorganize and clarify ideas.

Additional Drafts

After getting responses from a reader, the writer begins the second draft. And the third. And maybe the fourth. No one can predict how many drafts are necessary for a final essay, but very few writers get by with fewer than two or three drafts. Revision usually involves working first on the clear expression of ideas and later on revision for spelling, grammatical correctness, and good sentence structure.

Final Draft

The final draft is intended for public, rather than private, reading. It must be the writer's best effort. Most editors and teachers require final drafts to be double-spaced, neatly written or typed with wide margins, and clearly identified with the writer's name, the date, and information to locate the writer (such as class code or home address).

This brief overview sketches in some of the important steps in the writing process. But you don't want to lose the idea that writing is a process both of inspiration and of craft. Many writers have tried to explain how the two connect in their own particular efforts to create. The novelist and short story writer Katherine Anne Porter, for example, tells how inspiration becomes communication in her writing: "Now and again thousands of memories converge, harmonize, and arrange themselves around a central idea in a coherent form, and I write. . . ." Jean Cocteau, the playwright, asserts the need to shape inspiration into language for a page of writing: "To write, to conquer ink and paper, accumulate letters and paragraphs, divide them with periods and commas, is a different matter from carrying around the dream of a play or a book." The point made by Porter and Cocteau is that writing emerges from both creativity and skill, instruction and technique, talent and effort. As we said, writing is a process *and* craft.

The four writers in this chapter represent a variety of approaches to both the inspiration and the craft of writing. Amy Tan, for instance, finds *her* writer's voice when she realizes that her mother is the ideal audience. Like William Zinsser pleading for the preciseness that comes only with simplicity, Tan advises us to aim for direct and simple language instead of academic jargon or pretentious style. William Saroyan combines personal reminiscence with theories of art, while William Stafford urges paying much more attention to the process than to the product.

The four writers represented here also introduce expository techniques discussed in subsequent chapters. Careful examination of their sources of inspiration *and* their revelations about the nuts and bolts of how to get the writing done prepares the way for later chapters and writing assignments.

Finally, though films and floppy discs may seem to replace the printed page, the basic medium of communication is still words. Whether we scratch them onto stone tablets, draw them on parchment with turkey feathers, or charge them onto computer storage boards, we still use words. Without writing, we risk the loss of our political freedom and our personal history. With words, we pass ideas and values on from one generation to the next. The words of Henry Miller will always ring true: "Writing, like life itself, is a voyage of discovery."

Why I Write

William Saroyan

William Saroyan (1908–1981) won the 1939 Pulitzer Prize for his play *The Time of Your Life.* His novel *The Human Comedy* (1942) is both an ironic and an optimistic look at the human condition. In this essay, Saroyan writes of how tragedy, memory, and art have combined to bring meaning to his life.

Words to Watch

isolated (par. 2)   set apart
vineyards (par. 4)   fields for growing wine grapes
sorrow (par. 5)   sadness
impelled (par. 6)   driven to do something
impulse (par. 7)   sudden inclination prompting action
gradual (par. 10)   by degrees; little by little

1   It is a quarter of a century, almost, since my first book was published, but as I began to write when I was nine, I have been writing for forty years: that is to say, I have lived in a special way for forty years—the way that takes hold of a man who is determined to understand the meaning of his own life, and to be prepared to write about it.

2   But I think it goes even farther back than forty years. I think I began to live in my own special way when I became aware that I had memory. That happened before I was three. I also had a memory that went back to a time before I was *two,* but it was an isolated one. At that age I wasn't given to remembering *everything,* or rather I hadn't yet noticed that it had come to pass that I remembered.

3   In the past were some of the best things I had, several of them gone: my father, for instance, who had died before I was three.

4   My first memory, the one that went back to a time when I was not yet two, was of my father getting up onto a wagon, sitting beside my mother, and making a sound that told the horse to go.

My two sisters and my brother and I sat in the back of the wagon as it moved slowly down a dusty road between vineyards on a hot afternoon in the summertime. I remembered sensing sorrow and feeling *with*—with mine, my people—a father, a mother, two sisters, a brother, our horse, our wagon, our pots and pans and books. The rest is lost in the sleep that soon carried me away. The next thing I knew my father was gone, which I didn't understand.

I was fascinated by having memory, and troubled by the 5 sorrow of it. I refused to accept the theory that things end, including people, including my father. I refused to believe that my father was dead. (In the sense that every man *is* his father, I wasn't much mistaken.)

All the same, I felt impelled from the time I knew I had 6 memory to do something about the past, about endings, about human death.

My first impulse was simple. I wanted to cause the impossi- 7 ble to happen, because if I was able to do that, I knew I would be able to cause *anything* to happen. Thus, death would not be death, if anybody wanted it not to be.

I found two large empty cans. One I filled with water. The 8 empty can I placed two feet from the full can. I asked myself to cause the water in the full can to pass into the empty can, by itself, because I wanted it to.

The experiment failed. I had begun with the maximum, I 9 had failed, and so I began to consider what might be the next best.

For a long time there didn't appear to be *any* next best at 10 all. It was a matter of all or nothing, or at any rate the equivalent of nothing: continuous *gradual* loss, and finally total loss, or death.

What could a man do about this? Wait? That didn't seem to 11 be enough.

Why should I be troubled by memory at all if all memory 12 told me was that things change, fail, decline, end, and die? I didn't want good things to do that, and I didn't think they should. How could I seize a good thing when I saw it and halt its decline and death? As far as people were concerned, there just didn't seem to be *any* way.

And so I came to accept the theory that as far as I knew, as 13 far as *anybody* knew, as far as there appeared to be any order to the action of things at all, the end of the order was invariably and inevitably decline, disappearance, and death.

14   And yet the world was full of people all the time. And the earth, the sea, and the sky were full of all manner of other living things: plants, animals, fish, birds.

15   Thus, something *did* stay, something *was* constant, or appeared to be. It was the *kind* that stayed. *One* of a kind couldn't stay, and couldn't apparently be made to. I myself was one of a kind, and everybody I knew and loved was one of a kind, and so what about us? What could I do about our impermanence?

16   How could I halt this action? How had other men halted it?

17   I learned that they never had halted it. They had only pretended to.

18   They had done this by means of art, or the putting of limits upon the limitless, and thereby holding something fast and making it seem constant, indestructible, unstoppable, unkillable, deathless.

19   A great painter painted his wife, his son, his daughter, and himself, and then one by one they all moved along and died. But the painting remained. A sculptor did the same thing with stone, a composer with musical sounds, and a writer with words.

20   Therefore, as the next best thing, art in one form or another would have to be the way of my life, but which form of art?

21   Before I was eight I didn't think it could possibly be writing, for the simple reason that I couldn't read, let alone write, and everybody else I knew could do both. At last, though, I got the hang of reading and writing, and I felt (if I didn't think), "This is for me."

22   It had taken me so long to learn to write that I considered being able to write the greatest thing that could happen to anybody.

23   If I wrote something, it *was* written, it was itself, and it might continue to be itself forever, or for what passes as forever.

24   Thus, I could halt the action of things, after all, and at the same time be prepared to learn new things, to achieve new forms of halting, or art.

25   That is roughly how and why I became a writer.

26   In short, I began to write in order to get even on death.

27   I have continued to write for many reasons.

A long time ago I said I write because it is the only way I   28
am willing to survive.

Mainly, though, I write because I want to.   29

BUILDING VOCABULARY

1. The words below from the essay contain *prefixes* and *suffixes* (see
    Glossary) that can help you determine the meanings of the words
    themselves. For each word define the prefix or suffix in italics
    and then define the word.
    a. *de*cline (par. 12)
    b. *in*vari*ably* (par. 13)
    c. *in*evit*ably* (par. 13)
    d. *dis*appear*ance* (par. 13)
    e. *im*permanence (par. 15)
    f. limit*less* (par. 18)
    g. *in*destruct*ible* (par. 18)
    h. *un*stopp*able* (par. 18)
    i. *un*kill*able* (par. 18)
    j. death*less* (par. 18)
2. Write the *antonyms* (opposite meanings) for any five of the words
    in the exercise above. Then, use each antonym in an original sen-
    tence.

UNDERSTANDING THE WRITER'S IDEAS

1. How old is Saroyan at the time of writing this essay? How do
    you know?
2. In your own words, describe the "special way" in which Saroyan
    has lived? When did this "special way" of living begin for the au-
    thor?
3. From what age does Saroyan remember his first memory? Sum-
    marize the memory in your own words. What is the importance
    of memory for this writer?
4. In what sort of environment did Saroyan live as a child?
5. How was Saroyan affected by his father's death? Explain the

meaning of the parenthetical sentence: "(In the sense that every man *is* his father, I wasn't much mistaken)" (par. 5).

6. In paragraph 7, Saroyan writes, "I wanted to cause the impossible to happen." Why? How did this desire relate to his father's death? How did he go about trying to cause the impossible? Did he succeed?

7. What *definition* does Saroyan offer of "art"? Why did he choose art as a way of life? What relationship did this choice have to memory? To his father's death? How did he come to choose writing among all the arts?

8. The title may be read in two ways: (a) why Saroyan *started* to write, and (b) why he *continues* to write. Which seems predominant? Why? Cite the author's own reasons for both (a) and (b).

UNDERSTANDING THE WRITER'S TECHNIQUES

1. Is there a *thesis statement* (see Glossary) in this essay? Explain. Describe Saroyan's purpose for writing this essay. Who is his intended audience? Explain.

2. *Tone* (see Glossary) refers to the writer's attitude or stance toward his or her subject and is expressed in the word choices, rhythms, and overall "voice" of a piece of writing. How would you describe the tone of this essay? Point to three places in the essay that are particularly expressive of the tone.

3. What was your emotional response to reading the first paragraph of this essay? Explain what it was about Saroyan's writing that made you feel that way.

4. What idea is repeated in paragraphs 1 and 2? Why? For what effect?

5. A *process analysis* (see Chapter 9) tells the reader step by step how to do something. Trace the steps whereby Saroyan dealt with his father's death.

6. Paragraph 18 (just one sentence long) contains at least five words built from prefix, root, suffix combinations. What is the cumulative effect of all these words? Why do you think Saroyan has used them here?

7. Throughout this essay, Saroyan makes liberal use of italics. For

what reason does he use them? Which uses are most effective?
Are there any which you feel are unnecessary? Why?

8. This essay is composed of a series of relatively short paragraphs, some only one or two sentences long. What is the effect
of this type of writing? Do you feel any choppiness or incom-
pleteness? Why or why not?

9. Throughout the essay, the author asks a number of questions, especially in paragraphs 15 and 16. What is his purpose in asking
these questions? To whom are they addressed? What effect do
they create?

10. Do you think the title is meant as a question or as a statement?
Explain your answer in the context of the essay.

EXPLORING THE WRITER'S IDEAS

1. What is your earliest memory? How old were you? What lasting
effect has the memory had on you?

2. Compare the environment in which Saroyan lived with your own
childhood surroundings.

3. Was Saroyan's reaction to his father's death typical? How does it
compare with the way in which you have had to handle the loss
of a loved one?

4. Have any of the arts given you the sort of consolation or life direction that they provided for Saroyan? For example, at a time of
stress or sadness, has anything in music, literature, or the visual
arts ever changed your mood? Do you practice any art form, either professionally or as a hobby? If so, explain why you do it
and how it makes you feel.

IDEAS FOR WRITING

Guided Writing

Write an essay entitled "Why I _____." Fill in
the blank with an activity that is very important to you, that you
believe will remain so throughout your life, and that reflects your
creative talents. For example, you might want to write about

"Why I Paint," "Why I Play the Piano," or "Why I Cook"—or, if you prefer, "Why I Write."

1. Begin with a statement of why and for how long this activity has been important to you.
2. Dig deeply into your memory to relate an early memory that is tied to your choice to pursue this activity.
3. Tell about a particular incident or person that especially affected your choice of this activity.
4. Relate the process whereby you chose this "special way of living."
5. Throughout your essay use questions to help your reader understand your thought processes as you developed this way of life.
6. Write in a simple, direct way, using mainly very short paragraphs.
7. Try to maintain an emotionally charged, serious tone.
8. End your essay with a series of quick, direct statements, the last of which should relate positively to your future in this activity.

More Writing Projects

1. Start a journal for the term. In your first entry, record some of your earliest memories of various creative acts—for instance, writing out letters of the alphabet, toying with a musical instrument, playing with crayons and paint, and so forth. Try to capture the original sensations.
2. Summarize the main ideas presented by Saroyan in a paragraph of no more than 100 words. Then write another paragraph condensing the summary to 50 words.
3. Write a brief essay on what Saroyan calls the "fascination" and "sorrow" of memory.

Mother Tongue
Amy Tan

Amy Tan is a novelist and essayist who was born in California only two and a half years after her parents emigrated to the United States. Her first novel, *The Joy Luck Club* (1989), was extremely popular, and was followed by *The Kitchen God's Wife* (1991). Speaking and writing in standard English is essential, Tan argues, but the diversity of cultures in America requires that we acknowledge the different "Englishes" spoken by immigrants. As you read her essay, think about your own experience in learning English, and how you respond to the other Englishes you may have heard spoken by your family or neighbors. Consider why Tan chooses to write in standard English.

Words to Watch

intersection (par. 3)   crossroad

wrought (par. 3)   made; worked

belies (par. 7)   misrepresents; disguises

wince (par. 8)   cringe; shrink

empirical (par. 9)   relying on observation

guise (par. 10)   outward appearance

benign (par. 14)   not harmful

insular (par. 15)   like an island; isolated

I AM NOT a scholar of English or literature. I cannot give you 1 much more than personal opinions on the English language and its variations in this country or others.

I am a writer. And by that definition, I am someone who 2 has always loved language. I am fascinated by language in daily life. I spend a great deal of my time thinking about the power of language—the way it can evoke an emotion, a visual image, a complex idea, or a simple truth. Language is the tool of my trade. And I use them all—all the Englishes I grew up with.

Recently, I was made keenly aware of the different English- 3 es I do use. I was giving a talk to a large group of people, the same talk I had already given to half a dozen other groups. The nature of the talk was about my writing, my life, and my book,

The Joy Luck Club. The talk was going along well enough, until I remembered one major difference that made the whole talk sound wrong. My mother was in the room. And it was perhaps the first time she had heard me give a lengthy speech, using the kind of English I have never used with her. I was saying things like, "The intersection of memory upon imagination" and "There is an aspect of my fiction that relates to thus-and-thus"—a speech filled with carefully wrought grammatical phrases, burdened, it suddenly seemed to me, with nominalized forms, past perfect tenses, conditional phrases, all the forms of standard English that I had learned in school and through books, the forms of English I did not use at home with my mother.

4   Just last week, I was walking down the street with my mother, and I again found myself conscious of the English I was using, the English I do use with her. We were talking about the price of new and used furniture and I heard myself saying this: "Not waste money that way." My husband was with us as well, and he didn't notice any switch in my English. And then I realized why. It's because over the twenty years we've been together I've often used that same kind of English with him, and sometimes he even uses it with me. It has become our language of intimacy, a different sort of English that relates to family talk, the language I grew up with.

5   So you'll have some idea of what this family talk I heard sounds like, I'll quote what my mother said during a recent conversation which I videotaped and then transcribed. During this conversation, my mother was talking about a political gangster in Shanghai who had the same last name as her family's, Du, and how the gangster in his early years wanted to be adopted by her family, which was rich by comparison. Later, the gangster became more powerful, far richer than my mother's family, and one day showed up at my mother's wedding to pay his respects. Here's what she said in part:

6   "Du Yusong having business like fruit stand. Like off the street kind. He is Du like Du Zong—but not Tsung-ming Island people. The local people call putong, the river east side, he belong to that side local people. That man want to ask Du Zong father take him in like become own family. Du Zong father wasn't look down on him, but didn't take seriously, until that man big like become a mafia. Now important person, very hard to inviting

him. Chinese way, came only to show respect, don't stay for dinner. Respect for making big celebration, he shows up. Mean gives lots of respect. Chinese custom. Chinese social life that way. If too important won't have to stay too long. He come to my wedding. I didn't see. I heard it. I gone to boy's side, they have YMCA dinner. Chinese age I was nineteen."

You should know that my mother's expressive command of 7 English belies how much she actually understands. She reads the *Forbes* report, listens to *Wall Street Week,* converses daily with her stockbroker, reads all of Shirley MacLaine's books with ease—all kinds of things I can't begin to understand. Yet some of my friends tell me they understand 50 percent of what my mother says. Some say they understand 80 to 90 percent. Some say they understand none of it, as if she were speaking pure Chinese. But to me, my mother's English is perfectly clear, perfectly natural. It's my mother tongue. Her language, as I hear it, is vivid, direct, full of observation and imagery. That was the language that helped shape the way I saw things, expressed things, made sense of the world.

Lately, I've been giving more thought to the kind of English my 8 mother speaks. Like others, I have described it to people as "broken" or "fractured" English. But I wince when I say that. It has always bothered me that I can think of no way to describe it other than "broken," as if it were damaged and needed to be fixed, as if it lacked a certain wholeness and soundness. I've heard other terms used, "limited English," for example. But they seem just as bad, as if everything is limited, including people's perceptions of the limited English speaker.

I know this for a fact, because when I was growing up, my 9 mother's "limited" English limited *my* perception of her. I was ashamed of her English. I believed that her English reflected the quality of what she had to say. That is, because she expressed them imperfectly her thoughts were imperfect. And I had plenty of empirical evidence to support me: the fact that people in department stores, at banks, and at restaurants did not take her seriously, did not give her good service, pretended not to understand her, or even acted as if they did not hear her.

My mother has long realized the limitations of her English 10 as well. When I was fifteen, she used to have me call people on the phone to pretend I was she. In this guise, I was forced to ask for information or even to complain and yell at people who had been rude to her. One time it was a call to her stockbroker in New York. She had cashed out her small portfolio and it just so happened we were going to go to New York the next week, our very first trip outside California. I had to get on the phone and say in an adolescent voice that was not very convincing, "This is Mrs. Tan."

11   And my mother was standing in the back whispering loudly, "Why he don't send me check, already two weeks late. So mad he lie to me, losing me money."

12   And then I said in perfect English, "Yes, I'm getting rather concerned. You had agreed to send the check two weeks ago, but it hasn't arrived."

13   Then she began to talk more loudly. "What he want, I come to New York tell him front of his boss, you cheating me?" And I was trying to calm her down, make her be quiet, while telling the stockbroker, "I can't tolerate any more excuses. If I don't receive the check immediately, I am going to have to speak to your manager when I'm in New York next week." And sure enough, the following week there we were in front of this astonished stockbroker, and I was sitting there red-faced and quiet, and my mother, the real Mrs. Tan, was shouting at his boss in her impeccable broken English.

14   We used a similar routine just five days ago, for a situation that was far less humorous. My mother had gone to the hospital for an appointment, to find out about a benign brain tumor a CAT scan had revealed a month ago. She said she had spoken very good English, her best English, no mistakes. Still, she said, the hospital did not apologize when they said they had lost the CAT scan and she had come for nothing. She said they did not seem to have any sympathy when she told them she was anxious to know the exact diagnosis, since her husband and son had both died of brain tumors. She said they would not give her any more information until the next time and she would have to make another appointment for that. So she said she would not leave until the doctor called her daughter. She wouldn't budge. And when the doctor finally called her daughter, me, who spoke in perfect English—lo and behold—we had assurances the CAT scan would be found, promises that a conference call on Monday would be held,

and apologies for any suffering my mother had gone through for a most regrettable mistake.

I think my mother's English almost had an effect on limit- 15 ing my possibilities in life as well. Sociologists and linguists probably will tell you that a person's developing language skills are more influenced by peers. But I do think that the language spoken in the family, especially in immigrant families which are more insular, plays a large role in shaping the language of the child. And I believe that it affected my results on achievement tests, IQ tests, and the SAT. While my English skills were never judged as poor, compared to math, English could not be consid- ered my strong suit. In grade school I did moderately well, get- ting perhaps B's, sometimes B-pluses, in English and scoring perhaps in the sixtieth or seventieth percentile on achievement tests. But those scores were not good enough to override the opinion that my true abilities lay in math and science, because in those areas I achieved A's and scored in the ninetieth percentile or higher.

This was understandable. Math is precise; there is only one 16 correct answer. Whereas, for me at least, the answers on English tests were always a judgment call, a matter of opinion and person- al experience. Those tests were constructed around items like fill- in-the-blank sentence completion, such as, "Even though Tom was _____, Mary thought he was _____." And the correct answer always seemed to be the most bland combinations of thoughts, for example, "Even though Tom was shy, Mary thought he was charming," with the grammatical structure "even though" limiting the correct answer to some sort of semantic opposites, so you wouldn't get answers like, "Even though Tom was foolish, Mary thought he was ridiculous." Well, according to my mother, there were very few limitations as to what Tom could have been and what Mary might have thought of him. So I never did well on tests like that.

The same was true with word analogies, pairs of words 17 in which you were supposed to find some sort of logical, se- mantic relationship—for example, "*Sunset* is to *nightfall* as _____ is to _____." And here you would be pre- sented with a list of four possible pairs, one of which showed the same kind of relationship: *red* is to *stoplight, bus* is to *ar- rival, chills* is to *fever, yawn* is to *boring.* Well, I could never think that way. I knew what the tests were asking, but I could not block out of my mind the images already created by the first pair, *"sunset* is to *nightfall"*—and I would see a burst of colors against a darkening sky, the moon rising, the lowering of a curtain of stars. And all the other pairs of words—red, bus, stoplight, boring—just threw up a mass of confusing images, making it impossible for me to sort out something as logical as saying: "A sunset precedes nightfall" is the same as "a chill precedes a fever." The only way I would have gotten that answer right would have been to imagine an associative situation, for example, my being disobedient and staying out past sunset, catching a chill at night, which turns into feverish pneumonia as punishment, which indeed did happen to me.

18   I have been thinking about all this lately, about my mother's English, about achievement tests. Because lately I've been asked, as a writer, why there are not more Asian Americans represented in American literature. Why are there few Asian Americans enrolled in creative writing programs? Why do so many Chinese students go into engineering? Well, these are broad sociological questions I can't begin to answer. But I have noticed in surveys—in fact, just last week—that Asian students, as a whole, always do significantly better on math achievement tests than in English. And this makes me think that there are other Asian-American students whose English spoken in the home might also be described as "broken" or "limited." And perhaps they also have teachers who are steering them away from writing and into math and science, which is what happened to me.

19   Fortunately, I happen to be rebellious in nature and enjoy the challenge of disproving assumptions made about me. I became an English major my first year in college, after being enrolled as pre-med. I started writing nonfiction as a freelancer the week after I was told by my former boss that writing was my worst skill and I should hone my talents toward account management.

20   But it wasn't until 1985 that I finally began to write fiction. And at first I wrote using what I thought to be wittily crafted sentences, sentences that would finally prove I had mastery over the English language. Here's an example from the first draft of a story that later made its way into *The Joy Luck Club,* but without

this line: "That was my mental quandary in its nascent state." A terrible line, which I can barely pronounce.

Fortunately, for reasons I won't get into today, I later decided I should envision a reader for the stories I would write. And the reader I decided upon was my mother, because these were stories about mothers. So with this reader in mind—and in fact she did read my early drafts—I began to write stories using all the Englishes I grew up with: the English I spoke to my mother, which for lack of a better term might be described as "simple"; the English she used with me, which for lack of a better term might be described as "broken"; my translation of her Chinese, which could certainly be described as "watered down"; and what I imagined to be her translation of her Chinese if she could speak in perfect English, her internal language, and for that I sought to preserve the essence, but neither an English nor a Chinese structure. I wanted to capture what language ability tests can never reveal: her intent, her passion, her imagery, the rhythms of her speech and the nature of her thoughts.

21

Apart from what any critic had to say about my writing, I knew I had succeeded where it counted when my mother finished reading my book and gave me her verdict: "So easy to read."

22

BUILDING VOCABULARY

Tan uses technical words to distinguish standard English from the English her mother speaks. Investigate the meanings of the following terms, and find examples to illustrate them for your classmates.

1. nominalized forms
2. transcribed
3. imagery
4. linguists
5. semantic opposites
6. word analogies
7. quandary
8. nascent
9. scholar
10. freelancer

UNDERSTANDING THE WRITER'S IDEAS

1. Why does Tan start her essay by identifying who she is *not?* What does she see as the difference between a scholar and a writer?

2. What does Tan mean when she says, "Language is the tool of my trade"? What are the four ways she says language can work?

3. Tan speaks of "all the Englishes I grew up with" in paragraph 2, and later of the "different Englishes" she uses. Why does her mother's presence in the lecture room help her recall these Englishes? Why does she give us examples of what was "wrong" with her talk in paragraph 3?

4. In paragraph 4, Tan recognizes that she herself shifts from one English to another. Which English is "our language of intimacy"? Why?

5. Tan describes how she recorded her mother's words. Why does she give us her technique in paragraph 5 before presenting her mother's exact words in paragraph 6?

6. What do we know about Tan's mother when we learn she reads the *Forbes* report and various books? Why is it important for Tan to understand the way her mother sees the world? What connection does Tan make between the way we use language and the way we see the world?

7. In paragraph 8, Tan tries to find a suitable label for her mother's language. Why is she unwilling to use a description like "broken" or "limited" English? What does her mother's English sound like to you?

8. In what ways did outsiders (like bankers and waiters) make judgments on Tan's mother because of her language? Were the judgments deliberate or unconscious on their part?

9. How does Tan use humor as she contrasts the two Englishes in the telephone conversations she records? How does the tone change when Tan shifts to the hospital scene? Why do the authorities provide different service and different information when the daughter speaks than they do when the mother speaks?

10. How does Tan connect her math test scores with her mother's language? Why does she think she never did well on language tests? Why does she think the tests do not measure a student's language use very well? Why does Tan ultimately become an English major (par. 19)?

11. In paragraph 20, why does Tan show us the sentence: "That was my mental quandary in its nascent state"? How does it compare with the other sentences in her essay? What is wrong with this "terrible" sentence? What does it mean?

12. In her two final paragraphs, Tan returns to her mother. Why does selecting her mother as her reader help Tan learn to become a better writer? What are the elements of good writing her mother recognizes, even if she herself cannot write standard English?

UNDERSTANDING THE WRITER'S TECHNIQUES

1. What is the thesis statement in Tan's essay? Where does it appear?

2. Throughout her essay, Tan uses *dialogue,* the written reproduction of speech or conversation. Why does she do this? What is the effect of dialogue? Which sentences of dialogue do you find especially effective, and why?

3. In paragraph 3, Tan writes fairly long sentences until she writes, "My mother was in the room." Why is this sentence shorter? What is the effect of the short sentence on the reader?

4. *Narration* (see Chapter 4) is the telling of a story or series of events. *Anecdotes* are very short narrations, usually of an amusing or autobiographical nature. Point out uses of narration and anecdote in Tan's essay.

5. How does identifying her mother as her intended audience help Tan make her own language more effective? Does Tan suggest that all writing should be "simple"? Is her writing always "simple"? Why does her mother find it "easy" to read?

6. Why does Tan put quotation marks around "broken" and "limited"? What other words can describe this different English?

EXPLORING THE WRITER'S IDEAS

1. Why is an awareness of different kinds of English necessary for a writer? Why are writers so interested in "different Englishes"? Should all Americans speak and write the same English?

2. What is the role of parents in setting language standards for their

children? How did your parents or other relatives influence your
language use?

3. Reread Tan's essay, and look more carefully at her *point of view*
(see Glossary) about other Englishes. How do we know what her
point of view is? Does she state it directly or indirectly? Where?

4. Listen to someone who speaks a "different" English. Try to
record a full paragraph of the speech, as Tan does in paragraph 6.
Use a tape recorder and (or) a video camera so that you can re-
play the speech several times. Explain what the difficulties were
in capturing the sound of the speech exactly. Write a "translation"
of the paragraph into standard English.

5. Tan explores the special relation between mothers and daughters.
How would you describe the author's relation with her mother?
How did the daughter rebel from the career goals set for her by
her mother? Would you call Tan a feminist writer or not? Explain.

IDEAS FOR WRITING

Guided Writing

Write a narrative essay using first-person point of view in which
you contrast your language with the language of someone who
speaks differently from you.

1. Begin by making some notes on your own language and by deciding whom you will choose as your other subject. It should be
someone you can spend time with so that you can record his or
her speech.

2. Following Tan's model, create a narrative to frame your subject's
language. Tell who you are and why you speak the way you do.
Introduce the other speaker, and tell why his or her speech is different.

3. Use dialogue to provide examples of both Englishes.

4. Analyze how listeners other than yourself respond to both types
of speech. What are the social implications of speech differences?

5. Show how listening to the other speaker and to yourself has
helped you shape your own language and write your essay. What
can you learn about good writing from this project?

6. Be sure the essay has a clear thesis in the introduction. Add a strong conclusion that returns to the idea of the thesis.

More Writing Projects

1. In your journal, record examples of new words you have heard recently. Divide the list into columns according to whether the words are standard English or a different English. How many different Englishes can you find in your community and in college?
2. Reread question 1 in Exploring the Writer's Ideas, and write a one-paragraph response to it.
3. Tan's experience as a daughter of recent immigrants has clearly shaped her life in fundamental ways. She writes about the "shame" she once felt for her mother's speech. Write about a personal experience in which you were once embarrassed by someone close to you who was "different." Tell how you would feel about the same encounter if it happened today.

Writing
William Stafford

In this 1970 essay on writing, author William Stafford presents an important message to writers at all levels. Writing, he insists, is foremost a *process*. It is not, according to Stafford, "negotiable," not to be considered for its value as a product. And, he suggests, the ultimate guide for a writer must be "the self." Stafford's "process-rather-than-substance" message also relates well to creative endeavors other than writing, as well as to less-exalted processes like fishing, for example, which Stafford offers as an analogy.

Words to Watch

succession (par. 1)   series; sequence

unforeseen (par. 1)   unexpected; not anticipated

interval (par. 3)   fixed period of time

trivial (par. 3)   unimportant; superficial

resolutely (par. 4)   purposefully; in a determined manner

headlong (par. 4)   without pause or delay

justification (par. 5)   defense; vindication

successive (par. 6)   one after another

baffled (par. 7)   confused; dazed

stalled (par. 7)   temporarily stopped

negotiable (par. 9)   marketable; usable

eventuates (par. 9)   makes happen in the end

scope (par. 12)   range; area

elation (par. 12)   joy; great happiness

realm (par. 12)   domain; zone

1   A writer is not so much someone who has something to say as he is someone who has found a process that will bring about new things he would not have thought of if he had not started to say them. That is, he does not draw on a reservoir; instead, he engages in an activity that brings to him a whole succession of unforeseen stories, poems, essays, plays, laws, philosophies, religions, or—but wait!

Back in school, from the first when I began to try to write   2
things, I felt this richness. One thing would lead to another; the
world would give and give. Now, after twenty years or so of trying, I live by that certain richness, an idea hard to pin, difficult to
say, and perhaps offensive to some. For there are strange implications in it.

One implication is the importance of just plain receptivity.   3
When I write, I like to have an interval before me when I am
not likely to be interrupted. For me, this means usually the early
morning, before others are awake. I get pen and paper, take a
glance out the window (often it is dark out there), and wait. It is
like fishing. But I do not wait very long, for there is always a
nibble—and this is where receptivity comes in. To get started I
will accept anything that occurs to me. Something always occurs, of course, to any of us. We can't keep from thinking.
Maybe I have to settle for an immediate impression: it's cold, or
hot, or dark, or bright, or in between! Or—well, the possibilities
are endless. If I put down something, that thing will help the
next thing come, and I'm off. If I let the process go on, things
will occur to me that were not at all in my mind when I started.
These things, odd and trivial as they may be, are somehow connected. And if I let them string out, surprising things will happen.

If I let them string out . . . Along with initial receptivity,   4
then, there is another readiness: I must be willing to fail. If I am
to keep on writing, I cannot bother to insist on high standards. I
must get into action and not let anything stop me, or even slow
me much. By "standards" I do not mean "correctness"—spelling,
punctuation, and so on. These details become mechanical for
anyone who writes for a while. I am thinking about what many
people would consider "important" standards, such matters as social significance, positive values, consistency, etc. I resolutely
disregard these. Something better, greater, is happening! I am following a process that leads so wildly and originally into new ter-
ritory that no judgment can at the moment be made about values,
significance, and so on. I am making something new, something
that has not been judged before. Later others—and maybe I myself—will make judgments. Now, I am headlong to discover. Any
distraction may harm the creating.

So, receptive, careless of failure, I spin out things on the   5

page. And a wonderful freedom comes. If something occurs to
me, it is all right to accept it. It has one justification: it occurs to
me. No one else can guide me. I must follow my own weak, wan-
dering, diffident impulses.

6   A strange bonus happens. At times, without my insisting
on it, my writings become coherent; the successive elements
that occur to me are clearly related. They lead by themselves to
new connections. Sometimes the language, even the syllables
that happen along, may start a trend. Sometimes the materials
alert me to something waiting in my mind, ready for sustained
attention. At such times, I allow myself to be eloquent, or intentional, or for great swoops (treacherous! not to be trusted!) reasonable. But I do not insist on any of that; for I know that back
of my activity there will be the coherence of my self, and that
indulgence of my impulses will bring recurrent patterns and
meanings again.

7   This attitude toward the process of writing creatively suggests a problem for me, in terms of what others say. They talk
about "skills" in writing. Without denying that I do have experience, wide reading, automatic orthodoxies and maneuvers of various kinds, I still must insist that I am often baffled about what
"skill" has to do with the precious little area of confusion when I
do not know what I am going to say and then I found out what I
am going to say. That precious interval I am unable to bridge by
skill. What can I witness about it? It remains mysterious, just as
all of us must feel puzzled about how we are so inventive as to be
able to talk along through complexities with our friends, not
needing to plan what we are going to say, but never stalled for
long in our confident forward progress. Skill? If so, it is the skill
we all have, something we must have learned before the age of
three or four.

8   A writer is one who has become accustomed to trusting that
grace, or luck, or—skill.

9   Yet another attitude I find necessary: most of what I write,
like most of what I say in casual conversation, will not amount to
much. Even I will realize, and even at the time, that it is not negotiable. It will be like practice. In conversation, I allow myself
random remarks—in fact, as I recall, that is the way I learned to
talk—so in writing I launch many expendable efforts. A result of
this free way of writing is that I am not writing for others, most-

ly; they will not see the product at all unless the activity eventuates in something that later appears to be worthy. My guide is the
self, and its adventuring in the language brings about communication.

This process-rather-than-substance view of writing invites a 10
final, dual reflection:

1. Writers may not be special—sensitive or talented in any 11
usual sense. They are simply engaged in sustained use of a language skill we all have. Their "creations" come about through
confident reliance on stray impulses that will, with trust, find occasional patterns that are satisfying.

2. But writing itself is one of the great, free human activi- 12
ties. There is scope for individuality, and elation, and discovery,
in writing. For the person who follows with trust and forgiveness
what occurs to him, the world remains always ready and deep, an
inexhaustible environment, with the combined vividness of an
actuality and flexibility of a dream. Working back and forth between experience and thought, writers have more than space and
time can offer. They have the whole unexplored realm of human
vision.

BUILDING VOCABULARY

1. Use *context clues* (see Glossary) to determine the meanings of
   the words in italics below. Use a dictionary to check your definitions.
   a. strange *implications* (par. 2)
   b. initial *receptivity* (par. 4)
   c. *diffident* impulses (par. 5)
   d. strange *bonus* (par. 6)
   e. *sustained* attention (par. 6)
   f. *recurrent* patterns (par. 6)
   g. automatic *orthodoxies* (par. 7)
   h. *expendable* efforts (par. 9)
   i. stray *impulses* (par. 11)
   j. *inexhaustible* environment (par. 12)
2. Select five words from the Words to Watch section, and write
   original sentences that use each word correctly.

UNDERSTANDING THE WRITER'S IDEAS

1. In your own words, explain the meaning of the first two sentences.

2. What is the "richness" Stafford refers to in paragraph 2? Why is it "hard to pin"? Why "perhaps offensive to some"?

3. What does Stafford mean by "just plain receptivity" (par. 3)?

4. Outline the main steps in Stafford's process of writing. What does he mean when he writes of the first step that "It is like fishing" (par. 3)? What is his general attitude toward the overall process? When and how does he usually begin the process? Why?

5. According to Stafford, what are the important "standards" in writing? Which are *not* important? What is his attitude toward these standards? Why?

6. Why does Stafford say: "I must be willing to fail" (par. 4)?

7. Explain Stafford's use of the phrase "great swoops" (par. 6). Why does he follow the phrase with the parenthetical "(treacherous! not to be trusted!)"?

8. What is "that indulgence" of paragraph 6?

9. What is the author's opinion of the "skills" to which people refer when they talk about writing? What skill does he feel is the most valuable? Why?

10. What is Stafford's attitude toward his writing while he is in the midst of the process? Explain. What is his attitude toward his readers while he is writing? Explain.

11. Stafford offers two definitions of a writer. What are they? How do they relate to each other? In what ways are they similar? In what ways different? What relation does their placement in the essay have to Stafford's purpose in writing the essay? What relation to his main idea?

12. What does Stafford mean by "an inexhaustible environment, with the combined vividness of an actuality and flexibility of a dream" (par. 12)?

UNDERSTANDING THE WRITER'S TECHNIQUES

1. Is there one sentence in this essay that states the main idea, or *thesis* (see Glossary)? If so, what is it? Where does it appear in the development of the essay? Why?

2. What is the effect of "—but wait!" which ends paragraph 1? What relation does it have to the reader? Who is the intended audience (readership) for this essay?

3. In what ways does the first sentence of paragraph 3 serve as an effective *transition* (see Glossary) from the introduction to the body of this essay?

4. Throughout the essay, Stafford uses dashes. What is the usual purpose of this form of punctuation? How does Stafford's use of dashes affect meaning in this essay? How does it affect *tone* (see Glossary)?

5. Why does Stafford repeat the statement "if I let them string out" at the end of paragraph 3 and the beginning of paragraph 4? What does he mean by that clause?

6. What comparison does Stafford make between the process of writing and conversation? Explain the comparison in your own words.

7. Although most of the paragraphs in this essay are quite fully developed, Stafford makes use of 2, one-sentence paragraphs. Locate them, and discuss their usefulness and effectiveness.

8. To whom is the one-word question "Skill?" addressed in paragraph 7?

9. The title of this essay is simple and direct. Do you find it appropriate? If you were to give this essay a new title, what would it be?

10. What is the relation between the two aspects of the "dual reflection" (pars. 10–12) that concludes this essay?

11. Compare the tone of the opening (pars. 1–2), middle (pars. 3–9), and closing (pars. 10–12) sections of the essay. Are there any changes in tone? Support your answer with specific references to the text.

12. What is Stafford's purpose in writing this essay? How do you know?

13. In paragraph 1, Stafford refers to "A writer" and "he." But, in paragraph 12, the references are to "writers" and "They." What is the effect of this change in reference?

EXPLORING THE WRITER'S IDEAS

1. In the first sentence, Stafford indicates that the process of writing itself calls forth ideas that even the writer may not have

been aware of. Do you believe this is true? How have your experiences of writing—essays, letters, stories, poems—confirmed or
challenged this assertion?

2. Many writers, and creative artists in general, have a less-than-
favorable view of critics. Based on your reading of Stafford's
essay about the process of writing, what would you guess is his
attitude toward literary critics? Explain your response.

3. In paragraph 10, Stafford refers to his "process-rather-than-
substance view of writing." Throughout the essay, he is clearly
more concerned with the creative process than with the creative
product. Find examples throughout the essay that support this
attitude.

4. Stafford states: "Writers may not be special." Do you feel this
honestly sums up his attitude toward writers? Why? Compare
Stafford's attitude to William Saroyan's attitude that as a writer,
he felt that he had "lived in a special way" (page 6 in the essay
"Why I Write"). Would Stafford agree with the last sentence in
Saroyan's essay, in which he states: "Mainly, though, I write because I want to" (page 9)?

5. In general, do you think that creative processes such as writing,
painting, making music, and so on can be learned—or do you
think that people must be born with certain talents and abilities?
Discuss examples of talented people you know personally.

IDEAS FOR WRITING

Guided Writing

Write an essay about something that you do well in which the
process is more important to you than the product. For example,
you might choose singing, painting, weight lifting, public speaking, cooking, gardening, and so on.

1. Begin your essay with a definition of a person (for example, a
singer, a painter, a weight lifter) who engages in this activity. Relate your definition to the process.

2. Briefly state the most important feature of this process, and comment on how others may view it.

3. In well-developed paragraphs, outline the steps and most important concerns that guide you in the process. Explain how your
   concerns might contradict the more usually accepted attitudes toward the process of this activity.
4. Pay close attention to the ways in which you feel that you are developing your skills or achieving personal satisfaction while you
   are engaged in the process.
5. Use dashes here and there to set off parenthetical reflections.
6. Before beginning your conclusion, write another, more con-
   cise, one-sentence definition of a person who engages in this
   activity.
7. Organize your conclusion into two generalized, yet important,
   summary observations about the process of this activity.
8. Give your essay a simple, one- or two-word title.

More Writing Projects

1. In your journal, list the skills that you possess as a writer—as
   well as those skills that you would like to acquire.
2. Outline in a paragraph the processes you use in approaching a
   writing assignment. Explain which is the most satisfying and en-
   joyable. Which is the least so? Why?
3. Write a short essay to describe an activity in which the product,
   or end result, is *definitely more important* than the process by
   which you achieve it.

Simplicity
William Zinsser

In this chapter from *On Writing Well,* William Zinsser begins with a fairly pessimistic analysis of the clutter that pervades and degrades American writing, and he offers many examples to prove his point. Zinsser deals with almost all major aspects of the writing process—thinking, composing, awareness of the reader, self-discipline, rewriting, and editing—and concludes that simplicity is the key to them all.

Words to Watch

decipher (par. 2)   to make out the meaning of something obscure

adulterants (par. 3)   added substances which make something impure or inferior

mollify (par. 4)   to appease; to soothe

spell (par. 4)   a short period of time

assailed (par. 8)   attacked with words or physical violence

spruce (par. 8)   neat or smart in appearance

rune (par. 10)   character in an ancient alphabet

embarking (par. 12)   making a start

consolation (par. 13)   comfort; reduction of stress or misery

1 Clutter is the disease of American writing. We are a society strangling in unnecessary words, circular constructions, pompous frills and meaningless jargon.

2   Who can understand the viscous language of everyday American commerce and enterprise: the business letter, the interoffice memo, the corporation report, the notice from the bank explaining its latest "simplified" statement? What member of an insurance or medical plan can decipher the brochure that describes what the costs and benefits are? What father or mother can put together a child's toy—on Christmas Eve or any other eve—from the instructions on the box? Our national tendency is to inflate and thereby sound important. The airline pilot who announces that he is presently anticipating experiencing considerable precipitation wouldn't dream of saying that it may rain. The sentence is too simple—there must be something wrong with it.

But the secret of good writing is to strip every sentence to ₃
its cleanest components. Every word that serves no function,
every long word that could be a short word, every adverb that
carries the same meaning that's already in the verb, every passive
construction that leaves the reader unsure of who is doing what—
these are the thousand and one adulterants that weaken the
strength of a sentence. And they usually occur, ironically, in proportion to education and rank.

During the late 1960s the president of a major university ₄
wrote a letter to mollify the alumni after a spell of campus unrest.
"You are probably aware," he began, "that we have been experiencing very considerable potentially explosive expressions of
dissatisfaction on issues only partially related." He meant that the
students had been hassling them about different things. I was far
more upset by the president's English than by the students' potentially explosive expressions of dissatisfaction. I would have
preferred the presidential approach taken by Franklin D.
Roosevelt when he tried to convert into English his own government's memos, such as this blackout order of 1942:

> Such preparations shall be made as will completely obscure all Fed-
> eral buildings and non-Federal buildings occupied by the Federal
> government during an air raid for any period of time from visibility
> by reason of internal or external illumination.

"Tell them," Roosevelt said, "that in buildings where they ₅
have to keep the work going to put something across the windows."

Simplify, simplify. Thoreau said it, as we are so often re-
minded, and no American writer more consistently practiced ₆
what he preached. Open *Walden* to any page and you will find a
man saying in a plain and orderly way what is on his mind:

> I went to the woods because I wished to live deliberately, to front
> only the essential facts of life, and see if I could not learn what it had
> to teach, and not, when I came to die, discover that I had not lived. I
> did not wish to live what was not life, living is so dear; nor did I
> wish to practice resignation, unless it was quite necessary. I wanted
> to live deep and suck out all the marrow of life, to live so sturdily and
> Spartan-like as to put to rout all that was not life, to cut a broad swath
> and shave close, to drive life into a corner, and reduce it to its lowest
> terms, and, if it proved to be mean, why then to get the whole and
> genuine meanness of it, and publish its meanness to the world; or if it
> were sublime, to know it by experience, and be able to give a true ac-
> count of it.

7   How can the rest of us achieve such enviable freedom from clutter? The answer is to clear our heads of clutter. Clear thinking becomes clear writing; one can't exist without the other. It's impossible for a muddy thinker to write good English. You may get away with it for a paragraph or two, but soon the reader will be lost, and there's no sin so grave, for the reader will not easily be lured back.

8   Who is this elusive creature, the reader? The reader is someone with an attention span of about sixty seconds—a person assailed by forces competing for the minutes that might otherwise be spent on a magazine or a book. At one time these forces weren't so numerous or so possessive: newspapers, radio, spouse, home, children. Today they also include a "home entertainment center" (TV, VCR, video camera, tapes and CDs), pets, a fitness program, a lawn and a garden and all the gadgets that have been bought to keep them spruce, and that most potent of competitors, sleep. The person snoozing in a chair, holding a magazine or a book, is a person who was being given too much unnecessary trouble by the writer.

9   It won't do to say that the reader is too dumb or too lazy to keep pace with the train of thought. If the reader is lost, it's usually because the writer hasn't been careful enough. The carelessness can take any number of forms. Perhaps a sentence is so excessively cluttered that the reader, hacking through the verbiage, simply doesn't know what it means. Perhaps a sentence has been so shoddily constructed that the reader could read it in any of several ways. Perhaps the writer has switched pronouns in midsentence, or has switched tenses, so the reader loses track of who is talking or when the action took place. Perhaps Sentence B is not a logical sequel to Sentence A—the writer, in whose head the connection is clear, hasn't bothered to provide the missing link. Perhaps the writer has used an important word incorrectly by not taking the trouble to look it up. The writer may think that "sanguine" and "sanguinary" mean the same thing, but the difference is a bloody big one. The reader can only infer (speaking of big differences) what the writer is trying to imply.

10   Faced with such obstacles, readers are at first remarkably tenacious. They blame themselves—they obviously missed something, and they go back over the mystifying sentence, or over the whole paragraph, piecing it out like an ancient rune, making

guesses and moving on. But they won't do this for long. The writer is making them work too hard, and they will look for one who is better at the craft.

Writers must therefore constantly ask: What am I trying to   11
say? Surprisingly often they don't know. Then they must look at what they have written and ask: Have I said it? Is it clear to someone encountering the subject for the first time? If it's not, that's because some fuzz has worked its way into the machinery. The clear writer is someone clearheaded enough to see this stuff for what it is: fuzz.

I don't mean that some people are born clearheaded and   12
are therefore natural writers, whereas others are naturally fuzzy and will never write well. Thinking clearly is a conscious act that writers must force upon themselves, just as if they were embarking on any other project that requires logic: adding up a laundry list or doing an algebra problem. Good writing doesn't come naturally, though most people obviously think it does. The professional writer is constantly being bearded by strangers who say they'd like to "try a little writing some time"—meaning when they retire from their real profession, like insurance or real estate. Or they say, "I could write a book about that." I doubt it.

Writing is hard work. A clear sentence is no accident. Very   13
few sentences come out right the first time, or even the third time. Remember this as a consolation in moments of despair. If you find that writing is hard, it's because it *is* hard. It's one of the hardest things that people do.

BUILDING VOCABULARY

1. Zinsser uses a number of words and expressions drawn from areas other than writing; he uses them to make interesting combinations or comparisons in such expressions as *elusive creature* (par. 8) and *hacking through the verbiage* (par. 9). Find other such expressions in this essay. Write simple explanations for the two above and the others that you find.
2. List words or phrases in this essay that pertain to writing—the process, the results, the faults, the successes. Explain any with which you were unfamiliar.

Two pages of the final manuscript of this chapter. Although they look like a first draft, they have already been rewritten and retyped—like almost every other page—four or five times. With each rewrite I try to make what I have written tighter, stronger and more precise, eliminating every element that is not doing useful work, until at last I have a clean copy for the printer. Then I go over it once more, reading it aloud, and am always amazed at how much clutter can still be profitably cut.

---

is too dumb or too lazy to keep pace with the ~~writer's~~ train of thought. My sympathies are ~~entirely~~ with him.) ~~He's not so dumb.~~ (If the reader is lost, it is generally because the writer ~~of the article~~ has not been careful enough to keep him on the ~~proper~~ path.

(This carelessness can take any number of ~~different~~ forms. Perhaps a sentence is so excessively ~~long and~~ cluttered that the reader, hacking his way through ~~all~~ the verbiage, simply doesn't know what *it* ~~the writer~~ means. Perhaps a sentence has been so shoddily constructed that the reader could read it in any of *several* ~~two or three different~~ ways. ~~He thinks he knows what the writer is trying to say, but he's not sure.~~ Perhaps the writer has switched pronouns in mid-sentence, or ~~perhaps he~~ has switched tenses, so the reader loses track of who is talking ~~to whom,~~ or ~~exactly~~ when the action took place. Perhaps Sentence B is not a logical sequel to Sentence A -- the writer, in whose head the connection is ~~perfectly~~ clear, has not *bothered to provide* ~~given enough thought to providing~~ the missing link. Perhaps the writer has used an important word incorrectly by not taking the trouble to look it up ~~, and make sure.~~ He may think that "sanguine" and "sanguinary" mean the same thing, but) ~~I can assure you that~~ (the difference is a bloody big one ~~, to the~~

~~reader.~~ *The reader* ~~He~~ can only ~~try to~~ infer ~~what~~ (speaking of big differences) what the writer is trying to imply.

(Faced with *these* ~~such a variety of~~ obstacles, the reader
is at first a remarkably tenacious bird. He ~~tends to~~ blame^s
himself~~,~~ ~~H~~e obviously missed something, ~~he thinks,~~ and he goes
back over the mystifying sentence, or over the whole paragraph,
piecing it out like an ancient rune, making guesses and moving
on. But he won't do this for long. ~~He will soon run out of~~
~~patience.~~ (The writer is making him work too hard, ~~)~~ ~~harder~~
~~than he should have to work —~~ (and the reader will look for
~~a writer~~ *one* who is better at his craft.

(The writer must therefore constantly ask himself: What am
I trying to say? ~~in this sentence?~~ (Surprisingly often, he
doesn't know.) ~~And~~ Then he must look at what he has ~~just~~
written and ask: Have I said it? Is it clear to someone
encountering
~~who is coming upon~~ the subject for the first time~~,~~? If it's
not~~, clear~~, it is because some fuzz has worked its way into the
machinery. The clear writer is a person ~~who is~~ clear-headed
enough to see this stuff for what it is: fuzz.

(I don't mean ~~to suggest~~ that some people are born
clear-headed and are therefore natural writers, whereas
others
~~other people~~ are naturally fuzzy and will ~~therefore~~ never write
well. Thinking clearly is~~,~~ *a* ~~an entirely~~ conscious act that the
force
writer must~~,~~ ~~keep forcing~~ upon himself, just as if he were
embarking ~~starting out~~ on any other ~~kind of~~ project that~~,~~ *requires* ~~calls for~~ logic:
adding up a laundry list or doing an algebra problem ~~or playing~~
~~chess.~~ Good writing doeesn't ~~just~~ come naturally, though most
it does.
people obviously think ~~it's as easy as walking~~. The professional

UNDERSTANDING THE WRITER'S IDEAS

1. State simply Zinsser's meaning in the opening paragraph. What faults of "bad writing" does he mention in this paragraph?
2. To what is Zinsser objecting in paragraph 2?
3. What, according to the author, is the "secret of good writing"? Explain this "secret" in a few simple words of your own. What does Zinsser say detracts from good writing? What is the meaning of the word *ironically?* Why does Zinsser write that the incidence of these writing faults "occur, *ironically,* in proportion to education and rank"?
4. What was the "message" in the letter from the university president to the alumni? Why does Zinsser object to it? Was it more objectionable in form or in content?
5. Who was Thoreau? What is *Walden?* Why are references to the two especially appropriate to Zinsser's essay?
6. What, according to Zinsser, is the relation between clear thinking and good writing? Can you have one without the other? What is meant by a "muddy thinker" (par. 7)? Why is it "impossible for a muddy thinker to write good English"?
7. Why does the author think most people fall asleep while reading? What is his attitude toward such people?
8. Look up and explain the "big differences" between the words *sanguine* and *sanguinary*; *infer* and *imply*. What is Zinsser's point in calling attention to these differences?
9. In paragraph 11, Zinsser writes about a writer's necessary awareness of the composing process. What elements of the *process* of writing are included in that paragraph? In that discussion, Zinsser speaks of *fuzz* in writing. What does he mean by that word as it relates to the writing process? To what does Zinsser compare the writer's thinking process? Why does he use such simple comparisons?
10. Explain the meaning of the last sentence. What does it indicate about Zinsser's attitude toward his work?

UNDERSTANDING THE WRITER'S TECHNIQUES

1. What is the writer's thesis? Is it stated or implied?
2. Explain the use of the words *disease* and *strangling* in para-

graph 1. Why does Zinsser use these words in an essay about writing?

3. For what purpose does Zinsser use a series of questions in paragraph 2?

4. Throughout this essay, Zinsser makes extensive use of examples to support general opinions and attitudes. What attitude or opinion is he supporting in paragraphs 2, 3, 4, 5, and 9? How does he use examples in each of those paragraphs?

5. Analyze the specific structure and organization of paragraph 3:
   a. What general idea about writing does he propose?
   b. Where does he place that idea in the paragraph?
   c. What examples does he offer to support his general idea?
   d. With what new idea does he conclude the paragraph? How is it related to the beginning idea?

6. Why does Zinsser reproduce exactly portions of the writings of a past president of a major university, President Franklin D. Roosevelt, and Henry David Thoreau? How do these sections make Zinsser's writing clearer, more understandable, or more important?

7. What is the effect on the reader of the words "Simplify, simplify," which begin paragraph 6? Why does Zinsser use them at that particular point in the essay? What do they indicate about his attitude toward his subject? Explain.

8. Why does the author begin so many sentences in paragraph 9 with the word "Perhaps"? How does that technique help to *unify* (see Glossary) the paragraph?

9. For what reasons does Zinsser include the two pages of "rough" manuscript as a part of the finished essay? What is he trying to show the reader in this way? How does seeing these pages help you to understand better what he is writing about in the completed essay?

10. Overall, how would you describe Zinsser's attitude toward the process and craft of writing? What would you say is his overall attitude toward the future of American writing? Is he generally optimistic or pessimistic? On what does his attitude depend? Refer to specifics in the essay to support your answer.

11. Do you think Zinsser expected other writers, or budding writers, to be the main readers of this essay? Why or why not? If so, with what main idea do you think he would like them to come away from the essay? Do you think readers who were not somehow involved in the writing process would benefit equally from this essay? Why?

EXPLORING THE WRITER'S IDEAS

1. Do you think that Zinsser is ever guilty in this essay of the very "sins" against writing about which he is upset? Could he have simplified any of his points? Select one of Zinsser's paragraphs in the finished essay and explain how you might rewrite it more simply.

2. In the reading that you do most often, have you noticed overly cluttered writing? Or, do you feel that the writing is at its clearest level of presentation and understanding for its audience? Bring to class some examples of this writing, and be prepared to discuss it. In general, what do you consider the relation between the simplicity or complexity of a piece of writing and its intended readership?

3. In the note to the two rough manuscript pages included with this essay, Zinsser implies that the process of rewriting and simplifying may be endless. How do you know when to stop trying to rewrite an essay, story, or poem? Do you ever really feel satisfied that you've reached the end of the rewriting process?

4. Choose one of the rough manuscript paragraphs, and compare it with the finished essay. Which do you feel is better? Why? Is there anything Zinsser deleted from the rough copy that you feel he should have retained? Why?

5. Comment on Zinsser's assertion that "Thinking clearly is a conscious act that writers must force upon themselves" (par. 12). How does this opinion compare with the opinions of the three other writers in this chapter?

6. Reread William Stafford's essay "Writing" (pages 24–27). What similarities and differences do you note in Zinsser's and Stafford's writing processes?

IDEAS FOR WRITING

Guided Writing

In a 500- to 750-word essay, write about what you feel are some of the problems that you face as a writer.

1. In the first paragraph, identify the problems that you plan to discuss.

2. In the course of your essay, relate your problems more generally to society at large.

3. Identify what, in your opinion, is the "secret" of good writing. Give specific examples of what measures to take to achieve that secret process and thereby to eliminate some of your problems.

4. Try to include one or two accurate reproductions of your writing to illustrate your composing techniques.

5. Point out what you believe were the major causes of your difficulties as a writer.

6. Toward the end of your essay, explain the type of writer that you would like to be in order to succeed in college.

More Writing Projects

1. Over the next few days, listen to the same news reporter or talk-show host on television or radio. Record in your journal at least ten examples that indicate the use of "unnecessary words, circular constructions, pompous frills, and meaningless jargon." Or compile such a list from an article in a newspaper or magazine you read regularly. Then write an essay presenting and commenting on these examples.

2. Respond in a paragraph to Zinsser's observation, "Good writing doesn't come naturally."

3. In preparation for a writing assignment, collect with other class members various samples of junk mail and business correspondence that confirm Zinsser's statement that these tend to be poorly written. Write an essay describing your findings. Be certain to provide specific examples from the documents you have assembled.

SUMMING UP: CHAPTER 1

1. It sounds simple enough. Many writers, famous and unknown, have tried it at one time or another. Now, it's your turn. Write an essay simply titled "On Writing." Develop the essay in any way you please: you may deal with abstract or concrete ideas, philosophical or practical issues, emotional or intellectual processes, and so forth. Just use this essay to focus your own thoughts and to give your readers a clear idea of what writing means to you.

2. William Zinsser ("Simplicity") tells writers to simplify their writing. Select any writer from this section, and write an essay about whether you think the writer achieved (or did not achieve) simplicity. How did the writer achieve it? Where in the selection would you have preferred even more simplicity? Make specific references to the text.

3. Think about the message implicit in Amy Tan's essay on using her mother as an ideal audience. Find your own ideal listener. Then write a letter to that person in which you discuss your reactions to becoming a writer. Include observations you think your listener or reader will enjoy, such as your everyday life as a student, daydreams, descriptions of teachers, of cafeteria food, or of interesting people you have met.

4. Write a letter from William Stafford to Amy Tan on what skill has to do with good writing and on the value of many "Englishes." Draw on what you understand of Stafford's philosophy of writing from his essay "Writing," and what Amy Tan says in "Mother Tongue."

5. The writers in this chapter all give some sense of *why* they write. For the most part, their reasons are very personal. For example, William Stafford writes of the "scope for individuality, and elation, and discovery," while William Saroyan simply states, "I write because I want to." However, many writers (including many represented in this book) feel that writing entails a certain social responsibility. For example, when Albert Camus received the 1957 Nobel Prize for Literature, he was cited for "illuminating the problems of the human conscience of our time." And, in his acceptance speech, he stated, "[T]he writer's function is not without arduous duties. By definition, he cannot serve today those who make history; he must serve those who are subject to it."

What do you feel are writers' responsibilities to themselves and to others? Do you agree with Camus? Do you prefer writing that deals primarily with an individual's experience or with more general social issues?

Write an essay concerning the social responsibilities of writers. As you consider the issue, refer to points made by writers in this section.

CHAPTER 2

On Reading

WHAT IS READING?

"Reading had changed the course of my life forever," writes Malcolm X in one of the essays in this chapter. For many of us, the acquisition of reading skills may not have been quite as dramatic as it was for the author of "Prison Studies," but if we are to understand the value of literacy in today's society, Malcolm X's analysis of the power of the written word is vital. Reading allows us actively to engage the minds of many writers who have much to tell us and to hear a variety of viewpoints not always available on the cable channels, VCRs, and video forms that vie for our attention. Learning to read well means interacting with what you read. Such reading opens new universes, challenges your opinions, enhances your understanding of yourself and others and of your past, present, and future. Knowledge of books is the mark of a literate person.

But how do we learn this complex skill? Ellen Tashie Frisina's essay on teaching her grandmother to read may remind you of your own early experiences with printed words. Or, if you are a parent, you may be reading stories to your own children to help them learn to read. The joy of early reading experiences should remind us, though, that there are many levels of reading. As we become more mature readers, we read not just as we once did, for the story and its magical pleasures, but for information. We learn not to be passive readers but active ones.

That early love of stories, and the self-esteem that came with mastery of a once impossible task, is, however, only the first

step in understanding the power of reading. "Prison Studies" and
Margaret Atwood's "Survival" extend our understanding of what
reading is beyond the personal into the political and cultural
sphere. Both writers explore not only the power of reading to ex-
cite and inspire them, but also the ways in which language connects to social identity. Each uses reading, and later writing, to
challenge existing assumptions and find a place as an alert and
engaged member of society. Malcolm X argues that his reading
outside of school made him better educated than most formally
educated citizens in America. Atwood points out that what a
reader likes to read is often rooted in where she comes from and
what she sees in the outside world. Her growth as a reader argues
that reading and cultural identity are linked.

Reading gives us access to many printed stories and documents, old and new. By selecting and reading these records, we
can see beyond the highly edited sound bites and trendy images
that tempt us from the television screen. With a book, we can
read what we want when we want to read it. We can reread difficult passages to be sure we understand them. We have time to
question the author's idea, a luxury that high-speed visual media
usually deny us. We have time to absorb and analyze ideas not
only from contemporary life but also from ancient cultures and
distant places. The diverse materials in libraries allow us to select
what we read rather than be channeled into one TV director's
point of view.

Reading, then, lets us share ideas. Reading can teach us
practical skills that we need for survival in our complex world,
such as how to repair a computer or how to become a biology
teacher or a certified public accountant. Good reading can inspire
us, educate us, or entertain us. It can enrich our fantasy lives.
Reading critically also helps us analyze how society operates, how
power is distributed, how we can improve our local community or
the global environment. As Eudora Welty writes, reading can lead
to a lifelong love affair with books and stories. The beauty of the
written word and the stirrings of imagination and vision that the
printed page can produce are all part of what reading is.

HOW DO WE READ?

To become a good reader, we need to think about what we read
just as we think about what and how we write.

- What is the writer's primary purpose? Who is the intended audience?

We should first examine what we are about to read to determine what it is: Is it a romance? a history book? a religious tract? Who wrote it? Why was it written? When was it written? How do the answers to these questions shape our attitude toward the material? As readers of novels, for instance, we soon learn that a gothic romance with a cover featuring a heroine snatched from a fiery castle belongs to a particular genre, or type, of literature. As potential readers, we might prepare ourselves to be skeptical about the happy ending we know awaits us, but at the same time we are prepared for a romantic tale. In contrast, if we face a hard-covered glossy textbook entitled *Economics,* we prepare ourselves to read with far more concentration. We might enjoy the love story, but if we skip whole chapters it may not matter much. If, however, we skip chapters of the textbook, we may find ourselves confused. The first book *entertains* us, while the second *informs.* Only if we understand the *purpose* of a reading assignment are we ready to begin reading.

- What is the precise issue or problem that the writer treats?

Reading is often a process of analyzing and synthesizing. We read an entire chapter, and then we go back and look for the key points. We try to summarize the main idea. We look for subtopics that support the main idea. We identify the writer's *exact* topic. A writer's general topic might be the Battle of Gettysburg, for instance, but if she is writing about the women at Gettysburg, then her precise topic is narrower. What is she saying, we next ask, about these women?

- Who is the writer? For whom is he or she writing?

Clues to a writer's identity can often help us establish whether the material we are reading is reliable. Would we read a slave owner's account of life in slave quarters the same way we would read a slave's diary, for instance? If a Sioux writes about the effects of a treaty on Native-American family life, we might read the essay with a different eye than if the writer were General Custer. The *audience* is also important. If we are reading a handbook on immigration policies in the United States, we might read it differently if we knew it was written for officials at Ellis Island in 1990 than we would if it were written for Chinese men arriving to work on the railroads in the nineteenth century.

• What information, conclusions, and recommendations does the writer present?

The reader may find that note taking is helpful in improving understanding of a text. Creating an outline of materials after reading can help identify the writer's aims.

• How does the writer substantiate, or "prove," his or her case?

The reader must learn the difference between a writer who merely *asserts* an idea and one who effectively *substantiates* an idea. The writer who only asserts that the Holocaust never happened will be read differently from the writer who substantiates his or her claims that the Holocaust did exist with photographs of Germany in the 1940s, interviews with concentration camp survivors, military records of medical experiments, and eyewitness accounts of gas chambers.

• Is the total message successful, objective, valid, or persuasive?

Once you have answered all of the above questions, you are ready to *assess* the work you have read. As you make your evaluation, find specific evidence in the text to back up your position.

These steps will help you engage in an active conversation, or dialogue, with the writer, sharing ideas and debating issues. At the same time, becoming a better reader will help you become a better writer. Eudora Welty, Malcolm X, and Margaret Atwood all became readers as part of their apprenticeship to becoming world-renowned writers. For Ellen Tashie Frisina, reading remains, as it does for most of us, a personal achievement. For Welty, words came to her "as though fed . . . out of a silver spoon." Malcolm X tells us how reading was so powerful for him that it allowed him to break down prison walls. Atwood writes of her bittersweet discovery of literature in her native Canada. Frisina reminds us that literacy is not a birthright, but a skill that can be painstakingly learned, and taught, at any age.

Moon on a Silver Spoon
Eudora Welty

Eudora Welty, born in 1909, is among America's foremost writers, often focusing on the ways of life in rural Mississippi. Her novel *The Optimist's
Daughter* won the 1972 Pulitzer Prize, and her *Collected Stories* (1980) has
been widely acclaimed. In this selection from her autobiography, *One
Writer's Beginnings* (1984), Welty uses delightful descriptions and narrations of her childhood to tell how she developed her love for reading.

Words to Watch

sap (par. 4)   to drain away

gratitude (par. 10)   thankfulness

essential (par. 10)   absolutely necessary

keystone (par. 10)   something on which associated things depend for support

wizardry (par. 11)   magic

acute (par. 13)   very specific or serious

elders (par. 13)   older people

ailment (par. 14)   illness

insatiability (par. 16)   inability to be satisfied

lingers (par. 18)   stays with

On a visit to my grandmother's in West Virginia, I stood inside   1
the house where my mother had been born and where she grew
up.

"Here's where I first began to read my Dickens," Mother   2
said, pointing. "Under that very bed. Hiding my candle. To keep
them from knowing I was up all night."

"But where did it all *come* from?" I asked her at last. "All   3
that Dickens?"

"Why, Papa gave me that set of Dickens for agreeing to   4
let them cut off my hair," she said. "In those days, they thought
very long, thick hair like mine would sap a child's strength. I
said *No!* I wanted my hair left the very way it was. They offered me gold earrings first. I said *No!* I'd rather keep my hair.

Then Papa said, 'What about books? I'll have them send a whole set of Charles Dickens to you, right up the river from Baltimore, in a barrel.' I agreed."

5   My mother had brought that set of Dickens to our house in Jackson, Miss.; those books had been through fire and water before I was born, she told me, and there they were, lined up—as I later realized, waiting for *me.*

6   I learned from the age of two or three that any room in our house, at any time of day, was there to read in, or to be read to. My mother read to me. She'd read to me in the big bedroom in the mornings, when we were in her rocker together, which ticked in rhythm as we rocked, as though we had a cricket accompanying the story. She'd read to me in the dining room on winter afternoons in front of the coal fire, with our cuckoo clock ending the story with "Cuckoo," and at night when I'd got in my own bed. I must have given her no peace.

7   It had been startling and disappointing to me to find out that storybooks had been written by *people,* that books were not natural wonders, coming up of themselves like grass. Yet regardless of where they came from, I cannot remember a time when I was not in love with them—with the books themselves, cover and binding and the paper they were printed on, with their smell and their weight and with their possession in my arms, captured and carried off to myself.

8   Neither of my parents had come from homes that could afford to buy many books, but though it must have been something of a strain on his salary, my father was all the while carefully selecting and ordering away for what he and Mother thought we children should grow up with.

9   Besides the bookcase in the living room, which was always called the library, there were the encyclopedia tables and dictionary stand under windows in our dining room. There was a full set of Mark Twain and a short set of Ring Lardner in our bookcase, and those were the volumes that in time united us as parents and children.

10   I live in gratitude to my parents for initiating me—and as early as I begged for it, without keeping me waiting—into knowledge of the word, into reading and spelling, by way of the alphabet. They taught it to me at home in time for me to begin to

read before starting school. I believe the alphabet is no longer considered an essential piece of equipment for traveling through life. In my day it was the keystone to knowledge. You learned the alphabet as you learned "Now I lay me" and the Lord's Prayer, and your father's and mother's name and address and telephone number, all in case you were lost.

My love for the alphabet, which endures, grew out of reciting 11 it, but before that, out of seeing the letters on the page. In my own storybooks, before I could read them for myself, I fell in love with various winding, enchanted-looking initials at the heads of fairy tales. In "Once upon a time," an "O" had a rabbit running it as a treadmill, his feet upon flowers. When the day came, years later, for me to see the Book of Kells, Gospels from the ninth century, all the wizardry of letter, initial and word swept over me, a thousand times over, and the illustration, the gold, seemed a part of the word's beauty and holiness that had been there from the start.

In my sensory education I include my physical awareness 12 of the word. Of a certain word, that is; the connection it has with what it stands for. Around age six, perhaps, I was standing by myself in our front yard waiting for supper, just at that hour in a late summer day when the sun is already below the horizon and the risen full moon in the visible sky stops being chalky and begins to take on light. There comes the moment, and I saw it then, when the moon goes from flat to round. For the first time it met my eyes as a globe. The word "moon" came into my mouth as though fed to me out of a silver spoon. Held in my mouth the moon became a word. It had the roundness of a Concord grape that Grandpa took off his vine and gave me to suck out of its skin and swallow whole, in Ohio.

Long before I wrote stories, I listened for stories. Listening 13 *for* them is something more acute than listening *to* them. I suppose it's an early form of participation in what goes on. Listening children know stories are *there*. When their elders sit and begin, children are just waiting and hoping for one to come out, like a mouse from its hole.

When I was six or seven, I was taken out of school and put 14 to bed for several months for an ailment the doctor described as "fast-beating heart." I never dreamed I could learn away from the schoolroom, and that bits of enlightenment far-reaching in my life went on as ever in their own good time.

15   An opulence of storybooks covered my bed. As I read away, I was Rapunzel, or the Goose Girl, or the princess in one of the *Thousand and One Nights* who mounted the roof of her palace every night and of her own radiance faithfully lighted the whole city just by reposing there.

16   My mother was very sharing of this feeling of insatiability. Now, I think of her as reading so much of the time while doing something else. In my mind's eye *The Origin of Species* is lying on the shelf in the pantry under a light dusting of flour—my mother was a bread maker; she'd pick it up, sit by the kitchen window and find her place, with one eye on the oven.

17   I'm grateful, too, that from my mother's example, I found the base for worship—that I found a love of sitting and reading the Bible for myself and looking up things in it.

18   How many of us, the Southern writers-to-be of my generation, were blessed in one way or another if not blessed alike, in not having gone deprived of the King James Version of the Bible. Its cadence entered into our ears and our memories for good. The evidence, or the ghost of it, lingers in all our books.

19   "In the beginning was the Word."

BUILDING VOCABULARY

1. Identify the following references to authors, books, and stories from Welty's essay:
   a. Charles Dickens
   b. Mark Twain
   c. Ring Lardner
   d. the Book of Kells
   e. Gospels
   f. Rapunzel
   g. the Goose Girl
   h. the *Thousand and One Nights*
   i. *The Origin of Species*
   j. the King James Version of the Bible
2. Write definitions and your own sentences for the following words:
   a. initiating (par. 10)
   b. enchanted-looking (par. 11)

   c. treadmill (par. 11)
   d. holiness (par. 11)
   e. enlightenment (par. 14)
   f. opulence (par. 15)
   g. radiance (par. 15)
   h. reposing (par. 15)
   i. deprived (par. 18)
   j. cadence (par. 18)

UNDERSTANDING THE WRITER'S IDEAS

1. Where did Welty's grandmother come from? Where was Welty herself brought up? Why did Welty's grandparents want to cut off their daughter's hair?

2. For what reason did Welty's mother receive a set of Charles Dickens's works? What does this tell you about the attitude toward reading in Welty's family? What happened to the set of Dickens? Although Welty doesn't say so, what do you think she did with the books? Why?

3. How did the way Welty's mother felt toward books affect her child's attitude toward reading? In what ways did the conditions in Welty's home contribute to her attitude toward books?

4. Why does the author write of her mother, "I must have given her no peace" (par. 6)?

5. Why was it "startling and disappointing" for Welty to find out that storybooks were written by *people?* Where did she think they came from? Aside from the stories themselves, what is it that the author loves so much about books?

6. For what reasons does Welty feel that learning the alphabet is so important? To what other learning processes does she compare it? Before she learned to recite her alphabet, why was it so important to her?

7. Explain in your own words what Welty considers to be the relation between physical sensations and learning words. According to the author, why is it important for parents to read to their children?

8. For what reason was the young Welty taken out of school? How did this affect her attitude toward reading? How did her mother influence her at this time?

9. At the time of writing this piece, Welty was in her mid-seventies. Explain what she sees as the relation between the Bible and southern writers of her generation. By what descriptions and references in the essay does she indicate her feelings for the Bible?

10. Identify the source of the final sentence. Why is it especially significant to this essay?

UNDERSTANDING THE WRITER'S TECHNIQUES

1. What is the main idea of Welty's essay? Is there any point at which she directly states that main idea? Explain.

2. Why does Welty use an *image* (see Glossary) for her title instead of choosing a more straightforward one, such as William Stafford's "Writing" (pages 24–27), or William Saroyan's "Why I Write" (pages 6–9)? What effect does Welty achieve with the title? What does the title mean?

3. A *reminiscence* is a narrative account of a special memory. How does Welty use reminiscence in this essay?

4. The *tone* (see Glossary) of an essay is the expression of the writer's attitude toward the topic. Describe the tone of this essay. What specifically about the writing contributes to that tone?

5. *Description* helps the reader to "see" objects and scenes and to feel their importance through the author's eyes. *Narration*—the telling of a story—helps the reader follow a sequence of events. (See Chapters 3 and 4.) Both techniques rely on the writer's skill in choosing and presenting *details*. In what way does Welty make use of description and narration in this essay? How would you evaluate her use of details?

6. Placing words in *italics* emphasizes them. Where does the author use italics in this essay? Why does she use them?

7. What does Welty mean by the italicized phrase in the statement "Those books had been *through fire and water* before I was born" (par. 5)? How does the image contribute to the point she's making?

8. The writing of *dialogue* (see Glossary), often used as part of a narration, is the technique whereby a writer either reproduces words actually spoken or invents speech that logically fits into the

essay or story. How does Welty use dialogue here? In what ways does it affect your understanding or enjoyment of the writing?

9. *Similes* (see Glossary) are imaginative comparisons using the word "like" or "as." Use of similes often enlivens the writing and makes it memorable.

In your own words, explain what is being compared in the following similes (in italics) drawn from Welty's essay, and tell how they contribute to the essay:

a. . . . we were in her rocker together, which ticked in rhythm as we rocked, *as though we had a cricket accompanying the story.* (par. 6)

b. The word "moon" came into my mouth *as though fed to me out of a silver spoon.* (par. 12)

c. Listening children know stories are *there.* When their elders sit and begin, children are just waiting and hoping for one to come out, *like a mouse from its hole.* (par. 13)

10. Throughout this essay, Welty refers to "the word." Is she referring to a specific word or to a more abstract concept? Explain. Reread the essay, and find and list all references to "the word." What is the relation between them all? How do they work to keep the essay *coherent* and *unified* (see Glossary)? How do they build to the reference in the final sentence? Why is "the Word" capitalized there?

EXPLORING THE WRITER'S IDEAS

1. Welty believes that it is very important for parents to read to their children. Some specialists in child development even advocate reading to infants still in the womb and to babies before they've spoken their first words. For what reasons might such activities be important? Do you personally feel they are important or useful? Would you read to an unborn infant? Why or why not? If you would, *what* would you read?

2. Welty was born in 1909 and obviously belongs to a different generation from the vast majority of college students today. Do you feel that her type of love and advocacy of reading are as valid for the current generation, raised on television, video, cassettes, VCRs, CDs, satellite dishes, and MTV? Explain.

3. Welty describes her love of books as going beyond the words and
   stories they contain to their physical and visual attributes. What
   objects—not other people—do you love or respect with that
   intensity? Tell a little about why and how you have developed
   this feeling.

IDEAS FOR WRITING

Guided Writing

Write an essay that describes your own attitude toward reading.

1. In order to set the stage for the discussion of your attitude, begin
   by recalling details about a moment with a parent or other adult.
2. Use dialogue as part of this scene.
3. Go as far back in your childhood as you can possibly remember,
   and narrate two or three incidents that help explain the formation of your current attitude toward reading.
4. Use sensory language (color, sound, smell, touch, and taste) to
   show how the environment of the home where you grew up
   helped shape your attitude.
5. Tell about a particular, special childhood fascination with something you *saw*—not read—in a book.
6. Try to describe the first time you were conscious of the *meaning*
   of a particular word.
7. Use at least one *simile* in your essay.
8. Create and keep a consistent *tone* throughout the essay.
9. End your essay with an explanation of how a particular book
   has been continually influential to you as well as to others of
   your generation.
10. Give your essay an unusual title that derives from some descrip-
    tion in your essay.

More Writing Projects

1. Enter in your journal early memories of people who read to you
   or of books that you read on your own. Try to capture the sensation and importance of these early reading experiences.

2. Return to question 2 in Exploring the Writer's Ideas, and write a one-paragraph response to it.

3. Write an essay on the person who most influenced your childhood education. Did this person read to you, give you books, make you do your homework? Assess the impact of this person on your life.

Prison Studies
Malcolm X

Born Malcolm Little in Omaha, Nebraska, Malcolm X (1925–1965) was a charismatic leader of the black power movement and founded the Organization of Afro-American Unity. In prison, he became a Black Muslim. (He split with this faith in 1963 to convert to orthodox Islam.) "Prison Studies" is excerpted from the popular and fascinating *Autobiography of Malcolm X,* which he cowrote with *Roots* author Alex Haley. The essay describes the writer's struggle to learn to read as well as the joy and power he felt when he won that struggle.

Words to Watch

emulate (par. 2)   imitate, especially from respect

motivation (par. 2)   reason to do something

tablets (par. 3)   writing notebooks

bunk (par. 9)   small bed

rehabilitation (par. 10)   the process of restoring to a state of usefulness or constructiveness

inmate (par. 10)   prisoner

corridor (par. 13)   hallway; walkway

vistas (par. 15)   mental overviews

confers (par. 15)   bestows; gives ceremoniously

alma mater (par. 15)   the college that one has attended

1   Many who today hear me somewhere in person, or on television, or those who read something I've said, will think I went to school far beyond the eighth grade. This impression is due entirely to my prison studies.

2   It had really begun back in the Charlestown Prison, when Bimbi first made me feel envy of his stock of knowledge. Bimbi had always taken charge of any conversation he was in, and I had tried to emulate him. But every book I picked up had few sentences which didn't contain anywhere from one to nearly all of the words that might as well have been in Chinese. When I just

skipped those words, of course, I really ended up with little idea of what the book said. So I had come to the Norfolk Prison Colony still going through only book-reading motions. Pretty soon, I would have quit even these motions, unless I had received the motivation that I did.

I saw that the best thing I could do was get hold of a 3 dictionary—to study, to learn some words. I was lucky enough to reason also that I should try to improve my penmanship. It was sad. I couldn't even write in a straight line. It was both ideas together that moved me to request a dictionary along with some tablets and pencils from the Norfolk Prison Colony school.

I spent two days just riffling uncertainly through the 4 dictionary's pages. I'd never realized so many words existed! I didn't know which words I needed to learn. Finally, to start some kind of action, I began copying.

In my slow, painstaking, ragged handwriting, I copied into 5 my tablet everything printed on that first page, down to the punctuation marks.

I believe it took me a day. Then, aloud, I read back, to my- 6 self, everything I'd written on the tablet. Over and over, aloud, to myself, I read my own handwriting.

I woke up the next morning, thinking about those words— 7 immensely proud to realize that not only had I written so much at one time, but I'd written words that I never knew were in the world. Moreover, with a little effort, I also could remember what many of these words meant. I reviewed the words whose meanings I didn't remember. Funny thing, from the dictionary first page right now, that "aardvark" springs to my mind. The dictionary had a picture of it, a long-tailed, long-eared, burrowing African mammal, which lives off termites caught by sticking out its tongue as an anteater does for ants.

I was so fascinated that I went on—I copied the dictio- 8 nary's next page. And the same experience came when I studied that. With every succeeding page, I also learned of people and places and events from history. Actually the dictionary is like a miniature encyclopedia. Finally the dictionary's A section had filled a whole tablet—and I went on into the B's. That was the way I started copying what eventually became the entire dictionary. It went a lot faster after so much practice helped me to pick up handwriting speed. Between what I wrote in my tablet, and writing letters, during the rest of my time in prison I would guess I wrote a million words.

9   I suppose it was inevitable that as my word-base broadened, I could for the first time pick up a book and read and now begin to understand what the book was saying. Anyone who has read a great deal can imagine the new world that opened. Let me tell you something; from then until I left that prison, in every free moment I had, if I was not reading in the library, I was reading on my bunk. You couldn't have gotten me out of books with a wedge. Between Mr. Muhammad's teachings, my correspondence, my visitors—usually Ella and Reginald—and my reading of books, months passed without my even thinking about being imprisoned. In fact, up to then, I never had been so truly free in my life. . . .

10   As you can imagine, especially in a prison where there was heavy emphasis on rehabilitation, an inmate was smiled upon if he demonstrated an unusually intense interest in books. There was a sizable number of well-read inmates, especially the popular debaters. Some were said by many to be practically walking encyclopedias. They were almost celebrities. No university would ask any student to devour literature as I did when this new world opened to me, of being able to read and *understand*.

11   I read more in my room than in the library itself. An inmate who was known to read a lot could check out more than the permitted maximum number of books. I preferred reading in the total isolation of my own room.

12   When I had progressed to really serious reading, every night at about ten P.M. I would be outraged with the "lights out." It always seemed to catch me right in the middle of something engrossing.

13   Fortunately, right outside my door was a corridor light that cast a glow into my room. The glow was enough to read by, once my eyes adjusted to it. So when "lights out" came, I would sit on the floor where I could continue reading in that glow.

14   At one-hour intervals the night guards paced past every room. Each time I heard the approaching footsteps, I jumped into bed and feigned sleep. And as soon as the guard passed, I got back out of bed onto the floor area of that light-glow, where I would read for another fifty-eight minutes—until the guard ap-

proached again. That went on until three or four every morning. Three or four hours of sleep a night was enough for me. Often in the years in the streets I had slept less than that.

I have often reflected upon the new vistas that reading 15 opened to me. I knew right there in prison that reading had changed forever the course of my life. As I see it today, the ability to read awoke inside me some long dormant craving to be mentally alive. I certainly wasn't seeking any degree, the way a college confers a status symbol upon its students. My homemade education gave me, with every additional book that I read, a little bit more sensitivity to the deafness, dumbness, and blindness that was afflicting the black race in America. Not long ago, an English writer telephoned me from London, asking questions. One was, "What's your alma mater?" I told him, "Books." You will never catch me with a free fifteen minutes in which I'm not studying something I feel might be able to help the black man. . . .

Every time I catch a plane, I have with me a book that I 16 want to read—and that's a lot of books these days. If I weren't out here every day battling the white man, I could spend the rest of my life reading, just satisfying my curiosity—because you can hardly mention anything I'm not curious about. I don't think anybody ever got more out of going to prison than I did. In fact, prison enabled me to study far more intensively than I would have if my life had gone differently and I had attended some college. I imagine that one of the biggest troubles with colleges is there are too many distractions, too much panty-raiding, fraternities, and boola-boola and all of that. Where else but in prison could I have attacked my ignorance by being able to study intensely sometimes as much as fifteen hours a day?

BUILDING VOCABULARY

1. Throughout the selection, Malcolm X uses *figurative* and *colloquial language* (see Glossary). As you know, figurative language involves imaginative comparisons, which go beyond plain or ordinary statements. Colloquial language involves informal or conversational phrases and expressions.

The following are examples of some of the figurative and colloquial usages in this essay. Explain each italicized word group in your own words.

a. *going through* only *book-reading motions* (par. 2)
b. I was *lucky enough* (par. 3)
c. *Funny thing* (par. 7)
d. can imagine *the new world that opened* (par. 9)
e. *You couldn't have gotten me out of books with a wedge* (par. 9)
f. an inmate was *smiled upon* (par. 10)
g. to be practically *walking encyclopedias* (par. 10)
h. ask any student *to devour literature* (par. 10)
i. changed forever *the course of my life* (par. 15)
j. *some long dormant craving* to be *mentally alive* (par. 15)
k. *the deafness, dumbness, and blindness that was afflicting* the black race in America (par. 15)
l. Every time I *catch a plane* (par. 16)
m. every day *battling the white man* (par. 16)
n. just *satisfying my curiosity* (par. 16)
o. *boola-boola and all of that* (par. 16)
p. I have *attacked my ignorance* (par. 16)

2. Find the following words in the essay. Write brief definitions for them without using a dictionary. If they are unfamiliar to you, try to determine their meaning based on the context in which they appear.

a. riffling (par. 4)
b. painstaking (par. 5)
c. ragged (par. 5)
d. burrowing (par. 7)
e. inevitable (par. 9)
f. emphasis (par. 10)
g. distractions (par. 16)

UNDERSTANDING THE WRITER'S IDEAS

1. What was the highest level of formal education that the writer achieved? How is this different from the impression most people got from him? Why?
2. Who was Bimbi? Where did Malcolm X meet him? How was Bimbi important to the writer?

3. What does the author mean by writing that when he tried to read, most of the words "might as well have been in Chinese"? What happened when he skipped over such words? What motivated him to change his way of reading?

4. Why did Malcolm X start trying to improve his handwriting? How was it connected to his desire to improve his reading ability? Briefly describe how he went about this dual process. How did he feel after the first day of this process? Why?

5. How is the dictionary "like a miniature encyclopedia"?

6. Judging from this essay and his description of his "homemade education," how much time did Malcolm X spend in prison? Does the fact that he was in prison affect your appreciation of his learning process? How?

7. What is a "word-base" (par. 9)? What happened once the author's word-base expanded? How did this give him a sense of freedom?

8. Who is "Mr. Muhammad"?

9. Why did the prison officials like Malcolm X? What special privileges came to him as a result of this favorable opinion?

10. Why was Malcolm X angered with the "lights out" procedure? How did he overcome it?

11. What does the following sentence tell you about Malcolm X's life: "Often in the years in the streets I had slept less than that" (par. 14)?

12. Characterize the writer's opinion of a college education. How does he compare his education to a college degree? How did his education influence his understanding of his place and role in American society?

13. In your own words, describe the writer's attitude toward American blacks. Toward the relation between blacks and whites?

14. To what main purpose in life does the writer refer? What was the relation between this purpose and his feelings about reading? Use one word to describe Malcolm X's attitude toward reading.

15. What is the meaning of the conclusion?

UNDERSTANDING THE WRITER'S TECHNIQUES

1. What is the thesis? Where does the writer place it?

2. Later in the book, you will learn about the techniques of *process*

analysis (see Chapter 9) and *cause-and-effect analysis* (see Chapter 10). Briefly, process analysis tells the reader *how* something is done, while cause-and-effect analysis explains *why* one thing leads to or affects another.

For this essay, outline step by step the process whereby Malcolm X developed his ability to read and enthusiasm for reading. Next, for each step in your outline, explain why one step led to the next.

3. *Narration* (see Chapter 4) is the telling of a story or the orderly relating of a series of events. How does Malcolm X use narration in this essay? How does he order the events of his narration?

4. What is the effect of the author writing "Let me tell you something" in paragraph 9?

5. How is the author's memory of the first page of the dictionary like a dictionary entry itself? What does this say about the importance of this memory to the author?

6. *Tone* (see Glossary) is a writer's attitude toward his or her subject. Characterize the tone of this essay. What elements of the writing contribute to that tone? Be specific.

7. Which paragraphs make up the conclusion of this essay? How does the author develop his conclusion? How does he relate it to the main body of the essay? Do you feel that there is a change in tone (see question 6) in the conclusion? Explain, using specific examples.

8. What is Malcolm X's main purpose in writing this essay? For whom is it intended? How do you know?

EXPLORING THE WRITER'S IDEAS

1. Malcolm X writes about his newly found love of reading and ability to read: "In fact, up to then, I never had been so truly free in my life." Has learning any particular skill or activity ever given you such a feeling of freedom or joy? Explain.

2. What do you feel was the source of Malcolm X's attitude toward a college education? Do you think any of his points here are valid? Why? What are your opinions about the quality of the college education you are receiving?

3. The writer also implies that, in some ways, the educational opportunities of prison were superior to those he would have had at college. What is his basis for this attitude? Have you ever experienced a circumstance in which being restricted actually benefited you? Explain.

4. Malcolm X held very strong opinions about the relations between blacks and whites in America. Do some library research on him to try to understand his opinions. You might begin by reading *The Autobiography of Malcolm X,* from which this essay was excerpted. Do you agree or disagree with his feelings? Why?

5. Following Malcolm X's example, handwrite a page from a dictionary (a pocket dictionary will be fine), copying everything—including punctuation—*exactly!*

   How long did it take you? How did it make you feel? Did you learn anything from the experience?

IDEAS FOR WRITING

Guided Writing

Write an essay in which you tell about an activity that you can now perform but that once seemed impossible to you.

1. Open your essay with an example in which you compare what most people assume about your skill or background in the activity to what the reality is.

2. Mention someone who especially influenced you in your desire to master this activity.

3. Tell what kept you from giving up on learning this activity.

4. Explain, step by step, the *process* by which you learned more and more about the activity. Explain how and why one step led to the next.

5. Use *figurative* and *colloquial* language where you think it appropriate in your essay.

6. Describe in some detail how you overcame an obstacle, imposed by others, which could have impeded your learning process.

7. Use your conclusion to express a deeply felt personal opinion and to generalize your learning of this skill to the population at large.

More Writing Projects

1. Select any page of a standard dictionary and copy in your journal at least ten words, with definitions, that are new or somewhat unfamiliar to you. Then jot down some thoughts on the process.
2. Ask yourself formal, journalistic questions about Malcolm X's essay: *What* happened? *Who* was involved? *How* was it done? *Where* did it occur? *When* did it occur? *Why* did it happen? Write out answers to these questions, and then assemble them in a unified, coherent paragraph.
3. Form a group with three other classmates. Focus on the context of Malcolm X's essay and on his comment on "the deafness, dumbness, and blindness that was afflicting the black race in America" (par. 15). Discuss this issue and its connection to education. Then prepare a collaborative essay on the topic.

"See Spot Run": Teaching My Grandmother to Read

Ellen Tashie Frisina

Ellen Tashie Frisina writes about her "secret" project to teach her 70-year-old grandmother, who came to the United States from Greece in 1916, to read English. Frisina's narrative reveals the pleasures of reading and illustrates the importance of reading no matter what age the reader.

Words to Watch

differentiated (par. 1)   separated from; distinguished from
stealthily (par. 2)   secretly
monosyllabic (par. 3)   one syllable; short in length
vehemently (par. 8)   severely; intensely; angrily
phonetically (par. 14)   pronounced by sound
afghan (par. 15)   a blanket or shawl
crocheting (par. 15)   a type of needlework

When I was 14 years old, and very impressed with my teenage 1 status (looking forward to all the rewards it would bring), I set for myself a very special goal—a goal that so differentiated me from my friends that I don't believe I told a single one. As a teenager, I was expected to have deep, dark secrets, but I was not supposed to keep them from my friends.

My secret was a project that I undertook every day after 2 school for several months. It began when I stealthily made my way into the local elementary school—horror of horrors should I be seen; I was now in junior high. I identified myself as a *graduate* of the elementary school, and being taken under wing by a favorite fifth grade teacher, I was given a small bundle from a locked storeroom—a bundle that I quickly dropped into a bag, lest anyone see me walking home with something from the "little kids" school.

I brought the bundle home—proudly now, for within the 3 confines of my home, I was proud of my project. I walked into the living room, and one by one, emptied the bag of basic reading books. They were thin books with colorful covers and large print. The words were monosyllabic and repetitive. I sat down to the secret task at hand.

4   "All right," I said authoritatively to my 70-year-old grand-mother, "today we begin our first reading lesson."

5   For weeks afterward, my grandmother and I sat patiently side by side—roles reversed as she, with a bit of difficulty, sounded out every word, then read them again, piece by piece, until she understood the short sentences. When she slowly repeated the full sentence, we both would smile and clap our hands—I felt so proud, so grown up.

6   My grandmother was born in Kalamata, Greece, in a rocky little farming village where nothing much grew. She never had the time to go to school. As the oldest child, she was expected to take care of her brother and sister, as well as the house and meals, while her mother tended to the gardens, and her father scratched out what little he could from the soil.

7   So, for my grandmother, schooling was out. But she had big plans for herself. She had heard about America. About how rich you could be. How people on the streets would offer you a dollar just to smell the flower you were carrying. About how everyone lived in nice houses—not stone huts on the sides of mountains—and had nice clothes and time for school.

8   So my grandmother made a decision at 14—just a child, I realize now—to take a long and sickening 30-day sea voyage alone to the United States. After lying about her age to the pass-port officials, who would shake their heads vehemently at anyone under 16 leaving her family, and after giving her favorite gold earrings to her cousin, saying "In America, I will have all the gold I want," my young grandmother put herself on a ship. She landed in New York in 1916.

9   No need to repeat the story of how it went for years. The streets were not made of gold. People weren't interested in smelling flowers held by strangers. My grandmother was a for-eigner. Alone. A young girl who worked hard doing piecework to earn enough money for meals. No leisure time, no new gold ear-rings—and no school.

10   She learned only enough English to help her in her daily business as she traveled about Brooklyn. Socially, the "foreign-ers" stayed in neighborhoods where they didn't feel like foreign-ers. English came slowly.

My grandmother had never learned to read. She could make 11
out a menu, but not a newspaper. She could read a street sign, but
not a shop directory. She could read only what she needed to read
as, through the years, she married, had five daughters, and helped
my grandfather with his restaurant.

So when I was 14—the same age that my grandmother was 12
when she left her family, her country, and everything she knew—
I took it upon myself to teach my grandmother something, something I already knew how to do. Something with which I could
give back to her some of the things she had taught me.

And it was slight repayment for all she taught me. How to 13
cover the fig tree in tar paper so it could survive the winter. How
to cultivate rose bushes and magnolia trees that thrived on her
little piece of property. How to make baklava, and other Greek
delights, working from her memory. ("Now we add some milk."
"How much?" "Until we have enough.") Best of all, she had
taught me my ethnic heritage.

First, we phonetically sounded out the alphabet. Then, we 14
talked about vowels—English is such a difficult language to
learn. I hadn't even begun to explain the different sounds "gh"
could make. We were still at the basics.

Every afternoon, we would sit in the living room, my 15
grandmother with an afghan covering her knees, giving up her
crocheting for her reading lesson. I, with the patience that can
come only from love, slowly coached her from the basic reader
to the second-grade reader, giving up my telephone gossiping.

Years later, my grandmother still hadn't learned quite 16
enough to sit comfortably with a newspaper or magazine, but it
felt awfully good to see her try. How we used to laugh at her pro-
nunciation mistakes. She laughed more heartily than I. I never
knew whether I should laugh. Here was this old woman slowly
and carefully sounding out each word, moving her lips, not saying anything aloud until she was absolutely sure, and then, loudly, proudly, happily saying, "Look at Spot. See Spot run."

When my grandmother died and we faced the sad task of 17
emptying her home, I was going through her night-table drawer
and came upon the basic readers. I turned the pages slowly, remembering. I put them in a paper bag, and the next day returned
them to the "little kids" school. Maybe someday, some teenager
will request them again, for the same task. It will make for a lifetime of memories.

BUILDING VOCABULARY

Put the following phrases into your own words and explain what the writer means in the context of the essay:

1. "very impressed with my teenage status" (par. 1)
2. "No need to repeat the story of how it went for years." (par. 9) Why not? What is the implication of this sentence?
3. "doing piecework to earn enough money for meals." (par. 9) What was piecework?
4. "Best of all, she had taught me my ethnic heritage." (par. 13)
5. "First, we phonetically sounded out the alphabet." (par. 14)

UNDERSTANDING THE WRITER'S IDEAS

1. The author begins by saying that her project was a secret from her junior high school peers. Explain why a 14-year-old would not want to be seen carrying basic readers. What further reasons might the author have had for keeping her project a secret?
2. In paragraph 3, the author uses the words "proudly" and "proud." Why has her attitude changed?
3. How does teaching her grandmother to read change the relation between the two? How does Frisina speak to her grandmother in paragraph 4?
4. What are the myths about America that cause the grandmother to make her difficult decision to leave her family in Greece? How does the real America live up to the stories the grandmother had heard before she arrived? How common are experiences like the grandmother's for other immigrants?
5. What does Frisina imply in paragraph 10 about the daily life of immigrants in the early twentieth century? How is language usually acquired? What limits the grandmother's ability to learn English?
6. The author provides details of what her grandmother taught her for which the author is grateful. How do the specific details help the reader understand the kind of woman the grandmother was? What kind of life did the grandmother lead?
7. In paragraph 14, the author describes how hard it is to learn English. What in particular makes English a hard language to read?

What can you tell from paragraph 17 about how the grandmother felt about her reading? Why does the grandmother keep the schoolbooks in her night-table drawer? What does this tell you about how she felt about learning to read?

UNDERSTANDING THE WRITER'S TECHNIQUES

1. Where does the author place her thesis statement? Why does she put it where she does? Explain the thesis in your own words.
2. *Diction* (see Glossary) refers to a writer's choice and use of words. We classify *levels of diction*—"informal," "academic," "low-class," "snobbish," "conversational," and so forth. How would you describe the general level of diction in this essay? Does the level suit the subject matter? Why?
3. Why does the author rely on short paragraphs throughout her narrative? What does the paragraph length and diction tell you about the intended audience for this piece?
4. The writer assumes that the reader is familiar with the history of immigration in America in the early twentieth century. How do we know that she makes this assumption? Should she provide readers with more historical detail? Why or why not?
5. Describe the method the author uses to teach her grandmother to read. Is this the way you remember learning to read? Describe the first book you remember reading. How did your experience compare with the grandmother's?

EXPLORING THE WRITER'S IDEAS

1. The author uses the story of her grandmother's life to illustrate the experiences of many immigrants who came to America in the early twentieth century. How do those experiences compare with the arrival of immigrants to America today? Is it easier or more difficult to immigrate here now? What evidence can you provide to support your position?
2. Though the grandmother could barely read a newspaper, even her limited literacy seemed to give her pleasure. Why should learning to read be so important to an adult who cannot read? In a world

of television, movies, and other visual sources of information, is learning to read truly important for illiterate adults? Why or why not?

3. The effort to teach and learn reading helps bridge the gap between generations. Do you see any practical applications here for bringing old and young people together for more harmonious relations? How else can young people and old people be united?

IDEAS FOR WRITING

Guided Writing

Write an essay titled "Teaching _____ to _____." Fill in the blanks after considering your own experience with teaching someone something. You might choose one of these topics:

a. Teaching my daughter/son to read
b. Reading English as a second language (about your own experience or someone else's)
c. Working as a volunteer in a neighborhood literacy program

1. Begin your essay with a general discussion about the expectations you had when you started this learning project and the feelings you had when you accomplished it.
2. Define yourself as a reader. What age were you when you started the project? What kind of reading did you do? How did you feel about reading? Why?
3. Explain why you started the project of teaching someone to read or of changing the level of your own reading skill. What situation encouraged or required you to change or act?
4. Use examples and illustrations to show how you began the task. Give examples of words and sentences you worked with. Give the steps you used to carry out your project.
5. Describe the moment when a change happened—the first time your son or daughter read to you or the first time a difficult English sentence became clear. Use dialogue to capture the moment.
6. Analyze how you changed as a result of this moment, and why you remember it so vividly.
7. Conclude by describing your present status as a reader, or the

skills level of the person you taught to read. Was the project worthwhile?

More Writing Projects

1. In your journal, write down your ideas about what the difference is between reading "See Spot run" and reading a science textbook or a technical manual or a play by Shakespeare. Give steps by which a reader can increase his or her reading skills.
2. Write a paragraph in which you consider whether or not it is important to be a "good" reader to succeed in life.
3. Can teaching someone else, like a son or daughter, to read teach you to read better as well? Write an essay in which you discuss a parent's role in teaching his or her child to read. Consider what the child learns at school and what he or she learns at home about reading.

Survival

Margaret Atwood

Margaret Atwood is a Canadian poet and novelist whose works, such as *The Edible Woman* (1969) and *Bodily Harm* (1981), often deal with alienation and people's insensitivities toward one another and the environment. In this selection from her 1972 book, *Survival: A Thematic Guide to Canadian Literature*, Atwood explains how, even as a budding Canadian writer, she was almost ignorant of Canadian literature. However, through her richly detailed descriptions, she also communicates the delight she came to experience—and still experiences—in reading Canadian authors.

Words to Watch

enhanced (par. 1)   made more valuable

sniveled (par. 1)   acted in a whining or emotionally weak manner

artifacts (par. 3)   simple, usually handmade objects such as tools or ornaments (often refers to ancient objects)

stress (par. 4)   emphasis

snares (par. 4)   animal traps

posthaste (par. 4)   immediately

domestic (par. 5)   family- or home-related

menace (par. 5)   threat; danger

curricula (par. 6)   sets of academic courses

1   I started reading Canadian literature when I was young, though I didn't know it was that; in fact I wasn't aware that I lived in a country with any distinct existence of its own. At school we were being taught to sing "Rule, Britannia" and to draw the Union Jack; after hours we read stacks of Captain Marvel, Plastic Man and Batman comic books, an activity delightfully enhanced by the disapproval of our elders. However, someone had given us Charles G. D. Roberts' *Kings in Exile* for Christmas, and I sniveled my way quickly through these heart-wrenching stories of animals caged, trapped and tormented. That was followed by Ernest Thompson Seton's *Wild Animals I Have Known*, if anything more upsetting because the animals were more actual—

they lived in forests, not circuses—and their deaths more mundane: the deaths, not of tigers, but of rabbits.

No one called these stories Canadian literature, and I 2 wouldn't have paid any attention if they had; as far as I was concerned they were just something else to read, along with Walter Scott, Edgar Allan Poe and Donald Duck. I wasn't discriminating in my reading, and I'm still not. I read then primarily to be entertained, as I do now. And I'm not saying that apologetically: I feel that if you remove the initial gut response from reading—the delight or excitement or simply the enjoyment of being told a story—and try to concentrate on the meaning or the shape or the "message" first, you might as well give up, it's too much like all work and no play.

But then as now there were different levels of entertain- 3 ment. I read the backs of Shredded Wheat boxes as an idle pastime, Captain Marvel and Walter Scott as fantasy escape—I knew, even then, that wherever I lived it wasn't *there,* since I'd never seen a castle and the Popsicle Pete prizes advertised on the comic book covers either weren't available in Canada, or cost more—and Seton and Roberts as, believe it or not, something closer to real life. I *had* seen animals, quite a few of them; a dying porcupine was more real to me than a knight in armor or Clark Kent's Metropolis. Old mossy dungeons and Kryptonite were hard to come by where I lived, though I was quite willing to believe they existed somewhere else; but the materials for Seton's stick-and-stone artifacts and live-off-the-land recipes in *Wildwood Wisdom* were readily available, and we could make them quite easily, which we did. Most of the recipes were somewhat inedible, as you'll see if you try Cattail Root Stew or Pollen Pancakes, but the raw ingredients can be collected around any Canadian summer cottage.

However, it wasn't just the content of these books that felt 4 more real to me; it was their shapes, their patterns. The animal stories were about the struggle to survive, and Seton's practical handbook was in fact a survival manual: it laid much stress on the dangers of getting lost, eating the wrong root or berry, or angering a moose in season. Though it was full of helpful hints, the world it depicted was one riddled with pitfalls, just as the animal stories were thickly strewn with traps and snares. In this world, no Superman would come swooping out of the sky at the last minute to rescue you from the catastrophe; no rider would arrive posthaste with a pardon from the King. The main thing was to avoid dying, and only by a mixture of cunning, experience and narrow escapes could the animal—or the human relying on his own resources—manage that. And, in the animal stories at any rate, there were no final happy endings or ultimate solutions; if the animal happened to escape from the particular crisis in the story, you knew there would be another one later on from which it wouldn't escape.

5   I wasn't making these analytical judgments at the time, of course. I was just learning what to expect: in comic books and things like *Alice in Wonderland* or Conan Doyle's *The Lost World,* you got rescued or you returned from the world of dangers to a cozy safe domestic one; in Seton and Roberts, because the world of dangers was *the same* as the real world, you didn't. But when in high school I encountered—again as a Christmas present—something labeled more explicitly as Canadian Literature, the Robert Weaver and Helen James anthology, *Canadian Short Stories,* I wasn't surprised. There they were again, those animals on the run, most of them in human clothing this time, and those humans up against it; here was the slight mistake that led to disaster, here was the fatal accident; this was a world of frozen corpses, dead gophers, snow, dead children, and the ever-present feeling of menace, not from an enemy set over against you but from everything surrounding you. The familiar peril lurked behind every bush, and *I knew the names of the bushes.* Again, I wasn't reading this as Canlit, I was just reading it; I remember being elated by some stories (notably James Reaney's "The Bully") and not very interested in others. But these stories felt real to me in a way that Charles Dickens, much as I enjoyed him, did not.

6   I've talked about these early experiences not because I think that they were typical but because I think that—significantly—they weren't: I doubt that many people my age had even this much contact, minimal and accidental though it was, with their own literature. (Talking about this now makes me feel about 102, because quite a lot has changed since then. But though new curricula are being invented here and there across the country, I'm not convinced that the *average* Canadian child or high school student is likely to run across much more Canadian literature than I did. *Why* this is true is of course one of our problems.)

Still, although I didn't read much Canadian writing, what I ₇
did read had a shape of its own that felt different from the shapes
of the other things I was reading. What that shape turned out to
be, and what I felt it meant in terms of this country, became
clearer to me the more I read.

BUILDING VOCABULARY

1. A writer will often use *allusions* (see Glossary), or references to
   people, events, places, literature, and aspects of a particular culture or era. In order to better understand Atwood's essay, try to
   identify as many of the following allusions as you can:
   a. "Rule, Britannia," the Union Jack, Captain Marvel, Plastic
   Man, Batman, G. D. Roberts, Ernest Thompson Seton (par. 1)
   b. Walter Scott, Edgar Allan Poe, Donald Duck (par. 2)
   c. Shredded Wheat, Popsicle Pete, Clark Kent's Metropolis,
   Kryptonite (par. 3)
   d. *Alice in Wonderland,* Conan Doyle, Charles Dickens (par. 5)
2. Select the letter of the word following it that best defines the
   word in italics.

   1. *distinct*   **a.** wonderful   **b.** cloudy   **c.** well-defined
   d. careful

   2. *mundane*   **a.** common   **b.** tragic   **c.** horrible
   d. timely

   3. *initial*   **a.** nervous   **b.** warm   **c.** first   **d.** alphabetic

   4. *readily*   **a.** inexpensively   **b.** speedily   **c.** willingly
   d. really

   5. *inedible*   **a.** unfit for consumption   **b.** delicious
   c. difficult   **d.** different

   6. *depicted*   **a.** ridiculed   **b.** represented   **c.** longed for
   d. hated

   7. *cunning*   **a.** speed   **b.** trickery   **c.** cleverness
   d. cuteness

   8. *cozy*   **a.** comfortable   **b.** limited   **c.** familiar
   d. boring

   9. *explicitly*   **a.** precisely   **b.** sexually   **c.** unhappily
   d. hopelessly

10. *fatal*   **a.** deadly   **b.** fated   **c.** tragic   **d.** weary
11. *elated*   **a.** sad   **b.** gleeful   **c.** confused   **d.** welcome
12. *minimal*   **a.** short-lived   **b.** fortunate   **c.** minor
    d. major

UNDERSTANDING THE WRITER'S IDEAS

1. What point about the sense of national identity for Canadians of her generation (she was born in 1939) does Atwood make in the opening sentence? How does the next sentence illustrate that point? With what nation are "Rule, Britannia" and the Union Jack associated?

2. How did Atwood's parents' attitude toward comic books affect her enjoyment of them?

3. What nationality were the writers Charles G. D. Roberts and Ernest Thompson Seton? What did Atwood feel when she read them for the first time? Why did she read them? What were their respective subject matters?

4. Did the young Atwood enjoy reading? Was she choosy about what she read? What was her main reason for reading? What is it as an adult?

5. According to the writer, what happens if you concentrate too much on the "meaning" of what you are reading?

6. For what purpose would Atwood read things like Walter Scott or Captain Marvel? To where does the italicized *there* in paragraph 3 refer? How did writers such as Seton and Roberts, and the environments they described, feel to Atwood when she first read them? Why? Explain how her references to "Cattail Root Stew" and "Pollen Pancakes" connect with this feeling.

7. Summarize in your own words why it was not just Seton's and Roberts's subject matter, but also the "shapes" and "patterns" of their writing that held special significance for Atwood. What was their overview of life? What does their appeal tell you about Atwood's outlook as a child?

8. Contrast the two different types of "worlds of danger" discussed in paragraph 5.

9. How did Atwood react upon reading the anthology *Canadian Short Stories* when in high school? Why? Who are "those animals" (par. 5)? What is "Canlit"?

10. Does Atwood think that the majority of Canadians have a good sense of their national literature? Explain. How has the situation changed since she was a child? How has it remained the same? What is her idea about the connection between reading and self-image? Based on your understanding of the entire essay, what would you assume Atwood sees as "the shape" of Canadian literature as she refers to it in her conclusion?

UNDERSTANDING THE WRITER'S TECHNIQUES

1. Is there a single statement of the main idea of this essay? Explain. Which paragraphs comprise the introduction, body, and conclusion of this essay?

2. For whom did Atwood write this essay? Is it equally significant to both Canadian and non-Canadian readers? Why?

3. *Transitions* (see Glossary) enable writers to move from one idea to the next, or one paragraph to the next, while maintaining the *coherence* (logical connections) of their ideas. It is interesting to note that Atwood consistently uses grammatical negatives in the first sentences of the paragraphs of this selection.

Go through the essay and list some of the grammatical negatives that appear in the opening sentences of selected paragraphs. How does this pattern serve as a transition device? For what other reasons might she be using these constructions?

4. At the end of paragraph 2, why does the writer place the word "message" in quotation marks?

5. In paragraph 5, Atwood italicizes a statement of seemingly not much importance on its own: "*I knew the names of the bushes.*" Why does she place it in italics? How is it so significant to the paragraph or the essay?

6. The techniques of *description* and *illustration* (see Glossary) go hand in hand to make a writer's abstract ideas clear and vivid for readers. Generally, how does Atwood use description and illustration in this essay? Choose a particular paragraph and explain in detail what ideas the author's descriptions and illustrations make clear for you.

7. In the Building Vocabulary section, you identified various *allusions* (see page 75) in this essay. For what purpose did the author include so many allusions? Which were the most important to your understanding of the essay? Why?

8. Atwood uses four adjectives composed of between two and four words linked by hyphens. ("Stick-and-stone" in paragraph 3 is one example.) Find and list the other three. What single-word adjectives could she have used instead? How would that have altered the tone of the sentences in which these adjectives appear?

9. Paragraph 6 is at least half composed of an explanation in parentheses. What is the main point of paragraph 6? What is Atwood's reason for the parenthetical explanation? How would it have affected the paragraph's meaning if she had written all the same sentences but had omitted the parentheses?

10. What is the significance of the title of this essay? Are there possible multiple meanings? Explain your answer with specific references to the essay.

EXPLORING THE WRITER'S IDEAS

1. Clearly, Atwood is proud of her heritage as a Canadian, as well as of her status as a Canadian writer. Look up and define the following words: *nationalist, patriot, chauvinist.* Which word most closely describes Atwood's attitude in this essay? Why?

2. Atwood makes the point that if you try too hard to understand the "message" of a story, you are likely to miss its "delight or excitement." What different responses do you experience when reading for an assignment versus reading for your own reasons? Describe the differences. Which do you enjoy more? From which do you learn more? Explain. How do you feel that school reading assignments can be made more pleasurable?

3. Do you believe that different countries produce significantly different types of literature? Explain. Discuss some of the best-known authors from countries other than your own. How many have you read? In general, do you more enjoy reading works by authors from your own country (or region) or from elsewhere? Why? How are the two reading experiences different for you?

IDEAS FOR WRITING

Guided Writing

Write an essay that explains how you came to appreciate a particular aspect of your own national culture or ethnic background.

1. Begin by telling when you first became aware of this aspect of your culture. Tell how circumstances or the environment around you did not necessarily encourage your appreciation.
2. Introduce specific examples of this cultural aspect that were important in shaping your appreciation.
3. Where appropriate, use allusions as examples of other things that were more available to you than your own culture.
4. Use specific examples to support your point.
5. Throughout the essay, keep as an unstated purpose to educate your readers to the value and joy of this aspect of your culture.
6. Use clear transitions between paragraphs.
7. Describe how your initial attraction blossomed into a deep appreciation.
8. Explain to your readers your main reason for relating these early experiences. In this overall explanation, include a long parenthetical explanation.
9. Give your essay a one-word title.

More Writing Projects

1. Atwood writes about reading to be entertained rather than instructed. Write in your journal about books, television shows, and films that you have found entertaining —even if they haven't had a serious "message."
2. Describe in a paragraph your favorite story, book, or television program from childhood.
3. Do you think that publishers, film studios, and television producers have a responsibility to present entertainment reflecting the cultural diversity of the United States? Take a position on this issue and write an essay on it.

SUMMING UP: CHAPTER 2

1. In one way or another, all the writers in this chapter explain how reading has provided them with emotional ease or intellectual stimulation at some point in their lives. Which of these writers, alone or in combination, best reflects your own view of reading? Write an essay in which you address this question.

2. On the average, Americans are said to read less than one book per person annually. Take a survey of several people who are not students to find out how often and what kind of books they read. In an essay, analyze the results. Indicate the types of people you interviewed, and explain why your results either conformed to or differed from the norm. Indicate the types of books each person read.

3. List all the books you have read in the past six months. For each, write a brief two- or three-sentence reaction. Compare your list with those of your classmates. What reading trends do you notice? From these lists, what generalizations can you draw about college students' reading habits?

4. The United States ranks forty-ninth among nations in literacy. People often ask, "Why is there such a low rate of literacy in such an advanced nation?" What is your answer to this question? How do you think the writers in this chapter would respond to the question? Write an essay that explains your response by drawing on Welty, Malcolm X, Atwood, and Frisina. Suggest some ways to improve the rate of literacy in this country. You might want to consider this fact: By the time the average American finishes high school, he or she has spent 18,000 hours in front of a television set as compared to 12,000 hours in the classroom.

5. Using Welty or Atwood as an example, write an essay in which you reflect on your early memories of reading. Describe when you learned to read, when you experienced pleasure at being read to, or when you started appreciating a particular kind of reading. Call your essay "Reading When I Was Young."

CHAPTER 3

Description

WHAT IS DESCRIPTION?

Description is a technique for showing readers what the writer sees: objects, scenes, characters, ideas, and even emotions and moods. Good description relies on the use of *sensory language*—that is, language that evokes our five senses of sight, touch, taste, smell, and sound. In writing, description uses specific *nouns* and *adjectives* to create carefully selected vivid details. The word "vehicle" is neutral, but a "rusty, green 1959 Pontiac convertible" creates a picture. Description is frequently used to make *abstract* ideas more *concrete*. While the abstract word "liberty" may have a definition for each reader, a description of the Statue of Liberty gleaming in New York's harbor at twilight creates an emotional description of liberty. Description, then, is used by writers who want their readers to *see* what they are writing about. A travel writer, like William Least Heat Moon, uses description to re-create for the armchair traveler the landscape he has been privileged to see. A physician, like Richard Selzer, uses description to re-create the experience of a dying patient. Maxine Hong Kingston uses vivid description of her mother's collection of turtles, catfish, pigeons, skunks, and other unexpected food sources to re-create for her readers a culture different from their own. Gretel Ehrlich relies on description to capture her often spiritual journey in the wilderness tracing the source of a river. Each writer, then, uses description to help us, as readers, *see* the material about which he or she is writing. As writers, we can study their techniques to improve our own essays.

HOW DO WE READ DESCRIPTION?

Reading a descriptive essay requires us to

- Identify what the writer is describing, and ask why he or she is describing it.
- Look for the concrete nouns, supportive adjectives, or other sensory words that the writer uses to create vivid pictures.
- Find the perspective or angle from which the writer describes: Is it top to bottom, left to right, front to back? Or is it a mood description that relies on feelings? How has the writer *selected* details to create the mood?
- Determine how the writer has organized the description. Here we must look for a "dominant impression." This arises from the writer's focus on a single subject and the feelings that the writer brings to that subject. Each one should be identified.
- Identify the purpose of the description. What is the *thesis* of the writing?
- Determine what audience the writer is aiming toward. How do we know?

HOW DO WE WRITE DESCRIPTION?

After reading some of the selections of descriptive writing in this chapter, you should be ready to write your own description. Don't just read about Kingston's animals, though, or William Least Heat Moon's desert. Think critically about how you can adapt their methods to your needs.

Select a topic and begin to write a thesis statement, keeping in mind that you will want to give the reader information about what you are describing and what angle you are taking on the topic.

Sample thesis sentence:

For a first-time tourist in New York City, the subway trains can seem confusing and threatening, but the long-time resident finds the train system a clever, speedy network for traveling around the city.

Here, we see the thesis statement sets out a purpose and an audience. The purpose is to demonstrate the virtues of the New York transit system, and the audience is not the well-traveled New Yorker, but a visitor.

Collect a list of sensory words.

New York City's subway trains are noisy and crowded, labeled with brightly colored letters, made of shiny corrugated stainless steel, travel at 90 miles per hour, display colorful graffiti and advertising signs, run on electricity.

Use the five senses:

What are subways sounds? Music by street musicians, the screech of brakes, conductors giving directions over scratchy loudspeakers, people talking in different languages.

What are subway smells? Pretzels roasting, the sweaty odor of human bodies crowded together on a hot summer day.

What are subway textures? Colored metal straps and poles for balance, the crisp corner of a newspaper you're reading.

What are subway tastes? A candy bar or chewing gum you buy at the newsstand.

What are subway sights? Crowds of people rushing to work; the colorful pillars freshly painted in each station; the drunk asleep on a bench; the police officer in a blue uniform; the litter on the ground; the subway system maps near each token booth; the advertising posters on the walls and trains.

Plan a dominant impression and an order for arranging details. You might look at the subway from a passenger's point of view and describe the travel process from getting onto the train to arriving at the destination. Your impression might be that to the uninitiated, the subway system seems confusing, but to the experienced New Yorker, trains are the fastest and safest way to get around town.

Express a *purpose* for the description. The purpose might be to prepare a visitor from out of town for her first subway ride by writing a letter to her before she arrives in New York.

Identify the audience: Who will read the essay?

If you were writing to the Commissioner of Transportation in New York, or to a cousin from Iowa whom you know well, you would write differently in each case. Awareness of audience can help you choose a level of diction and formality. Knowing your audience can also help you decide which details to include and which your readers might know. It is always best to assume that the audience knows less than you do and to include details even if they seem obvious to you.

For example, even if you, as a native New Yorker, know that subway trains run twenty-four hours a day, your cousin from Iowa would not be expected to know this, so you should include it as part of your description of how efficient the system is.

Writing the Draft

Use the thesis statement to set up an introductory paragraph. Then plan the body paragraphs so that they follow the order you decided on—from beginning the journey to arriving, from the top of a subway car to the bottom, or from the outside of the train to the inside. Include as many details in the first draft as possible; it is easier to take them out in a second or third draft than to add them later. Then plan the conclusion to help the reader understand what the purpose of the description has been.

Reading and Revising the Draft

Read your first draft, circling each description word. Then go back and add *another* description word after the ones already in the essay. If you can't think of any more words, use a *thesaurus* to find new words.

If possible, read your essay aloud to a classmate. Ask him or her to tell you if the details are vivid. Have your classmate suggest where more details are needed. Check to see that you have included some description in each sensory category: sight, sound, taste, touch, and smell.

Proofread your essay for correctness.

Make a clean, neat final copy.

Arizona 87
William Least Heat Moon

In this chapter from his 1982 book, *Blue Highways,* William Least Heat Moon presents a bittersweet, richly detailed description of the landscape he sees while driving his truck, Ghost Dancing, through the southwestern United States. As he drives through central Arizona, his careful eye photographs both the natural and the human landscape around him. In converting these snapshots to language, Least Heat Moon relies upon rich sensory detail and especially vivid and original comparisons.

Words to Watch

friable (par. 1)   easily crushed or pulverized

persnickety (par. 1)   fussy about small details

pollinate (par. 3)   to carry pollen to fertilize plant seeds

aerial (par. 3)   occurring in the air

kamikaze (par. 3)   a member of a corps of Japanese pilots assigned to make a suicidal crash at a target

cache (par. 4)   something hidden

marauding (par. 6)   roaming about in search of plunder

Apaches (par. 6)   a tribe of Native Americans of the southwestern United States

rodeo (par. 6)   a performance featuring cowboy stunts

badger (par. 7)   a burrowing animal with long claws

unobtrusively (par. 9)   not very obviously

escarpment (par. 9)   a long cliff

coalesced (par. 12)   came together

I don't suppose that saguaros mean to give comic relief to the 1 otherwise solemn face of the desert, but they do. Standing on the friable slopes they are quite persnickety about, saguaros mimic men as they salute, bow, dance, raise arms to wave, and grin with faces carved in by woodpeckers. Older plants, having survived odds against their reaching maturity of sixty million to one, have every right to smile.

The saguaro is ninety percent water, and a big, two- 2

hundred-year-old cactus may hold a ton of it—a two-year supply. With this weight, a plant that begins to lean is soon on the ground; one theory now says that the arms, which begin sprouting only after forty or fifty years when the cactus has some height, are counterweights to keep the plant erect.

3   The Monday I drove northeast out of Phoenix, saguaros were in bloom—comparatively small, greenish-white blossoms perched on top of the trunks like undersized Easter bonnets; at night, long-nosed bats came to pollinate them. But by day, cactus wrens, birds of daring aerial skill, put on the show as they made kamikaze dives between toothpick-size thorns into nest cavities, where they were safe from everything except the incredible ascents over the spines by black racers in search of eggs the snakes would swallow whole.

4   It was hot. The only shade along Arizona 87 lay under the bottomsides of rocks; the desert gives space then closes it up with heat. To the east, in profile, rose the Superstition Mountains, an evil place, Pima and Maricopa Indians say, which brings on diabolic possession to those who enter. Somewhere among the granite and greasewood was the Lost Dutchman gold mine, important not for whatever cache it might hide as for providing a white dream.

5   North of the Sycamore River, saguaro, ocotillo, paloverde, and cholla surrendered the hills to pads of prickly pear the size of a man's head. The road climbed and the temperature dropped. At Payson, a mile high on the northern slope of the Mazatzal Mountains, I had to pull on a jacket.

6   Settlers once ran into Payson for protection from marauding Apaches; after the Apache let things calm down, citizens tried to liven them up again by holding rodeos in the main street. Now, streets paved, Payson lay quiet but for the whine of sawmills releasing the sweet scent of cut timber.

7   I stopped at an old log hotel to quench a desert thirst. A sign on the door: NO LIVE ANIMALS ALLOWED. I guess you could bring in all the dead ones you wanted. A woman shouted, "Ain't servin' now." Her unmoving eyes, heavy as if cast from lead, watched suspiciously for a live badger under my jacket or a weasel up my pantleg.

8   "This is a fine old hotel," I said. She ignored me. "Do you mind if I look at your big map?" She shrugged and moved away, safe from any live animal attack. I was hunting a place to go

next. Someone had marked the Hopi Reservation to the north in red. Why not? As I left, I asked where I could water my lizard. She ignored that too.

Highway 260, winding through the pine forests of central 9 Arizona, let the mountains be boss as it followed whatever avenues they left open, crossing ridges only when necessary, slipping unobtrusively on narrow spans over streams of rounded boulders. But when 260 reached the massive escarpment called the Mogollon Rim, it had to challenge geography and climb the face.

I shifted to low, and Ghost Dancing pulled hard. A man 10 with a dusty, leathery face creased like an old boot strained on a bicycle—the old style with fat tires. I called a hello, he said nothing. At the summit, I waited to see whether he would make the ascent. Far below lay two cars, crumpled wads. Through the clear air I could count nine ranges of mountains, each successively grayer in a way reminiscent of old Chinese woodblock prints. The Mogollon was a spectacular place; the more so because I had not been anesthetized to it by endless Kodachromes. When the cyclist passed, I called out, "Bravo!" but he acknowledged nothing. I would have liked to talk to a man who, while his contemporaries were consolidating their little empires, rides up the Mogollon Rim on a child's toy. Surely he knew something about desperate men.

The top of the great scarp, elevation sixty-five hundred feet, 11 lay flat and covered with big ponderosas standing between dirty snowdrifts and black pools of snowmelt. I began anticipating Heber, the next town. One of the best moments of any day on the road was, toward sunset, looking forward to the last stop. At Heber I hoped for an old hotel with a little bar off to the side where they would serve A-1 on draft under a stuffed moosehead; or maybe I'd find a grill dishing up steak and eggs on blue-rimmed platters. I hoped for people who had good stories, people who sometimes took you home to see their collection of carved peach pits.

That was the hope. But Heber was box houses and a dingy 12 sawmill, a couple of motels and filling stations, a glass-and-Formica cafe. Heber had no center, no focus for the eye and soul: neither a courthouse, nor high church steeple, nor hotel. Nothing has done more to take a sense of civic identity, a feeling of community, from small-town America than the loss of old hotels to the motel business. The hotel was once where things coalesced, where you could meet both townspeople and travelers. Not so in a motel. No matter how you build it, the motel remains a haunt of the quick and dirty, where the only locals are Chamber of Commerce boys every fourth Thursday. Who ever heard the returning traveler exclaim over one of the great motels of the world he stayed in? Motels can be big, but never grand.

BUILDING VOCABULARY

1. *Compound words* are made up of two separate words joined together. They help intensify description by focusing on the connection between two words. Some compounds are formed by joining two nouns (*photograph, chairperson*); others combine nouns with nonnoun prefixes, suffixes, or combining forms (*childlike, self-pity*). Some compounds use hyphens between the two words, although the general current trend is to omit the hyphens. For example, such words as *today* or *tomorrow* were regularly hyphenated just 100 years ago. However, many compound words are still acceptable in all three steps of development: two separate words, a single hyphenated word, a single nonhyphenated word *(war monger, war-monger, warmonger)*.

   Locate at least ten compound words that in Least Heat Moon's essay are formed by joining two nouns. Use each in a sentence of your own.

2. *Denotation* refers to the dictionary definition of a word; *connotation* refers to the various shades of meaning and feeling readers bring to a word or phrase. (See Glossary.) Look up and write dictionary definitions for each of the words in italics below. Then, explain in your own words the connotative meaning of each sentence or phrase.

   a. the otherwise *solemn* face of the desert (par. 1)
   b. to *quench* a desert thirst (par. 7)
   c. it had to *challenge* geography (par. 9)
   d. I had not been *anesthetized* by endless *Kodachromes* (par. 10)
   e. glass-and-*Formica* cafe (par. 12)

3. Least Heat Moon is a careful observer of the plants, rocks, and wildlife of the Arizona landscape. List some of the words drawn from this landscape and write dictionary definitions of them.

UNDERSTANDING THE WRITER'S IDEAS

1. What are the saguaros? What are the odds of their reaching full growth? How old may saguaros become? At what age do they begin to sprout arms?
2. For what purpose do the cactus wrens use the saguaros? What is the major danger to these birds?
3. Explain the sentence: "The only shade along Arizona 87 lay under the bottom sides of rocks." (par. 4)
4. What is the American Indian legend about Superstition Mountains? Explain the "diabolic possession." What is supposedly hidden in these mountains and what is its importance? What is meant by "a white dream"?
5. How was the weather in Payson different from the weather when the writer started driving through the desert? What used to be the atmosphere in Payson? What is it like now?
6. Paragraph 9 describes the route of Highway 260. In your own words, how does the highway relate to the environment that surrounds it?
7. What is Moon's attitude toward the man on the bicycle? What do we learn about the man's appearance? How does the man react to Moon? What does Moon describe as "a child's toy"? Why?
8. How do we know that some cars fell off the Mogollon Rim?

UNDERSTANDING THE WRITER'S TECHNIQUES

1. Does the essay have a thesis? If so, where is it? Is the thesis stated or implied?
2. Writers often sharpen descriptions by making unusual comparisons. In this essay Least Heat Moon makes many such comparisons. Locate and explain the meaning of what each of the following things is compared to:
   a. the shape and look of the saguaros
   b. the saguaro blossoms
   c. the dives of the cactus wrens
   d. the appearance of the nine mountain ranges
   Locate and explain other comparisons in the essay.
3. How does Moon use elements of space and time to order details

in this description? Why is this method effective? Why does he introduce himself ("I drove") in paragraph 3? Why does he wait until then to introduce himself?

4. What is the effect of the short sentence "It was hot" (par. 4) coming as it does after a number of much longer sentences in preceding paragraphs?

5. *Imagery* (see Glossary) refers to clear, vivid description rooted in sensory detail. List several images of vivid details that employ the senses: sight (color and action), sound, smell, touch, and taste.

6. In describing the old log hotel in paragraphs 7 and 8, Moon uses *dialogue* (see Glossary), or accurate recordings of actual conversations. What is the effect of dialogue on that descriptive scene?

7. Least Heat Moon makes use of humor to make biting observations about the hotel in Payson. Explain what he means by "I guess you could bring in all the dead ones you wanted" (par. 7) and "As I left, I asked where I could water my lizard" (par. 8). Why does the woman ignore him? Why does he use biting humor in this way?

8. Least Heat Moon does not simply present factual details of the Arizona desert. Instead, his descriptions are highly subjective, colored with personal emotions. Locate five sentences of highly subjective description. Why is he so subjective? What impression does he give you of the scenes he describes? How does his subjectivity help create the *tone* (see Glossary) of this essay? What is that tone?

9. Do you find the ending suitable? Is it too abrupt or is it consistent with the rest of the selection? Explain. Remember, this selection is a complete chapter of a book by the author.

EXPLORING THE WRITER'S IDEAS

1. In the final paragraph Least Heat Moon writes about the disappearance of "civic identity" or "a feeling of community" from small-town America. He blames this loss on the replacement of once-bustling hotels with impersonal motels. Do you think the writer believes this is the only reason for the change? In your experience, how else have American small towns lost their unique flavors or identities?

2. In paragraph 10, in discussing the bicyclist, the author writes, "Surely he knew something about desperate men." Why do you think he feels this way about the cyclist?

IDEAS FOR WRITING

Guided Writing

Write a short essay describing a landscape you traveled through at one time. This can be a city, suburban, or countryside landscape.

1. Begin by concentrating on a particular or dominant element of the landscape.
2. Focus on the environmental conditions and the weather. Note any changes of the climate.
3. Arrange your description as you travel in time from place to place in the landscape.
4. Include at least one interaction with another person who helped you to formulate your feelings about the place.
5. Use concrete sensory detail as you write images of color, action, sound, smell, touch, and taste.
6. Use vivid and varied comparisons to describe what you saw.
7. Conclude your essay with a description and explanation of something that either greatly disappointed or excited you about your travels through this place.

More Writing Projects

1. Concentrating on both the setting and the person, enter in your journal a short description of a chance encounter with someone, as Least Heat Moon does with the bicyclist on the Mogollon Rim. End by coming to a conclusion about this person's personality.
2. Least Heat Moon writes, "Motels can be big, but never grand." Use this sentence as a thesis for a paragraph describing a specific motel you are familiar with. If you prefer to vary the lead sentence to focus on other travel facilities, feel free to do so.
3. Describe in an essay a particular place that you feel has been changed very much by modernization. Include descriptions of both the old and the new ways the place looks and feels. Also include your reactions to both the old and the new.

Catfish in the Bathtub

Maxine Hong Kingston

In this selection from her best-selling *The Woman Warrior* (1976), Chinese-American author Maxine Hong Kingston describes various strange eating habits of her childhood. The author skillfully blends techniques of personal narration and rich sensory detailing to create a fascinating impression of another culture's daily life-style.

Words to Watch

dromedaries (par. 1)   one-humped camels

sensibility (par. 1)   ability to receive sensations

perched (par. 1)   resting on a bird's roost

scowls (par. 1)   expressions of displeasure

dismembering (par. 1)   taking apart bodily limbs and innards

sprains (par. 2)   sudden twists of joints such as ankles or wrists

unsettle (par. 3)   make uneasy or uncomfortable

tufts (par. 4)   small patches of hair

awobble (par. 6)   unsteady, teetering

toadstools (par. 7)   mushrooms

revulsion (par. 8)   a strong reaction away from something

1 My mother has cooked for us: raccoons, skunks, hawks, city pigeons, wild ducks, wild geese, black-skinned bantams, snakes, garden snails, turtles that crawled about the pantry floor and sometimes escaped under refrigerator or stove, catfish that swam in the bathtub. "The emperors used to eat the peaked hump of purple dromedaries," she would say. "They used chopsticks made from rhinoceros horn, and they ate ducks' tongues and monkeys' lips." She boiled the weeds we pulled up in the yard. There was a tender plant with flowers like white stars hiding under the leaves, which were like the flower petals but green. I've not been able to find it since growing up. It had no taste. When I was as tall as the washing machine, I stepped out on the back porch one night, and some heavy, ruffling, windy, clawed thing dived at me. Even after getting chanted back to sensibility, I shook when I recalled

that perched everywhere there were owls with great hunched shoulders and yellow scowls. They were a surprise for my mother from my father. We children used to hide under the beds with our fingers in our ears to shut out the bird screams and the thud, thud of the turtles swimming in the boiling water, their shells hitting the sides of the pot. Once the third aunt who worked at the laundry ran out and bought us bags of candy to hold over our noses; my mother was dismembering skunk on the chopping block. I could smell the rubbery odor through the candy.

In a glass jar on a shelf my mother kept a big brown hand 2 with pointed claws stewing in alcohol and herbs. She must have brought it from China because I do not remember a time when I did not have the hand to look at. She said it was a bear's claw, and for many years I thought bears were hairless. My mother used the tobacco, leeks, and grasses swimming about the hand to rub our sprains and bruises.

Just as I would climb up to the shelf to take one look after 3 another at the hand, I would hear my mother's monkey story. I'd take my fingers out of my ears and let her monkey words enter my brain. I did not always listen voluntarily, though. She would begin telling the story, perhaps repeating it to a homesick villager, and I'd overhear before I had a chance to protect myself. Then the monkey words would unsettle me; a curtain flapped loose inside my brain. I have wanted to say, "Stop it. Stop it," but not once did I say, "Stop it."

"Do you know what people in China eat when they have 4 the money?" my mother began. "They buy into a monkey feast. The eaters sit around a thick wood table with a hole in the middle. Boys bring in the monkey at the end of a pole. Its neck is in a collar at the end of the pole, and it is screaming. Its hands are tied behind it. They clamp the monkey into the table; the whole table fits like another collar around its neck. Using a surgeon's saw, the cooks cut a clean line in a circle at the top of its head. To loosen the bone, they tap with a tiny hammer and wedge here and there with a silver pick. Then an old woman reaches out her hand to the monkey's face and up to its scalp, where she tufts some hairs and lifts off the lid of the skull. The eaters spoon out the brains."

Did she say, "You should have seen the faces the monkey 5 made"? Did she say, "The people laughed at the monkey screaming"? It was alive? The curtain flaps closed like merciful black wings.

6   "Eat! Eat!" my mother would shout at our heads bent over bowls, the blood pudding awobble in the middle of the table.

7   She had one rule to keep us safe from toadstools and such: "If it tastes good, it's bad for you," she said. "If it tastes bad, it's good for you."

8   We'd have to face four- and five-day-old leftovers until we ate it all. The squid eye would keep appearing at breakfast and dinner until eaten. Sometimes brown masses sat on every dish. I have seen revulsion on the faces of visitors who've caught us a meals.

9   "Have you eaten yet?" the Chinese greet one another.

10   "Yes, I have," they answer whether they have or not. "And you?"

11   I would live on plastic.

BUILDING VOCABULARY

1. Go through this essay again and list every animal mentioned. Then, write a short description of each, using the dictionary or encyclopedia if necessary.
2. Use any five of the Words to Watch in sentences of your own.

UNDERSTANDING THE WRITER'S IDEAS

1. What is Kingston saying about her childhood? How does her opening catalogue of foods that her mother prepared, combined with further descriptions of foods, support this point? What are some of the "strange" foods that she ate but that are not mentioned in this first paragraph?
2. Who are "the emperors" mentioned in paragraph 1? What were some of their more unusual dishes?
3. What attacks and frightens the young Kingston on her back porch? Where did they come from? How do we know that she was a young girl at the time? Explain the meaning of "even after getting chanted back to sensibility."
4. At the end of the first paragraph, the author mentions methods

she and her siblings used to shut out unpleasant sensory input. What were they?

5. For what purpose did her mother keep a bear's claw in a glass jar? Where did Kingston think it came from? Why?

6. What are "the monkey words"? Summarize the "monkey words" in your own language. Kingston says that she wanted to say "Stop it" to the monkey words, but didn't. Why didn't she?

7. What was Kingston's mother's attitude toward the taste of things in relation to their healthfulness?

8. Why would there sometimes be "revulsion on the faces of visitors" who watched the author's family eating?

9. What is the traditional Chinese greeting?

10. What is the author's overall attitude toward her mother? Explain.

UNDERSTANDING THE WRITER'S TECHNIQUES

1. Does Kingston ever make a direct *thesis statement?* Why or why not?

2. In this essay, Kingston seems to shift in and out of various tenses deliberately. For example, in paragraph 3, she writes: ". . . a curtain *flapped* loose inside my brain. I *have wanted* to say. . . ." Why do you think that Kingston uses such a technique? List three other examples of such tense shifts.

3. Comment on Kingston's use of transitions here. How do they contribute to the overall *coherence* (see Glossary) of the essay?

4. How does Kingston use the five senses to create descriptive imagery? Give examples of her use of sounds, tastes, smells, sights, and feelings. Which are the most effective?

5. Eliminating the specific references to China, how do we know that the author is of Chinese background? Which details or references contribute to this understanding?

6. Evaluate the use of *dialogue* (records of spoken words or conversations) in this essay. What effect does it have on the flow of the writing? On our understanding of Kingston's main point?

7. In paragraph 1, why does the author give so much attention to the white flower stars with no taste? Is she merely describing yet another thing she ate, or does she have some other purpose? Explain.

8. Although other incidents or ideas are described rather briefly, Kingston devotes a full, detailed paragraph to a description of the monkey feast. Why?

9. Throughout the essay, Kingston combines very realistic description (the bear's claw, the turtles thudding against the cook pot, the monkey feast) with various *similes* and *metaphors* (see Glossary). Explain the meaning of the following uses of *figurative language* (see Glossary):

   a. a curtain flapped loose inside by brain (par. 3)

   b. The curtain flaps closed like merciful black winds. (par. 5)

   c. Sometimes brown masses sat on every dish. (par. 8)

10. What is the effect of the series of questions in paragraph 5? Why are some in quotations and others not?

11. Explain the meaning of the last sentence. How does it relate to Kingston's *purpose* (see Glossary) in this essay?

EXPLORING THE WRITER'S IDEAS

1. Kingston certainly describes some "strange" foods and eating habits in this essay. But, what makes particular foods "strange"? What are some of the strangest foods you have ever eaten? Where did they come from? Why did you eat them? How did you react to them? What foods or eating habits that are common to your everyday life might be considered strange by people from other cultures?

2. In this essay, Kingston concentrates on her mother, mentioning her father only once. Speculate on why she excludes her father in this way, but base your speculation on the material of the essay.

3. As we all know, different cultures have very different customs. In this essay, for example, the author describes the Chinese way of greeting one another as well as the monkey feast, both of which are quite foreign to American culture. Describe different cultural customs that you have observed in your school, among your friends, in places around your city or town. How do you feel when you observe customs different from the ones you are familiar with? Do you believe that any particular custom is "right" or "wrong"? Why? Which custom among your own culture's would you most like to see changed? Why?

4. Describe you reaction to the monkey feast description.

5. For what reason do you think the Chinese greet each other with the words "Have you eaten yet?" Attempt to do further research into this custom. List as many different ways as you know of people greeting one another.

IDEAS FOR WRITING

Guided Writing

Write an essay entitled "Food" in which you describe its importance to you, your family, and your cultural background.

1. Begin with a list of important foods related to your family's lifestyle.
2. Show the role of your parents or other relatives in relation to these foods.
3. Briefly tell about an incident involving food that affected you deeply.
4. Create strong sensory imagery. Attempt to use at least one image for each of the five senses.
5. If possible, relate food customs to your family's ethnic or cultural background.
6. Use dialogue in your essay, including some of the dialogue of your "inner voice."
7. Use transitions to make the parts of your essay cohere.
8. Mention how outsiders experienced this custom.
9. End your essay with a direct statement to summarize your current attitude toward the food you have described and those times in your life.

More Writing Projects

1. In your journal, write a description of an interesting custom or activity that you witnessed, a custom coming from outside your own cultural or social background. Include vivid sensory details.
2. Describe in detail the most wonderful meal you have ever eaten.
3. Research and write a short report about the food and eating customs of a culture other than your own.

The Discus Thrower

Richard Selzer

Richard Selzer, a surgeon, gives his readers vivid insights into the excitement as well as the pathos of the world of medicine. His books include *Rituals of Surgery* (1974) and *Mortal Lessons* (1977). His essays are widely published in magazines, including *Esquire, Harper's,* and *Redbook.* In this essay, Selzer dramatically describes a patient's final day.

Words to Watch

furtive (par. 1)   sly

pruned (par. 2)   cut back; trimmed

facsimile (par. 2)   an exact copy

forceps (par. 19)   an instrument used in operations for holding or pulling

shard (par. 19)   a broken piece; fragment

athwart (par. 20)   leaning across

probes (par. 32)   investigates thoroughly

hefts (par. 32)   tosses; heaves

1 I spy on my patients. Ought not a doctor to observe his patients by any means and from any stance, that he might the more fully assemble evidence? So I stand in the doorways of hospital rooms and gaze. Oh, it is not all that furtive an act. Those in bed need only look up to discover me. But they never do.

2   From the doorway of Room 542 the man in the bed seems deeply tanned. Blue eyes and close-cropped white hair give him the appearance of vigor and good health. But I know that his skin is not brown from the sun. It is rusted, rather, in the last stage of containing the vile repose within. And the blue eyes are frosted, looking inward like the windows of a snowbound cottage. This man is blind. This man is also legless—the right leg missing from midthigh down, the left from just below the knee. It gives him the look of a bonsai, roots and branches pruned into the dwarfed facsimile of a great tree.

3   Propped on pillows, he cups his right thigh in both hands. Now and then he shakes his head as though acknowledging the

intensity of his suffering. In all of this he makes no sound. Is he mute as well as blind?

The room in which he dwells is empty of all possessions— 4
no get-well cards, small, private caches of food, day-old flowers, slippers, all the usual kick-shaws of the sickroom. There is only the bed, a chair, a nightstand, and a tray on wheels that can be swung across his lap for meals.

"What time is it?" he asks.   5
"Three o'clock."   6
"Morning or afternoon?"   7
"Afternoon."   8
He is silent. There is nothing else he wants to know.   9
"How are you?" I say.   10
"Who is it?" he asks.   11
"It's the doctor. How do you feel?"   12
He does not answer right away.   13
"Feel?" he says.   14
"I hope you feel better," I say.   15
I press the button at the side of the bed.   16
"Down you go," I say.   17
"Yes, down," he says.   18

He falls back upon the bed awkwardly. His stumps, un- 19
weighted by legs and feet, rise in the air, presenting themselves. I unwrap the bandages from the stumps, and begin to cut away the black scabs and the dead, glazed fat with scissors and forceps. A shard of white bone comes loose. I pick it away. I wash the wounds with disinfectant and redress the stumps. All this while, he does not speak. What is he thinking behind those lids that do not blink? Is he remembering a time when he was whole? Does he dream of feet? Of when his body was not a rotting log?

He lies solid and inert. In spite of everything, he remains 20
impressive, as though he were a sailor standing athwart a slanting deck.

"Anything more I can do for you?" I ask.   21
For a long moment he is silent.   22
"Yes," he says at last and without the least irony. "You can 23
bring me a pair of shoes."

In the corridor, the head nurse is waiting for me.   24
"We have to do something about him," she says. "Every 25

morning he orders scrambled eggs for breakfast, and, instead of eating them, he picks up the plate and throws it against the wall."

26   "Throws his plate?"

27   "Nasty. That's what he is. No wonder his family doesn't come to visit. They probably can't stand him any more than we can."

28   She is waiting for me to do something.

29   "Well?"

30   "We'll see," I say.

31   The next morning I am waiting in the corridor when the kitchen delivers his breakfast. I watch the aide place the tray on the stand and swing it across his lap. She presses the button to raise the head of the bed. Then she leaves.

32   In time the man reaches to find the rim of the tray, then on to find the dome of the covered dish. He lifts off the cover and places it on the stand. He fingers across the plate until he probes the eggs. He lifts the plate in both hands, sets it on the palm of his right hand, centers it, balances it. He hefts it up and down slightly, getting the feel of it. Abruptly, he draws back his right arm as far as he can.

33   There is the crack of the plate breaking against the wall at the foot of his bed and the small wet sound of the scrambled eggs dropping to the floor.

34   And then he laughs. It is a sound you have never heard. It is something new under the sun. It could cure cancer.

35   Out in the corridor, the eyes of the head nurse narrow.

36   "Laughed, did he?"

37   She writes something down on her clipboard.

38   A second aide arrives, brings a second breakfast tray, puts it on the nightstand, out of his reach. She looks over at me shaking her head and making her mouth go. I see that we are to be accomplices.

39   "I've got to feed you," she says to the man.

40   "Oh, no you don't," the man says.

41   "Oh, yes I do," the aide says, "after the way you just did. Nurse says so."

42   "Get me my shoes," the man says.

43   "Here's oatmeal," the aide says. "Open." And she touches the spoon to his lower lip.

44   "I ordered scrambled eggs," says the man.

45   "That's right," the aide says.

I step forward. 46

"Is there anything I can do?" I say. 47

"Who are you?" the man asks. 48

In the evening I go once more to that ward to make my 49 rounds. The head nurse reports to me that Room 542 is deceased. She has discovered this quite by accident, she says. No, there had been no sound. Nothing. It's a blessing, she says.

I go into his room, a spy looking for secrets. He is still 50 there in his bed. His face is relaxed, grave, dignified. After a while, I turn to leave. My gaze sweeps the wall at the foot of the bed, and I see the place where it has been repeatedly washed, where the wall looks very clean and very white.

BUILDING VOCABULARY

1. In this essay, Selzer uses a few words that derive from languages other than English. Look up the following words and tell what language they come from. Then, write a definition for each:
   a. *bonsai*
   b. *kick-shaws*
   c. *caches*
2. Use these words from the essay in complete sentences of your own: *vile, repose, dwarfed, glazed, inert, accomplices.*

UNDERSTANDING THE WRITER'S IDEAS

1. What reason does Selzer give for a doctor's spying on his patients?
2. What does the man in Room 542 look like? Why is his skin brown? How does Selzer know he is blind? Why does Selzer think the patient may be mute? When do we know that he is not mute?
3. What is the author's meaning of the phrase "vile repose"?
4. How do we know that this patient does not receive many visitors?
5. Aside from wanting to know the time of day, what is the patient's one request? Do you think he is serious about his request? Why?
6. Why does the patient hurl his food tray against the wall?
7. For what reason does the head nurse complain about the patient?
8. What does Selzer feel and think about the patient? How do you know?

UNDERSTANDING THE WRITER'S TECHNIQUES

1. What is the author's thesis? Where is it stated?

2. Throughout the essay, Selzer asks a number of questions. Locate at least three of these questions that are not a part of the dialogue. To whom do you think they are addressed? What is their effect on the reader?

3. Like William Least Heat Moon, Selzer heightens the description by making vivid and unusual comparisons. Locate and explain in your own words three comparisons that you feel are especially descriptive and intriguing.

4. Selzer uses some very short sentences interspersed among longer ones. Locate at least four very short sentences. How do they draw your attention to the description?

5. Locate in Selzer's essay at least five examples of vivid description (imagery) relating to illness. What is their emotional effect on the reader?

6. How does Selzer use *dialogue* to reveal the personality of the patient? of the doctor? of the head nurse?

7. In paragraph 23, Selzer states that the patient delivers his request "without the least irony." *Irony* (see Glossary) is saying what is opposite to what one means. Why might Selzer have expected irony from the patient? Why might someone in the sick man's condition use irony? What do you think the man means by his request "You can bring me a pair of shoes"—if, in fact, the remark is not an ironical one?

8. What does the title of the essay mean? What is a discus thrower? Why has Selzer chosen an ancient image of an athlete as the title of this essay? In what way is the title ironic?

9. Why does Selzer use such an unusual word as *kick-shaws* (par. 4)?

10. *Double entendre* is a French expression that indicates that something has a double meaning, each equally valid. What might be the two meanings of the nurse's words "It's a blessing"?

11. In this essay, the author uses a *framing* device: that is, he opens and closes the essay with a similar image or idea. What is that idea? Why is it effective? What are the differences in the use of this idea in the opening and closing paragraphs?

12. The heart of this essay is the patient's insistence upon throwing

his breakfast plate at the wall, and yet Selzer does not attempt to explain the man's reasons for such an act. Why do you think the man hurls his breakfast across the room each morning—and why does he laugh? Why does Selzer not provide an analysis of the action? How does the title help us see Selzer's attitude toward the man's act?

EXPLORING THE WRITER'S IDEAS

1. In the beginning of the essay Selzer asks, "Ought not a doctor to observe his patients by any means from any stance, that he might more fully assemble evidence?" Do you feel that a doctor should have this right? Why? What rights do you believe patients should have in a hospital?
2. The head nurse in Selzer's description seems fed up with the patient in Room 542. Why do you think she feels this way? Do you think that a person in her position has the right to express this feeling on his or her job? Why or why not?
3. The patient's attitude is influenced by his physical state and his nearness to death. How have physical ailments or handicaps changed the attitudes of people you have known? How has an illness influenced your thoughts at any time?

IDEAS FOR WRITING

Guided Writing

Describe a person you have observed who was seriously ill, in danger, or under great stress.

1. Base your description upon close observation of the person during a short but concentrated span of time: a morning or afternoon, an hour or two, even a few minutes.
2. Begin with a short, direct paragraph in which you introduce the person and the critical situation he or she faces.
3. Include yourself ("I") in the description.
4. Describe the vantage point from which you are "spying" or observing, and focus on the particular subject of the scene.
5. Throughout your essay, ask key questions.

6. Use imagery and original comparisons to highlight the description of your subject.
7. Include some dialogue with either the subject or another person.
8. Describe at least one very intense action performed by your subject.
9. Tell how the subject and scene had changed when you next saw them.

More Writing Projects

1. In your journal, describe a hospital room in which you stayed or visited some other person. Focus on your sensory perceptions of the place.
2. Describe in an extended paragraph an interaction you had with a person who was blind or deaf or was disabled in some other way. In your description, focus closely on the person's features. Write about your reactions during and after the interaction.
3. Using both description and commentary, analyze the people you observe in one of the following situations: a bus or train during rush hour; breakfast at a diner or restaurant; a sports event or concert. Incorporate the description and observation into a five-paragraph essay.

A River's Route

Gretel Ehrlich

Montana resident Gretel Ehrlich celebrates nature in this highly personal, often spiritual description of her journey along a river in the Absaroka Mountains. In this essay, which was part of the introduction to the 1989 Sierra Club wilderness calendar, notice how Ehrlich not only writes strikingly clear images of the *places* she visits, but also writes of their deep effects on her. Ehrlich is also the author of *The Solace of Open Spaces.*

Words to Watch

articulation (par. 2)   interrelationship; connecting

ascent (par. 3)   rising; upward motion

verdant (par. 3)   green

archaic (par. 4)   out-of-date; antiquated

beeline (par. 4)   a straight, direct course

pitons (par. 6)   metal spikes for a rope in mountain climbing

crampons (par. 6)   spiked iron shoe plates to prevent slipping

desiccated (par. 7)   dried up

gluttony (par. 8)   excessive eating and drinking

hedonism (par. 8)   doctrine that pleasure is the highest good

cirque (par. 8)   a steep-walled basin in a mountain

vertiginous (par. 10)   causing dizziness

emanation (par. 11)   an emergence

redolent (par. 11)   full of

riffles (par. 15)   small waves

It's morning in the Absaroka Mountains. The word *absaroka* 1 means "raven" in the Crow language, though I've seen no ravens in three days. Last night I slept with my head butted against an Engelmann spruce, and on waking the limbs looked like hundreds of arms swinging in a circle. The trunk is bigger than an elephant's leg, bigger than my torso. I stick my nose against the bark. Tiny opals of sap stick to my cheeks and the bark breaks up, textured: red and gray, coarse and smooth, wet and flaked.

2   A tree is an aerial garden, a botanical migration from the
sea, from those earliest plants, the seaweeds; it is a purchase on
crumbled rock, on ground. The human, standing, is only a different upsweep and articulation of cells. How tree-like we are, how
human the tree.

3   But I've come here to seek out the source of a river, and as
we make the daylong ascent from a verdant valley, I think about
walking and wilderness. We use the word "wilderness," but perhaps we mean wildness. Isn't that why I've come here? In
wilderness, I seek the wildness in myself—and in so doing, come
on the wildness everywhere around me because, being part of nature, I'm cut from the same cloth.

4   Following the coastline of a lake, I watch how wind picks
up water in dark blasts and drops it again. Ducks glide in Vs
away from me, out onto the fractured, darkening mirror. I stop. A
hatch of mayflies powders the air and the archaic, straight-
winged dragonflies hang, blunt-nosed, above me. A friend talks
about aquatic bugs: water beetles, spinners, assassin bugs, and
one that hatches, mates, and dies in a total life-span of two hours.
At the end of the meadow, the lake drains into a fast-moving
creek. I quicken my pace and trudge upward. Walking is also an
ambulation of mind. The human armor of bones rattles, fat rolls,
and inside this durable, fleshy prison of mine, I make a beeline
toward otherness, lightness, or, maybe like a moth, toward flame.

5   Somewhere along the trail I laugh out loud. How shell-like
the body seems suddenly—not fleshy at all, but inhuman and
hard. And farther up, I step out of my body though I'm still held
fast by something, but what? I don't know.

6   How foolish the preparations for wilderness trips seem
now. We pore over our maps, chart our expeditions. We "gear
up" at trailheads with pitons and crampons, horsepacks and back-
packs, fly rods and cameras, forgetting the meaning of simply
going, of lifting thought-covers, of disburdenment. I look up
from these thoughts. A blue heron rises from a gravel bar and
glides behind a gray screen of dead trees, appears in an opening
where an avalanche downed pines, and lands again on water.

7   I stop to eat lunch. Ralph Waldo Emerson wrote, "The
Guatama said that the first men ate the earth and found it sweet."
I eat baloney and cheese and think about eating the earth. It's an-
other way of framing our wonder in which the width of the

mouth stands for the generous palate of consciousness. I cleanse
my palate with miner's lettuce and stream water and try to imagine what kinds of sweetness the earth provides: the taste of
glacial flour, or the mineral taste of basalt, the fresh and foul bou-
quets of rivers, the desiccated, stinging flavor of a snowstorm—
like eating red ants, my friend says.

As I begin to walk again it occurs to me that this notion of 8
"eating the earth" is not about gluttony, hedonism, or sin, but,
rather, unconditional love. Everywhere I look I see the possibility
of love. To find wildness, I must first offer myself up, accept all
that comes before me: a bullfrog breathing hard on a rock; moose
tracks under elk scats; a cloud that looks like a clothespin; a seep
of water from a high cirque, black on brown rock, draining down
from the brain of the world.

At tree line, birdsong stops. I'm lifted into another move- 9
ment of music, one with no particular notes, only windsounds becoming watersounds, becoming windsounds. Above, a cornice
crowns a ridge and melts into a teal and turquoise lake, like a
bladder leaking its wine.

On top of Marston Pass I'm in a ruck of steep valleys and 10
gray, treeless peaks. The alpine carpet, studded with red paint-
brush and alpine buttercups, gives way to rock. Now all the way
across a vertiginous valley, I see where water oozes from moss
and mud, how, at its source, it quickly becomes something else.

Emerson also said: "Every natural fact is an emanation, and 11
that from which it emanates is an emanation also, and from every
emanation is a new emanation." The ooze, the source of a great
river, is now a white chute tumbling over soft folds of conglom-
erate rock—brown bellies. Now wind tears at it, throwing sheets
of water to another part of the mountainside; soft earth gives way
under my feet, clouds spill upward and spit rain. Isn't everything
redolent with loss, with momentary radiance, a coming to different ground? Stone basins catch the waterfall, spill it again, like
thoughts strung together, laddered down.

I see where meltwater is split by a rock—half going west to 12
the Pacific, the other going east to the Atlantic, for this is the
Continental Divide. Down the other side the air I gulp feels soft-
er. Ice spans and tunnels the creek, then, when night comes but
before the full moon, falling stars have the same look as that
white chute of water, falling against the rock of night.

13   To rise above tree line is to go above thought and after, the descent back into birdsong, bog orchids, willows, and firs, is to sink into the preliterate parts of ourselves. It is to forget discontent, undisciplined needs. Here the world is only space, raw loneliness, green valleys hung vertically. Losing myself to it—if I can—I do not fall . . . or, if I do, I'm only another cataract of water.

14   Wildness has no conditions, no sure routes, no peaks or goals, no source that is not instantly becoming something more than itself, then letting go of that, always becoming. It cannot be stripped of its complexity by CAT scan or telescope. Rather, it is a many-pointed truth, almost a bluntness, a sudden essence like the wild strawberries strung along the ground on scarlet runners under my feet. Wildness is source and fruition at once, as if every river circled round, the mouth eating the tail—and the tail, the source.

15   Now I am camped among trees again. Four yearling moose, their chestnut coats shiny from a summer's diet of willow shoots, tramp past my bedroll and drink from a spring that issues sulfurous water. The ooze, the white chute, the narrow stream—now almost a river—joins this small spring and slows into skinny oxbows and deep pools before breaking again on rock, a stepladder of sequined riffles.

16   To trace the history of a river, or a raindrop, as John Muir would have done, is also to trace the history of the soul, the history of the mind descending and arising in the body. In both, we constantly seek and stumble on divinity, which, like the cornice feeding the lake and the spring becoming a waterfall, feeds, spills, falls, and feeds itself over and over again.

BUILDING VOCABULARY

1. Determine the meaning of the words in italics from context clues—clues in the surrounding words and sentences. Do not use a dictionary until *after* you make your guess. Return to the indicated paragraph for more clues.

   a. my head *butted* against an Engelmann spruce (par. 1)

   b. The human, standing, is only a different *upsweep* and *articulation* of cells. (par. 2)

    c. Walking is also an *ambulation* of mind. (par. 4)

    d. the generous *palate* of consciousness (par. 7)

    e. a *cornice* crowns a ridge (par. 9)

    f. *studded* with red paintbrush (par. 10)

    g. folds of *conglomerate* rock (par. 11)

    h. that white *chute* of water (par. 12)

    i. the *descent* back into birdsong . . . is to sink into the *pre-literate* parts of ourselves (par. 13)

2. This essay contains many references to nature. Look through the essay again, and list two or three nature references for each category below:

    a. vegetation

    b. water

    c. animals

    d. rock or geographic formations

    e. the sky

UNDERSTANDING THE WRITER'S IDEAS

1. Where does the name of the Absaroka Mountains come from? Who are the Crow? For what reason has Ehrlich come to the Absaroka Mountains? Does she achieve her purpose? Explain.

2. Explain the sentence, "How tree-like we are, how human the tree" (par. 2). What is its relevance to the overall message of the essay?

3. During what period of time does the author's journey take place? Outline the various stages of her journey. Where does she begin and end her journey?

4. Why does Ehrlich write, "We use the word 'wilderness,' but perhaps we mean wildness" (par. 3)? How does this statement relate to the purpose of her journey? What is the difference between *wilderness* and *wildness?*

5. Is Ehrlich alone on this journey? How do you know? Why does she not include others very much in her description?

6. Identify Ralph Waldo Emerson and John Muir. How do they relate to this essay and to Ehrlich's purpose?

7. Why does she "laugh out loud" at one point on the trip? Where is she when she does?

8. Does she go into the wilderness totally unprepared and "natural"? Explain.
9. How is the wilderness/wildness "source and fruition at once" (par. 14)?

UNDERSTANDING THE WRITER'S TECHNIQUES

1. Is there a *thesis statement* (see Glossary) in this essay? How would you state the thesis? Explain.
2. In this essay, Ehrlich makes vivid use of *imagery* (see Glossary) related to the five senses. List images related to each of these senses. On which senses does she concentrate most? Why? Which images do you find most effective? Why?
3. What is the *dominant impression* (see page 82) of this essay? Explain. What is the *tone* (see Glossary) of the essay? Give examples to support your response.
4. How does Ehrlich organize her description? How does she maintain *coherence* (see Glossary)?
5. Which paragraphs constitute the introduction? The body? The conclusion? How does Ehrlich *frame* her description? That is, what descriptive elements are similar in the beginning and ending of the essay?
6. Identify and explain the author's use of *definition* (see Glossary and Chapter 7) in paragraphs 1, 2, and 14. Where else does she use definition? Would you characterize her definitions as *denotative* or *connotative* (see Glossary)? Explain.
7. What is the *stated purpose* of her trip? What is the *implied purpose?* Explain the difference. What is her *purpose* (see Glossary) in writing this essay?
8. This essay is part of the introduction to the 1989 Sierra Club wilderness calendar. Do you think Ehrlich's *audience* (see Glossary) is limited to like-minded environmentalists? Why? What is the intended audience?
9. In general, Ehrlich uses the first-person ("I") *point of view* (see Glossary) throughout the essay. Yet, at a few points, she uses the plural "we." Where does she change pronoun references? How do the changes affect the essay?

10. Where in the essay does the author use literary *allusions* (see Glossary)? What is their effect?

11. Ehrlich makes use of a wide range of *figurative language* in this essay, including *similes* and *metaphors* (see Glossary). Point out the most visual and original figures.

12. Explain the conclusion of the essay.

EXPLORING THE WRITER'S IDEAS

1. Clearly, this is a highly *subjective* (see *objective* in Glossary) description of the author's journey through nature. In general, when you are reading about nature or travels, do you enjoy such subjective description, or do you prefer more objective, realistic ones? Why? What are the advantages and disadvantages of each?

2. Examine a recent issue of *National Geographic* magazine. Do you feel this essay would be appropriate to appear in *National Geographic?* Why? Explain the differences or similarities in writing styles, choice of subject, and so on.

3. In the 1992 presidential campaign, Albert Gore's promise to be an "environmentalist" vice-president helped focus on what is clearly a major concern of many people. Generally, where do you stand on environmental issues? What global environmental issues are of most concern to you? What local issues?

IDEAS FOR WRITING

Guided Writing

Write a subjective description of a recent experience you had in nature that took place over a period of only one day.

1. Begin your essay with the morning when you awoke. Describe the entire day.

2. Write a clear description of your starting point.

3. Continue to describe each stage and place of your experience as it occurred.

4. Clearly state the purpose of your experience.

5. Use vivid, personal imagery encompassing all five senses. Try to make your imagery include a variety of natural focuses.

6. Make your description as personal as possible. Write about what you saw, how it made you feel, and what other things it made you think about.
7. Include at least one *allusion* (see Glossary) to a person or thing not present but somehow connected to the experience.
8. Use definition as needed in your essay. At one point, redefine a common phrase to stress your personal interpretation of it.
9. Organize your essay so that it has a clear introduction, body, and conclusion. The conclusion should sum up your experience and its meaning for you.

More Writing Projects

1. For a journal entry, select a special time of day and write about it in such a way that the description captures the moods that the scene evokes in you.
2. Describe in a paragraph a highly "unnatural" urban scene that affected you deeply.
3. Write an objective description of the same experience you wrote about in the Guided Writing exercise.

SUMMING UP: CHAPTER 3

1. As you have discovered in this chapter, one of the keys to writing effective description is the selection and creation of vivid and relevant images. How do the writers in this chapter use imagery? Which writer's images do you find most concrete, original, vivid, and creative? For each of the four essays of description in this chapter, write a paragraph in which you evaluate the writer's use of imagery.
2. In this chapter, William Least Heat Moon and Gretel Ehrlich write about their solitary experience in a particular *place*—what they expected, what they found, and how it affected them emotionally.

   In *Nothing to Declare,* a book about her experiences as a woman traveling alone, novelist and essayist Mary Morris writes: "I felt ready for a change. . . . I went in search of a place where the land and the people and the time in which they lived were somehow connected—where life would begin to make sense to me again."

Write an essay about a place you know well that reflects some of the same criteria for which Least Heat Moon and Ehrlich were searching.

3. Least Heat Moon and Selzer provide vivid descriptions of people. What general guidelines for describing people do you derive from these writers? Write a short essay called "How to Describe People," basing your observations on Least Heat Moon's and Selzer's techniques.

4. William Least Heat Moon's steady companion in his journey through America—a journey recorded in *Blue Highways*—was a half-ton Ford van he called Ghost Dancing. In many ways, Least Heat Moon's work is a tribute to the American automobile, not just a vehicle but also a place in which to live, a companion, a symbol of success or achievement or escape. Consider the role of the automobile in your immediate world and write an essay exploring its value as an essential (or nonessential) element of modern life.

5. Ehrlich celebrates the river in her essay, but today many waterways are threatened by industrial pollution. What problems affect the rivers and lakes in your home state or near your college? Take a trip to a water site not far from your campus or home. Read articles about local waterways in your newspaper. Write an essay called "The Fate of Our Waters."

6. Maxine Hong Kingston and William Least Heat Moon both write from their experience as members of a multicultural society. Is there any evidence that their choice of subject or method of description is shaped by their ethnic backgrounds? Write a short essay on the relation between the writers' backgrounds and the nature of their descriptions.

CHAPTER 4

Narration

WHAT IS NARRATION?

Narration is the telling of a story. As a technique in essay writing, it normally involves a discussion of events that are "true" or real, events that take place over a period of time. Narration helps a writer explain things and, as such, it is an important skill for the kind of writing often required of you.

Narration often includes the use of *description* in order to make the *purpose* of the story clear. A good narrative, then, must have a *thesis*. The thesis tells the reader that the narrative goes beyond just telling a story for entertainment. Like description, the narrative has a purpose, and an audience. The writer puts forth a main idea through the events and details of the story. For example, a writer might decide to *narrate* the events that led her to leave her native country and come to the United States as an immigrant. She would establish her thesis—her main point—quickly, and then use the body of the essay to tell about the event itself. She would use narration as the means to an end—to make a significant statement about the important decision that changed her life.

Writer Elizabeth Wong uses narrative to explore the pitfalls of divorcing herself from her cultural heritage as she tells about events in her youth with the purpose of pointing out the dangers of becoming "All-American." In his comic narrative "Salvation," Langston Hughes reveals his disillusionment as he cannot find Jesus as his family expects him to. Parent Michael Dorris uses the narrative of chasing down a special Christmas

114

present for his daughters to make a point about the changing roles of fathers in a gender-conscious society. The renowned writer George Orwell narrates events at a hanging he witnessed in Burma to call attention to how all too often we can take the value of life for granted. Each writer, then, whose work you will read in this chapter, uses narrative to tell a story of events that take place over a period of time, but also to put forward a thesis or main idea that comes directly out of events in the story.

HOW DO WE READ NARRATIVE?

Reading narrative requires us to look for more than the story, but not to overlook the story. So, as we read, we should ask ourselves:

- What are the main events in the narrative or story?
- What is the writer's purpose in telling us about these events, as stated in the thesis?
- How is the story organized? Is it chronological? Does the writer use *flashback* (see Glossary)? How much time is covered in the narrative?
- Does the author use description to make the narrative more vivid for a reader?
- What point of view does the author use? Are events told through his or her own eyes, or from a detached and objective point of view? Why did the writer make this choice about point of view? How would altering the point of view alter the purpose of the narrative?
- What transitions of time does the writer use to connect events? Look for expressions that link events: *next, soon after, a day later, suddenly, after two years*. These expressions act like bridges to connect the various moments in the narrative pattern.
- Does the writer use dialogue? What is the effect of dialogue in the narrative?
- What audience is the author aiming at? How do we know?

HOW DO WE WRITE NARRATIVE?

After reading the selections of narrative writing in this chapter, you should be ready to try narrative writing on your own. Fortunately, most individuals have a basic storytelling ability and know how to develop stories that make a point. Once you master narration as a writing pattern, you will be able to use it in a variety of situations.

Select the event you want to tell a story about. Begin with a thesis statement that gives the reader the purpose of the narrative.

Sample thesis statement:

My year studying abroad in Paris was an adventure that taught me not only skills in a foreign language but a new respect for people with cultural values different from my own.

Decide which point of view you will use: first person? third person? Think about how your audience is, and choose the point of view best suited for that audience. If you are writing to a friend, first person may be more informal. If your are writing to address a wider public audience, as Orwell is, third person might be more effective.

First person: I saw a man hanged, and the experience changed my views on capital punishment.

Third person: Spending a day at a Planned Parenthood clinic would help opponents of abortion understand the other side's fervent commitment to choice.

Determine the purpose of the narrative in relation to your audience. If you were writing for a Roman Catholic newspaper, for instance, your audience would be different from the audience you'd address in a feminist magazine like *Ms.;* the purpose would be different as well. In one case, you might be trying to get readers to change their views through your description. In another case, you might be showing how weak the opposition was by the way you described them.

Plan the scope of the piece: How much time will events cover? Can you describe all the events within the required length of the essay? Notice that Michael Dorris's narrative, for instance, concentrates on one incident—the purchase of a gift—even though the article refers to other aspects of family life at Christmas.

Plan to include dialogue. Here, you might include a few fragments of conversation between lost or confused freshmen to give our "first day at school" story real-life flavor:

"Did you buy your books yet?"

"No, I couldn't find the bookstore!"

"Well, I already spent $125, and that was only for two courses. I'm going to have to ask my Mom for more money."

"Yeah, I'm thinking maybe I'm going to need a part-time job."

"Yeah, maybe we can work in the bookstore and get a discount."

Make a list of *transitions* that show the passage of time and use as many as you need to help your reader follow the sequence of events in the narrative. Check that there are transitions between events: *after that, a few hours later, by the time the day ended.*

State your *thesis.* Write out the thesis statement so that you know the *subject* and the *purpose* of the essay. Then make a list of the major events in the story. You might begin with why you chose the college you did, and how you felt when you got accepted. Or, you might begin with your arrival on the first day of classes, and go through the main events of the day—going to class, buying books, meeting other new students, evaluating teachers, having lunch, and so forth.

Plan an arrangement of events: chronological? use of flashback? Again, in the Dorris piece, he looks back to pre-Christmas excitement, and ends on Christmas day, but the main idea of the story is about shopping and what he learns from the choice of gift.

Writing the Draft

Once you have structured your essay, build your ideas by including descriptive details. Insert as many descriptive words as possible to help a reader *see* the campus, the students, the cafeteria, and so on:

the bright-colored sofas in the student lounge, filled with cigarette burns

the smells of french fries from the cafeteria, with its long rows of orange tables

the conversations of the biology majors at the next table, who were talking about cutting up frogs

the large, imposing library, with its rows of blue computer terminals and its hushed whispered noises

Discuss how these events made you feel about your decision. Did you choose the right college?

Write a conclusion that reinforces the purpose of the essay. Make a direct statement of the way the events in the narrative changed you, or how your expectations for the day compare with what really happened.

Reading and Revising the Draft

Read the essay aloud to a classmate who is also a new freshman. Ask your listener if his or her day was the same as yours. Did you put the events in a logical sequence? Can your listener suggest more ideas to add? Have you included enough details so that a reader who was not a member of the college community could see the events as you saw them?

Proofread carefully for correctness and make a neat final copy.

The Struggle to Be an All-American Girl

Elizabeth Wong

In this poignant remembrance, Elizabeth Wong tells of the hurts and sorrows of her bicultural upbringing. Wong effectively blends concrete description and imaginative comparisons to give a vivid look into the life of a child who felt she had a Chinese exterior but an American interior.

Words to Watch

stoically (par. 1)   without showing emotion

dissuade (par. 2)   to talk out of doing something

ideographs (par. 7)   Chinese picture symbols used to form words

disassociate (par. 8)   to detach from association

vendors (par. 8)   sellers of goods

gibberish (par. 9)   confused, unintelligible speech or language

pidgin (par. 10)   simplified speech that is usually a mixture of two or more languages

It's still there, the Chinese school on Yale Street where my brother and I used to go. Despite the new coat of paint and the high wire fence, the school I knew 10 years ago remains remarkably, stoically the same. 1

Every day at 5 P.M., instead of playing with our fourth- and fifth-grade friends or sneaking out to the empty lot to hunt ghosts and animal bones, my brother and I had to go to Chinese school. No amount of kicking, screaming, or pleading could dissuade my mother, who was solidly determined to have us learn the language of our heritage. 2

Forcibly, she walked us the seven long, hilly blocks from our home to school, depositing our defiant tearful faces before the stern principal. My only memory of him is that he swayed on his heels like a palm tree, and he always clasped his impatient twitching hands behind his back. I recognized him as a repressed maniacal child killer, and knew that if we ever saw his hands we'd be in big trouble. 3

4   We all sat in little chairs in an empty auditorium. The room smelled like Chinese medicine, an imported faraway mustiness. Like ancient mothballs or dirty closets. I hated that smell. I favored crisp new scents. Like the soft French perfume that my American teacher wore in public school.

5   There was a stage far to the right, flanked by an American flag and the flag of the Nationalist Republic of China, which was also red, white and blue but not as pretty.

6   Although the emphasis at the school was mainly language—speaking, reading, writing—the lessons always began with an exercise in politeness. With the entrance of the teacher, the best student would tap a bell and everyone would get up, kowtow, and chant, "Sing san ho," the phonetic for "How are you, teacher?"

7   Being ten years old, I had better things to learn than ideographs copied painstakingly in lines that ran right to left from the tip of a *moc but,* a real ink pen that had to be held in an awkward way if blotches were to be avoided. After all, I could do the multiplication tables, name the satellites of Mars, and write reports on "Little Women" and "Black Beauty." Nancy Drew, my favorite book heroine, never spoke Chinese.

8   The language was a source of embarrassment. More times than not, I had tried to disassociate myself from the nagging loud voice that followed me wherever I wandered in the nearby American supermarket outside Chinatown. The voice belonged to my grandmother, a fragile woman in her seventies who could outshout the best of the street vendors. Her humor was raunchy, her Chinese rhythmless, patternless. It was quick, it was loud, it was unbeautiful. It was not like the quiet, lilting romance of French or the gentle refinement of the American South. Chinese sounded pedestrian. Public.

9   In Chinatown, the comings and goings of hundreds of Chinese on their daily tasks sounded chaotic and frenzied. I did not want to be thought of as mad, as talking gibberish. When I spoke English, people nodded at me, smiled sweetly, said encouraging words. Even the people in my culture would cluck and say that I'd do well in life. "My, doesn't she move her lips fast," they would say, meaning that I'd be able to keep up with the world outside Chinatown.

My brother was even more fanatical than I about speaking 10
English. He was especially hard on my mother, criticizing her,
often cruelly, for her pidgin speech—smatterings of Chinese
scattered like chop suey in her conversation. "It's not 'What it
is,' Mom," he'd say in exasperation. "It's 'What *is* it, what *is* it,
what *is* it!'" Sometimes Mom might leave out an occasional
"the" or "a," or perhaps a verb of being. He would stop her in
mid-sentence: "Say it again, Mom. Say it right." When he
tripped over his own tongue, he'd blame it on her: "See, Mom,
it's all your fault. You set a bad example."

What infuriated my mother most was when my brother cor- 11
nered her on her consonants, especially "r." My father had played
a cruel joke on Mom by assigning her an American name that her
tongue wouldn't allow her to say. No matter how hard she tried,
"Ruth" always ended up "Luth" or "Roof."

After two years of writing with a *moc but* and reciting 12
words with multiples of meanings, I finally was granted a cultural divorce. I was permitted to stop Chinese school.

I thought of myself as multicultural. I preferred tacos to egg 13
rolls; I enjoyed Cinco de Mayo more than Chinese New Year.

At last, I was one of you; I wasn't one of them. 14

Sadly, I still am. 15

BUILDING VOCABULARY

For each of the words in italics, choose the letter of the word or
expression that most closely matches its meaning.

1. the *stern* principal (par. 3)   **a.** military   **b.** very old   **c.** im-
moral   **d.** strict

2. *repressed* maniacal child killer (par. 3)   **a.** quiet   **b.** ugly
c. held back   **d.** retired

3. an imported faraway *mustiness* (par. 4)   **a.** country   **b.** moth
balls   **c.** chair   **d.** staleness

4. a *fragile* woman (par. 8)   **a.** elderly   **b.** frail   **c.** tall   **d.**
inconsistent

5. her humor was *raunchy* (par. 8)   **a.** obscene   **b.** unclear   **c.**
childish   **d.** very funny

6. quiet *lilting* romance of French (par. 8)   **a.** musical   **b.** tilting   **c.** loving   **d.** complicated

7. thought of as *mad* (par. 9)   **a.** foreign   **b.** angry   **c.** stupid   **d.** crazy

8. what *infuriated* my mother most (par. 11)   **a.** angered   **b.** humiliated   **c.** made laugh   **d.** typified

UNDERSTANDING THE WRITER'S IDEAS

1. What did Elizabeth Wong and her brother do every day after school? How did that make them different from their friends? What was their attitude toward what they did? How do you know?

2. What does Wong mean when she says of the principal "I recognized him as a repressed child killer"? Why were she and her brother afraid to see his hands?

3. What was the main purpose of going to Chinese school? What did Wong feel she had learned at "regular" American school? Which did she feel was more important? What are *Little Women, Black Beauty,* and Nancy Drew?

4. In the first sentence of paragraph 8, what language is "the language"?

5. What was Wong's grandmother like? What was Wong's attitude toward her? Why?

6. When Wong spoke English in Chinatown, why did the others think it was good that she moved her lips quickly?

7. What was her brother's attitude toward speaking English? How did he treat their mother when she tried to speak English? Why was it unfortunate that the mother had the American name *Ruth?* Who gave her that name? Why?

8. Explain the expression "he tripped over his own tongue" (par. 10).

9. In paragraph 13, Wong states, "I thought of myself as multicultural." What does that mean? What are tacos, egg rolls, and Cinco de Mayo? Why is it surprising that Wong includes those items as examples of her multiculturalism?

10. Who are the "you" and "them" of paragraph 14? Explain the significance of the last sentence. What does it indicate about Wong's attitude toward Chinese school from the vantage point of being an adult?

UNDERSTANDING THE WRITER'S TECHNIQUES

1. Wong does not state a thesis directly in a thesis sentence. How does her title imply a thesis? If you were writing a thesis sentence of your own for this essay, what would it be?

2. What is Wong's purpose in writing this narrative? Is the technique of narration an appropriate one to her purpose? Why or why not?

3. This narrative contains several stories. The first one ends after paragraph 7 and tells about Wong's routine after 5 P.M. on school days. Paragraphs 8 and 9, 10 and 11, and 12 and 13 offer other related narratives. Summarize each of these briefly. How does Wong help the reader shift from story to story?

4. The writer of narration will present *time* in a way that best fulfills the purpose of the narration. This presentation may take many forms: a single, personal event; a series of related events; a historical occurrence; an aging process. Obviously Wong chose a series of related events. Why does she use such a narrative structure to make her point? Could she have chosen an alternative plan, do you think? Why or why not?

5. Writers of narration often rely upon descriptive details to flesh out their stories. Find examples of sensory language here that makes the scene come alive for the reader.

6. Writers often use figurative comparisons to enliven their writing and to make it more distinctive. A *simile* is an imaginative form of figurative comparison using "like" or "as" to connect two items. One thing is similar to another in this figure. A *metaphor* is a figure of speech in which the writer compares two items not normally thought of as similar, but unlike in a simile, the comparison is direct—that is, it does not use "like" or "as." In other words, one thing is said to be the other thing, not merely to be like it. For example, if you wanted to compare love to a rose, you might use these two comparisons:

Simile:
   My love is *like* a red, red rose.
Metaphor:
   My love *is* a red, red rose.

In Wong's essay, find the similes and metaphors in paragraphs 2, 3, 4, 10, and 12. For each, name the two items compared and explain the comparison in your own words.

7. Narratives often include lines of spoken language—that is, one person in the narrative talking alone or to another. Wong uses quoted detail sparsely here. Why did she choose to limit the dialogue? How effective is the dialogue that appears here? Where do you think she might have used more dialogue to advance the narrative?

8. The last two paragraphs are only one sentence each. Why do you think the author chose this technique?

9. What is the *irony* (see Glossary) in the last sentence of the essay? How would the meaning of the last sentence change if you eliminated the word "sadly"? What is the irony in the title of the essay?

10. What is the *tone* (see Glossary) of this essay? How does Wong create that tone?

EXPLORING THE WRITER'S IDEAS

1. Wong and her brother deeply resented being forced to attend Chinese school. When children very clearly express displeasure or unhappiness, should parents force them to do things anyway? Why or why not?

2. On one level this essay is about a clash of cultures, here the ancient Chinese culture of Wong's ancestry and the culture of twentieth-century United States. Is it possible for someone to maintain connections to his or her ethnic or cultural backgrounds and at the same time to become an all-American girl or boy? What do people of foreign backgrounds gain when they become completely Americanized? What do they lose?

3. Because of their foreign ways, the mother and grandmother clearly embarrassed the Wong children. Under what other conditions that you can think of do parents embarrass children? Children, parents?

IDEAS FOR WRITING

Guided Writing

Write a narration in which you tell about some difficult moment that took place in grade school or high school, a moment that taught you something about yourself, your needs, or your cultural background.

1. Provide a concrete description of the school.
2. Tell in correct sequence about the event.
3. Identify people who play a part in this moment.
4. Use concrete, sensory description throughout your essay.
5. Use original similes and metaphors to make your narrative clearer and more dramatic.
6. Use dialogue (or spoken conversation) appropriately in order to advance the narrative.
7. In your conclusion, indicate what your attitude toward this moment is now that you are an adult.
8. Write a title that implies your thesis.

More Writing Projects

1. Did you have any problems in grade school or high school because of your background or ancestry? Did you know someone who had such problems? Record a specific incident in your journal.
2. Write a narrative paragraph explaining some basic insights about your heritage or culture.
3. Get together with other classmates in a small group and brainstorm or bounce ideas off one another on troubling ethnic, racial, or cultural issues on campus. Write down all the incidents. Then write a narrative essay tracing one episode or connecting a series of them.

Salvation
Langston Hughes

For more than forty years, Langston Hughes (1902–1967) was a major figure in American literature. In poetry, essays, drama, and fiction he attempt-
ed, as he said himself, "to explain and illuminate the Negro condition in
America." This selection from his autobiography, *The Big Sea* (1940), tells
the story of his "conversion" to Christ. Salvation was a key event in the life
of his community, but Hughes tells comically how he bowed to pressure by
permitting himself to be "saved from sin."

Words to Watch

dire (par. 3)   terrible; disastrous

gnarled (par. 4)   knotty; twisted

rounder (par. 6)   watchman; policeman

deacons (par. 6)   members of the clergy or laypersons who are appointed
    to help the minister

serenely (par. 7)   calmly; tranquilly

knickerbockered (par. 11)   dressed in short, loose trousers that are gath-
    ered below the knees

1   I was saved from sin when I was going on thirteen. But not really
saved. It happened like this. There was a big revival at my Auntie
Reed's church. Every night for weeks there had been much
preaching, singing, praying, and shouting, and some very hard-
ened sinners had been brought to Christ, and the membership of
the church had grown by leaps and bounds. Then just before the
revival ended, they held a special meeting for children, "to bring
the young lambs to the fold." My aunt spoke of it for days ahead.
That night I was escorted to the front row and placed on the
mourners' bench with all the other young sinners, who had not
yet been brought to Jesus.

2   My aunt told me that when you were saved you saw a light,
and something happened to you inside! And Jesus came into your
life! And God was with you from then on! She said you could
see and hear and feel Jesus in your soul. I believed her. I had
heard a great many old people say the same thing and it seemed

to me they ought to know. So I sat there calmly in the hot, crowded church, waiting for Jesus to come to me.

The preacher preached a wonderful rhythmical sermon, all 3 moans and shouts and lonely cries and dire pictures of hell, and then he sang a song about the ninety and nine safe in the fold, but one little lamb was left out in the cold. Then he said: "Won't you come? Won't you come to Jesus? Young lambs, won't you come?" And he held out his arms to all us young sinners there on the mourners' bench. And the little girls cried. And some of them jumped up and went to Jesus right away. But most of us just sat there.

A great many old people came and knelt around us and 4 prayed, old women with jet-black faces and braided hair, old men with work-gnarled hands. And the church sang a song about the lower lights are burning, some poor sinners to be saved. And the whole building rocked with prayer and song.

Still I kept waiting to *see* Jesus.   5

Finally all the young people had gone to the altar and were 6 saved, but one boy and me. He was a rounder's son named Westley. Westley and I were surrounded by sisters and deacons praying. It was very hot in the church, and getting late now. Finally Westley said to me in a whisper: "God damn! I'm tired o' sitting here. Let's get up and be saved." So he got up and was saved.

Then I was left all alone on the mourners' bench. My aunt 7 came and knelt at my knees and cried, while prayers and songs swirled all around me in the little church. The whole congregation prayed for me alone, in a mighty wail of moans and voices. And I kept waiting serenely for Jesus, waiting, waiting—but he didn't come. I wanted to see him, but nothing happened to me. Nothing! I wanted something to happen to me, but nothing happened.

I heard the songs and the minister saying: "Why don't you 8 come? My dear child, why don't you come to Jesus? Jesus is waiting for you. He wants you. Why don't you come? Sister Reed, what is this child's name?"

"Langston," my aunt sobbed.   9

"Langston, why don't you come? Why don't you come and 10 be saved? Oh, Lamb of God! Why don't you come?"

Now it was really getting late. I began to be ashamed of 11 myself, holding everything up so long. I began to wonder what

God thought about Westley, who certainly hadn't seen Jesus either, but who was now sitting proudly on the platform, swinging
his knickerbockered legs and grinning down at me, surrounded
by deacons and old women on their knees praying. God had not
struck Westley dead for taking his name in vain or for lying in
the temple. So I decided that maybe to save further trouble, I'd
better lie, too, and say that Jesus had come, and get up and be
saved.

12   So I got up.

13   Suddenly the whole room broke into a sea of shouting, as
they saw me rise. Waves of rejoicing swept the place. Women
leaped in the air. My aunt threw her arms around me. The minister took me by the hand and led me to the platform.

14   When things quieted down, in a hushed silence, punctuated by a few ecstatic "Amens," all the new young lambs were
blessed in the name of God. Then joyous singing filled the
room.

15   That night, for the last time in my life but one—for I was a
big boy twelve years old—I cried. I cried, in bed alone, and
couldn't stop. I buried my head under the quilts, but my aunt
heard me. She woke up and told my uncle I was crying because
the Holy Ghost had come into my life, and because I had seen
Jesus. But I was really crying because I couldn't bear to tell her
that I had lied, that I had deceived everybody in the church, that I
hadn't seen Jesus, and that now I didn't believe there was a Jesus
any more, since he didn't come to help me.

BUILDING VOCABULARY

1. Throughout this essay, Hughes selects words dealing with religion to emphasize his ideas. Look the following words up in a
   dictionary. Then tell what *connotations* (see Glossary) the words
   have for you.
   a. sin (par. 1)
   b. mourner (par. 1)
   c. lamb (par. 3)
   d. salvation (title)
2. Locate additional words that deal with religion.

3. When Hughes talks about lambs in the fold—and lambs in general—he is using a figure of speech, a comparison (see Chapter 6). What is being compared? How does religion enter into the comparison? Why is it useful as a figure of speech?

UNDERSTANDING THE WRITER'S IDEAS

1. According to Hughes's description, what is a revival meeting like? What is the effect of the "preaching, singing, praying, and shouting" on the "sinners" and the "young lambs"?
2. Why does Westley "see" Jesus? Why does Langston Hughes come to Jesus?
3. How does the author feel after his salvation? Does Hughes finally believe in Christ after his experience? How do you know?

UNDERSTANDING THE WRITER'S TECHNIQUES

1. Is there a thesis statement in the essay? Where is it located?
2. How does the first paragraph serve as an introduction to the narrative?
3. What is the value of description in this essay? List several instances of vivid description that contribute to the narrative.
4. Where does the main narration begin? How much time passes in the course of the action?
5. In narration, it is especially important to have effective *transitions*—or word bridges—from stage to stage in the action. Transitions help the reader shift easily from idea to idea, event to event. List several transition words that Hughes uses.
6. A piece of writing has *coherence* if all its parts relate clearly and logically to one another. Each sentence grows naturally from the sentence before it; each paragraph grows naturally from the paragraph before it. Is Hughes's essay coherent? Which transitions help advance the action and relate the parts of a single paragraph to one another? Which transitions help connect paragraphs together? How does the way Hughes organized this essay help establish coherence?

7. A story (whether it is true or fiction) has to be told from the first-person ("I, we"), second-person ("you"), or third-person ("he, she, it, they") *point of view.* Point of view in narration sets up the author's position in regard to the action, making him either a part of the action or an observer of it.

   a. What is the point of view in "Salvation"—is it first, second, or third person?

   b. Why has Hughes chosen this point of view instead of any other? Can you think of any advantages to this point of view?

8. What is your opinion about the last paragraph, the conclusion of this selection? What does it suggest about the mind of a twelve-year-old boy? What does it say about adults' misunderstanding of the activities of children?

9. What does the word "conversion" mean? What conversion really takes place in this piece? How does that compare with what people usually mean when they use "conversion" in a religious sense?

EXPLORING THE WRITER'S IDEAS

1. Hughes seems to suggest that we are forced to do things because of social pressures. Do you agree with his suggestion? Do people do things because their friends or families expect them to? To what extent are we part of the "herd"? Is it possible for a person to retain individuality under pressure from a group? When did you bow to group pressures? When did you resist?

2. Do you find the religious experience in Hughes's essay unusual or extreme? Why or why not? How do *you* define religion?

3. Under what circumstances might a person lie in order to satisfy others? Try to recall a specific episode in which you or someone you know was forced to lie in order to please others.

IDEAS FOR WRITING

Guided Writing

Narrate an event in your life where you (or someone you know) gave in to group pressure or were forced to lie in order to please those around you.

1. Start with a thesis statement.
2. Set the stage for your narrative in the opening paragraph by telling where and when the incident took place. Use specific names for places.
3. Try to keep the action within as brief a time period as possible. If you can write about an event that took no more than a few minutes, so much the better.
4. Use description to sketch in the characters around you. Use colors, actions, sounds, smells, sensations of touch to fill in details of the scene.
5. Use effective transitions of time to link sentences and paragraphs.
6. Use the last paragraph to explain how you felt immediately after the incident.

More Writing Projects

1. Explain in a journal entry an abstract word like "salvation," "sin," "love," or "hatred" by narrating an event that reveals the meaning of the word to you.
2. Write an extended paragraph on an important event that affected your relationship with family, friends, or your community during your childhood.
3. Make a list of all the important details that you associate with some religious occasion in your life. Then write a narrative essay on the experience.

The Minnie Mouse Kitchen

Michael Dorris

Michael Dorris is a novelist and author of *The Broken Cord* (1989). This essay presents the dilemma of a father who wants to raise his daughters without gender stereotypes. Note how he uses dialogue from both himself and his daughters to present both sides of the dilemma.

Words to Watch

horizons (par. 1)   outlooks; visions
collective (par. 2)   common; joint
gender-neutral (par. 3)   without sexual stereotypes
aspiration (par. 6)   hope
suffrage (par. 6)   right to vote
inequities (par. 6)   inequalities; injustices
teetered (par. 16)   shook back and forth; wobbled
facades (par. 20)   exteriors; appearances

1   My wife, Louise, and I, well-intentioned parents of two young daughters, are ever vigilant lest our girls limit their horizons because of sexist stereotyping. Each, we believe, should aim for whatever her talents and inclinations dictate—be it president or Nobel Prize physicist, Supreme Court justice or space-shuttle pilot.

2   So, what did we do last year when, for their special Christmas present, five-year-old Persia and four-year-old Pallas's collective wish was for the complete Minnie Mouse kitchen?

3   Despair. Despite all of our gender-neutral picture books, they had clearly already been molded by the subtle messages of media and popular culture. White aprons, not lab coats, loomed in their future.

4   How about a chess set? we suggested. A magic kit? An ant farm?

5   No. Persia was firm, Pallas obdurate: It was Minnie Mouse or nothing. Tucked under the pillow of their imaginations was the page torn from a wish book in which two future mommies happi-

ly baked miniature angel foods, washed tiny plastic dishes, and planned the week's menu by perusing their stock of brand-name products.

Early December became the time for an unstated battle of wills, a contest of aspiration over who knew best what two of us wanted. Louise and I made the issue a symbol that spanned from suffrage to the Equal Rights Amendment. Our daughters, however, remained steadfast in their inclination toward home ec, though ultimately they seemed to resign themselves to the inequities of power. Their complaints would be saved, no doubt, for some future psychoanalyst. 6

Then on Christmas Eve, as I was preparing my grandmother's special sweet-potato balls (whipped, flavored with brandy, formed around a marshmallow, and dredged in cornflake crumbs) and Louise was making a family favorite, wild-rice stuffing for the turkey, a string of startling insights simultaneously occurred to us: *We* loved to cook. *We* spent lots of time doing it. *We* were Minnie Mouse. 7

Yikes! It was almost 4:00 P.M., and the stores would soon close. 8

A gentle snow had begun to fall, and here and there as I drove along the road toward town, colored Christmas lights twinkled through the windows of houses with smoking chimneys. New England in winter can, at such moments, seem like one giant Hollywood set, a Currier and Ives scene ready for a heartwarming story to happen. In this version, my part would have been played by Jimmy Stewart: awkward, stalwart, the honest gallumpf who carried the American dream like a red, white, and blue banner. He was out to do a deed, to accomplish one of those minor miracles that make life wonderful and annually bring a smile to Donna Reed's eyes. 9

The problem was, every store within a hundred miles was sold out of the Minnie Mouse kitchen. 10

"The last one went ten minutes ago," the salesman noted, driving a stake through my heart as I finally stood at the head of a long line of shoppers. 11

I was a poor excuse for a father. I looked from right to left in search of any idea, and there it was, suspended by wires from the ceiling: every one of Minnie's treasures—stove, sink, and "frigerator," its doors invitingly ajar. 12

13   "How about that one?" I pleaded.

14   "Oh, no," the man said. "That's the display model."

15   "It's not for me," I argued, perhaps unnecessarily. "It's for my little girls. They're only four and five." I paused dramatically, then fired my best shot: "It's Christmas Eve."

16   The man hesitated as Minnie teetered between us: rules, or little girls' dreams come true?

17   "Sell it to him," the grandmother behind me snarled menacingly. "What are you, Mr. Scrooge?"

18   "Call the manager," protested a man waiting to buy a snow shovel.

19   "Climb up there and take it down," demanded a very pregnant young woman with an ominously quiet voice. "Or I will."

20   There were holes in the plywood facades of Minnie's major appliances where the hooks had been, but no matter. They fit into the backseat, jauntily red and white. Jimmy Stewart drove home singing carols with the radio.

21   After our daughters were in bed, Louise and I arranged the kitchen beneath the tree, amid the puzzles and books and telescopes. Then we rose early to witness the girls' reaction. Right on cue they ran into the room, stopped still, and stared. What would each do first? Cook? Scour a pot? Clean out the freezer? Anything was possible.

22   Persia and Pallas held hands for what seemed a long time. Then, as one, they turned to where we sat and ran to squeeze between us.

23   "We knew you would," Persia said.

24   And Pallas nodded in agreement. "We knew it all the time."

BUILDING VOCABULARY

1. The author uses several "-ly" adverbs to modify sentence meanings. Give definitions for each word below.
   a. clearly (par. 3)
   b. ultimately (par. 6)
   c. simultaneously (par. 7)
   d. finally (par. 11)

    e. invitingly (par. 12)
    f. unnecessarily (par. 15)
    g. menacingly (par. 17)
    h. ominously (par. 19)

2. The words below refer to various degrees of strength or weakness in character or action. Write definitions for each word; then classify the word in one of the two groups.
    a. vigilant (par. 1)
    b. obdurate (par. 5)
    c. steadfast (par. 6)
    d. stalwart (par. 9)

UNDERSTANDING THE WRITER'S IDEAS

1. When does the narrative take place? Where does the writer live? What kind of economic and social class does he come from? Where in the narrative do we find out?

2. What is the author's first response when his daughters ask for a toy kitchen set? Why does he react this way? What makes him change his mind about his daughters' request? Why does he give us the recipe for his grandmother's sweet-potato balls?

3. In paragraph 7, the author highlights "we" when he writes, "*We* loved to cook. *We* spent lots of time doing it. *We* were Minnie Mouse." Who is the "we"? Why is "we" in italics? Who did the author previously think had influenced his daughters' choice of presents?

4. What does the essay suggest about the role of the father in the family? Why does the author say very little about the mother's role and emphasize his behavior instead? Where in the essay do we learn most about this father's role as a parent?

5. Toward the end of the essay, why does the author include the comments of the other shoppers in the toy store: the "grandmother behind me," the man waiting to buy a snow shovel, the pregnant woman?

6. In your own words, explain what makes the father decide to buy the Minnie Mouse kitchen after all. Do you think he made the right choice? Why?

UNDERSTANDING THE WRITER'S TECHNIQUES

1. What is the thesis of Dorris's essay?
2. Dorris uses his personal experience as a father to communicate his ideas about being a parent. Is using personal experience an effective technique to communicate the author's ideas? Why?
3. *Chronological order* in narration refers to the arrangement of events in the time order that they occurred, beginning with the one in the most distant past. How does Dorris use chronological order in his essay? Outline the chronology. What transitions does he use to tie together that chronology?
4. The writer uses *allusions* to expand the reader's picture of events in the story. Who is "Mr. Scrooge" (par. 17), and how does this allusion help develop the theme of the story? What other allusions do you find—in paragraph 9, for example? What does Dorris mean by the image of Jimmy Stewart who "carried the American dream like a red, white, and blue banner"? Why does the writer imagine such patriotic scenes at this point in his story? What is meant by the American dream?
5. For what audience is this essay intended? How do you know? How does this audience shape the way the writer plans his narrative? Explain.
6. What is the main point of Dorris's tale about his choice of a Christmas present for his daughters? Does he state it directly or do we have to *infer* it from the events in the narrative?

EXPLORING THE WRITER'S IDEAS

1. Langston Hughes writes in "Salvation" that he came to a point where he stopped believing in the ideas he had been raised to take for granted. In what ways does Dorris have to reassess his acceptance of cultural values of a different type?
2. Throughout his essay, Dorris contrasts his ideas about his daughters' wishes with their own ideas. Although the daughters do not speak directly until the last lines of the essay, their point of view is understood throughout. Which point of view do you think is

more accurate? What are the limitations to each point of view, and what are the strengths? Would you have bought the kitchen set or not? Why?

3. The setting for this story is a "typical" middle-class family in America, emphasized by allusions to classic Hollywood images of such families. Does this setting in any way undervalue your appreciation of the author's dilemma? Is "gender-neutral" parenting something that only middle-class families can afford to be concerned about, or does the issue cross boundaries of class and race?

IDEAS FOR WRITING

Guided Writing

Write a narrative essay that focuses on an incident from your experience that involved a parent and child. Take the point of view of either the parent or the child. Through your narrative, show how the incident had lasting effects on you because it helped you understand yourself and your values better, solve a conflict, or become a better parent (or child).

1. Begin by identifying the family situation about which you are writing. What is your status (single parent? only child?). In what economic and social setting does the incident occur?
2. Use allusions to familiar films or television programs that will help the reader identify the setting.
3. Tell what the focus of the incident was: a dilemma or conflict you had to resolve that lead you to a new self-awareness, for example.
4. Explain how the behavior of the various people involved (you, your parents or children, neighbors, teachers) was in part conditioned by the social assumptions under which they lived.
5. Use dialogue from a variety of people to make the events vivid.
6. Use chronological order in your narration of the incident.
7. Throughout the narration, contrast your perceptions of this problem with those of the other person involved.
8. In the conclusion, show who was right, and why the incident remains important to you today.

More Writing Projects

1. In your journal, recollect a memorable incident involving a holiday gift. Use narration and description.
2. Narrate in a paragraph an incident in which you changed your mind about something important.
3. Write an essay about something you did that made another person's life happier or better.

A Hanging

George Orwell

One of the masters of English prose, George Orwell (1903–1950) often used narration of personal events to explore important social issues. Notice here how he involves the reader in a simple yet fascinating and tragic story, almost as if he were writing fiction. Orwell takes a brief time span and expands that moment with specific language. At one point, as you will see, the purpose of the narrative comes into sharp focus.

Words to Watch

sodden (par. 1)   heavy with water

absurdly (par. 2)   ridiculously

desolately (par. 3)   gloomily; lifelessly; cheerlessly

prodding (par. 3)   poking or thrusting at something

Dravidian (par. 4)   any member of a group of intermixed races of southern India and Burma

pariah (par. 6)   outcast; a member of a low caste of southern India and Burma

servile (par. 11)   slavelike; lacking spirit or independence

reiterated (par. 12)   repeated

abominable (par. 13)   hateful; disagreeable; unpleasant

timorously (par. 15)   fearfully

oscillated (par. 16)   moved back and forth between two points

garrulously (par. 20)   in a talkative manner

refractory (par. 22)   stubborn

amicably (par. 24)   in a friendly way; peaceably

It was in Burma, a sodden morning of the rains. A sickly light, 1 like yellow tinfoil, was slanting over the high walls into the jail yard. We were waiting outside the condemned cells, a row of sheds fronted with double bars, like small animal cages. Each cell measured about ten feet by ten and was quite bare within except for a plank bed and a pot of drinking water. In some of them brown silent men were squatting at the inner bars, with their blankets draped round them. These were the condemned men, due to be hanged within the next week or two.

2   One prisoner had been brought out of his cell. He was a Hindu, a puny wisp of a man, with a shaven head and vague liquid eyes. He had a thick, sprouting moustache, absurdly too big for his body, rather like the moustache of a comic man on the films. Six tall Indian warders were guarding him and getting him ready for the gallows. Two of them stood by with rifles with fixed bayonets, while the others handcuffed him, passed a chain through his handcuffs and fixed it to their belts, and lashed his arms tight to his sides. They crowded very close about him, with their hands always on him in a careful, caressing grip, as though all the while feeling him to make sure he was there. It was like men handling a fish which is still alive and may jump back into the water. But he stood quite unresisting, yielding his arms limply to the ropes, as though he hardly noticed what was happening.

3   Eight o'clock struck and a bugle call, desolately thin in the wet air, floated from the distant barracks. The superintendent of the jail, who was standing apart from the rest of us, moodily prodding the gravel with his stick, raised his head at the sound. He was an army doctor, with a grey toothbrush moustache and a gruff voice. "For God's sake hurry up, Francis," he said irritably. "The man ought to have been dead by this time. Aren't you ready yet?"

4   Francis, the head jailer, a fat Dravidian in a white drill suit and gold spectacles, waved his black hand. "Yes sir, yes sir," he bubbled. "All iss satisfactorily prepared. The hangman iss waiting. We shall proceed."

5   "Well, quick march, then. The prisoners can't get their breakfast till this job's over."

6   We set out for the gallows. Two warders marched on either side of the prisoner, with their files at the slope; two others marched close against him, gripping him by arm and shoulder, as though at once pushing and supporting him. The rest of us, magistrates and the like, followed behind. Suddenly, when we had gone ten yards, the procession stopped short without any order or warning. A dreadful thing had happened—a dog, come goodness knows whence, had appeared in the yard. It came bounding among us with a loud volley of barks, and leapt round us wagging its whole body, wild with glee at finding so many human beings together. It was a large woolly dog, half Airedale, half pariah. For a moment it pranced round us, and then, before anyone

could stop it, it had made a dash for the prisoner, and jumping up tried to lick his face. Everyone stood aghast, too taken aback even to grab at the dog.

"Who let that bloody brute in here?" said the superinten- 7 dent angrily. "Catch it, someone!"

A warder, detached from the escort, charged clumsily after 8 the dog, but it danced and gambolled just out of his reach, taking everything as part of the game. A young Eurasian jailer picked up a handful of gravel and tried to stone the dog away, but it dodged the stones and came after us again. Its yaps echoed from the jail walls. The prisoner, in the grasp of the two warders, looked on incuriously, as though this was another formality of the hanging. It was several minutes before someone managed to catch the dog. Then we put my handkerchief through its collar and moved off once more, with the dog still straining and whimpering.

It was about forty yards to the gallows. I watched the bare 9 brown back of the prisoner marching in front of me. He walked clumsily with his bound arms, but quite steadily, with that bobbing gait of the Indian who never straightens his knees. At each step his muscles slid neatly into place, the lock of hair on his scalp danced up and down, his feet printed themselves on the wet gravel. And once, in spite of the men who gripped him by each shoulder, he stepped slightly aside to avoid a puddle on the path.

It is curious, but till that moment I had never realised what 10 it means to destroy a healthy, conscious man. When I saw the prisoner step aside to avoid the puddle, I saw the mystery, the unspeakable wrongness, of cutting a life short when it is in full tide. This man was not dying, he was alive just as we were alive. All the organs of his body were working—bowels digesting food, skin renewing itself, nails growing, tissues forming—all toiling away in solemn foolery. His nails would still be growing when he stood on the drop, when he was falling through the air with a tenth of a second to live. His eyes saw the yellow gravel and the grey walls, and his brain still remembered, foresaw, reasoned—reasoned even about puddles. He and we were a party of men walking together, seeing, hearing, feeling, understanding the same world; and in two minutes, with a sudden snap, one of us would be gone—one mind less, one world less.

11   The gallows stood in a small yard, separate from the main grounds of the prison, and overgrown with tall prickly weeds. It was a brick erection like three sides of a shed, with planking on top, and above that two beams and a crossbar with the rope dangling. The hangman, a grey-haired convict in the white uniform of the prison, was waiting beside his machine. He greeted us with a servile crouch as we entered. At a word from Francis the two warders, gripping the prisoner more closely than ever, half led, half pushed him to the gallows and helped him clumsily up the ladder. Then the hangman climbed up and fixed the rope round the prisoner's neck.

12   We stood waiting, five yards away. The warders had formed in a rough circle round the gallows. And then, when the noose was fixed, the prisoner began crying out on his god. It was a high, reiterated cry of "Ram! Ram! Ram! Ram!", not urgent and fearful like a prayer or a cry for help, but steady, rhythmical, almost like the tolling of a bell. The dog answered the sound with a whine. The hangman, still standing on the gallows, produced a small cotton bag like a flour bag and drew it down over the prisoner's face. But the sound, muffled by the cloth, still persisted, over and over again: "Ram! Ram! Ram! Ram! Ram!"

13   The hangman climbed down and stood ready, holding the lever. Minutes seemed to pass. The steady, muffled crying from the prisoner went on and on, "Ram! Ram! Ram!" never faltering for an instant. The superintendent, his head on his chest, was slowly poking the ground with his stick; perhaps he was counting the cries, allowing the prisoner a fixed number—fifty, perhaps, or a hundred. Everyone had changed colour. The Indians had gone grey like bad coffee, and one or two of the bayonets were wavering. We looked at the lashed, hooded man on the drop, and listened to his cries—each cry another second of life; the same thought was in all our minds: oh, kill him quickly, get it over, stop that abominable noise!

14   Suddenly the superintendent made up his mind. Throwing up his head he made a swift motion with his stick. "Chalo!" he shouted almost fiercely.

15   There was a clanking noise, and then dead silence. The prisoner had vanished, and the rope was twisting on itself. I let go of the dog, and it galloped immediately to the back of the gallows; but when it got there it stopped short, barked, and then re-

treated into a corner of the yard, where it stood among the weeds, looking timorously out at us. We went round the gallows to inspect the prisoner's body. He was dangling with his toes pointed straight downwards, very slowly revolving, as dead as a stone.

The superintendent reached out with his stick and poked 16 the bare body; it oscillated, slightly. "*He's* all right," said the superintendent. He backed out from under the gallows, and blew out a deep breath. The moody look had gone out of his face quite suddenly. He glanced at his wristwatch. "Eight minutes past eight. Well, that's all for this morning, thank God."

The warders unfixed bayonets and marched away. The dog, 17 sobered and conscious of having misbehaved itself, slipped after them. We walked out of the gallows yard, past the condemned cells with their waiting prisoners, into the big central yard of the prison. The convicts, under the command of warders armed with lathis, were already receiving their breakfast. They squatted in long rows, each man holding a tin pannikin, while two warders with buckets marched round ladling out rice; it seemed quite a homely, jolly scene, after the hanging. An enormous relief had come upon us now that the job was done. One felt an impulse to sing, to break into a run, to snigger. All at once everyone began chattering gaily.

The Eurasian boy walking beside me nodded towards the 18 way we had come, with a knowing smile: "Do you know, sir, our friend (he meant the dead man), when he heard his appeal had been dismissed, he pissed on the floor of his cell. From fright— Kindly take one of my cigarettes, sir. Do you not admire my new silver case, sir? From the boxwallah, two rupees eight annas. Classy European style."

Several people laughed—at what, nobody seemed certain.   19

Francis was walking by the superintendent, talking garru- 20 lously: "Well, sir, all hass passed off with the utmost satisfactoriness. It wass all finished—flick! like that. It iss not always so— oah, no! I have known cases where the doctor wass obliged to go beneath the gallows and pull the prisoner's legs to ensure decease. Most disagreeable!"

"Wriggling about, eh? That's bad," said the superintendent.   21

"Ach, sir, it iss worse when they become refractory! One 22 man, I recall, clung to the bars of hiss cage when we went to take him out. You will scarcely credit, sir, that it took six warders to dislodge him, three pulling at each leg. We reasoned with him. 'My dear fellow,' we said, 'think of all the pain and trouble you are causing to us!' But no, he would not listen! Ach, he wass very troublesome!"

23   I found that I was laughing quite loudly. Everyone was laughing. Even the superintendent grinned in a tolerant way. "You'd better all come out and have a drink," he said quite genially. "I've got a bottle of whisky in the car. We could do with it."

24   We went through the big double gates of the prison, into the road. "Pulling at his legs!" exclaimed a Burmese magistrate suddenly, and burst into a loud chuckling. We all began laughing again. At that moment Francis's anecdote seemed extraordinarily funny. We all had a drink together, native and European alike, quite amicably. The dead man was a hundred yards away.

BUILDING VOCABULARY

1. Use *context clues* (see Glossary) to make an "educated guess" about the definitions of the following words in italics. Before you guess, look back to the paragraph for clues. Afterward, check your guess in a dictionary.
   a. *condemned* men (par. 1)
   b. puny *wisp* of a man (par. 2)
   c. Indian *warders* (par. 2)
   d. careful *caressing* grip (par. 2)
   e. stood *aghast* (par. 6)
   f. it danced and *gambolled* (par. 8)
   g. *solemn* foolery (par. 10)
   h. armed with *lathis* (par. 17)
   i. a tin *pannikin* (par. 17)
   j. quite *genially* (par. 23)

2. What are definitions for the words below? Look at words within them, which you may be able to recognize.
   a. moodily
   b. dreadful
   c. Eurasian
   d. incuriously
   e. formality

UNDERSTANDING THE WRITER'S IDEAS

1. The events in the essay occur in Burma, a country in Asia. Describe in your own words the specific details of the action.
2. Who are the major characters in this essay? Why might you include the dog as a major character?
3. In a narrative essay the writer often tells the events in chronological order. Examine the following events from "A Hanging." Arrange them in the order in which they occurred.
   a. A large wooly dog tries to lick the prisoner's face.
   b. A Eurasian boy talks about his silver case.
   c. The superintendent signals "Chalo!" to the hangman.
   d. One prisoner, a Hindu, is brought from his cell.
   e. Francis discusses with the superintendent a prisoner who had to be pulled off the bars of his cage.
   f. The prisoner steps aside to avoid a puddle as he marches to the gallows.
4. What is the author's opinion of *capital punishment* (legally killing someone who has disobeyed the laws of society)? How does the incident with the puddle suggest that opinion, even indirectly?

UNDERSTANDING THE WRITER'S TECHNIQUES

1. What is the main point that the writer wishes to make in this essay? Which paragraph tells the author's thesis most clearly? Which sentence in that paragraph best states the main idea of the essay?
2. In the first paragraph of the essay, we see clear images such as "brown silent men were squatting at the inner bars, with their blankets draped around them." The use of color and action make an instant appeal to our sense of sight.
   a. What images in the rest of the essay do you find most vivid?
   b. Which sentence gives the best details of sound?
   c. What word pictures suggest action and color?
   d. Where do you find words that describe a sensation of touch?
3. In order to make their images clearer, writers use *figurative language* (see Glossary). "A Hanging" is especially rich in *similes,* which are comparisons using the word "like" or "as".

a. What simile does Orwell use in the first paragraph in order to let us see how the light slants over the jail yard walls? How does the simile make the scene clearer?

b. What other simile does Orwell use in the first paragraph?

c. Discuss the similes in the paragraphs listed below. What are the things being compared? Are the similes, in your opinion, original? How do they contribute to the image the author intends to create?

  (1) It was like men handling a fish. . . . (par. 2)

  (2) A thick sprouting moustache . . . rather like the moustache of a comic man on the films (par. 2)

  (3) It was a high, reiterated cry. . . like the tolling of a bell. (par. 12)

  (4) The Indians had gone grey like bad coffee. . . . (par. 13)

  (5) He was dangling with his toes pointed straight downwards, slowly revolving, as dead as a stone. (par. 15)

4. You know that an important feature of narration is the writer's ability to look at a brief span of time and to expand that moment with specific language.

a. How has Orwell limited the events in "A Hanging" to a specific moment in time and place?

b. How does the image "a sodden morning of the rains" in paragraph 1 set the mood for the main event portrayed in the essay? What is the effect of the image "brown silent men"? Why does Orwell describe the prisoner as "a puny wisp of a man, with a shaven head and vague liquid eyes" (par. 2)? Why does the author present him in almost a comic way?

c. What is the effect of the image about the bugle call in paragraph 3? Why does Orwell create the image of the dog trying to lick the prisoner's face (par. 6)? How does it contribute to his main point? In paragraph 12, Orwell tells us that the dog whines. Why does he give that detail? Discuss the value of the images about the dog in paragraphs 15 and 17.

d. Why does Orwell offer the image of the prisoner stepping aside "to avoid a puddle on the path"? How does it advance the point of the essay? What is the effect of the image of the superintendent poking the ground with his stick (par. 13)?

e. What is the importance of the superintendent's words in paragraph 3? What is the value of the Eurasian boy's conversation in paragraph 18? How does the dialogue in paragraphs 20 to 24 contribute to Orwell's main point?

   f. Why has Orwell left out information about the crime the prisoner committed? How would you feel about the prisoner if you knew he were, say, a rapist, a murderer, a molester of children, or a heroin supplier?

5. Analyze the point of view in the essay. Is the "I" narrator an observer, a participant, or both? Is he neutral or involved? Support your opinion.

6. In "A Hanging," Orwell skillfully uses several forms of *irony* to support his main ideas. Irony, in general, is the use of language to suggest the opposite of what is said. First, there is *verbal irony,* which involves a contrast between what is said and what is actually meant. Second, there is *irony of situation,* where there is a contrast between what is expected or thought appropriate and what actually happens. Then, there is *dramatic irony,* in which there is a contrast between what a character says and what the reader (or the audience) actually knows or understands.

   a. In paragraph 2, why does Orwell describe the prisoner as a *comic* type? Why does he emphasize the prisoner's *smallness?* Why does Orwell write that the prisoner "hardly noticed what was happening"? Why might this be called ironic?

   b. When the dog appears in paragraph 6, how is its behavior described? How do the dog's actions contrast with the situation?

   c. What is the major irony that Orwell analyzes in paragraph 10?

   d. In paragraph 11, how does the fact that one prisoner is being used to execute another prisoner strike you?

   e. Why is the superintendent's remark in paragraph 16—"*He's all right*"—a good example of verbal irony?

   f. After the hanging, the men engage in seemingly normal actions. However, Orwell undercuts these actions through the use of irony. Find at least three examples of irony in paragraphs 17 to 24.

EXPLORING THE WRITER'S IDEAS

1. Orwell is clearly against capital punishment. Why might you agree or disagree with him? Are there any crimes for which capital punishment is acceptable to you? If not, what should society do with those convicted of serious crimes?

2. Do you think the method used to perform capital punishment has anything to do with the way we view it? Is death by hanging or firing squad worse than death by gas or by the electric chair? Or are they all the same? Socrates—a Greek philosopher convicted of conspiracy—was forced to drink *hemlock,* a fast-acting poison. Can you accept that?

3. Orwell shows a variety of reactions people have to an act of execution. Can you believe the way the people behave here? Why? How do you explain the large crowds that gathered to watch public executions in Europe in the sixteenth and seventeenth centuries?

IDEAS FOR WRITING

Guided Writing

Write a narrative essay in which you tell about a punishment you either saw or received. Use sensory language, selecting your details carefully. At one point in your paper—as Orwell does in paragraph 10—state your opinion or interpretation of the punishment clearly.

1. Use a number of images that name colors, sounds, smells, and actions.

2. Try to write at least three original similes. Think through your comparisons carefully. Make sure they are logical. Avoid overused comparisons like "He was white as a ghost."

3. Set your narrative in time and place. Tell the season of the year and the place in which the event occurred.

4. Fill in details of the setting. Show what the surroundings look like.

5. Name people by name. Show details of their actions. Quote some of their spoken dialogue.

6. Use the first-person point of view.

More Writing Projects

1. Narrate in your journal an event that turned out differently from what you expected—a blind date, a picnic, a holiday. Try to stress the irony of the situation.

2. Write a narrative paragraph that describes a vivid event in which you hid your true feelings about the event, such as a postelection party, the wedding of someone you disliked, a job interview, a visit to the doctor.

3. Write an editorial for your college newspaper supporting or attacking the idea of capital punishment. Communicate your position through the use of real or hypothetical narration of a relevant event.

SUMMING UP: CHAPTER 4

1. Orwell's essay has remained one of the outstanding essays of the century, widely anthologized and frequently taught in English writing classes. How do you account for its popularity? Would you consider it the best essay in this chapter? in the four chapters you have read so far? Write an essay in which you analyze and evaluate "A Hanging."

2. Elizabeth Wong and Michael Dorris both challenge cultural assumptions behind being an "all-American girl." Use their narratives as a starting point, and write an essay about a particular time in your childhood when you tried to ignore or defy a given cultural or social expectation.

3. You are Richard Selzer (author of "The Discus Thrower," pages 98–101) and you have been asked by a local newspaper to write a short review of George Orwell's "A Hanging." Basing your insights on the philosophy of "The Discus Thrower," write the review. Or, if you choose, be George Orwell and write a review of Selzer's "The Discus Thrower."

4. What have you learned about writing strong narratives from the writers in this chapter? What generalizations can you draw? What "rules" can you derive? Write an essay called "How to Write Narratives" based on what you have learned from Wong, Hughes, Dorris, and (or) Orwell. Make specific references to the writer(s) of your choice.

5. Hughes's essay highlights the role of religion in life. Write an essay in which you narrate an important religious experience that you remember. You might want to narrate the story of your own "conversion."

CHAPTER 5

Illustration

WHAT IS ILLUSTRATION?

One convenient way for writers to present and to support a point is through *illustration*—that is, by means of several examples to back up an idea. Illustration (or *exemplification*) helps a writer put general or abstract thoughts into specific examples. As readers, we often find that we are able to understand a writer's point more effectively because we respond to the concrete examples. We are familiar with illustration in everyday life. If a police officer is called a racist, the review board will want *illustrations* of the racist behavior. The accuser will have to provide concrete examples of racist language, or present arrest statistics that show the officer was more likely to arrest Koreans, for instance, than Italian Americans.

Writing that uses illustration is most effective if it uses *several* examples to support the thesis. A single, isolated example might not convince anyone easily, but a series of examples builds up a stronger case. Writers can also use an *extended example,* which is one example that is developed at length.

For instance, you might want to illustrate your thesis that American patchwork quilts are an important record of women's history. Since your reader might not be familiar with quilts, you would have to illustrate your argument with examples such as these:

- Baltimore album quilts were given to eastern women heading west in the nineteenth century, and contain signatures and dates stitched in the squares to mark the event.

- Women used blue and white in quilt patterns to show their support for the temperance movement that opposed sale of alcohol.
- Women named patterns after geographic and historical events, creating such quilts as Rocky Road to Kansas and Abe Lincoln's Platform.
- African-American quilters adapted techniques from West Africa to make blankets for slave quarters.
- One quilter from Kentucky recorded all the deaths in her family in her work. The unusual quilt contains a pattern of a cemetery and coffins with names for each family member!

If you visited a museum and there was only one painting on the wall, you would probably feel that you hadn't gotten your money's worth. You expect a museum to be a *collection* of paintings, so that you can study a variety of types of art or several paintings by the same painter in order to understand the whole field of art. In the same way, through the accumulation of illustrations, the writer builds a case for the thesis.

In this chapter Ray Bradbury *illustrates* how important a holiday Halloween was for him when he was growing up in Illinois in 1928. He gives examples of costumes, and customs, including many sensory details. Brent Staples, an African-American journalist, illustrates the ways in which his mere presence on a street at night is perceived by some as a threat through his examples of events during his walks to chase away insomnia. Patricia Volk uses humorous examples to illustrate the ingenuity of American inventors, not just providing one invention, but dozens. Finally, Lewis Thomas uses examples from his experience as a surgeon to illustrate how death is a natural part of the life cycle. Each writer knows that one example is insufficient to create a case, but that multiple examples yield a convincing essay.

HOW DO WE READ ILLUSTRATION?

Reading illustration requires us to ask ourselves these questions:

- What is the writer's thesis? What is the *purpose* of the examples?
- What audience is the writer addressing? How do we know?
- What other techniques is the writer using? Is there narration? description? How are these used to help the illustration?

- In what order has the writer arranged the examples? Where is the most important example placed?
- How does the writer use *transitions?* Often, transitions in illustration essays enumerate: *first, second, third*; *one, another.*

HOW DO WE WRITE WITH ILLUSTRATIONS?

Read the selections critically to see the many ways in which writers can use illustrations to support an idea. Notice how many illustrations each writer provides, and plan to do the same in your essay.

Select your topic and write a thesis sentence that tells the reader what you are going to illustrate and what your main idea is about the subject.

Sample thesis statement:

Quilts have long been cherished for their beautiful colors and patterns, but few collectors recognize the history stitched into the squares.

Make a list of *examples* to support the thesis.

- Examples by quilt types:

Baltimore album quilts, political quilts, suffrage quilts, slave quilts, graveyard quilts

- Examples by quilt pattern names:

Radical Rose; Drunkard's Path; Memory Blocks; Old Maid's Puzzle: Wheel of Mystery; Log Cabin; Rocky Road to Kansas; Slave Chain; Underground Railroad; Delectable Mountains; Union Star; Jackson Star; Old Indian Trail; Trip around the World

Determine who the audience will be: a group of experienced quilters? museum curators? a PTA group? Each is a different audience with different interests and needs.

Plan an arrangement of the examples. Begin with the least important and build up to the most important. Or arrange the examples in chronological order.

Plan to use other techniques (such as description), especially if your audience is unfamiliar with your subject. If you are writing the quilt paper and using the example of the Baltimore album quilt, you would then have to *describe* it for readers who did not know what such a quilt looked like.

Be sure that the *purpose* of the illustrations is clearly stated, especially in the conclusion. In the quilt essay, for instance, different quilt patterns might be illustrated in order to encourage readers to preserve and study quilts.

Writing and Revising the Draft

Use the first paragraph to introduce the subject and to set up a clear thesis. You might introduce an *abstract* idea, such as forgotten history, that will be *illustrated* in the examples.

Plan the body to give the reader lots of examples, and to develop the examples if necessary. Use narration, description, and dialogue to enhance the illustrations. Write a conclusion that returns to the abstract idea you began with in the introduction.

Write a second draft for reading aloud.

Revise, based on your listener's comments. Proofread the essay carefully. Check spelling and grammar. Make a final copy.

Tricks! Treats! Gangway!

Ray Bradbury

Ray Bradbury is noted for his science fiction writing—you may have read *Farenheit 451* or have seen the movie—but in this piece he is recalling a special time of year for a boy who grew up in the Midwest in the 1920s and 1930s. Illustrations drawn from his childhood show what a grand time Halloween really was in Illinois.

Words to Watch

corrupted (par. 2) spoiled; ruined

induce (par. 2) cause; bring about

climax (par. 6) the highest point of interest or excitement

corn shocks (par. 7) bunches of corn sheaves drawn together to dry

grisly renderings (par. 8) terrifying examples

crump-backed (par. 8) creased; humpbacked

caldron (par. 10) a large kettle

banshee (par. 10) a female spirit that warns of death

bereavements (par. 10) losses of people through death

serpentines (par. 10) coils

papier-mâché (par. 10) a material made of paper pulp that can be molded into objects when moist

vulnerable (par. 15) open to attack

disemboweled (par. 17) with the bowels or entrails removed

1 Halloweens I have always considered wilder and richer and more important than even Christmas morn. The dark and lovely memories leap back at me as I see once again my ghostly relatives, and the lurks and things that creaked stairs or sang softly in the hinges when you opened a door.

2 For, you see, I have been most fortunate in the selection of my aunts and uncles and midnight-minded cousins. My grandma gave me her old black-velvet opera cape to cut into batwings and fold about myself when I was eight. My aunt gave me some white candy fangs to stick in my mouth and make delicious and most terrible smiles. A great-aunt encouraged me in my witch-

crafts by painting my face into a skull and stashing me in closets to induce cardiac arrest in passing cousins or upstairs boarders. My mother corrupted me completely by introducing me to Lon Chaney in *The Hunchback of Notre Dame* when I was three.

In sum, Halloween has always been *the* celebration for me 3 and mine. And those Halloweens in the late 1920s and early '30s come back to me now at the least scent of candlewax or aroma of pumpkin pies.

Autumns were a combination of that dread moment when 4 you see whole windows of dime stores full of nickel pads and yellow pencils meaning School is Here—and also the bright promise of October, that stirring stuff which lurks in the blood and makes boys break out in joyful sweats, planning ahead.

For we *did* plan ahead in the Bradbury houses. We were three 5 families on one single block in Waukegan, Ill. My grandma and, until he died in 1926, grandpa, lived in the corner house; my mom and dad, and my brother Skip and I, in the house next south of that; and around the block my Uncle Bion, whose library was wise with Edgar Rice Burroughs and ancient with H. Rider Haggard.

1928 was one of the prime Halloween years. Everything 6 that was grandest came to a special climax that autumn.

My Aunt Neva was 17 and just out of high school, and she 7 had a Model-A Ford. "Okay, kiddo," she said around about October 20. "It's coming fast. Let's make plans. How do we use the attics? Where do we put the witches? How many corn shocks do we bring in from the farms? Who gets bricked up in the cellar with the Amontillado?"

"Wait, wait, wait!" I yelled—and we made a list. Neva 8 drew pictures and made paintings of the costumes we would all wear to make the holiday truly fascinating and horrible. That was Costume Painting Night. When Neva finished, there were sketches of Grandma as the nice mother in "The Monkey's Paw," paintings of my dad as Edgar Allan Poe, some fine grisly renderings of my brother as crump-backed Quasimodo, and myself playing my own xylophone skeleton as Dr. Death.

After that came, in one flying downpour, Costume Cutting 9 Night, Mask Painting Night, Cider Making Night, Candle Dippling and Taffy Pulling Night, and Phonograph Playing Night, when we picked the spookiest music. Halloween, you see, didn't just stroll into our yards. It had to be seized and shaped and *made* to happen!

10   My grandparents' home, then, was a caldron to which we might bring hickory sticks that looked like witches' broken arms and leaves from the family graveyard out where the banshee trains ran by at night souling the air with bereavements. To their house, upstairs and down, must be fetched corn shocks from fields just beyond the burying tombs, and pumpkins. And from Woolworth's, orange-black crepe serpentines, and bags of black confetti which you tossed on the wind, yelling, "A witch just sneezed!" and papier-mâché masks that smelled like a sour dog's fur after you had snuffed in and out while running. All of it had to be fetched, carried, touched, held, sniffed, crunched along the way.

11   October 29 and 30 were almost as great as October 31, for those were the late afternoons, the cool, spicy dusks when Neva and Skip and I went out for the Slaughter and final Gathering.

12   "Watch out, pumpkins!"

13   I stood by the Model A as the sun furnaced the western sky and vanished, leaving spilled-blood and burnt-pumpkin colors behind. "Pumpkins, if they had any brains, would hide tonight!" said I.

14   "Yeah," said Skip. "Here comes the Smiler with the Knife!" I beamed, feeling my Boy Scout knife in my pocket.

15   We reached our uncles' farms and went out to dance around the corn shocks and grab great armfuls and wrestle them like dry Indian ghosts back to the rumble seat. Then we went back to get the harvest-moon pumpkins. They burrowed in the cereal grass, but they could not escape the Smiler and his friends. Then home, with the cornstalks waving their arms wildly in the wind behind us, and the pumpkins thudding and running around the floorboards trying to escape. Home toward a town that looked vulnerable under burning clouds, home past real graveyards with real cold people in them, your brother and sister, and you thinking of them suddenly and knowing the true, deep sense of Halloween.

16   The whole house had to be done over in a few short, wildly laughing hours. All staircases must be eliminated by grabbing leaves out of dining-room tables and covering the steps so you could only scrabble and slip up and then slide, shrieking, down, down, down into night. The cellar must be mystified with sheets hung on lines in a ghostly maze through which giggling and screaming banshees must blunder and flee, children suddenly searching for mothers, and finding spiders. The icebox must be

stashed with chicken viscera, beef hearts, ox tongues, tripe, chicken legs and gizzards, so that at the height of the party the participants, trapped in the coal cellar, might pass around the "parts" of the dead witch: "Here's her heart! . . . Here's her finger! . . . Here's her eyeball!"

Then, everything set and placed and ready, you run out late 17 from house to house to make certain-sure that each boy-ghost remembers, that each girl-become-witch will be there tomorrow night. Your gorilla fangs in your mouth, your winged cape flapping, you come home and stand in front of your grandparents' house and look at how great and spooky it has become, because your sappy aunt and your loony brother and you yourself have magicked it over, doused the lights, lit all the disemboweled pumpkins and got it ready like a dark beast to devour the children as they arrive through its open-mouth door tomorrow night.

You sneak up on the porch, tiptoe down the hall, peer into 18 the dim pumpkin-lit parlor and whisper: "Boo."

And that's *it*.   19

Oh, sure, Halloween arrived. Sure, the next night was wild 20 and lovely and fine. Apples swung in doorways to be nibbled by two dozen hungry mice-children. Apples and gargling kids almost drowned in water tubs while ducking for bites.

But the party was almost unimportant, wasn't it? Prepara 21 tion was 70 percent of the lovely, mad game. As with most holidays, the getting set, the gathering sulfur for the explosion, was sweeter, sadder, lovelier than the stampede itself.

That Halloween of 1928 came like the rusted moon up in 22 the sky—sailing, and then down like that same moon. And it was over. I stood in the middle of my grandma's living room and wept.

On the way home across the lawn to my house, I saw the pile 23 of leaves I had made just that afternoon. I ran and dived in, and vanished. I lay there under the leaves, thinking. This is what it's like to be dead. Under grass, under dirt, under leaves. The wind blew and stirred the grand pile. Way out in farm country, a train ran past, wailing its whistle. The sound cut my soul. I felt the tears start up again. I knew if I stayed I would never get out of the grass and leaves; I would truly be dead. I jumped up, yelling, and ran in the house.

Later, I went to bed. "Darn," I said in the middle of the 24 night.

25   "Darn what?" asked my brother, awake in bed beside me.

26   "365 darn days until Halloween again. What if I die, waiting?"

27   "Why, then," said my brother, after a long silence, "you'll *be* Halloween. Dead people *are* Halloween."

28   "Hey," said I, "I never *thought* of that."

29   "Think," said my brother.

30   I thought: 365 days from now . . .

31   Gimme a pad, some paper. Neva, rev up that Model A! Skip, hunch your back! Farmyards, grow pumpkins! Graveyards, shiver your stones! Moon, rise! Wind, hit the trees, blow up the leaves! Up, now, run! Tricks! Treats! Gangway!

32   And a small boy in midnight Illinois, suddenly glad to be alive, felt something on his face. Between the snail-tracks of his tears . . . a smile.

33   And then he slept.

BUILDING VOCABULARY

1. Bradbury has often used informal expressions in this essay. First, explain the meaning of the words in italics in the following groups. Then suggest a word or phrase that an author who wished to be more formal might have used instead.

   a. *"Okay, kiddo"* (par. 7)

   b. when we picked the *spookiest* music (par. 9)

   c. your *sappy* aunt and your *loony* brother and yourself have *magicked* it over (par. 17)

   d. *Gangway!* (par. 31)

2. A number of *figurative expressions* (see Glossary) spark this essay. In the list of examples of simile, metaphor, and personification below, explain each figure. (Personification is giving an object, thing, or idea lifelike or human qualities.) What is being compared to what? What other figures can you find in the essay?

   a. Halloween, you see, didn't just stroll into our yards. It had to be seized and shaped and *made* to happen! (*personification*) (par. 9)

   b. My grandparents' home, then, was a caldron (*metaphor*) to which we might bring hickory sticks that looked like witches' broken arms. . . . (*simile*) (par. 10)

c. where the *banshee* trains *ran* by at night (*metaphor*) (par. 10)

d. papier-mâché masks that smelled *like* a *sour dog's fur* (*simile*) (par. 10)

e. the sun *furnaced* the western sky (*personification*) and vanished, leaving *spilled blood* and *burnt-pumpkin colors* behind (*metaphor*) (par. 13)

UNDERSTANDING THE WRITER'S IDEAS

1. What part of the essay most clearly states the author's purpose?

2. What two things did autumn signify to Bradbury?

3. What were some of the various activities for the Bradburys before October 29?

4. Why were October 29 and 30 almost as great as October 31? What did Bradbury and Neva and Skip do?

5. What is the "true, deep sense of Halloween"?

6. How did the young Bradburys change the house into a Halloween place?

7. How do the activities before Halloween compare with the activities after it? Which activities did the narrator prefer?

8. Why does the author say "Darn" in the middle of the night after Halloween? Why is he unhappy?

9. How does his brother ease Bradbury's unhappiness?

10. Why does the author smile just before he goes to sleep?

UNDERSTANDING THE WRITER'S TECHNIQUES

1. What is the author's thesis? Is it stated or implied?

2. How is this essay an example of *illustration?* What examples does Bradbury give to show he has been lucky to have Halloween-minded relatives? How does he illustrate that "1928 was one of the prime Halloween years"?

3. The examples Bradbury offers to show the quality of the 1928 Halloween vary in their length and degree of development. Which examples are developed most fully?

4. In any essay of illustration the writer will often provide a simple listing of examples to demonstrate a point he is trying to make.

Paragraph 15 offers a listing of details, but none of the examples is fully developed. Why does Bradbury use this technique here? What other paragraphs offer a listing of details to illustrate a point?

5. Check your responses to question 2 in Building Vocabulary. How do all the figurative expressions contribute to Bradbury's topic? How are most of the metaphors and similes related to the topic and to each other?

6. Underline some sentences that you think have the best sensory details. Where does the author use color? action? sound? smell?

7. Look at the last sentence in paragraph 10: "All of it had to be fetched, carried, touched, held, sniffed, crunched along the way." Why has Bradbury used so many verbs? What is the effect upon the reader?

8. It is clear that the style here is simple, direct, and informal. Why has the writer chosen such a style? How is it related to the topic of the essay? to the character represented in it?

9. What is the meaning of the title? Why do you think Bradbury selected it? How does it reflect the personality of a young boy?

10. To enrich the meaning of an essay, a writer will often use references or *allusions* (see Glossary) to some other work in literature. The question posed by Aunt Neva, "Who gets bricked up in the cellar with the Amontillado?" in paragraph 7 is an allusion to a short story by Edgar Allan Poe, "The Cask of Amontillado." What is that brief story about? Why would Bradbury want to allude to Poe in this essay about Halloween? What other references to literature does the writer make (see paragraphs 2 and 8)? Explain them, or ask your instructor to if you are not familiar with them.

11. In what sequence has Bradbury presented the events in this essay? How has he used the order he selects to create a kind of suspense, a building up from minor events to major ones?

12. Before he states his purpose in this essay, Bradbury offers a couple of paragraphs of introduction. What information does he deal with in his introduction? How does that information set the stage for the real point of the essay?

EXPLORING THE WRITER'S IDEAS

1. It is a strong statement to make that Halloween is "wilder and richer and more important than Christmas morn." Does Bradbury support his point well? In your experience, is Halloween so wild, so rich, and so important a holiday? Why? In your family, is there a special holiday for which everyone makes grand preparations? Describe it.

2. Bradbury's wild view of Halloween was, to a large degree, encouraged by his relatives' reaction to the holiday too. How do your views about some holiday—like the Fourth of July, Thanksgiving, even Halloween—compare with or differ from the views of your relatives? In what cases do your relatives enrich your appreciation? detract from it?

3. What is the real significance of Halloween (check the dictionary or encyclopedia)? Why does that holiday still have a hold on the imagination of children today? Bradbury says that passing by a graveyard, he knew from the dead the "true, deep sense of Halloween." Do you agree? Is *that* the true sense of Halloween?

4. Bradbury says in paragraph 21 that the party was less important than the preparation for it. Would you agree, in general, that the *preparation* for an event—such as a holiday, a wedding, a party—is often more important than the event itself? Explain your answer by giving a specific example from your own life.

5. How are Bradbury's feelings after Halloween is over typical of feelings any young child would have? How is he able to overcome these feelings? Are children generally able to cope with disappointment in the way young Bradbury has?

IDEAS FOR WRITING

Guided Writing

Write an essay of 500 words in which you *illustrate* the personal value of some holiday that you celebrate.

1. Write an introduction that builds up to your thesis, as Bradbury has. State in your thesis sentence just how you feel about the holiday. Is it a wild time, like Bradbury's Halloween, or deeply reli-

gious, or just a time of nonstop fun with marvelous meals and parties?

2. Decide on an effective order for the illustrations you present. If you offer examples to support an idea about one particular holiday (the Christmas of 1991, for example) you might want to use chronology. If you present several examples (drawn over a number of years) to show why one holiday is important to you, you might again use chronology. But you might also want to tell the events according to their importance, saving the most important for last.

3. Depending upon how many examples you offer, develop your illustrations with enough details. Some of your illustrations will require expanded treatment; others will not. In any case, offer at least three examples to support your point.

4. Since you are drawing from your own experience, you will want to use sensory language—colors, smells, actions, sounds, images of touch. Try to use figurative expressions as effectively as Bradbury has.

5. After you present and develop your illustrations, discuss in your conclusion how you feel after the holiday is over.

More Writing Projects

1. Write a journal entry in which you show how one relative shared in the joys or pains of your childhood experiences. Select as illustration important moments that you can narrate clearly and in concrete, sensory language.

2. In recent years, Halloween has become a rather dangerous holiday where innocent children often come to harm by thoughtless, mean adults. Write an extended paragraph to illustrate the dangers of Halloween. Or, write an essay in which you show by means of illustration what steps your town or community takes to prevent Halloween accidents.

3. Do some research about a local festival, the preparations for it, and the activities involved in its celebration. Or, you might choose to investigate a more remote festival in another part of the country, such as the chili contest in Texas, sausage festival in Wisconsin, or pie-eating contest associated with state fairs. After you collect your research, write a four- or five-paragraph essay illustrating different features of this festival.

Night Walker
Brent Staples

Brent Staples is an editorial writer for *The New York Times* and holds a Ph.D. in psychology from the University of Chicago. Yet, since his youth, he has instilled fear and suspicion in many just by taking nighttime walks to combat his insomnia. In this essay, which appeared in the *Los Angeles Times* in 1986, Staples explains how others perceive themselves as his potential victim simply because he is a black man in "urban America."

Words to Watch

affluent (par. 1)   wealthy
discreet (par. 1)   showing good judgment; careful
quarry (par. 2)   prey; object of a hunt
dismayed (par. 2)   discouraged
taut (par. 4)   tight; tense
warrenlike (par. 5)   like a crowded tenement district
bandolier (par. 5)   gun belt worn across the chest
solace (par. 5)   relief; consolation; comfort
retrospect (par. 6)   review of past event
ad hoc (par. 7)   unplanned; for the particular case at hand
labyrinthine (par. 7)   like a maze
skittish (par. 9)   nervous; jumpy
constitutionals (par. 10)   regular walks

My first victim was a woman—white, well dressed, probably in 1 her early 20s. I came upon her late one evening on a deserted street in Hyde Park, a relatively affluent neighborhood in an otherwise mean, impoverished section of Chicago. As I swung onto the avenue behind her, there seemed to be a discreet, uninflammatory distance between us. Not so. She cast back a worried glance. To her, the youngish black man—a broad six feet two inches with a beard and billowing hair, both hands shoved into the pockets of a bulky military jacket—seemed menacingly close. She picked up her pace and was soon running in earnest. Within seconds she disappeared into a cross street.

2   That was more than a decade ago. I was 22 years old, a graduate student newly arrived at the University of Chicago. It was in the echo of that terrified woman's footfalls that I first began to know the unwieldy inheritance I'd come into—the ability to alter public space in ugly ways. It was clear that she thought herself the quarry of a mugger, a rapist, or worse. Suffering a bout of insomnia, however, I was stalking sleep, not defenseless wayfarers. As a softy who is scarcely able to take a knife to a raw chicken—let alone hold one to a person's throat—I was surprised, embarrassed, and dismayed all at once. Her flight made me feel like an accomplice in tyranny. It also made it clear that I was indistinguishable from the muggers who occasionally seeped into the area from the surrounding ghetto. I soon gathered that being perceived as dangerous is a hazard in itself: Where fear and weapons meet—and they often do in urban America—there is always the possibility of death.

3   In that first year, my first away from my hometown, I was to become thoroughly familiar with the language of fear. At dark, shadowy intersections, I could cross in front of a car stopped at a traffic light and elicit the *thunk, thunk, thunk, thunk* of the driver—black, white, male, female—hammering down the door locks. On less traveled streets after dark, I grew accustomed to but never comfortable with people crossing to the other side of the street rather than pass me. Then there were the standard unpleasantries with policemen, doormen, bouncers, cabdrivers, and others whose business it is to screen out troublesome individuals *before* there is any nastiness.

4   I moved to New York nearly two years ago and I have remained an avid night walker. In central Manhattan, the near-constant crowd covers the tense one-on-one street encounters. Elsewhere, things can get very taut indeed.

5   After dark, on the warrenlike streets of Brooklyn where I live, I often see women who fear the worst from me. They seem to have set their faces on neutral, and with their purse straps strung across their chests bandolier-style, they forge ahead as though bracing themselves against being tackled. I understand, of course, that the danger they perceive is not a hallucination. Women are particularly vulnerable to street violence, and young black males are drastically overrepresented among the perpetrators of that violence. Yet these truths are no solace against the

alienation that comes of being ever the suspect, an entity with whom pedestrians avoid making eye contact.

It is not altogether clear to me how I reached the ripe old 6 age of 22 without being conscious of the lethality nighttime pedestrians attributed to me. Perhaps it was because in Chester, Pa., the small, angry industrial town where I came of age in the 1960s, I was scarcely noticeable against a backdrop of gang warfare, street knifings, and murders. I grew up one of the good boys, had perhaps a half-dozen fistfights. In retrospect, my shyness of combat has clear sources. As a boy, I saw countless tough guys locked away; I have since buried several, too. They were babies, really—a teen-age cousin, a brother of 22, a childhood friend in his mid-20s—all gone down in episodes of bravado played out in the streets. I chose, perhaps unconsciously, to remain a shadow—timid, but a survivor.

The fearsomeness mistakenly attributed to me in public 7 places often has a perilous flavor. The most frightening of these confusions occurred in the late 1970s and early 1980s, when I worked as a journalist in Chicago. One day, rushing into the office of a magazine I was writing for with a deadline story in hand, I was mistaken for a burglar. The office manager called security and, with an ad hoc posse, pursued me through the labyrinthine halls, nearly to my editor's door. I had no way of proving who I was. I could only move briskly toward the company of someone who knew me.

Relatively speaking, however, I never fared as badly as an- 8 other black male journalist. He went to nearby Waukegan, Ill., a couple of summers ago to work on a story about a murderer who was born there. Mistaking the reporter for the killer, police officers hauled him from his car at gunpoint and but for his press credentials would probably have tried to book him. Such episodes are not uncommon. Black men trade tales like this all the time.

Over the years, I learned to smother the rage I felt at so 9 often being mistaken for a criminal. Not to do so would surely have led to madness. I now take precautions to make myself less threatening. I move about with care, particularly late in the evening. I give a wide berth to nervous people on subway platforms during the wee hours. If I happen to be entering a building behind some people who appear skittish, I may walk by, letting

them clear the lobby before I return, so as not to seem to be following them. I have been calm and extremely congenial on those
rare occasions when I've been pulled over by the police.

10 And on late-evening constitutionals I employ what has
proved to be an excellent tension-reducing measure: I whistle
melodies from Beethoven and Vivaldi and the more popular clas-
sical composers. Even steely New Yorkers hunching toward
nighttime destinations seem to relax, and occasionally they even
join in the tune. Virtually everybody seems to sense that a mugger wouldn't be warbling bright, sunny selections from Vivaldi's
"Four Seasons." It is my equivalent of the cowbell that hikers
wear when they are in bear country.

BUILDING VOCABULARY

1. Use context clues to determine the meaning of each word in italics. Return to the appropriate paragraph in the essay for more
   clues. Then, if necessary, check your definitions in a dictionary
   and compare the dictionary meaning with the meaning you derived from the context.

   a. seemed *menacingly* close (par. 1)
   context _____
   dictionary _____

   b. I was *indistinguishable* from the muggers who occasionally
   seeped into the area (par. 2)
   context _____
   dictionary _____
   context _____
   dictionary _____

   c. I have remained an *avid* night walker (par. 4)
   context _____
   dictionary _____

   d. they *forge* ahead (par. 5)
   context _____
   dictionary _____

   e. Women are particularly *vulnerable* to street violence (par. 5)
   context _____
   dictionary _____

   f. the *lethality* nighttime pedestrians attributed to me (par. 6)
   context _____

    dictionary _____

g. episodes of *bravado* played out in the streets (par. 6)
    context _____
    dictionary _____

h. I learned to *smother* the rage I felt . . . so often (par. 9)
    context _____
    dictionary _____

i. I now take *precautions* to make myself less threatening (par. 9)
    context _____
    dictionary _____

j. Even *steely* New Yorkers *hunching* toward nighttime destinations (par. 10)
    context _____
    dictionary _____
    context _____
    dictionary _____

2. Reread paragraph 1. List all the words suggesting action and all words involving emotion. What is the cumulative effect?

UNDERSTANDING THE WRITER'S IDEAS

1. Explain in your own words the incident Staples narrates in paragraph 1. Where does it take place? When? How old was the author at the time? What was he doing? During the incident, why did the woman "cast back a worried glance"? Was she really his "victim"? Explain. What was Staples's reaction to the incident?

2. How does Staples describe himself in paragraph 1? What point is he making by such a description?

3. What is the "unwieldy inheritance" mentioned in paragraph 2? What is Staples's definition of it? What is the implied meaning?

4. How would you describe Staples's personality? What does he mean when he describes himself as "a softy"? How does he illustrate the fact that he is "a softy"? Why did he develop this personality?

5. Explain the meaning of the statement, "I soon gathered that being perceived as dangerous is a hazard in itself" (par. 2).

6. What is "the language of fear" (par. 3)? What examples does Staples provide to illustrate this "language"?

7. Why did car drivers lock their doors when the author walked in front of their cars? How did Staples feel about that?

8. Where did Staples grow up? Did he experience the same reactions there to his nighttime walks as he did in Chicago? Why? How was Manhattan different from Chicago for the author? How was Brooklyn different from Manhattan?

9. What has been Staples's reaction to the numerous incidents of mistaken identity? How has he dealt with that reaction? What "precautions" does he take to make himself "less threatening"?

10. Summarize the example Staples narrates about the black journalist in Waukegan.

11. What has been the author's experiences with the police? Explain.

12. Does the author feel that all the danger people attribute to him when he takes night walks is unfair or unwarranted? Explain.

13. Why does his whistling selections from Beethoven and Vivaldi seem to make people less afraid of the author?

UNDERSTANDING THE WRITER'S TECHNIQUES

1. What is Staples's thesis in this essay?

2. How do the title and opening statement of this essay grasp and hold the reader's interest?

3. Reread the first paragraph. What *mood* or *tone* does Staples establish here? How? Does he sustain that mood? Is there a shift in tone? Explain.

4. How does the author use *narration* in paragraph 1 as a way to illustrate a point? What point is illustrated? Where else does he use narration?

5. What is the effect of the two-word sentence "Not so" in paragraph 1?

6. Staples uses *description* in this essay. Which descriptions serve as illustrations? Explain what ideas they support.

7. *Onomatopoeia* is the use of words whose sounds suggest their sense or action. Where in the essay does Staples use this technique? What action does the sound represent? Why does the author use this technique instead of simply describing the action?

8. What examples from Staples's childhood illustrate why he developed his particular adult personality?

9. Explain the meaning of the final sentence in the essay.

10. *Stereotypes* are oversimplified, uncritical judgments about people, races, issues, events, and so forth. Where in this essay does the author present stereotypes? For what purpose?

11. For whom was this article intended? Why do you think so? Is it written primarily for a white or black audience? Explain.

EXPLORING THE WRITER'S IDEAS

1. In this essay, Staples gives not only examples of his own experiences but also those of other black men. It is interesting, however, that he does not include examples of the experiences of black women. Why do you think he omitted these references? How do you feel about the omission? Are there any recent news stories, either in your city or in others, which might be included as such illustrations?

2. What prejudices and stereotypes about different racial and cultural groups do people in your community hold? Where do these prejudices and stereotypes come from? Do you think any are justified?

3. What everyday situations do you perceive as most dangerous? Why do you perceive them as such? How do you react to protect yourself? Do you feel your perceptions and reactions are realistic? Explain.

IDEAS FOR WRITING

Guided Writing

Write an essay that illustrates how something about your personality has been incorrectly perceived at some time or over a period of time.

1. Begin your essay by narrating a single incident that vividly illustrates the misperception. Begin this illustration with a statement.

2. Explain the time context of this incident as it fits into your life or into a continuing misperception.

3. Describe and illustrate "who you really are" in relation to this misperception.

4. Explain how this misperception fits into a larger context outside your immediate, personal experience of it.
5. Write a series of descriptive illustrations to explain how this misperception has continued to affect you over time.
6. Explain how you first became aware of the misperception.
7. If possible, offer illustrations of others who have suffered the same or similar misperceptions of themselves.
8. Write about your emotional reaction to this overall situation.
9. Illustrate how you have learned to cope with the situation.
10. Give your essay a "catchy" title.

More Writing Projects

1. Usually stereotypes are thought of as negative. Illustrate at least three *positive* stereotypes in your latest journal entry.
2. Write a paragraph in which you illustrate your family's or friends' misconceptions about your girlfriend/boyfriend, wife/husband, or best friend.
3. Discuss in a small class group productive ways in which to solve the key problems raised by Brent Staples. Take notes, and then write an essay illustrating the problems and their possible solutions.

A Family of Firsts

Patricia Volk

Patricia Volk, author of the novel *White Light* (1992), writes this humorous essay to describe her ethnic identity and her awareness of what it means to achieve in America. The family tree of inventors she describes is like a funny Eastern European folktale, yet it serves to remind us that being clever is often a key to survival for immigrants.

Words to Watch

bon mots (par. 2)   clever words
criterion (par. 2)   standard of judgment
imprint (par. 6)   impression; mark
folklore (par. 6)   tales or stories based on legend or tradition
eulogized (par. 9)   honored
inverted (par. 12)   turned inside out

1   In my family, success is weighed by a single standard: The ability to be first. It does not matter what you are first at as long as you are first at something.

2   My relatives came from Europe at the height of the Machine Age. Every day, something else in America was new and first. The first flush toilet, the first emery board, the first air-conditioned hat. My family got first fever. Recipes, bon mots and good ideas all counted. Styles, inventions, slogans, too. The sole criterion for being first at something was simply not having heard that someone else had done it. Then you earned the right to say the magic words: "I did it first!"

3   My great-grandfather on my mother's mother's side invented the toodle. The toodle is a little square of waxed paper rolled into a cone with a dollop of mustard in it. You could take a toodle to work in the morning with a piece of cold meat and squeeze a squiggle of fresh mustard on it at lunch.

4   This great-grandfather, the toodle inventor, had three daughters: Ruthie, the first girl who ever made a lace curtain into a shawl; Gertie, the first girl who ever made a lace shawl into a

curtain, and Polly, my grandmother, who perfected a brush to clean the inside of a faucet. "Just because you can't see it doesn't mean it isn't dirty," she was fond of saying.

5 Polly was proud of the fact that every inch of her apartment was touched by human hand at least twice a year. She even dusted the tops of doors, using a top-of-the-door duster made of old stockings with runs in them, stuffed with old stockings with runs in them. Old stockings with runs in them have always been perceived as a challenge by my family. My mother uses hers as an onion bag, an idea she says she invented. She also takes credit for being the first person to use pantyhose simultaneously, one leg for onions, one leg for potatoes or garlic. But I am getting ahead of myself.

6 Perhaps my most famous relative of all, the one who really left his imprint on America, was Reb Sussel, my great-grandfather on my father's father's side. According to family folklore, he brought the pastrami sandwich to the New World. In 1879, Reb Sussel left his native Lithuania to find fame and fortune on the streets of New York. He had been a miller in Vilna, but, finding the wheat business too much of a grind, became a tinker, selling pots and pan off his back. He had no home and would sleep in the stables or basements of the people he sold pots to. While praying one morning he was kicked by a horse, which made him tear his hair and shout, "My life lacks dignity!"

7 Being a religious man, Reb Sussel knew how to butcher meat, so he opened a small butcher shop on Delancey Street. The first week, a Rumanian friend stopped by and asked if he could store a trunk in the back of the shop. "I'm just going back to Rumania for a few years," he said. "If you store my trunk, I'll give you the recipe for pastrami." As the story goes, Great-Grandpa took the trunk and the recipe and began selling hunks of pastrami over the counter. Soon he was selling it by the slice. Then, between two pieces of rye. He met up with my great-grandfather on my mother's side, who introduced him to the toodle, and before long, people were coming to Sussman Volk's for sandwiches more than they were coming for meat.

8 Legend has it that about this time my Great-Great-Uncle Albert, working independently, became the first man to stir scallions into cream cheese.

My paternal grandfather, Jacob Volk, took credit for the 9
wrecking ball. According to James Thurber, who eulogized him
in The New Yorker in March 1929, Jake was a housewrecker out
of "Herculean mythology." (In our family, Jake is also famous
for inventing the caviar sandwich eaten on a soda cracker. Until
then, everyone ate caviar on pumpernickel with a little chopped
egg and onion.)

Jake took his wrecking ball all over lower Manhattan. His 10
slogan, painted on the sides of all his trucks, was "The Most Destructive Force on Wall Street." He married Granny Ethel, who
was such a knockout she did not have to be first at anything. She
was, though—the first calendar girl in Princeton, N.J. In the early
1900's, her picture was used by a bank there for its first calendar.
That's where Grandpa met her, in the bank. She was so beautiful,
she once received a letter addressed:

Postman, Postman
Do your duty
Deliver this letter
To the Princeton beauty.

It was dropped off right at her front door.

The union between Jake and the prettiest girl in Princeton 11
produced my father, the 1938 shag-dancing champion at the University of West Virginia. He invented the six-color retractable
pen and pencil set, but was sold out by his partner, the mention of
whose name in our family is still followed by spitting. My father
did receive patents for the hydraulic-powered garbage-can brush
and the two-sided lighter so you never have to worry about
which side is up when you go to light. But perhaps most impressive, my father made the first illuminated Lucite single-shaft
fender guide, which clamped on to your car and facilitated nighttime parking by showing you where your fender ended.

My mother invented the Pinch Code, a series of pinches 12
that had clear interpretations: Don't stare! Don't say that! Be
quiet! How do you know? She's lying! Clean your plate! Watch
that tone of voice! No, you may not! I heard that! We'll talk
about it later! A dresser of local renown, my mother went around
in Great Aunt Bertha's blouses. Bertha claimed to have invented
the reverse tuck, a sewing technique that created parallel rows of
inverted pleats. The style was favored by First Lady Eleanor

Roosevelt, who, according to Aunt Bertha, once said she felt she could go anywhere in a Bertha Brecher blouse.

13   My maternal grandmother invented the shoe pocket. It was her belief that if you always kept a nickel in your shoe, nothing bad would happen to you. You could always make a phone call. You could always buy something. You would never be broke. But the nickel could slide around. And if it could slide around, it could slide out. So she constructed a small pocket that fit under the arch and fastened to the inner sole. That way, any pair of shoes could have its own bankroll. Her nephew, Cousin Wally, is said to have been the first soldier to have had a sponge left in his back during surgery after World War II. He was fine as long as he didn't sit. This forced him to look for work he could do standing up. That's how he found his second first: Cousin Wally was the first cameraman for the first live cooking show in television.

14   When Wally's uncle, my Grandpa Herman, came to this country in the 1800's at the age of 12, he made a promise to himself. Leaning over the railing of his ship, watching the Statue of Liberty fade in and out of the mist, he swore he would never speak German or Polish again, that the little town he came from in the Tatra Mountains that was sometimes German and sometimes Polish would no longer be a part of his life. He would never go back, never see his parents again, never climb the mountains of Nowy Targ. Herman Morgen would be American now. He would bathe every day. He would chew gum. He would invent something.

15   Herman got a job sweeping the floor of a restaurant, then he became a busboy, then a waiter, then a manager, then the owner, and then he found his first: He was the first man to carve meat in a window. It brought the customers in. It began a restaurant business that lasted for 60 years.

16   Me, I have yet to make my mark. I am still waiting to find a first. Sometimes I think my life is too cozy. Why should I mother an invention if all my necessities are met? But then something nudges me. How hard it is to start a roll of toilet paper! How annoying it is when dental floss gets stuck between the teeth! What a waste it is throwing out old light bulbs, egg shells and typewriter ribbons! Should bobby pins be used only in the hair? Why isn't there anything on the wheels of the bed frame to stop you from stubbing your toe? If Saran Wrap has a longer life ex-

pectancy than I do, why is it thrown out after using just once? Could dust balls really have been put on this earth for no reason?

When you come from a family of firsts, whether you like it 17 or not, you're thinking all the time.

When you come from a family of firsts, you never forget 18 the burden and the inspiration of our past.

BUILDING VOCABULARY

1. In paragraph 3, the author uses *definition* to introduce us to a new word, "toodle." Create your own word for a common, everyday object, and write a definition.
2. The author uses many words that come from her Eastern European heritage. Make a list of these words. How many of them have become common in American English? How many are new to you? Look up all the unfamiliar words in a dictionary.

UNDERSTANDING THE WRITER'S IDEAS

1. What is the *tone* in which this essay is written? How do you know that this is the intended tone?
2. What is the writer's ethnic heritage? What clues to this heritage does she provide?
3. What are some of the inventions the author accredits to her ancestors? What kinds of inventions are these? Why does she describe them in such detail?
4. The author refers to Lithuania in paragraph 6 and Rumania in paragraph 7. Where are these countries?
5. Why are so many of the inventions related to food? Why might food be especially important to immigrants? List all the food types mentioned in the essay.
6. In the conclusion, the author says, "When you come from a family of firsts, you never forget the burden and the inspiration of your past." What does she mean here? Why is the past both a "burden" and an "inspiration"? Does the *tone* of the writing change at this point? Explain.
7. What does Volk imply brings immigrants to the United States? Find evidence in the essay to support your answer.

8. Volk writes a family history, using humor and folklore to explain her own identity. In what ways is her story typical of the histories of other immigrant families? In what ways is it different?

UNDERSTANDING THE WRITER'S TECHNIQUES

1. What is the thesis of the essay? Where is it located?
2. What details does Volk use to illustrate the ingenuity of her ancestors? Which inventions seem most practical to you? Which ones seem imaginary? Why does she include so many inventions?
3. How does the author illustrate the economic and social status of her family through the inventions? In paragraph 5, the author describes her mother's use of old stockings as onion bags, for instance. Why does it seem important to the mother that she is the "first" to do this? In what way is "being first" related to the mother's heritage as an immigrant?
4. The writer creates not just one, but many illustrations of her family's inventions. How do the number of examples help the writer shape her paragraphs? What kind of detail does she use in the body of each illustration paragraph?
5. What transitional devices does the writer use when she shifts from one example to the next? Identify the transitional device used for each body paragraph.

EXPLORING THE WRITER'S IDEAS

1. Volk implies that both women and men are inventors. What sorts of devices do the women invent? What do the men invent? What seems to motivate the inventions?
2. Has Volk fairly presented the conditions of life for immigrants in America? In selecting a humorous tone, has she disgraced her heritage? Do you think that immigrants who settled in New York were better or worse off than those who left the city and settled elsewhere in the country?
3. Volk suggests that achieving the American dream can be as much a matter of self-assertion as of originality or wealth. If you *say*

you invented the toodle, you create self-esteem and respect for yourself. Do you agree with her analysis? Is success in America this easy for all immigrants? Can the immigrant's ethnic identity be a disadvantage in "making it" in America? Explain.

4. In paragraph 14, Volk describes her Grandpa Herman's dream of America: "He would bathe every day. He would chew gum. He would invent something." In your own words, tell what *you* think "being an American" means to recent immigrants. Is there any serious meaning to Grandpa Herman's images?

5. Compare Patricia Volk's ideas about the life of immigrants with those presented by Ellen Tashie Frisina in "'See Spot Run': Teaching My Grandmother to Read" (pages 65–67). Which story is more vivid? Why?

IDEAS FOR WRITING

Guided Writing

On a separate sheet of paper, fill in the blanks in the following sentence and then write an essay of 350 to 500 words in which you use illustration to present your ideas: Being from a family of _____, you never forget the _____ and _____ of your past.

1. For the blank spaces, select words that reflect important aspects of your own family and heritage. You can be either humorous or serious. You might say, "Being from a family of strong women, you never forget the beauty and perseverance of your past." Or you might follow one of the suggestions listed below if you cannot think of one of your own. But be sure to avoid overused and vague words: good, nice, stupid, interesting, fantastic.

   a. Being from a family of African Americans, you never forget the traditions and responsibilities of your past.

   b. Being from a family of New Yorkers, you never forget the tenement life and ethnic food of your past.

   c. Being from a family with a handicapped person, you never forget the misunderstanding and struggle of the past.

2. Use the sentence you have written as the thesis sentence of your essay. Build an introduction paragraph around it.

3. Illustrate your thesis with examples drawn from your family's history. Provide at least three detailed illustrations.
4. If your illustrations require narrative, follow the techniques you learned in Chapter 4 about good narration.
5. If you have to use description, make sure you follow the suggestions in Chapter 3 about good description. Use concrete, sensory language to help your reader see your points clearly. Remember the kind of language Volk uses to describe her inventions. Reread her illustrations and underline all the adjectives to remind yourself to include many concrete words in your essay.
6. Connect the different illustrations in your essay by referring to the main point in your thesis. Use transitional devices between paragraphs.
7. Conclude the essay by telling the reader what your family's greatest contribution to your own identify has been.

More Writing Projects

1. For a journal entry, consider your goals in life in light of your immediate family background. Support your general goals with specific examples drawn from family life and legend.
2. Write a paragraph of illustration in which you show how aspirations toward a better life shaped your family's decisions. You might think about a decision to move to a better neighborhood, or for a family member to go to college. Illustrate, for instance, how your mother got a second job in order to pay your tuition.
3. Write an essay in which you provide illustrations to show what brings immigrants to America. You may want to select illustrations from your own experience or observation or family history. Or you might want to use other sources, like newspaper articles, books, magazines, and presentations on radio or television.

Death in the Open
Lewis Thomas

Dr. Lewis Thomas is president of the Memorial Sloan-Kettering Cancer Center in New York City. He has written numerous articles about science, medicine, and life structures and cycles geared for the lay reader. His observations often bring fascinating clarity to the cycles of life and death on our planet. The following essay, a brilliant inquiry into the "natural marvel" of death, appears in his book *Lives of a Cell* (1974), which won the National Book Award for Arts and Letters in 1975.

Words to Watch

voles (par. 1)   the members of any one of several species of small rodents

impropriety (par. 2)   an improper action or remark

progeny (par. 4)   descendants or offspring

mutation (par. 4)   a sudden genetic change

amebocytes (par. 4)   one-celled organisms

stipulated (par. 6)   made a special condition for

incongruity (par. 6)   something which is not consistent with its environment

conspicuous (par. 7)   very obvious

inexplicably (par. 7)   unexplainably

anomalies (par. 10)   irregularities

notion (par. 11)   an idea

detestable (par. 11)   hateful

synchrony (par. 11)   simultaneous occurrence

Most of the dead animals you see on highways near the cities are   1
dogs, a few cats. Out in the countryside, the forms and coloring
of the dead are strange; these are the wild creatures. Seen from a
car window they appear as fragments, evoking memories of
woodchucks, badgers, skunks, voles, snakes, sometimes the mysterious wreckage of a deer.

It is always a queer shock, part a sudden upwelling of grief,   2
part unaccountable amazement. It is simply astounding to see an
animal dead on a highway. The outrage is more than just the lo-

cation; it is the impropriety of such visible death, anywhere. You do not expect to see dead animals in the open. It is the nature of animals to die alone, off somewhere, hidden. It is wrong to see them lying out on the highway; it is wrong to see them anywhere.

3   Everything in the world dies, but we only know about it as a kind of abstraction. If you stand in a meadow, at the edge of a hillside, and look around carefully, almost everything you can catch sight of is in the process of dying, and most things will be dead long before you are. If it were not for the constant renewal and replacement going on before your eyes, the whole place would turn to stone and sand under your feet.

4   There are some creatures that do not seem to die at all; they simply vanish totally into their own progeny. Single cells do this. The cell becomes two, then four, and so on, and after a while the last trace is gone. It cannot be seen as death; barring mutation, the descendants are simply the first cell, living all over again. The cycles of the slime mold have episodes that seem as conclusive as death, but the withered slug, with its stalk and fruiting body, is plainly the transient tissue of a developing animal; the free-swimming amebocytes use this organ collectively in order to produce more of themselves.

5   There are said to be a billion billion insects on the earth at any moment, most of them with very short life expectancies by our standards. Someone has estimated that there are 25 million assorted insects hanging in the air over every temperate square mile, in a column extending upward for thousands of feet, drifting through the layers of the atmosphere like plankton. They are dying steadily, some by being eaten, some just dropping in their tracks, tons of them around the earth, disintegrating as they die, invisibly.

6   Who ever sees dead birds, in anything like the huge numbers stipulated by the certainty of the death of all birds? A dead bird is an incongruity, more startling than an unexpected live bird, sure evidence to the human mind that something has gone wrong. Birds do their dying off somewhere, behind things, under things, never on the wing.

7   Animals seem to have an instinct for performing death alone, hidden. Even the largest, most conspicuous ones find ways to conceal themselves in time. If an elephant missteps and dies in an open place, the herd will not leave him there; the others will pick him up and carry the body from place to place, finally

putting it down in some inexplicably suitable location. When elephants encounter the skeleton of an elephant out in the open, they methodically take up each of the bones and distribute them, in a ponderous ceremony, over neighboring acres.

It is a natural marvel. All of the life of the earth dies, all of 8 the time, in the same volume as the new life that dazzles us each morning, each spring. All we see of this is the odd stump, the fly struggling on the porch floor of the summer house in October, the fragment on the highway. I have lived all my life with an embarrassment of squirrels in my backyard, they are all over the place, all year long, and I have never seen, anywhere, a dead squirrel.

I suppose it is just as well. If the earth were otherwise, and 9 all the dying were done in the open, with the dead there to be looked at, we would never have it out of our minds. We can forget about it much of the time, or think of it as an accident to be avoided, somehow. But it does make the process of dying seem more exceptional than it really is, and harder to engage in at the times when we must ourselves engage.

In our way, we conform as best we can to the rest of na- 10 ture. The obituary pages tell us of the news that we are dying away, while the birth announcements in finer print, off at the side of the page, inform us of our replacements, but we get no grasp from this of the enormity of scale. There are 3 billion of us on the earth, and all 3 billion must be dead, on a schedule, within this lifetime. The vast mortality, involving something over 50 million of us each year, takes place in relative secrecy. We can only really know of the deaths in our households, or among our friends. These, detached in our minds from all the rest, we take to be unnatural events, anomalies, outrages. We speak of our own dead in low voices; struck down, we say, as though visible death can only occur for cause, by disease or violence, avoidably. We send off for flowers, grieve, make ceremonies, scatter bones, unaware of the rest of the 3 billion on the same schedule. All of that immense mass of flesh and bone and consciousness will disappear by absorption into the earth, without recognition by the transient survivors.

Less than a half century from now, our replacements will 11 have more than doubled the numbers. It is hard to see how we can continue to keep the secret, with such multitudes doing the dying. We will have to give up the notion that death is catastrophe, or detestable, or avoidable, or even strange. We will need to learn more about the cycling of life in the rest of the system, and about our connection to the process. Everything that comes alive seems to be in trade for something that dies, cell for cell. There might be some comfort in the recognition of synchrony, in the information that we all go down together, in the best of company.

BUILDING VOCABULARY

1. Thomas makes imaginative and often unique use of adjectival expressions. Explain the meaning of each of adjective in the phrases below:
   a. *queer* shock (par. 2)
   b. *unaccountable* amazement (par. 2)
   c. *visible* death (pars. 2 and 10)
   d. *transient* tissue (par. 4)
   e. *ponderous* ceremony (par. 7)
   f. *neighboring* acres (par. 7)
   g. *natural* marvel (par. 8)
   h. *vast* mortality (par. 10)
   i. *relative* secrecy (par. 10)
   j. *transient* survivors (par. 11)
2. An *idiom* is an expression that has a special meaning only when taken as a whole; taken separately, the words may not make sense. What are the meanings of the following idioms?
   a. upwelling of grief (par. 2)
   b. catch sight of (par. 3)
   c. on the wing (par. 6)
   d. in time (par. 7)
   e. no grasp . . . of (par. 10)
   f. for cause (par. 10)

UNDERSTANDING THE WRITER'S IDEAS

1. Why does Thomas feel that it is strange to see dead animals in the countryside? How are dead animals more varied in the country than in the city? According to Thomas, for what reason is it a shock to see a dead animal on the road?

2. In paragraph 3, Thomas suggests that death is often an "abstraction." What does he mean by this statement? How does he suggest we can make death something more real? In your own words, for what reasons does he suggest we accept the life-death cycle as a more concrete idea?

3. Why, according to Thomas, do single cells seem not to die?

4. What is the meaning of the question at the beginning of paragraph 6? How does it relate to the theme of the essay? To what does the author compare seeing a dead bird? Why does he call it an "incongruity"? How is it "sure evidence . . . that something has gone wrong"?

5. Explain the process of death among elephants as Thomas describes it.

6. Explain the meaning of "the odd stump" in paragraph 8. What two examples of "the odd stump" does Thomas offer?

7. What example from personal experience does Thomas give to show that dead animals seem "to disappear"?

8. Explain the meaning of the first sentence of paragraph 9. In your own words, tell why Thomas feels the way he does.

9. What is the "secret" in paragraph 11?

10. In paragraph 10 Thomas says, "In our own way, we conform as best we can to the rest of nature." What does he mean? What supporting examples does he offer? What is the result? What examples does Thomas give of our reactions to the death of other human beings?

11. Why does Thomas say we must change our attitude toward death? How does he suggest that we do so?

UNDERSTANDING THE WRITER'S TECHNIQUES

1. What is Thomas's thesis in this essay? In what way is it reinforced by the concluding paragraph?

2. Study the introductory paragraphs. Why does the author offer several examples? Why is "the mysterious wreckage of a deer" an especially effective example?

3. Are there any clear illustrations in paragraph 2? Why or why not? What is the effect? Explain the connection between paragraphs 2 and 3.

4. Paragraphs 4 to 8 use illustrations to support a series of generalizations or topic sentences. Put a check mark by the topic sentence in these paragraphs and identify the generalization. Then analyze the illustrations used to support each one. Which examples are the most specific? the most visual? the most personal? Are there any extended examples?

5. How does paragraph 9 serve as a transition to the topic of paragraph 10? Why does Thomas use statistics in paragraph 10? How do they drive his point home?

6. Examine the author's use of pronouns in this essay. First, trace the use of first-person pronouns ("I," "we," "my," "our"). Why does Thomas use such pronouns? Why is their use in paragraph 8 especially effective? Next, consider Thomas's frequent use of the pronoun *it.* (Beginning writers are often instructed to minimize their use of such pronouns as *it, this,* and *that* because they are not specific and may leave the reader confused.) Explain what the word *it* stands for in paragraphs 2, 4, 8, and 9. Why does Thomas use a word whose meaning may be confusing?

7. Thomas uses *figurative language* (see Glossary) in this essay, particularly *similes* and *metaphors* (see Glossary). Explain in your own words the meanings of the following similes and metaphors:
   a. *the mysterious wreckage* of a deer (par. 1)
   b. episodes that seem *as conclusive as death* (par. 4)
   c. drifting through the layers of the atmosphere *like plankton* (par. 5)

8. We may say that the expression "dropping in their tracks" in paragraph 5 is a kind of pun. (A *pun* is a humorous use of a word or an expression that suggests two meanings.) What is the popular expression using the words *dropping* and *flies* that Thomas's phrase puns on?

9. Thomas makes use of a technique called "repetition with a difference"—that is, saying *almost* the same thing for added emphasis. Explain how repetition with a difference adds effectiveness to the sentences in which each of the following expressions is used:
   a. alone, hidden (par. 7)
   b. each morning, each spring (par. 8)
   c. unnatural events, anomalies, outrages (par. 10)

     d. catastrophe, or detestable, or avoidable, or even strange (par. 11)

10. *Parallelism* (see Glossary) is a type of sentence structure within a paragraph that creates a balance in the presentation of ideas and adds emphasis. It often uses a repeating pattern of subjects and verbs, prepositional phrases, questions, and so on. How does Thomas use parallelism in paragraph 3? paragraph 10? paragraph 11?

EXPLORING THE WRITER'S IDEAS

1. We might say that Thomas's title, "Death in the Open," is a double entendre (that is, has a double meaning). In what two ways may we interpret the phrase "in the open" as it relates to the contents of the essay? How do the two meanings relate to the philosophical points Thomas makes, especially in the two opening paragraphs and in the conclusion? Do you feel it is important to be more "open" about death? Why?

2. In paragraph 10, Thomas writes, "We speak of our own dead in low voices; struck down, we . . ." "Struck down" is used here as a *euphemism* (see Glossary) in place of other words that might be upsetting or distasteful. What other euphemisms do we have for death? Euphemisms for dying are often used to explain death to children. Do you think it is right, or necessary, to use such "guarded language" with youngsters? Why? For what other words or expressions do we commonly use euphemisms?

3. At the end of the essay, Thomas suggests that we might be less comfortable with death if we understood it more as a natural, common occurrence. What are your feelings about this philosophy?

4. According to Thomas's views in paragraph 9, because we don't often see dead animals "in the open," we are less prepared when we do encounter death. Do you think this reasoning is correct? Why or why not?

5. In paragraph 7 Thomas explains the process of death among elephants. What is your impression of the elephant herd's behavior at the death of one of its members? Why does Thomas call it "a natural marvel"? Have you ever heard the expression "the elephant dying grounds"? What does it mean?

6. Reread Gretel Ehrlich's "A River's Route" (pages 105–108). What similarities do you find between Thomas's and Ehrlich's visions of nature? Discuss them with specific references to the essays. How are the visions different? alike? Which author's ideas most closely resemble your own view of nature?

IDEAS FOR WRITING

Guided Writing

Write an essay in which you illustrate "_____ in the Open." Fill the blank with a word of your choice, a word that reflects some phenomenon, emotion, or idea whose features are often hard to understand. You might write about birth in the open, concerts in the open, love in the open, fear in the open, or war in the open, for example.

1. Develop an introduction with general examples that are relevant to your topic.
2. Add one or two paragraphs in which you speculate or philosophize on the phenomenon you are writing about.
3. Point out how the topic is most common throughout nature, society, or the world.
4. Give at least three extended examples that illustrate your topic.
5. Use the first-person pronouns "I" and "we" to add emphasis.
6. Illustrate ways in which people are generally unaware of certain features of the topic or tend to hide these features.
7. Try to include at least one statistic in your essay.
8. Use some idiomatic expressions in your essay.
9. Conclude your essay with some examples of how and why we can become more "open" about the topic.

More Writing Projects

1. For a journal entry, use examples to tell of your first experiences with death. You may want to write about the death of a relative, a friend, an acquaintance, a celebrity, or a pet.
2. Visit a place in the countryside (or a park) for one hour. Make a written record as you walk around detailing all evidence of natural death that you come across. Then write an illustrative paragraph on natural death as you observed it.

3. In your library, explore various burial practices among different races, religions, or ethnic groups and write an essay in which you illustrate several of these practices.

SUMMING UP: CHAPTER 5

1. In this chapter, Patricia Volk and Ray Bradbury each write about the inventiveness of people without a great deal of money. Both writers describe worlds in which imagination was supreme. Write an essay of illustration about some time in your life when imagination or inventiveness either replaced commercial products or invented new ones.

2. From this chapter select the essay that you think best uses the mode of illustration. Write an essay in which you analyze the writer's techniques and strategies. Make specific references to the text.

3. Richard Selzer ("The Discus Thrower," pages 98–101), Lewis Thomas ("Death in the Open," pages 179–182), and George Orwell ("A Hanging," pages 139–144) all deal with death and dying. Write your own essay about the issue, drawing on points from these three authors to illustrate your own position.

4. The world of the night, the environment of Staples's "Night Walker," challenges our senses and our perceptions, simply because it is so different from the typical daytime worlds we usually inhabit. What unusual nighttime experiences have you had? How do you feel about the night? Write an essay of illustration to address these questions.

CHAPTER 6

Comparison and Contrast

WHAT IS COMPARISON AND CONTRAST?

When we compare two things, we look for similarities. When we contrast, we look for differences. The comparison-contrast writing strategy, then, is a way of analyzing likenesses and differences between two or more subjects. Usually, the purpose is to evaluate or judge which is superior. Thus we might appreciate soccer if we compare it with football; we understand Roman Catholicism better if we see it in light of Buddhism.

Writers who use the comparison-contrast technique know that careful planning is required to *organize* the likenesses and differences into logical patterns. Some authors might use only *comparison,* to look at the similarities between subjects. Others might use only *contrast*. Often, writers combine the two in a carefully structured essay that balances one with the other.

Like many of the writing and reading strategies you have learned, comparison and contrast is familiar from everyday life. If you were about to buy a new car, for instance, you would look at several models before you made a choice. You might consider price, size, horsepower, options, safety features, status, and dependability before you spent such a large amount of money. If you were deciding whether to send your daughter to a public school or a private school, you would compare and contrast the features of each type of institution: cost, teacher quality, class size, location, curriculum, and composition of the student body might all be considered. If you were an art historian, you might compare and contrast an early picture by Matisse with one he completed late in life in order to understand his development as an artist.

Writing a comparison-contrast essay requires more careful planning, however, than the everyday life application technique. Both call for common sense. You wouldn't compare parochial schools with an Oldsmobile, for instance; they simply don't relate. But you would compare The Dalton School with Public School 34, or a Cutlass Supreme with a Volvo, a Matisse with a Cezanne. Clearly, any strong pattern of comparison and contrast treats items that are only in the same category or class. Moreover, there always has to be a basis for comparison; in other words, you compare or contrast two items in order to try to deal with all-important aspects of the things being compared before arriving at a final determination. These commonsense characteristics of comparison and contrast apply to our pattern of thought as well as our pattern of writing.

Author Rachel Carson, for instance, contrasts two visions of the future for planet earth: a flourishing environment or a devastated landscape. Thus she has a common category: the condition of the global ecology. She can use *contrast* because she has a common ground for her analysis. Ellen Goodman looks at friendships, Alice Walker at two landscapes, and Bruno Bettelheim at two kinds of children's stories. Each author sets up a formal pattern for contrasting and comparing subjects within a related class. One side of the pattern helps us understand the other. Finally, we may establish a preference for one or the other subject.

HOW DO WE READ COMPARISON AND CONTRAST?

Reading comparison and contrast requires us to ask ourselves these questions:

- What subjects has the author selected? Are they from a similar class or category?
- What is the basis for the comparison or contrast? What is the writer's *thesis*?
- What is the arrangement of topics? How has the writer organized each paragraph? Notice where transitional expressions *(on the one hand, on the other hand, similarly, in contrast)* are used to help the reader follow the writer's train of thought.

- Is the writer fair to each subject, devoting an equal amount of space to each side? Make an outline of one of the reading selections to see how the writer has balanced the two subjects.
- Has the writer used narration, description, or illustration to develop the comparison? What other techniques has the author used?
- Does the conclusion show a preference for one subject over the other? Is the conclusion justified by the evidence in the body?

HOW DO WE WRITE COMPARISON AND CONTRAST?

After reading the professional writers in this chapter, you will be better prepared to organize your own essay. Begin by clearly identifying the subjects of your comparison and by establishing the basis for it. The thesis sentence performs this important function for you.

Sample thesis statement:

Living in a small town is better than living in a big city because life is safer, friendlier, and cheaper.

Plan a strategy for the comparison and contrast. Writers can use one of three main techniques: block, alternating, or combination. The *block method* requires that the writer put all the points about one side (the small town in this case) in one part of the essay, and put the points about the other side (big city life) together in another part of the essay. In the *alternating method,* the writer explains one point about small-town life and then immediately gives the contrasting point about big-city life. The *combination* pattern allows the writer to use both alternating and block techniques.

Make a careful outline. For each point about one side, try to find a balancing point about the other. If, for instance, you write about the housing available in a small town, write about housing in the big city. Although it may be impossible to manage exact matches, try to be as fair as possible to each side.

Writing and Revising the Draft

Set up a purpose for the comparison and contrast in the thesis sentence.

Write an outline using paragraph blocks to indicate subject A and subject B. For instance, if you were going to write in the block form, your outline would look like this:

Introduction (with thesis)

Block A: Small Town
　　　1. housing
　　　2. jobs
　　　3. social life
Block B: Big City
　　　1. housing
　　　2. jobs
　　　3. social life
Conclusion

If you were going to use the alternating form, the outline would look as follows:

Introduction (with thesis)

Block A: Housing
　　　1. big city
　　　2. small town
Block B: Jobs
　　　1. big city
　　　2. small town
Block C: Social Life
　　　1. big city
　　　2. small town
Conclusion

Use many transitional devices, especially with the alternating form. Each time you shift from one subject to the other, use a transition: *like, unlike, on the one hand, on the other hand, in contrast, similarly.*

In the conclusion, offer your determination about the two subjects.

Proofread carefully. Check the draft for clarity and correctness and make a final copy.

A Fable for Tomorrow
Rachel Carson

Rachel Carson wrote a number of books and articles in the 1950s and 1960s that alerted Americans to dangers facing our natural environment. In this section from *Silent Spring* (1962), look for the ways in which Carson establishes a series of contrasts for her imaginary American town.

Words to Watch

migrants (par. 2)   people, animals, or birds that move from one place to another

blight (par. 3)   a disease or condition that kills or checks growth

maladies (par. 3)   illnesses

moribund (par. 4)   dying

pollination (par. 5)   the transfer of pollen (male sex cells) from one part of the flower to another

granular (par. 7)   consisting of grains

specter (par. 9)   a ghost; an object of fear or dread

stark (par. 9)   bleak; barren; standing out in sharp outline

1   There was once a town in the heart of America where all life seemed to live in harmony with its surroundings. The town lay in the midst of a checkerboard of prosperous farms, with fields of grain and hillsides of orchards where, in spring, white clouds of bloom drifted above the green fields. In autumn, oak and maple and birch set up a blaze of color that flamed and flickered across a backdrop of pines. Then foxes barked in the hills and deer silently crossed the fields, half hidden in the mists of the fall mornings.

2   Along the roads, laurel, viburnum and alder, great ferns and wildflowers delighted the traveler's eye through much of the year. Even in winter the roadsides were places of beauty, where countless birds came to feed on the berries and on the seed heads of the dried weeds rising above the snow. The countryside was, in fact, famous for the abundance and variety of its bird life, and when the flood of migrants was pouring through in spring and fall people traveled from great distances to observe them. Others

came to fish the streams, which flowed clear and cold out of the hills and contained shady pools where trout lay. So it had been from the days many years ago when the first settlers raised their houses, sank their wells, and built their barns.

Then a strange blight crept over the area and everything 3 began to change. Some evil spell had settled on the community: mysterious maladies swept the flocks of chickens; the cattle and sheep sickened and died. Everywhere was a shadow of death. The farmers spoke of much illness among their families. In the town the doctors had become more and more puzzled by new kinds of sickness appearing among their patients. There had been several sudden and unexplained deaths not only among adults but even among children, who would be stricken suddenly while at play and die within a few hours.

There was a strange stillness. The birds, for example— 4 where had they gone? Many people spoke of them, puzzled and disturbed. The feeding stations in the backyards were deserted. The few birds seen anywhere were moribund; they trembled violently and could not fly. It was a spring without voices. On the mornings that had once throbbed with the dawn chorus of robins, catbirds, doves, jays, wrens, and scores of other bird voices there was now no sound; only silence lay over the fields and woods and marsh.

On the farms the hens brooded, but no chicks hatched. 5 The farmers complained that they were unable to raise any pigs— the litters were small and the young survived only a few days. The apple trees were coming into bloom but no bees droned among the blossoms, so there was no pollination and there would be no fruit.

The roadsides, once so attractive, were now lined with 6 browned and withered vegetation as though swept by fire. These, too, were silent, deserted by all living things. Even the streams were now lifeless. Anglers no longer visited them, for all the fish had died.

In the gutters under the eaves and between the shingles of 7 the roofs, a white granular powder still showed a few patches; some weeks before it had fallen like snow upon the roofs and the lawns, the fields and streams.

No witchcraft, no enemy action had silenced the rebirth of 8 new life in this stricken world. The people had done it themselves.

This town does not actually exist, but it might easily have a 9 thousand counterparts in America or elsewhere in the world. I know of no community that has experienced all the misfortunes I describe. Yet every one of these disasters has actually happened somewhere, and many real communities have already suffered a substantial number of them. A grim specter has crept upon us almost unnoticed, and this imagined tragedy may easily become a stark reality we all shall know.

BUILDING VOCABULARY

1. In the second paragraph, find at least five concrete words that relate to trees, birds, and vegetation. How many of these objects could you identify? Look in a dictionary for the meanings of those words you do not know.
2. Try to identify the italicized words through the *context clues* (see Glossary) provided by the complete sentence.
   a. half-hidden in the *mists.* (par. 1)
   b. when the first settlers *raised* their houses. (par. 2)
   c. *stricken* suddenly while at play. (par. 3)
   d. the hens *brooded,* but no chicks hatched. (par. 5)
   e. *Anglers* no longer visited them, for all the fish had died. (par. 6)

UNDERSTANDING THE WRITER'S IDEAS

1. What is the quality of the world that Carson describes in her opening paragraph? If you had to describe it in just one or two words, which would you use?
2. What are some of the natural objects that Carson describes in her first two paragraphs? Why does she not focus on simply one aspect of nature—like animals, trees, or flowers?
3. How does Carson describe the "evil spell" that settles over the countryside?
4. What does Carson mean when she declares, "It was a spring without voices" (par. 4)? Why does she show that the critical action takes place in the springtime?
5. What do you think is the "white granular powder" that Carson refers to in paragraph 7? Why does she not explain what it is or where it came from?
6. In paragraph 9, the author states her basic point. What is it? Does she offer a solution to the problem that she poses?

UNDERSTANDING THE WRITER'S TECHNIQUES

1. A *fable* is a story with a moral; in other words, a fable is a form of teaching narrative. How does Carson structure her narrative in this essay? What *is* the "moral" or thesis?
2. What is the purpose of the description in this essay? Why does the writer use such vivid and precise words?
3. Where in this essay does Carson begin to shift from an essentially optimistic tone to a negative one?
4. Does Carson rely on comparison or contrast in this essay?
5. In the *block method* of comparison and contrast, the writer presents all information about one subject, and then all information about a second subject, as in the following diagram:

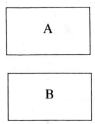

   a. How does Carson use this pattern in her essay?
   b. Are there actually two subjects in this essay, or two different aspects of one subject? How does chronology relate to the block structure?
   c. Are the two major parts of Carson's essay equally weighted? Why or why not?
   d. In the second part of the essay, does Carson ever lose sight of the objects introduced in the first part? What new terms does she introduce?
6. How can you explain paragraphs 8 and 9—which do not involve narration, description, or comparison and contrast—in relation to the rest of the essay? What is the nature of Carson's conclusion?

EXPLORING THE WRITER'S IDEAS

1. Today chemicals are used to destroy crop insects, to color and preserve food, and to purify our water, among other things. Would Carson term this "progress"? Would you? Do you think that there are inadequate safeguards and controls in the use of chemicals? What recent examples of chemical use have made the news?

2. Why would you agree or disagree that factories and corporations should protect the environment that they use? Should a company, for example, be forced to clean up an entire river that it polluted? What about oil spills?

3. Have there been any problems with the use of chemicals and the environment in your own area? Describe them. How do local citizens feel about these problems?

4. Do you think that it will be possible in the future for Americans "to live in harmony" with their natural surroundings? Why do you believe what you do?

IDEAS FOR WRITING

Guided Writing

Write a fable (an imaginary story with a moral) in which you contrast one aspect of the life of a person, community, or nation with another.

1. Begin with a phrase similar to Carson's "There was once . . . ." so that the reader knows you are writing a narrative fable.

2. Relate your story to an American problem.

3. Use the block method in order to establish your contrast. Write first about one aspect of the topic and then about the other.

4. Use sensory detail in order to make your narrative clear and interesting.

5. Make certain that you establish an effective transition as you move into the contrast.

6. In the second part of your essay, be sure to refer to the same points you raised in the first part.

7. Use the conclusion to establish the "moral" of your fable.

More Writing Projects

1. In a journal entry, describe a place you know well, one that has changed for better or worse. Contrast the place as it once was with the way it is now. Use concrete images that appeal to color, action, sound, smell, taste, and touch.
2. Examine in two block paragraphs the two sides of a specific ecological issue today—for instance, acid rain, the global warming trend, or the use of nuclear energy.
3. Using the block method, compare and contrast Carson's fable with the fable you wrote in Guided Writing.

The Place Where I Was Born

Alice Walker

Alice Walker is a novelist, poet, essayist, short story writer, and, in her own term, a "womanist." She has won both the American Book Award and the Pulitzer Prize for her novel *The Color Purple* (1982). As her essay reveals, she grew up in Eatonton, Georgia, but now lives in northern California. In comparing and contrasting her birthplace with her adopted home, Walker examines the persistence of racism in American society, and the decisions it forces victims of racial oppression to make.

Words to Watch

displaced (par. 1)   cast out from; removed from
expanse (par. 1)   large stretch or space
discreet (par. 1)   careful in speech; tactful
enigmatic (par. 1)   puzzling; mysterious
nostalgic (par. 1)   meditative; longing for what is not present
dell (par. 5)   small, secluded valley
bustles (par. 9)   moves about briskly

1   I am a displaced person. I sit here on a swing on the deck of my house in northern California admiring how the fog has turned the valley below into a lake. For hours nothing will be visible below me except this large expanse of vapor; then slowly, as the sun rises and gains in intensity, the fog will start to curl up and begin its slow rolling drift toward the ocean. People here call it the dragon; and, indeed, a dragon is what it looks like, puffing and coiling, winged, flaring and in places thin and discreet, as it races before the sun, back to its ocean coast den. Mornings I sit here in awe and great peace. The mountains across the valley come and go in the mist; the redwoods and firs, oaks and giant bays appear as clumpish spires, enigmatic shapes of green, like the stone forests one sees in Chinese paintings of Guilin.

2   It is incredibly beautiful where I live. Not fancy at all, or exclusive. But from where I sit on my deck I can look down on the backs of hawks, and the wide, satiny wings of turkey vultures

glistening in the sun become my present connection to ancient Egyptian Africa. The pond is so still below me that the trees reflected in it seem, from this distance, to be painted in its depths.

All this—the beauty, the quiet, the cleanliness, the peace— 3 is what I love. I realize how lucky I am to have found it here. And yet, there are days when my view of the mountains and redwoods makes me nostalgic for small rounded hills easily walked over, and for the look of big-leaf poplar and the scent of pine.

I am nostalgic for the land of my birth, the land I left forev- 4 er when I was 13—moving first to the town of Eatonton, Georgia, and then, at 17, to the city of Atlanta.

I cried one day as I talked to a friend about a tree I loved as a 5 child. A tree that had sheltered my father on his long cold walk to school each morning: It was midway between his house and the school and because there was a large cavity in its trunk, a fire could be made inside it. During my childhood, in a tiny, overcrowded house in a tiny dell below it, I looked up at it frequently and felt reassured by its age, its generosity despite its years of brutalization (the fires, I knew, had to hurt), and its tall, old-growth pine nobility. When it was struck by lightning and killed, and then was cut down and made into firewood, I grieved as if it had been a person. Secretly. Because who among the members of my family would not have laughed at my grief?

I have felt entirely fortunate to have had this companion, 6 and even today remember it with gratitude. But why the tears? my friend wanted to know. And it suddenly dawned on me that perhaps it *was* sad that it was a tree and not a member of my family to whom I was so emotionally close.

As a child I assumed I would always have the middle Georgia 7 landscape to live in, as Br'er Rabbit, a native also, and relative, had his brier patch. It was not to be. The pain of racist oppression, and its consequence, economic impoverishment, drove me to the four corners of the earth in search of justice and peace, and work that affirmed my whole being. I have come to rest here, weary from travel, on a deck—not a southern front porch—overlooking another world.

I am content; and yet, I wonder what my life would have 8 been like if I had been able to stay home.

I remember early morning fogs in Georgia, not so dramatic 9 as California ones, but magical too because out of the southern fog of memory tramps my dark father, smiling and large, glowing with rootedness, and talking of hound dogs, biscuits and coons. And my equally rooted mother bustles around the corner of our house preparing to start a wash, the fire under the black wash pot extending a circle of warmth in which I, a grave-eyed child, stand. There is my sister Ruth, beautiful to me and dressed elegantly for high school in gray felt skirt and rhinestone brooch, hurrying up the road to catch the yellow school bus which glows like a large glowworm in the early morning fog.

BUILDING VOCABULARY

1. Walker uses many references to nature as she describes and compares her two places. Identify the following natural elements in her scenes:
   a. redwoods
   b. firs
   c. oaks
   d. giant bays
   e. hawks
   f. turkey vultures
   g. big-leaf poplar
   h. pine
2. Walker alludes to other cultures and traditions in her essay. What does she mean by each of the following:
   a. Egyptian Africa
   b. Chinese paintings of Guilin
   c. Br'er Rabbit

UNDERSTANDING THE WRITER'S IDEAS

1. Why does the author consider herself a "displaced person"? What is the difference between being displaced and buying a new home?
2. What are the features of Walker's California home that make her content to live there?
3. Why does she cry when she remembers her childhood in Georgia? Why is the tree so important?

4. In paragraph 4, what does the author list as the consequences of her being an African American? Why did she have to leave Georgia?

5. Walker uses the natural world, particularly landscape, to create images of her past and present life. Why does she look so closely at the trees? Why does she use the metaphors of "rooted" and "rootedness" to describe her parents (par. 6)?

UNDERSTANDING THE WRITER'S TECHNIQUES

1. Where does the author place her thesis statement? What is her thesis?

2. Does Walker use *contrast* or *comparison* in her essay as her primary mode? What key words does she use to indicate that she is dealing primarily with similarities or differences?

3. Examine the structure of Walker's essay. How does she use the block method (see page 195) to organize her essay? Create an outline of Walker's essay.

4. What is the purpose of paragraph 7? Why is it so short? What key transition words does Walker use?

5. As well as presenting the two physical worlds of California and Georgia, Walker describes the two emotional worlds of the present time, and her nostalgia for the past. How does the memory of her sister, presented in the conclusion, contrast with the tone of the first sentence of the essay?

6. How is the structure of Walker's essay similar to or different from that used by Rachel Carson in "A Fable for Tomorrow" (pages 192–194)?

7. Reread paragraph 5. How does Walker introduce the *cause* of her being "displaced" by using contrast? Why is she "on a deck," and not "a southern front porch"? How do these two contrasting sites make concrete her political experience?

8. Note Walker's use of both abstract and concrete language. In paragraph 7, she relies on abstract words: "racist oppression," "economic impoverishment," "justice and peace." In paragraph 9, she uses concrete words: "hound dogs, biscuits and coons." Why does she include both types of language?

EXPLORING THE WRITER'S IDEAS

1. Walker implies that landscape is an essential part of our identity. She suggests that where we have lived, or where we live now, is a clue to who we are. Do you agree with her? Can we always control our landscape? Can we live where we choose? Do we ever outgrow our childhood landscapes, and leave them, not like Walker because we are compelled to, but because they seem too confining?

2. Walker describes herself as "nostalgic" (par. 3). In what ways might nostalgia be a false key to the past? Is nostalgia the same as memory? What are the *connotations* (see Glossary) of the word "nostalgic"?

3. As an African-American woman writer, Walker is keenly aware of the history of "displacement" of oppressed peoples. She has written, for instance, about Native Americans who were displaced from their ancestral lands by European settlers. What other racial or ethnic groups might be considered "displaced"? How can the idea of displacement be applied to urban dwellers? Because of her success as a writer, Walker was able to find a new home. What happens to displaced people who do not have her talent?

4. Do you think Walker would be content, as an adult, to return to Eatonton if circumstances were different, and she did not feel that the racism would make her life painful? Can we return to our "home" of childhood?

IDEAS FOR WRITING

Guided Writing

Write an essay in which you contrast two places you know very well.

1. In your first paragraph, write a clear thesis statement that uses key words to indicate the contrast your essay will make.

2. Give the two places names and define the special quality of each place by comparing it with a familiar painting or story.

3. Write an outline using the block method of organization.

4. Base your essay on your personal associations with the two places. Don't write a tourist brochure.
5. Make sure each paragraph has only one main point.
6. Use transitions between paragraphs.
7. Write one paragraph in which you reveal which place you prefer, and why. Why have you moved from one place to the other?

More Writing Projects

1. In your journal, develop characteristics of two places: where you are now, and your ideal place. Label the lists as "real" and "ideal."
2. In two paragraphs, compare and contrast two experiences, one in which you experienced prejudice or were discriminated against, and the other in which an incident took place that overcame prejudice or discrimination.
3. Using the comparison-contrast method, write an essay in which you examine your attitudes to a particular "ism"—racism, sexism, ageism—and the attitudes of another generation, such as your parents' or grandparents' generation. Or compare your attitudes with those of someone you recently met, attitudes that either surprised or offended you.

The Tapestry of Friendships

Ellen Goodman

Syndicated columnist for the *Boston Globe, Washington Post,* and other newspapers, Ellen Goodman presents a thought-provoking comparison of two categories of human relations in this selection from her book *Close to Home.* Notice especially how she blends personal experience with a clipped, direct journalistic style to examine the ways in which "friends" and "buddies" relate to one another.

Words to Watch

slight (par. 1)   not having much substance

fragility (par. 2)   condition of being easily broken or harmed

resiliency (par. 2)   condition of being able to recover easily from misfortune or change

binge (par. 4)   spree; indulgence

atavistic (par. 5)   manifesting a throwback to the past

culled (par. 5)   chosen from

palpably (par. 8)   in a way that can be touched or felt

loathsome (par. 10)   detestable; hateful

wretched (par. 13)   miserable; woeful

claustrophobic (par. 16)   uncomfortable at being confined in small places

1   It was, in many ways, a slight movie. Nothing actually happened. There was no big-budget chase scene, no bloody shoot-out. The story ended without any cosmic conclusions.

2   Yet she found Claudia Weill's film *Girlfriends* gentle and affecting. Slowly, it panned across the tapestry of friendship— showing its fragility, its resiliency, its role as the connecting tissue between the lives of two young women.

3   When it was over, she thought about the movies she'd seen this year—*Julia, The Turning Point* and now *Girlfriends.* It seemed that the peculiar eye, the social lens of the cinema, had drastically shifted its focus. Suddenly the Male Buddy movies had been replaced by the Female Friendship flicks.

4   This wasn't just another binge of trendiness, but a kind of *cinéma vérité.* For once the movies were reflecting a shift, not

just from men to women but from one definition of friendship to another.

Across millions of miles of celluloid, the ideal of friendship 5 had always been male—a world of sidekicks and "pardners," of Butch Cassidys and Sundance Kids. There had been something almost atavistic about these visions of attachments—as if producers culled their plots from some pop anthropology book on male bonding. Movies portrayed the idea that only men, those direct descendants of hunters and Hemingways, inherited a primal capacity for friendship. In contrast, they portrayed women picking on each other, the way they once picked berries.

Well, that duality must have been mortally wounded in 6 some shoot-out at the You're OK, I'm OK Corral. Now, on the screen, they were at least aware of the subtle distinction between men and women as buddies and friends.

About 150 years ago, Coleridge had written, "A woman's 7 friendship borders more closely on love than man's. Men affect each other in the reflection of noble or friendly acts, whilst women ask fewer proofs and more signs and expressions of attachment."

Well, she thought, on the whole, men had buddies, while 8 women had friends. Buddies bonded, but friends loved. Buddies faced adversity together, but friends faced each other. There was something palpably different in the way they spent their time. Buddies seemed to "do" things together; friends simply "were" together.

Buddies came linked, like accessories, to one activity or 9 another. People have golf buddies and business buddies, college buddies and club buddies. Men often keep their buddies in these categories, while women keep a special category for friends.

A man once told her that men weren't real buddies until 10 they'd been "through the wars" together—corporate or athletic or military. They had to soldier together, he said. Women, on the other hand, didn't count themselves as friends until they'd shared three loathsome confidences.

Buddies hang tough together; friends hang onto each other. 11

It probably had something to do with pride. You don't show 12 off to a friend; you show need. Buddies try to keep the worst from each other; friends confess it.

13   A friend of hers once telephoned her lover, just to find out if he were home. She hung up without a hello when he picked up the phone. Later, wretched with embarrassment, the friend moaned, "Can you believe me? A thirty-five-year-old lawyer, making a chicken call?" Together they laughed and made it better.

14   Buddies seek approval. But friends seek acceptance.

15   She knew so many men who had been trained in restraint, afraid of each other's judgment or awkward with each other's affection. She wasn't sure which. Like buddies in the movies, they would die for each other, but never hug each other.

16   She'd reread *Babbitt* recently, that extraordinary catalogue of male grievances. The only relationship that gave meaning to the claustrophobic life of George Babbitt had been with Paul Riesling. But not once in the tragedy of their lives had one been able to say to the other: You make a difference.

17   Even now men shocked her at times with their description of friendship. Does this one have a best friend? "Why, of course, we see each other every February." Does that one call his most intimate pal long distance? "Why, certainly, whenever there's a real reason." Do those two old chums ever have dinner together? "You mean alone? Without our wives?"

18   Yet, things were changing. The ideal of intimacy wasn't this parallel playmate, this teammate, this trenchmate. Not even in Hollywood. In the double standard of friendship, for once the female version was becoming accepted as the general ideal.

19   After all, a buddy is a fine life-companion. But one's friends, as Santayana once wrote, "are that part of the race with which one can be human."

BUILDING VOCABULARY

1. The first six paragraphs of this essay use many words and expressions related to film. Explain the meaning or connotation of each of the following words and expressions. Pay special attention to their context in Goodman's article.

   a. big-budget chase scene (par. 1)

   b. bloody shoot-out (par. 1)

   c. it panned (par. 2)

   d. the peculiar eye (par. 3)

    e. the social lens of the cinema (par. 3)
    f. shifted its focus (par. 3)
    g. flicks (par. 3)
    h. *cinéma vérité* (par. 4)
    i. millions of miles of celluloid (par. 5)
    j. plots (par. 5)
    k. on the screen (par. 6)
2. Write an *antonym* (word with an opposite meaning) for each of the following words from the Words to Watch section. Then use each antonym in a sentence.

    slight
    fragility
    resiliency
    atavistic
    palpably
    loathsome
    wretched

UNDERSTANDING THE WRITER'S IDEAS

1. What does the author mean when she writes that the movie "ended without any cosmic conclusions" (par. 1)? Is she being critical or descriptive in this statement? Explain.

2. Who is the "she" first mentioned at the beginning of paragraph 2 and referred to throughout the essay?

3. What pattern of change does the author note in the same-year releases of the films *Julia, The Turning Point,* and *Girlfriends?* Does she feel this is a superficial or real change? How do you know?

4. What is the author's main complaint about the ways in which movies have traditionally portrayed friendships? What example does she offer? Explain the meaning of the sentence, "Movies portrayed the idea that only men, those direct descendants of hunters and Hemingway, inherited a primal capacity for friendship" (par. 5). What is "male bonding"?

5. What two allusions does Goodman combine to produce the expression "the You're OK, I'm OK Corral"? Explain the full meaning of the sentence in which that expression appears.

6. According to Goodman, what is the main difference between male and female friendships? Which type do you think she prefers? Why?
7. What quality of friendships is suggested by the title?
8. What is meant by "the double standard of friendship"?
9. How does Goodman's conclusion support her preference for male or female types of friendships?

UNDERSTANDING THE WRITER'S TECHNIQUES

1. What is the main idea of this essay? Which sentence serves as the thesis statement? What two subjects form the basis for comparison in this essay?
2. Like most well-constructed essays, this one has three clear sections: introduction, body, conclusion. Specify which paragraphs make up each section. Does this seem a good balance? Explain.
3. How would you describe the effect of the writing in the opening paragraph? Does it give you a clear idea of the subject of this essay? Is that important in this essay? Why?
4. In the beginning, Goodman uses a number of *metaphors* (see Glossary), including the title. Explain the following metaphors in your own words:
   a. The Tapestry of Friendships (title and par. 2)
   b. the connecting tissue between the lives of two young women (par. 2)

   In what ways do the two metaphors convey similar ideas? Which do you prefer? Why?
5. What is the effect of the use of the pronoun "she" throughout the essay? Why do you suppose Goodman chose to use "she" rather than "I"?
6. Among the main purposes of a comparison-contrast essay are (a) *to explain* something unfamiliar in terms of something already familiar, (b) *to understand* better two things already known by comparing them point for point, (c) *to evaluate* the relative value of two things. Which of these objectives most closely describes Goodman's purpose? Explain.

7. Which of the three methods of writing comparison essays—block, alternating, or combination—dominates in this essay? Explain.

8. Who is the intended audience for this essay? Why?

9. There are four literary *allusions* (see Glossary) in this essay: (a) Hemingway, (b) Coleridge, (c) *Babbitt,* and (d) Santayana. Identify each and explain why Goodman chose to include it.

10. Throughout the essay, Goodman uses short, direct sentences and relatively short paragraphs. What is her purpose for that? Does it allow for adequate development of this subject matter? Why or why not?

11. At what points does Goodman make use of relatively *extended illustrations*?

12. Goodman chooses to point out the contrasts between her two subjects in short, directly opposing sentences or clauses, beginning with paragraph 8: ". . . men had buddies, while women had friends. Buddies bonded, but friends loved."

    Go through the essay and list all such opposing statements. How do these statements affect your reading of the essay?

13. How does Goodman use *repetition* as a transitional device in the essay?

14. What is the effect of the series of questions that comprise paragraph 17? How is it like a dialogue? Why are some of the questions in quotation marks and others not?

15. A good conclusion for an essay of comparison or contrast will either (a) restate the main idea, (b) offer a solution, or (c) set a new frame of reference by generalizing from the thesis. Which approach or combination of approaches does Goodman use? How effective is her conclusion? Why?

EXPLORING THE WRITER'S IDEAS

1. Do you agree with Goodman's basic distinction between female and male friendships? How closely does it relate to your own experiences? Do you have any friendships that don't fit into either of the two categories she describes?

2. In the beginning of this essay, Goodman refers to the "binge of trendiness" toward pop anthropology and psychology. Such periodicals, books, and syndicated columns as *Psychology Today, Women Who Love Too Much,* and Dr. Joyce Brothers—to name just a few—are widely read. What's more, radio call-in shows offering on-the-air advice are nationally syndicated and immensely popular.

   What are your feelings about such media presentations? Do you think they are useful? Are there instances when they might be harmful? Why do you think they are so popular?
3. Why does Goodman avoid any discussion of friendship between men and women? Do you feel this omission in any way affects the forcefulness or completeness of her essay? Explain.

IDEAS FOR WRITING

Guided Writing

Write an essay that contrasts the ways in which men and women perceive or approach some aspect of interpersonal relationships. You might choose, for example, dating, parenting, expressing affection, or divorce.

1. Begin with a description of some depiction of the subject in the contemporary media (for example, a film, TV program, book, video, commercial).
2. Staying with the same medium, give other examples that illustrate how the medium is shifting away from the old, established ways of viewing the subject. Use language specific to that medium.
3. In the rest of your introductory section, use a few metaphors.
4. As a transitional device, cite a statement from a well-known authority (not necessarily on the particular subject).
5. State the main idea of your essay at the beginning of the body section.
6. Develop your contrast using short, direct, opposing statements that summarize the different approaches of men and women.
7. Develop at least two of these opposing statements through extended personal examples.
8. Make your preference for either approach *implicit* (subtle) rather than *explicit* (obvious) throughout.

9. Make the last paragraph of the body of your essay a series of questions that form an internal dialogue.
10. Conclude with a statement that generalizes the main differences and your evaluation of the two approaches.

More Writing Projects

1. Compare and contrast in a journal entry two films or books, plays, or television programs that portray contrasting views of friendship, love, or marriage.
2. Compare in one or two paragraphs the ways you relate to two close friends.
3. Write an essay that compares and/or contrasts what was considered physically attractive in two different time periods in America. You may either focus your essay on one sex or attempt to discuss both.

Fairy Tales and Modern Stories

Bruno Bettelheim

Bruno Bettelheim was born in Austria in 1903 and came to the United States in 1939. For many years he was one of the major child psychologists in the world. In this selection, taken from *The Uses of Enchantment* (1976), Bettelheim compares fairy tales and realistic stories, analyzing the effect that they have on both children and adults. As you read this essay, keep in mind the various stories he is comparing.

Words to Watch

realistic (par. 1)   having to do with real things

props (par. 1)   supports

elaboration (par. 1)   a thing worked out in detail

rankled (par. 1)   caused pain or resentment

idyllic (par. 2)   pleasing and simple

protracted (par. 2)   drawn out

gratifications (par. 2)   things that cause satisfaction

sustained (par. 3)   maintained; supported; comforted

effected (par. 4)   brought to pass; accomplished

consolation (par. 5)   comfort

vagaries (par. 5)   odd notions; unexpected actions

extricating (par. 5)   setting free; getting out of; releasing

prevail (par. 5)   to triumph; to gain the advantage

asocial (par. 5)   not social

1   The shortcomings of the realistic stories with which many parents have replaced fairy tales is suggested by a comparison of two such stories—"The Little Engine That Could" and "The Swiss Family Robinson"—with the fairy tale of "Rapunzel." "The Little Engine That Could" encourages the child to believe that if he tries hard and does not give up, he will finally succeed. A young adult has recalled how much impressed she was at the age of seven when her mother read her this story. She became convinced that one's attitude indeed affects one's achieve-

ments—that if she would now approach a task with the conviction that she could conquer it, she would succeed. A few days later, this child encountered in first grade a challenging situation: she was trying to make a house out of paper, gluing various sheets together. But her house continually collapsed. Frustrated, she began to seriously doubt whether her idea of building such a paper house could be realized. But then the story of "The Little Engine That Could" came to her mind; twenty years later, she recalled how at that moment she began to sing to herself the magic formula "I think I can, I think I can, I think I can . . ." So she continued to work on her paper house, and it continued to collapse. The project ended in complete defeat, with this little girl convinced that she had failed where anybody else could have succeeded, as the Little Engine had. Since "The Little Engine That Could" was a story set in the present, using such common props as engines that pulled trains, this girl had tried to apply its lesson directly in her daily life, without any fantasy elaboration, and had experienced a defeat that still rankled twenty years later.

Very different was the impact of "The Swiss Family Robinson" on another little girl. The story tells how a shipwrecked family manages to live an adventurous, idyllic, constructive, and pleasurable life—a life very different from this child's own existence. Her father had to be away from home a great deal, and her mother was mentally ill and spent protracted periods in institutions. So the girl was shuttled from her home to that of an aunt, then to that of a grandmother, and back home again, as the need arose. During these years, the girl read over and over again the story of this happy family who lived on a desert island, where no member could be away from the rest of the family. Many years later, she recalled what a warm, cozy feeling she had when, propped up by a few large pillows, she forgot all about her present predicament as she read this story. As soon as she had finished it, she started to read it over again. The happy hours she spent with the Family Robinson in that fantasy land permitted her not to be defeated by the difficulties that reality presented to her. She was able to counteract the impact of harsh reality by imaginary gratifications. But since the story was not a fairy tale, it merely gave her a temporary escape from her problems; it did not hold out any promise to her that her life would take a turn for the better.

3   Consider the effect that "Rapunzel" had on a third girl. This girl's mother had died in a car accident. The girl's father, deeply upset by what had happened to his wife (he had been driving the car), withdrew entirely into himself and handed the care of his daughter over to a nursemaid, who was little interested in the girl and gave her complete freedom to do as she liked. When the girl was seven, her father remarried, and, as she recalled it, it was around that time that "Rapunzel" became so important to her. Her stepmother was clearly the witch of the story, and she was the girl locked away in the tower. The girl recalled that she felt akin to Rapunzel because the witch had "forcibly" taken possession of her, as her stepmother had forcibly worked her way into the girl's life. The girl felt imprisoned in her new home, in contrast to her life of freedom with the nursemaid. She felt as victimized as Rapunzel, who, in her tower, had so little control over her life. Rapunzel's long hair was the key to the story. The girl wanted her hair to grow long, but her stepmother cut it short; long hair in itself became the symbol of freedom and happiness to her. The story convinced her that a prince (her father) would come someday and rescue her, and this conviction sustained her. If life became too difficult, all she needed was to imagine herself as Rapunzel, her hair grown long, and the prince loving and rescuing her.

4   "Rapunzel" suggests why fairy tales can offer more to the child than even such a very nice children's story as "The Swiss Family Robinson." In "The Swiss Family Robinson," there is no witch against whom the child can discharge her anger in fantasy and on whom she can blame the father's lack of interest. "The Swiss Family Robinson" offers escape fantasies, and it did help the girl who read it over and over to forget temporarily how difficult life was for her. But it offered no specific hope for the future. "Rapunzel," on the other hand, offered the girl a chance to see the witch of the story as so evil that by comparison even the "witch" stepmother at home was not really so bad. "Rapunzel" also promised the girl that her rescue would be effected by her own body, when her hair grew long. Most important of all, it promised that the "prince" was only temporarily blinded—that he would regain his sight and rescue his princess. This fantasy continued to sustain the girl, though to a less intense degree, until she fell in love and married, and then she no longer needed it. We can

understand why at first glance the stepmother, if she had known the meaning of "Rapunzel" to her stepdaughter, would have felt that fairy tales are bad for children. What she would not have known was that unless the stepdaughter had been able to find that fantasy satisfaction through "Rapunzel," she would have tried to break up her father's marriage and that without the hope for the future which the story gave her she might have gone badly astray in life.

It seems quite understandable that when children are asked ⁵ to name their favorite fairy tales, hardly any modern tales are among their choices. Many of the new tales have sad endings, which fail to provide the escape and consolation that the fearsome events in the fairy tale require if the child is to be strengthened for meeting the vagaries of his life. Without such encouraging conclusions, the child, after listening to the story, feels that there is indeed no hope for extricating himself from his despairs. In the traditional fairy tale, the hero is rewarded and the evil person meets his well-deserved fate, thus satisfying the child's deep need for justice to prevail. How else can a child hope that justice will be done to him, who so often feels unfairly treated? And how else can he convince himself that he must act correctly, when he is so sorely tempted to give in to the asocial proddings of his desires?

BUILDING VOCABULARY

1. *Jargon* (see Glossary) is specialized vocabulary that appears in a certain profession or discipline. Bettelheim uses some jargon from psychology. Try to figure out what he means by the following terms:
   a. fantasy elaboration (par. 1)
   b. imaginary gratifications (par. 2)
   c. escape fantasies (par. 4)
   d. fantasy satisfaction (par. 4)
   e. asocial proddings (par. 5)
2. Write sentences in which you use the following words correctly:
   a. impressed (par. 1)
   b. conviction (par. 1)
   c. impact (par. 2)

   d. predicament (par. 2)
   e. victimized (par. 3)
   f. astray (par. 4)
   g. sorely (par. 5)

UNDERSTANDING THE WRITER'S IDEAS

1. Check in the children's book section of your library to summarize the stories and fairy tales Bettelheim discusses. How many stories is he examining in this essay?
2. What is the most important similarity between *The Little Engine That Could* and *The Swiss Family Robinson?*
3. What is the effect on children of *The Little Engine That Could?* How does it influence the adult whom Bettelheim introduces in paragraph 1?
4. How does Bettelheim summarize the story of *The Swiss Family Robinson?* Does this story, according to the author, have a beneficial effect on adults with problems?
5. Explain why "Rapunzel" was so important to the girl who had lost her mother in the car accident.
6. Why do traditional fairy tales benefit readers more than modern fairy tales and realistic stories? What do traditional fairy tales provide?
7. What does Bettelheim mean by his last sentence, "And how else can he convince himself that he must act correctly, when he is so sorely tempted to give in to the asocial proddings of his desires"?

UNDERSTANDING THE WRITER'S TECHNIQUES

1. Where does Bettelheim state his main point? How clear is his statement of it? Does he indicate in his thesis sentence his plan of development for the essay?
2. How does Bettelheim order his essay in terms of comparison and contrast? What is interesting about the pattern he chooses?
3. Where does the writer use narration? Why does he use it? How does it support the technique of comparison and contrast?

4. What is the function of paragraph 1? of paragraph 2? of paragraph 3?
5. How does the writer organize paragraph 4?
6. Is the same amount of emphasis given to "Rapunzel" as to the two "realistic" tales? Why or why not?
7. In concluding paragraphs of comparison and contrast papers, it is common to bring the two subjects together for a final observation. Does Bettelheim follow this strategy? How does he organize his subjects in the last paragraph?
8. How does Bettelheim achieve clear transitions from paragraph to paragraph? Discuss some of the words he uses so that his ideas are connected together clearly.

EXPLORING THE WRITER'S IDEAS

1. Bettelheim suggests that certain types of fairy tales help us cope with problems. Do you agree or disagree? What particular fairy tale do you remember that might help a child deal with his or her problems?
2. Why do most children clearly take delight from traditional fairy tales?
3. Look again at Bettelheim's psychoanalysis of the three children whom he uses as examples in his essay. Do you accept his explanations of their behavior? How might his ideas be criticized by other psychologists?
4. Which fairy tales—traditional or modern—appealed to you as a child? Why were you so fond of them?
5. If exposure to certain types of fairy tales can affect us seriously, then what can we conclude about our exposure to stories on television, on film, and in other types of media? Is it fair to generalize about television from Bettelheim's argument?

IDEAS FOR WRITING

Guided Writing

Write an essay in which you compare and/or contrast two or three fairy tales or stories that you remember from early childhood. Or do the same for two films, two television programs, two newspapers, or two subjects from another media form.

1. State the purpose of your comparison as soon as you can.
2. Decide on the best pattern of development (block, alternating, or a combination of both) for your purposes.
3. List the point of comparison or contrast that you plan to cover for each subject.
4. Be certain to support each point with substantial detail. Summarize parts of stories that bear out your point. Quote where you have to.
5. Make certain that, in the closing paragraph, you draw conclusions about all the subjects treated.

More Writing Projects

1. Compare and contrast in a journal entry the style of writing of any two writers in this section.
2. Select two heroes or heroines from popular children's stories or fairy tales; in an extended paragraph compare and contrast the two characters in regard to personality and behavior.
3. Write an essay in which you compare or contrast two newspapers or magazines. Be prepared to compare and contrast their contents, and also to indicate the type of audience at which they are aimed. Write a comparative paper on your findings.

SUMMING UP: CHAPTER 6

1. In the essays you have read thus far in this book, you have learned much about the personal lives of many of the authors. Select two whose lives seem very different, and write an essay in which you contrast their lives. In your essay, use only illustrations that you can cite or derive from the selections; that is, do not do research or use other outside information about the authors.
2. In this chapter both Bettelheim and Carson deal with two very old fictional forms: *fable* and *fairy tale*. Check definitions of the terms. Then, write an essay in which you explore the authors' use of the words.

3. Which author in this chapter do you think most successfully uses the comparison-contrast form? Write an essay in which you analyze the best comparison-contrast essay as you see it. Indicate the techniques and strategies that you feel work best. Make specific references to the essay you have chosen as a model.

4. Rachel Carson ("A Fable for Tomorrow," pages 192–194) and Gretel Ehrlich ("A River's Route," pages 105–108) both express deep environmental concerns in their essays. Write your own essay to compare and contrast these concerns. How are the two writers' treatments similar? How are they different?

5. In the manner of Rachel Carson, write your own "Fable for Tomorrow," in which you show how today's indifference to the environment will affect the future. Remember: *Silent Spring* was written in 1962, and many scholars believe that the way people abuse the environment today is even more serious than it was then.

CHAPTER 7

Definition

WHAT IS DEFINITION?

We are used to opening a dictionary when we want to *define* a word. Often, however, the dictionary definition is brief, and does not fully explain the meaning of a word as an individual writer sees it. An *extended definition* is necessary when a writer wishes to convey the full meaning of a word that is central to the writer's or a culture's thought. When an entire essay focuses on the meaning of a key word or group of related words, extended definition becomes the primary method of organization.

Definition can look at the *denotation* of a word, which is its literal meaning, or at the *connotations,* which are the variety of meanings associated with the word through common use. (See Glossary.) Denotation is generally available in the dictionary. Connotation, on the other hand, requires that the writer examine not only the denotation but also the way the word is used. In defining, a writer can also explore levels of *diction* (see Glossary), such as standard English, colloquial expressions, and slang. The word "red," for example, denotes a primary color. The connotations, however, are varied: In the early twentieth century Communists were called "Reds" because of the color of the Russian flag. We also associate red with the color of Valentine's cards, with passion and romance. "Redneck" derives from the sunburned skin of a white person who works outdoors and connotes a life-style associated with outdoor living and conservative political views. "Redskin" was a pejorative term used by European settlers to describe Native Americans.

We need extended definition to help us fully understand the complexity of our language. Most often, we use definition when words are abstract, controversial, or complex. Terms like "freedom," "pornography," "affirmative action," "bisexual," and "feminism" demand extended definition because they are often confused with some other word or term; because they are so easily misunderstood; or because they are of special importance to the writer, who chooses to redefine the term for his or her own purposes.

Although we can, of course, offer an extended definition just for the sake of definition, we usually go through the trouble of defining because we have strong opinions about complex and controversial words; consequently, we try to provide an extended definition for the purpose of illuminating a thesis for readers. Writer Alice Walker, for instance, once wrote an essay about feminism and African-American women. In her extended definition, she said that the meaning of "feminism" was restricted to white, upper- and middle-class women. As a result, the word did not apply to black women. She created the term "womanist," and wrote her essay to define it. Because of the controversial nature of her definition of "feminist," Walker relied on extended definition to support her thesis that the women's movement needed to pay more attention to women of color.

It *is* possible to give an objective definition of "feminism," with the writer tracing its history, explaining its historic applications, and describing its various subdivisions, such as "radical feminism." However, most of the time, writers have strong opinions. They would want to develop a thesis about the term, perhaps covering much of the same ground as the objective account but taking care that the reader understands the word as they do. It is normal for us to have our own opinions about any word, but in all instances we must make the reader understand fully what we mean by it.

In this chapter Gloria Naylor, an African-American woman, uses extended definition to confront the hate word "nigger." Her many *illustrations* of how and where the word is used show how definition is often determined by context. Writer Richard

Rodriguez tackles the related issue of skin color as he defines "complexion." In a more humorous vein, Jack Denton Scott provides an extended definition of "bagel," and Suzanne Britt Jordan has fun defining "fun."

HOW DO WE READ DEFINITION?

Reading definition requires us to ask ourselves these questions:

- What is the writer's thesis? Determine if the definition is *objective* or *subjective* (see Glossary).
- Does the writer state the definition directly, or expect the reader to understand it from the information the writer gives? When you finish reading the essay, write out a one-sentence definition of the term the writer has defined.
- What are the various techniques the writer uses, such as illustration with examples, description, narrative? The writer may also use *negation,* a technique of defining a word by what it does *not* mean. In addition, a writer may use a strategy of defining some general group to which the subject belongs (for instance, an orange is a member of the larger group of citrus), and to show how the word differs from all other words in the general group (by its color, acid content, size, and so forth).
- What is the writer's tone? Is the definition comic, or serious? Does it rely on *irony* (see Glossary)?

HOW DO WE WRITE A DEFINITION?

Reading the variety of *definitions* in this chapter will prepare you to write your own. The skill required in good definition writing is to make abstract ideas concrete. Writing good definitions allows you to practice many of the other writing strategies you already know, including narration, description, and illustration.

The thesis for your definition does not have to appear in the introduction, but it is helpful to write it out for yourself before you begin.

- Select the word: for example, *multiculturalism.*
- Place it in a class: Multiculturalism is a *belief,* or *system of values,* or *philosophy.*

- Distinguish it from other members of that class: Multiculturalists favor recognition and celebration of differences among various social groups instead of seeking similarities.
- Use negation: Multiculturalism is not the "melting pot" metaphor of how American society is constituted.

By arranging these pieces, and revising the language, you can create a working thesis.

Sample thesis statement:

> Multiculturalism supports the preservation and celebration of differences among people of diverse cultures rather than urging them to replace their ethnic identities with one single "American" identity.

Select support to illustrate, narrate, and describe the term. The selection of evidence can demonstrate the writer's *point of view* on the term. Is multiculturalism splitting the nation into separate groups, or is it affirming the identity of both minority and majority citizens? Look at how the term is used in a variety of settings, such as education, government, social services agencies, and religious institutions.

You might want to visit the library to see how a reference book's definition compares with your own. Libraries have a variety of dictionaries. Depending on the kind of word you are researching, you might want to look at a dictionary of slang, or even a dictionary of quotations to read some famous opinions about abstract words like "love," "hope," and "truth."

What is the *purpose* of the definition? Decide whether you want to show support for the policy or argue against its effectiveness.

Who is the audience? The writer would choose different language for addressing a PTA meeting than for writing to Congress.

Plan an arrangement of the supporting evidence. Unlike comparison and contrast, for instance, definition does not require a formal method of outlining. Examples can be arranged to suit the kind of word being defined, and the mood of the writer. Because so many methods can be applied effectively in an essay of extended definition, you should be able to organize and develop this type of composition easily.

Review the *transitions* you have used in other essays and see which ones apply here. You might want to focus on transitions that show addition: another, in addition, furthermore.

Writing and Revising the Draft

Think about where to put the thesis. What is the effect of placing it at the end rather than at the beginning?

Plan your strategy. Arrange the examples so that they most effectively create the extended definition you want. Your essay should have *coherence*. Avoid an unrelated collection of definitions.

Read your essay to a classmate who has defined a similar word. Decide whose definition is more successful, and why.

Revise. Revision may require that you reorganize, moving the examples and other supporting evidence to different sentences and paragraphs to make your argument more effective for a reader.

Proofread for correctness and make a final copy of your work.

What's a Bagel?

Jack Denton Scott

Author and bagel lover Jack Denton Scott combines a variety of expository techniques, statistics, and citations from experts to define what has now become one of America's most popular foods. In the process of definition, he explains why the bagel can no longer be considered only an East Coast ethnic food as America becomes "bagelized."

Words to Watch

aficionados (par. 1)   fans; devotees

phenomenon (par. 2)   observable fact or event

consumers (par. 2)   users of goods

croissant (par. 4)   French crescent-shaped pastry

hearth (par. 5)   brick fireplace or oven

automated (par. 6)   mechanical

quirky (par. 7)   peculiar; eccentric

tutus (par. 9)   short skirts worn by ballerinas

spirited (par. 14)   lively

If bread is the staff of life, the bagel may be the laugh of life. 1 "Brooklyn jawbreakers," "crocodile teething rings," even "doughnuts with rigor mortis" are affectionate terms invoked by bagel aficionados.

For those who haven't tried one, the flavorful bagel is a 2 shiny, hard, crisp yet chewy roll with a hole in the middle, and it is booming in popularity. Eight million are consumed daily in the United States—worth about $400 million a year. Bakery experts call the phenomenon "the Americanization of the bagel." To bagel believers it's "the bagelization of America." In the past four years retail sales of bagels have about doubled. Over 80 percent of these sales are now to non-Jewish consumers, a dramatic sociological switch. Moreover, the "bagel belt," always on the East Coast, is starting to stretch across the country. In fact, the world's largest bagel bakery is now located in Mattoon, Ill., producing over a million rolls a day.

3   Walter Heller of *Progressive Grocer* magazine calls the bagel's rise to stardom an example of "America's current love affair with ethnic foods." Yet, unless sliced in half, toasted and eaten warm, the bagel isn't easy to handle. It may make messy sandwiches and challenge the teeth. What's more, bagels become stale and hard after 12 hours—"something you can fight wars with," as one bagel expert said.

4   For the health-conscious, however, the bagel has a lot going for it. The plain, two-ounce toaster-size has just 150 calories and one gram of fat. (The popular buttery croissant, by comparison, contains 235 calories and 12 grams of fat.) Furthermore, the plain bagel has no cholesterol, preservatives, or artificial color.

5   Bagels are made with unbleached, protein-rich, high-gluten flour, lightly seasoned with malt, salt and sugar, and raised with yeast. They then get a brief bath in boiling water. This results in the shiny surface after they are baked. (Most are hearth-baked to give them a crusty exterior and chewy interior.)

6   Some U.S. bakeries still use the Old World method of rolling and shaping the stiff dough by hand. This requires about six months to learn, but one expert bagel baker can whip out about 700 an hour. (One automated machine can turn out up to 9000 an hour.)

7   Where did this quirky roll originate? One version has the bagel created by an Austrian baker in 1683, honoring the king of Poland who had defeated Turkish invaders. It was first formed to resemble a stirrup (*beugel,* from the German *bügel,* for stirrup), because the king's favorite hobby was riding.

8   Another account puts the bagel in Cracow, Poland, in 1610, where poor Jews, who normally ate coarse black bread, considered their uncommon white-flour roll a delicacy. Bagels were officially approved as presents for women after childbirth, and mothers used them as teething rings for their children. In the 1600s in Russia, bagels were looped on strings, and were thought to bring good luck and have magical powers.

9   Bagels were brought to New York City and New Jersey by Jewish immigrants about 1910. Among the most successful immigrant bagel bakers was Harry Lender, who arrived from Lublin, Poland, in 1927 and settled in New Haven, Conn. His sons—Sam, Murray and Marvin—have almost made Lender's Bagels household words by using humor to push sales. For their

bakery's 55th anniversary party, Murray and the executive staff attended a ballet class for two months; then, dressed in orange leotards and yellow tutus, they gracefully tiptoed to what was announced as "The Dance of the Bagels."

Today the baffling bagel surge to the top is even inspiring 10 bagel restaurants. They offer as many as 17 flavors, from raisin and honey to zippy onion, plus bagel sandwiches, burgers, clubs, grilled cheese, French toast, salad sandwich combos, an egg-and-sausage bagelwich and a rancher's bagel breakfast. Big also are bagelettes—one-inch bagels—served by the basket with dinners. Then there are hero, hoagie, pizza and taco bagels—even Bagel Dogs. Where there's a bagel, there's a way.

Bagel bakeries are opening in Alaska, England, Japan and 11 Israel. Ron Stieglitz, founder of the New York Bagels bakery in London, where few people had ever seen a bagel, had trouble raising money from banks. "A lot of them thought we were a football team," he said. But the bakery now supplies four large retail chains and many small shops and restaurants.

Lyle Fox, from Chicago, sees more potential for the bagel 12 in Japan than in the United States. Young Japanese view the bagel as trendy and upscale—so much so that he easily sells 6000 a day. Fox discovered that the Japanese associate the bagel with New York, and New York with fashion. Thus, a lot of his customers are young women who consider the bagel as "sort of another accessory." A long-time bagel lover, Fox says his stomach does a sickly flip when Japanese customers ask for lox and cream cheese on a cinnamon-raisin bagel.

Cashing in on the new bagel awareness, innovators have 13 come up with some really neat twists. Three Philadelphians started Bagels in Bed, a home-delivery business. Mike Bretz, owner of Simon Brothers Bakery in Skokie, Ill., has borrowed an idea from Chinese fortune cookies. He stuffs slips with Yiddish wisdom into his Schlepper Simon's Yiddish Fortune Bagels. One cheerfully advises, "Smile, bubeleh, success is assured."

A spirited cookbook, *The Bagels' Bagel Book* (Acropolis 14 Books), has recipes like "Mexicali Bagel Fondue," the "Kojak Bagel" with feta cheese and Greek olives, "Tofu Bagels," and "Delhi Bagels" with whipped cream cheese, curry and chutney. The book also captures some of the laughter inspired by baking's most remarkable roll. Here's comedienne Phyllis Diller:

"President Reagan was so gung-ho to get ethnic votes, he went into a deli and ordered a bagel. The waiter asked, 'How would you like that?' Ronnie said, 'On rye.'"

15   What's a bagel? Fun you can eat.

BUILDING VOCABULARY

1. Scott uses a variety of informal expressions that are fairly common in daily conversation and media talk or writing. Explain the following expressions in your own words.
   a. it is booming in popularity (par. 2)
   b. whip out (par. 6)
   c. household words (par. 9)
   d. to push sales (par. 9)
   e. trendy and upscale (par. 12)
   f. cashing in on (par. 13)
   g. gung-ho (par. 14)
2. List all the ethnic foods (other than bagels) mentioned in this essay and explain what they are.

UNDERSTANDING THE WRITER'S IDEAS

1. In paragraph 1, Scott uses a number of very colorful phrases to define bagels. Try to explain the following in your own words.
   a. Brooklyn jawbreakers
   b. crocodile teething rings
   c. doughnuts with rigor mortis
2. What ethnic group is traditionally associated with bagels? What "dramatic sociological switch" has occurred over the past few years?
3. What is meant by "the bagel belt"? Where has it traditionally been located? How is that location changing? Where is the world's largest bagel factory? Why is that surprising?
4. What are "ethnic foods"? How does the bagel figure in "America's current love affair with ethnic foods"?
5. For what reasons can a bagel be considered a food for the health conscious?

6. What is the process of making bagels? Explain the phrase "the Old World method"? What is the "Old World"?

7. In your own words, summarize the two stories concerning the origin of the bagel. What accounts for the shape of the modern bagel? Why were bagels considered delicacies among the poor Jews of Cracow? Does Scott seem to favor either story about the bagel's origins? Explain.

8. Where, when, and by whom were bagels first brought to the United States? How have these "bagel pioneers" continued to promote bagels?

9. Identify the origins of these take-offs on familiar sayings:
   a. If bread is the staff of life, the bagel may be the laugh of life (par. 1).
   b. Where there's a bagel, there's a way (par. 10).

10. In what other parts of the world are bagel factories operating? What was the problem in starting up a bagel business in London? Why are bagels so popular in Japan? Why does bagel manufacturer Lyle Fox get a little sick when the Japanese ask for lox and cream cheese on a cinnamon-raisin bagel?

11. Explain the meaning of the joke that concludes the essay. What serious point does it make about the bagel business?

12. Explain the meaning of the last paragraph: "What's a bagel? Fun you can eat."

UNDERSTANDING THE WRITER'S TECHNIQUES

1. What are Scott's *purpose* and *thesis* in this essay? How does the title indicate his purpose? Who is his *intended audience?* Explain.

2. Does Scott ever give a simple definition of a bagel? If so, where? Is it an objective or a subjective definition? Explain.

3. What is the general *tone* (see Glossary) of this essay? What is it about Scott's writing style that creates this tone? Is the tone appropriate to the subject and audience? Why?

4. Even a lighthearted essay can benefit from the use of *statistics* and *authorities* on the subject at hand. What statistics concerning bagels and their manufacture does Scott present? What authorities does he cite? What effect does the use of statistics and

authorities have on the essay? Would the essay have been as effective without them? Explain.

5. Throughout the essay, Scott makes use of many of the other expository techniques discussed in this book. Explain where Scott
uses each of the techniques below.
   a. definition (Chapter 7)
   b. process analysis (Chapter 9)
   c. comparison and contrast (Chapter 6)
   d. narration (Chapter 4)
   e. illustration (Chapter 5)
   What is the effect of using all these techniques in the essay?

6. Some information in this essay is contained in parentheses. Identify all the parenthetical information. Why does Scott choose to
set off this material from the main text? Is it necessary to do so?
Explain.

7. Scott uses various *allusions* (see Glossary). Explain or identify
the origin of each allusion below:
   a. "The Dance of the Bagels"
   b. Yiddish
   c. Kojak
   d. Delhi
   e. Phyllis Diller
   f. President Reagan

EXPLORING THE WRITER'S IDEAS

1. Over the past few years, a wide diversity of foods has become
available to Americans all over the country. Most supermarkets
carry a full complement of ethnic foods, and even small towns
are likely to have at least one "ethnic" restaurant. Like Scott,
some believe this is a positive trend because it allows Americans to enjoy and learn about other cultures. Others bemoan
the demise of regional American foods. What is your opinion?
How has the increased availability of ethnic foods affected
your area?

2. Discuss with your classmates some of the most exotic foods
you've ever eaten.

3. Eating habits are among the most deeply rooted of all cultural be-
haviors. What may be perfectly acceptable in one culture may be

considered quite rude in another. Research some of the eating habits of other cultures and compare them with those of your own culture. Discuss this issue with your classmates.

4. When did you eat your first bagel? Describe the situation. What did you eat with it? Did you like it? Which of Scott's descriptions conform with your own feelings about bagels? Do you regularly eat bagels now? Why or why not?

IDEAS FOR WRITING

Guided Writing

Write a definition essay entitled "What's a _____?" Fill in the blank with the name of something which was once thought to belong exclusively to a particular ethnic, cultural, or social group but now has become "Americanized" or "standardized." You might choose an article of clothing, a type of music, a cooking utensil, and so forth. (You may also choose a type of food.)

1. Begin your essay with some colorful definitions of your subject. (These may be definitions you've heard or ones you make up.)
2. Give a straightforward, objective definition of this item.
3. Explain how the item has become "Americanized." In your explanation, try to use at least three expository techniques other than definition.
4. Include some references to statistics and (or) authorities on the subject.
5. Describe the origin of this item. If possible, find out how and when it first appeared in the United States.
6. Keep an amusing tone throughout your essay.
7. Include several allusions to other cultures.
8. Conclude with a subjective definition that derives from the material presented throughout your essay.

More Writing Projects

1. Record in your journal all the associations connected with your favorite color. Then, using this list, write a definition of it.

2. Write an extended one-paragraph definition of a particular emotion.
3. Discuss with other class members all connotations related to the word "pizza." List all these associations on the chalkboard. Select the most appropriate items on the list and write an essay defining pizza.

Fun, Oh Boy. Fun. You Could Die from It.

Suzanne Britt Jordan

Most of us never really consider exactly what it means to have a good time. Suzanne Britt Jordan, a writer who claims she "tries to have fun, but often fails," offers an extended definition of the word "fun" by pointing out what it is *not*.

Words to Watch

puritan (par. 3)   one who practices or preaches a stricter moral code than that which most people now follow

selfless (par. 4)   unselfish; having no concern for oneself

fetish (par. 5)   something regarded with extravagant trust or respect

licentiousness (par. 9)   a lack of moral restraints

consumption (par. 9)   act of taking in or using up a substance; eating or drinking

epitome (par. 11)   an ideal; a typical representation

capacity (par. 12)   the ability to hold something

damper (par. 13)   something that regulates or that stops something from flowing

reverently (par. 13)   respectfully; worshipfully

blaspheme (par. 13)   to speak of without reverence

weary (par. 14)   tired; worn-out

horizon (par. 14)   the apparent line where the earth meets the sky

scan (par. 14)   to examine something carefully

Fun is hard to have. 1

Fun is a rare jewel. 2

Somewhere along the line people got the modern idea that 3 fun was there for the asking, that people deserved fun, that if we didn't have a little fun every day we would turn into (sakes alive!) puritans.

"Was it fun?" became the question that overshadowed all 4 other questions: good questions like: Was it moral? Was it kind?

Was it honest? Was it beneficial? Was it generous? Was it necessary? And (my favorite) was it selfless?

5   When the pleasure got to be the main thing, the fun fetish was sure to follow. Everything was supposed to be fun. If it wasn't fun, then by Jove, we were going to make it fun, or else.

6   Think of all the things that got the reputation of being fun. Family outings were supposed to be fun. Sex was supposed to be fun. Education was supposed to be fun. Work was supposed to be fun. Walt Disney was supposed to be fun. Church was supposed to be fun. Staying fit was supposed to be fun.

7   Just to make sure that everybody knew how much fun we were having, we put happy faces on flunking test papers, dirty bumpers, sticky refrigerator doors, bathroom mirrors.

8   If a kid, looking at his very happy parents traipsing through that very happy Disney World, said, "This ain't fun, ma," his ma's heart sank. She wondered where she had gone wrong. Everybody told her what fun family outings to Disney World would be. Golly gee, what was the matter?

9   Fun got to be such a big thing that everybody started to look for more and more thrilling ways to supply it. One way was to step up the level of danger or licentiousness or alcohol or drug consumption so that you could be sure that, no matter what, you would manage to have a little fun.

10   Television commercials brought a lot of fun and fun-loving folks into the picture. Everything that people in those commercials did looked like fun: taking Polaroid snapshots, swilling beer, buying insurance, mopping the floor, bowling, taking aspirin. We all wished, I'm sure, that we could have half as much fun as those rough-and-ready guys around the locker room, flicking each other with towels and pouring champagne. The more commercials people watched, the more they wondered when the fun would start in their own lives. It was pretty depressing.

11   Big occasions were supposed to be fun. Christmas, Thanksgiving and Easter were obviously supposed to be fun. Your wedding day was supposed to be fun. Your wedding night was supposed to be a whole lot of fun. Your honeymoon was supposed to be the epitome of fundom. And so we ended up going through every Big Event we ever celebrated, waiting for the fun to start.

It occurred to me, while I was sitting around waiting for the 12 fun to start, that not much is, and that I should tell you just in case you're worried about your fun capacity.

I don't mean to put a damper on things. I just mean we 13 ought to treat fun reverently. It is a mystery. It cannot be caught like a virus. It cannot be trapped like an animal. The god of mirth is paying us back for all those years of thinking fun was everywhere by refusing to come to our party. I don't want to blaspheme fun anymore. When fun comes in on little dancing feet, you probably won't be expecting it. In fact, I bet it comes when you're doing your duty, your job, or your work. It may even come on a Tuesday.

I remember one day, long ago, on which I had an especially 14 good time. Pam Davis and I walked to the College Village drug store one Saturday morning to buy some candy. We were about 12 years old (fun ages). She got her Bit-O-Honey. I got my malted milk balls, chocolate stars, Chunkys, and a small bag of M & M's. We started back to her house. I was going to spend the night. We had the whole day to look forward to. We had plenty of candy. It was a long way to Pam's house but every time we got weary Pam would put her hand over her eyes, scan the horizon like a sailor and say, "Oughta reach home by nightfall," at which point the two of us would laugh until we thought we couldn't stand it another minute. Then after we got calm, she'd say it again. You should have been there. It was the kind of day and friendship and occasion that made me deeply regretful that I had to grow up.

It was fun. 15

BUILDING VOCABULARY

1. *Trite language* refers to words and expressions that have been overused and, consequently, have lost much of their effectiveness. People do rely on trite language in their conversations, but writers usually avoid overused expressions. However, a good writer will be able to introduce such vocabulary at strategic points. Examples of trite language in Jordan's essay appear below. Explain in your own words what they mean:
   a. a rare jewel (par. 2)
   b. by Jove (par. 5)

    c. golly gee (par. 8)

    d. his ma's heart sank (par. 8)

2. For each of the following words drawn from Jordan's essay, write
a denotative definition. Then list four *connotations* (see Glossary)
that each word has for you.

    a. overshadow (par. 4)

    b. flunking (par. 7)

    c. traipsing (par. 8)

    d. swilling (par. 10)

    e. mirth (par. 13)

3. Select five words from the Words to Watch section and use them
in sentences of your own.

UNDERSTANDING THE WRITER'S IDEAS

1. What are some of the things Jordan says fun is not?

2. What does Jordan suggest we did to something if it wasn't already fun? Identify some of the things she says are "supposed" to
be fun.

3. In paragraph 9, Jordan lists some common things that certainly
aren't any fun. How does she say people made them fun anyway?

4. What are some of the ways people make fun even more thrilling?

5. What does Jordan list as looking like fun on television commercials?

6. Discuss the relationship between big occasions and the experience of fun. Explain the meaning of the statement, "It may even
come on a Tuesday."

7. Describe Jordan's attitude concerning how much in life really is
fun. According to Jordan, how should we treat fun? Why? Is it
something she says can be experienced only at special times?

8. How old was Jordan at the time she remembers having an especially good time with her friend Pam? Describe in your own
words why she had such a good time that day. What are some of
the candies she remembers buying? Why was it especially funny
when Pam would say, "Oughta reach home by nightfall"?

9. For what reason does Jordan feel regretful at the end of the
essay? Although she is regretful, do you think she is actually sad?
Why?

UNDERSTANDING THE WRITER'S TECHNIQUES

1. What is the author's thesis? Where is it placed?

2. Does Jordan ever offer a single-sentence definition of "fun"? Where? Is that sentence sufficient to define the concept? Why?

3. Jordan employs the technique of *negation*—defining a term through showing what it is *not*—so strongly in this essay that the writing verges on *irony*. Irony is using language to suggest the opposite of what is said (see Glossary). Explain the irony in paragraphs 9, 10, and 11.

4. Why does the author continually point out things that are supposed to be fun? What is she trying to tell us about these things?

5. Writers usually avoid vague language such as "everything" and "everybody" in their writing, yet Jordan uses these words frequently in her essay. Explain her purpose in deliberately avoiding concrete terms.

6. What is the *tone* (see Glossary) of this essay? Is it fun? How does Jordan create the tone? Much of the writing in this essay has a very conversational quality to it, as though the author were speaking directly to the reader. Locate five words or phrases that have this quality.

7. Why does Jordan use so many examples and illustrations in this essay? Which paragraphs use multiple illustrations with special effectiveness?

8. There is a definite turning point in this essay where Jordan switches from an ironic to an affirmative point of view and begins to explain what fun *can be* rather than what it *is not*. One paragraph in particular serves as the transition between the two attitudes. Which one is it? Which is the first paragraph to be mostly affirmative? What is the result of this switch?

9. Jordan uses specific brand names in the essay. Locate at least four of them. Why do you think she uses these brand names instead of names that simply identify the object?

10. What is the function of narration in the development of this essay? Where does the author *narrate* an imagined incident? Where does she use a real incident? Why does Jordan use narration in this paper?

11. Compare the effects of the two simple, direct statements that begin and end the essay. Why does Jordan not develop a more elaborate introduction and conclusion?

EXPLORING THE WRITER'S IDEAS

1. Jordan begins her essay by stating, "Fun is hard to have." At one point she indicates, "Fun got to be such a big thing that everybody started looking for more and more thrilling ways to supply it" (par. 9). Do you think that fun is hard to have? Why or why not? What relationship does the epidemic use of drugs and alcohol have to our difficulties in having fun today?

2. The author raises the question of how at big events we are sometimes left "waiting for the fun to start" (par. 11). What functions do events or occasions such as holidays, weddings, or birthdays play in our society? Why is there an emphasis placed on having fun at those events? Do you think there should be such an emphasis? Why?

3. This essay appeared as a guest editorial in *The New York Times*. We do not usually think of *The New York Times* as a "fun" newspaper, but rather as one that deals with serious issues of international significance. Jordan's article might be considered popular writing or light reading. Do you feel there is a place in the media—newspapers, magazines, radio, television—for a mixture of "heavy" and "light" attitudes? What well-respected newspapers or magazines that you know include articles on popular topics? What subjects do you think would currently be most appealing to popular audiences?

4. At the end of the essay, Jordan seems to imply that it is easier for children to have fun than it is for grownups. Do you agree? Is the basic experience of fun any different for kids or for adults? Do you feel it was any easier for people to have fun in days past than it is now? Why?

IDEAS FOR WRITING

Guided Writing

Select one of the following highly connotative terms for various types of experiences and write an extended definition about it: love, creativity, alienation, prejudice, fidelity.

1. Prepare for your essay by consulting a good dictionary for the lexical definition (denotation) of the term. However, instead of beginning with this definition, start with some catchy, interesting opening statements related to the definition.
2. Write a thesis sentence that names the word you will define and that tells the special opinion, attitude, or point of view you have about the word.
3. Attempt to establish the importance of your subject by considering it in terms of our current understanding of fun.
4. Use the technique of negation (see page 222) by providing various examples and illustrations of what your topic *is not* in order to establish your own viewpoint of what it *is*.
5. Use other strategies—description, narration, comparison and contrast, and so forth—to aid in clearly establishing an extended definition of your topic.
6. At the end of your essay dramatize through narration at least one personal experience that relates the importance of the topic to your life.

More Writing Projects

1. Sit someplace on campus and observe people having fun. Record in your journal their behavior—actions, gestures, noises, and so forth. Then turn these notes into a definition of "campus fun."
2. Write a brief one-paragraph definition of a "funny person." Use vivid details to create this portrait.
3. From a book of popular quotations (*Bartlett's Familiar Quotations,* the *Oxford Dictionary of Quotations*) check under the heading "fun" and select a number of statements about fun by professional writers. Then write an essay in which you expand one of those definitions. Draw upon your own experiences or readings to support the definition you choose to expand.

A Word's Meaning

Gloria Naylor

Gloria Naylor is best known for her novel *The Women of Brewster Place* (1982). She has also published *Mama Day* (1986) and *Bailley's Cafe* (1992) to critical acclaim. As an African-American woman and a writer, Naylor has found that words can change their meaning, depending on who defines them. Telling of a confrontation with an angry classmate who called her a "nigger" in the third grade, Naylor develops an extended definition of the word and its multiple meanings. As you read, think about other words that depend on context for their meaning.

Words to Watch

transcendent (par. 1)   rising above

fleeting (par. 1)   moving quickly

intermittent (par. 2)   alternate; repeated

consensus (par. 2)   agreement

verified (par. 3)   confirmed

gravitated (par. 4)   moved toward

inflections (par. 5)   pitch or tone of voice

endearment (par. 9)   expression of affection

disembodied (par. 9)   separated from the body

unkempt (par. 10)   messy

social stratum (par. 14)   status

1 Language is the subject. It is the written form with which I've managed to keep the wolf away from the door and, in diaries, to keep my sanity. In spite of this, I consider the written word inferior to the spoken, and much of the frustration experienced by novelists is the awareness that whatever we manage to capture in even the most transcendent passages falls far short of the richness of life. Dialogue achieves its power in the dynamics of a fleeting moment of sight, sound, smell and touch.

2   I'm not going to enter the debate here about whether it is language that shapes reality or vice versa. That battle is doomed to be waged whenever we seek intermittent reprieve from the

chicken and egg dispute. I will simply take the position that the spoken word, like the written word, amounts to a nonsensical arrangement of sounds or letters without a consensus that assigns "meaning." And building from the meanings of what we hear, we order reality. Words themselves are innocuous; it is the consensus that gives them true power.

I remember the first time I heard the word nigger. In my 3 third-grade class, our math tests were being passed down the rows, and as I handed the papers to a little boy in back of me, I remarked that once again he had received a much lower mark than I did. He snatched his test from me and spit out that word. Had he called me a nymphomaniac or a necrophiliac, I couldn't have been more puzzled. I didn't know what a nigger was, but I knew that whatever it meant, it was something he shouldn't have called me. This was verified when I raised my hand, and in a loud voice repeated what he had said and watched the teacher scold him for using a "bad" word. I was later to go home and ask the inevitable questions that every black parent must face— "Mommy, what does 'nigger' mean?"

And what exactly did it mean? Thinking back, I realize that 4 this could not have been the first time the word was used in my presence. I was part of a large extended family that had migrated from the rural South after World War II and formed a close-knit network that gravitated around my maternal grandparents. Their ground-floor apartment in one of the buildings they owned in Harlem was a weekend mecca for my immediate family, along with countless aunts, uncles and cousins who brought along as- sorted friends. It was a bustling and open house with assorted neighbors and tenants popping in and out to exchange bits of gossip, pick up an old quarrel or referee the ongoing checkers game in which my grandmother cheated shamelessly. They were all there to let down their hair and put up their feet after a week of labor in the factories, laundries and shipyards of New York.

Amid the clamor, which could reach deafening propor- 5 tions—two or three conversations going on simultaneously, punctuated by the sound of a baby's crying somewhere in the back rooms or out on the street—there was still a rigid set of rules about what was said and how. Older children were sent out of the living room when it was time to get into the juicy details about "you-know-who" up on the third floor who had gone and gotten herself "p-r-e-g-n-a-n-t!" But my parents, knowing that I could spell well beyond my years, always demanded that I follow the others out to play. Beyond sexual misconduct and death, everything else was considered harmless for our young ears. And so among the anecdotes of the triumphs and disappointments in the various workings of their lives, the word nigger was used in my presence, but it was set within contexts and inflections that caused it to register in my mind as something else.

6   In the singular, the word was always applied to a man who had distinguished himself in some situation that brought their approval for his strength, intelligence or drive:

7   "Did Johnny *really* do that?"

8   "I'm telling you, that nigger pulled in $6,000 of overtime last year. Said he got enough for a down payment on a house."

9   When used with a possessive adjective by a woman—"my nigger"—it became a term of endearment for husband or boyfriend. But it could be more than just a term applied to a man. In their mouths it became the pure essence of manhood—a disembodied force that channeled their past history of struggle and present survival against the odds into a victorious statement of being: "Yeah, that old foreman found out quick enough—you don't mess with a nigger."

10   In the plural, it became a description of some group within the community that had overstepped the bounds of decency as my family defined it: Parents who neglected their children, a drunken couple who fought in public, people who simply refused to look for work, those with excessively dirty mouths or unkempt households were all "trifling niggers." This particular circle could forgive hard times, unemployment, the occasional bout of depression—they had gone through all of that themselves—but the unforgivable sin was a lack of self-respect.

11   A woman could never be a "nigger" in the singular, with its connotation of confirming worth. The noun "girl" was its closest equivalent in that sense, but only when used in direct address and regardless of the gender doing the addressing. "Girl" was a token of respect for a woman. The one-syllable word was drawn out to sound like three in recognition of the extra ounce of wit, nerve or daring that the woman had shown in the situation under discussion.

12   "G-i-r-l, stop. You mean you said that to his face?"

But if the word was used in a third-person reference or 13
shortened so that it almost snapped out of the mouth, it always
involved some element of communal disapproval. And age became an important factor in these exchanges. It was only between
individuals of the same generation, or from an older person to a
younger (but never the other way around), that "girl" would be
considered a compliment.

I don't agree with the argument that use of the word nigger 14
at this social stratum of the black community was an internalization of racism. The dynamics were the exact opposite: the people
in my grandmother's living room took a word that whites used to
signify worthlessness or degradation and rendered it impotent.
Gathering there together, they transformed "nigger" to signify the
varied and complex human beings they knew themselves to be. If
the word was to disappear totally from the mouths of even the
most liberal of white society, no one in that room was naïve
enough to believe it would disappear from white minds. Meeting
the word head-on, they proved it had absolutely nothing to do
with the way they were determined to live their lives.

So there must have been dozens of times that the "nigger" 15
was spoken in front of me before I reached the third grade. But I
didn't "hear" it until it was said by a small pair of lips that had already learned it could be a way to humiliate me. That was the
word I went home and asked my mother about. And since she
knew that I had to grow up in America, she took me in her lap
and explained.

BUILDING VOCABULARY

1. In paragraph 3, Naylor says the word "nigger" is as puzzling to
   her as "necrophiliac" and "nymphomaniac." Using a dictionary,
   find both the meanings of these two terms and find their etymology, or roots.
2. In paragraph 14, Naylor writes, "I don't agree with the argument
   that use of the word nigger at this social stratum of the black
   community was an internalization of racism." Put Naylor's idea
   into your words. Use the context of the sentence to understand
   key terms such as "social stratum" and "internalization."

UNDERSTANDING THE WRITER'S IDEAS

1. What is the original situation in which Naylor recognizes that "nigger" can be a hate word? What clues from outside the dictionary meaning of the word help her to recognize this meaning? What confirms her suspicion that the word is "bad"?
2. In paragraph 4, Naylor gives us information about her family and background. In your own words, what kind of family did Naylor come from? Where did she grow up? What economic and social class did her family come from? How do you know?
3. In paragraph 5, Naylor explains the values of her group. What was considered appropriate and what was inappropriate for children to hear? What kind of behavior was condemned by the group?
4. Naylor defines at least five contexts in which the word "nigger" might be used. Make a list giving the five contexts, and write a sentence putting the use of the word into your own definition.
5. Explain one context in which Naylor says "nigger" was never used (paragraph 11). How are age and gender important in determining how the word was used?
6. When Naylor says in paragraph 14 that blacks' use of the word "nigger" about themselves rendered the word "impotent," what does she mean? How do they "transform" the meaning of the word?
7. In the last paragraph, Naylor recalls her mother's reaction to the experience of hearing a third-grade classmate use the word to humiliate her. What do you think the mother explained?

UNDERSTANDING THE WRITER'S TECHNIQUES

1. Where is the thesis statement of Naylor's essay? How do you know?
2. Why does Naylor begin with two paragraphs about language, in a very general or theoretical way? Explain what these two paragraphs tell us about the writer's authority to define words. How does she use her introduction to make herself sound like an expert on the problem of defining words?
3. In paragraph 3, the author shifts tone. She moves from the formal language of the introduction to the personal voice as she retells her childhood experience. What is the effect of this transition on the reader? Why?

4. Look closely at the examples of usage Naylor provides in paragraphs 8, 9, 10, and 11. Why does she give dialogue to illustrate the various contexts in which she heard the word "nigger" used? In what way is this variety of speakers related to her thesis statement?

5. Naylor uses grammatical terms to clarify differences in meaning, such as "in the singular" (par. 6), "possessive adjective" (par. 9), "plural" (par. 10), and "third-person reference" (par. 13). Why does she use these technical terms? What does it reveal about the audience for whom she is writing? What does it reveal about Naylor's understanding of that audience?

6. What do you think about the last sentence of the essay? Why does the author return to the simple and direct language of her childhood experience in order to conclude rather than using the theoretical and technical language of other parts of the essay?

EXPLORING THE WRITER'S IDEAS

1. Naylor chooses to define a difficult and controversial word in her essay. Does she define it in a way that makes you think again about the meaning of the word "nigger"? Have you used the word in any of the ways she defines? How have contemporary rap musicians used the word in ways to suggest that Naylor's definition is accurate?

2. Naylor argues that the definition of words emerges from consensus. So, if the third-grader used "nigger" to humiliate his classmate, we must draw the conclusion that that little boy's society consented to the racism he intended by using the word. How does this idea get reinforced in the last paragraph of the essay? What attitude toward racism does the mother seem to reveal when she picks up her daughter? Does Naylor's definition essay offer any solutions to the negative meaning the word carries?

3. The classic American novel *The Adventures of Huckleberry Finn* by Mark Twain uses the word "nigger" almost 200 times. For this reason, some school libraries want to ban the book. Does Naylor's definition essay offer any solutions to this censorship debate?

4. In what way does Naylor's discussion of language raise issues similar to those discussed by Amy Tan in "Mother Tongue" (pages 13–19)? While Tan is dealing with language among im-

migrants and Naylor is addressing the varieties of meaning of words to native speakers of English, both writers deal with the politics of language. How does each writer define the relationship between language and power?

IDEAS FOR WRITING

Guided Writing

Choose a word that you have recently heard used that offended you because it was sexist, racist, homophobic, or otherwise objectionable. Write a definition essay in which you define the word, show examples of its power to offend, and conclude by offering alternate words.

1. Use an anecdote to show whom you heard using the word, where it was used, and how you felt when you heard it used. Explain who you are, and who the other speaker was in your introduction.
2. In your thesis give the word and give an expanded definition of what the word means to you.
3. Explain the background of the word's negative use. Who uses it? What is the dictionary meaning of the word? How do you think the word got corrupted?
4. Give examples to expand your thesis that the word has negative meanings. Show who uses it, and for what purpose. Draw your examples from people at work, the media, or historical figures.
5. Use another example to show how the word can change meaning if the speaker deliberately uses it in order to mock its usual meaning or "render it impotent" as Naylor says.
6. If possible, try to define the word by negation—that is, by what it does not mean.
7. Connect your paragraphs with transitions that relate one idea thoughtfully to the next.
8. In your conclusion, place the term in a broader perspective, one that goes beyond the specific word to the power of language to shape reality or control behavior.

More Writing Projects

1. In your journal, record an incident in which someone addressed you with an offensive word. Explain how you reacted and why.
2. Write a one-paragraph definition of a word or phrase by which you would feel comfortable being labeled. Are you a single parent? an Italian-American? an honor student? Write a sharp thesis to define the term, and then expand the definition with examples.
3. The term "multicultural" refers to a perspective on society that values the differences among people of varying ethnic origin, religious belief, sexual preference, and social class. In an essay write an extended definition of the term "multicultural society." Draw upon your own experiences and (or) your readings to support your definition.

Complexion
Richard Rodriguez

In this excerpt from *Hunger of Memory* (1982) writer Richard Rodriguez uses autobiography to show the subtle ways in which his family's definition of his dark skin color as ugly led him to feel shame. His extended definition of "complexion" uses a variety of techniques to suggest the way in which a word can change a boy's life.

Words to Watch

buoyant (par. 1)   floating

incessantly (par. 2)   without stopping

menial (par. 4)   low level; for a servant

sensational (par. 6)   related to the five senses

braceros (par. 7)   manual workers

sarcasm (par. 8)   mocking remark; ridicule

scorn (par. 8)   contempt

stammering (par. 9)   uneven speech pattern

precocious (par. 9)   maturing early

effeminate (par. 10)   showing female qualities; unmanly

1   Complexion. My first conscious experience of sexual excitement concerns my complexion. One summer weekend, when I was around seven years old, I was at a public swimming pool with the whole family. I remember sitting on the damp pavement next to the pool and seeing my mother, in the spectators' bleachers, holding my younger sister on her lap. My mother, I noticed, was watching my father as he stood on a diving board, waving to her. I watched her wave back. Then saw her radiant, bashful, astonishing smile. In that second I sensed that my mother and father had a relationship I knew nothing about. A nervous excitement encircled my stomach as I saw my mother's eyes follow my father's figure curving into the water. A second or two later, he emerged. I heard him call out. Smiling, his voice sounded, buoyant, calling me to swim to him. But turning to see him, I caught my mother's eye. I heard her shout over to me. In Spanish she

called through the crowd: 'Put a towel on over your shoulders.'
In public, she didn't want to say why. I knew.

That incident anticipates the shame and sexual inferiority I 2
was to feel in later years because of my dark complexion. I was
to grow up an ugly child. Or one who thought himself ugly.
(Feo.) One night when I was eleven or twelve years old, I locked
myself in the bathroom and carefully regarded my reflection in
the mirror over the sink. Without any pleasure I studied my skin.
I turned on the faucet. (In my mind I heard the swirling voices of
aunts, and even my mother's voice, whispering, whispering incessantly about lemon juice solutions and dark, *feo* children.)
With a bar of soap, I fashioned a thick ball of lather. I began
soaping my arms. I took my father's straight razor out of the
medicine cabinet. Slowly, with steady deliberateness, I put the
blade against my flesh, pressed it as close as I could without cutting, and moved it up and down across my skin to see if I could
get out, somehow lessen, the dark. All I succeeded in doing,
however, was in shaving my arms bare of their hair. For as I
noted with disappointment, the dark would not come out. It remained. Trapped. Deep in the cells of my skin.

Throughout adolescence, I felt myself mysteriously marked. 3
Nothing else about my appearance would concern me so much as
the fact that my complexion was dark. My mother would say how
sorry she was that there was not money enough to get braces to
straighten my teeth. But I never bothered about my teeth. In three-
way mirrors at department stores, I'd see my profile dramatically
defined by a long nose, but it was really only the color of my skin
that caught my attention.

I wasn't afraid that I would become a menial laborer be- 4
cause of my skin. Nor did my complexion make me feel especially vulnerable to racial abuse. (I didn't really consider my dark
skin to be a racial characteristic. I would have been only too
happy to look as Mexican as my light-skinned older brother.)
Simply, I judged myself ugly. And, since the women in my family had been the ones who discussed it in such worried tones, I felt
my dark skin made me unattractive to women.

Thirteen years old. Fourteen. In a grammar school art class, 5
when the assignment was to draw a self-portrait, I tried and I
tried but could not bring myself to shade in the face on the paper
to anything like my actual tone. With disgust then I would come

face to face with myself in mirrors. With disappointment I located myself in class photographs—my dark face undefined by the camera which had clearly described the white faces of classmates. Or I'd see my dark wrist against my long-sleeved white shirt.

6　　　I grew divorced from my body. Insecure, overweight, listless. On hot summer days when my rubber-soled shoes soaked up the heat from the sidewalk, I kept my head down. Or walked in the shade. My mother didn't need anymore to tell me to watch out for the sun. I denied myself a sensational life. The normal, extraordinary, animal excitement of feeling my body alive—riding shirtless on a bicycle in the warm wind created by furious self-propelled motion—the sensations that first had excited in me a sense of my maleness, I denied. I was too ashamed of my body. I wanted to forget that I had a body because I had a brown body. I was grateful that none of my classmates ever mentioned the fact.

7　　　I continued to see the *braceros,* those men I resembled in one way and, in another way, didn't resemble at all. On the watery horizon of a Valley afternoon, I'd see them. And though I feared looking like them, it was with silent envy that I regarded them still. I envied them their physical lives, their freedom to violate the taboo of the sun. Closer to home I would notice the shirtless construction workers, the roofers, the sweating men tarring the street in front of the house. And I'd see the Mexican gardeners. I was unwilling to admit the attraction of their lives. I tried to deny it by looking away. But what was denied became strongly desired.

8　　　In high school physical education classes, I withdrew, in the regular company of five or six classmates, to a distant corner of a football field where we smoked and talked. Our company was composed of bodies too short or too tall, all graceless and all—except mine—pale. Our conversation was usually witty. (In fact we were intelligent.) If we referred to the athletic contests around us, it was with sarcasm. With savage scorn I'd refer to the 'animals' playing football or baseball. It would have been important for me to have joined them. Or for me to have taken off my shirt, to have let the sun burn dark on my skin, and to have run barefoot on the warm wet grass. It would have been very important. Too important. It would have been too telling a gesture—to admit the desire for sensation, the body, my body.

Fifteen, sixteen. I was a teenager shy in the presence of 9
girls. Never dated. Barely could talk to a girl without stammering. In high school I went to several dances, but I never managed to ask a girl to dance. So I stopped going. I cannot remember high school years now with the parade of typical
images: bright drive-ins or gliding blue shadows of a Junior
Prom. At home most weekend nights, I would pass evenings
reading. Like those hidden, precocious adolescents who have
no real-life sexual experiences, I read a great deal of romantic
fiction. 'You won't find it in your books,' my brother would
playfully taunt me as he prepared to go to a party by freezing
the crest of the wave in his hair with sticky pomade. Through
my reading, however, I developed a fabulous and sophisticated
sexual imagination. At seventeen, I may not have known how
to engage a girl in small talk, but I had read *Lady Chatterley's
Lover.*

It annoyed me to hear my father's teasing: that I would 10
never know what 'real work' is; that my hands were so soft. I
think I knew it was his way of admitting pleasure and pride in
my academic success. But I didn't smile. My mother said she
was glad her children were getting their educations and would
not be pushed around like *los pobres.* I heard the remark ironically as a reminder of my separation from *los braceros.* At
such times I suspected that education was making me effeminate. The odd thing, however, was that I did not judge my
classmates so harshly. Nor did I consider my male teachers in
high school effeminate. It was only myself I judged against
some shadowy, mythical Mexican laborer—dark like me, yet
very different.

BUILDING VOCABULARY

1. Rodriguez *defines* complexion in part by enumerating the sensual
activities that he associated with skin color. In paragraph 1, he
identifies his mother's "radiant, bashful, astonishing smile" as
she admires his father's body in the swimming pool. He uses adjectives—sensory words— in many other places to describe the
pleasures he felt his dark skin denied him. Identify at least five

words that Rodriguez uses to define complexion in this way, and write your own sentences with these words.

2. Rodriguez uses Spanish words: *feo,* meaning ugly; *los braceros,* meaning the workmen (literally those who work with their arms); *los pobres,* or the poor. Why does he include the Spanish word instead of an English word? Does the context help you translate the words if you do not know their meaning? Explain.

UNDERSTANDING THE WRITER'S IDEAS

1. What is the thesis of the essay? Where is it?
2. What assumptions about skin color does the author recognize when his mother tells him to cover himself with a towel in paragraph 1? Are these assumptions explicit or implicit? Why does the author connect complexion with sexual excitement?
3. What does the author mean when he says he became "divorced from my body" in paragraph 6? Write a sentence in your own words explaining what Rodriguez felt and why.
4. In paragraph 7, the author defines himself in part when he says that in some ways he resembled *los braceros,* but in another way he did not resemble them at all. Explain how he was similar to them and in what specific ways he was different.
5. In paragraphs 8 and 9, the author defines himself in another way by showing which groups of his peers he does and does not belong to. How does he define himself by negation, by what he cannot do?
6. In paragraph 9, Rodriguez continues his self-definition as he creates the individual class or group he does belong to—readers. Why does reading help him to achieve definition of who he is? What does he read? How do his parents define him because of his reading? In what way is he "very different" (par. 10)?

UNDERSTANDING THE WRITER'S TECHNIQUES

1. A writer can use one of several techniques to develop an extended definition. They include (a) showing how a particular term

differs from others that belong to the same category, (b) developing the etymology of a term (its origin and history in the language), and (c) using negation to show what the term does not mean.

Which of these three techniques best describes Rodriguez's predominant approach in this essay? Does he make use of either of the other two techniques? If so, where?

Write a paragraph-by-paragraph outline that traces the development of the predominant technique throughout the essay.

2. Rodriguez organizes his essay by showing how his *definition* of himself and his complexion developed from the time he was about seven years old until he reached young adulthood. How does this chronological organization create an expanded definition?

3. Rodriguez also uses anecdotes to develop his definition. In paragraph 2 he tells of trying to use a razor to shave off his skin color. What other anecdotes does Rodriguez use to expand his definition?

4. Rodriguez uses first-person narrative to tell his story, since it is personal experience. But we hear the voices of others as well. How does he bring in the aunts, and the parents, as participants in his definition? How do they contribute to his definition even though we don't hear them speak directly?

5. Rodriguez further relies on visual images to develop his definition. He uses mirrors, and photographs, for example, to emphasize the narrator's sensitivity to his skin color. What other visual images does he use? What sounds contribute to his definition of himself as ugly?

6. What is the *stated* attitude toward his complexion in Rodriguez's essay? Yet what is *implied* about his attitude toward his complexion by the fact that he writes the essay? Has his attitude changed? Explain.

7. Who is Rodriguez's intended audience for the essay? How do you know?

8. Describe the author's purpose in writing this essay.

9. Describe the overall *tone* (see Glossary) of the essay. Does this tone suit the subject? Explain.

10. Would you characterize this essay as primarily *objective* or *subjective* (see Glossary)? Why?

11. How does Rodriguez create transitions from one paragraph to the next? Give examples of transitional devices.

EXPLORING THE WRITER'S IDEAS

1. Rodriguez does not provide a dictionary definition of "complexion." Look up the word in a full-sized reference work, such as the *Oxford English Dictionary,* in your library. Compare the dictionary definition of "complexion" with the extended definition that Rodriguez provides. Explain how they are the same and where they differ.
2. Rodriguez implies that words are not merely defined literally; the culture in which they are used adds to the definition. Make a list of all the phrases in English that you can think of that include "black" and "white"—such as "white lie" and "black comedy." Define what these terms mean. What does the "complexion" of the word reveal about cultural attitudes toward color?
3. Rodriguez identifies himself as "different" not only because his skin is dark within his family, but because he is in a school with mostly white classmates. In paragraph 7, he says that when he looks at the *braceros,* he "feared looking like them" but that "it was with silent envy that I regarded them still. . . . I was unwilling to admit the attraction of their lives. I tried to deny it by looking away. But what was denied became strongly desired." What is Rodriguez saying about "difference"? In what way is this attraction to difference in conflict with Rodriguez's reading habits?
4. In "A Word's Meaning" (pages 240–243), Gloria Naylor writes about the internalization of racism within the African-American community. In what way is that problem similar to what Rodriguez defines in the Latino community in which he grew up?

IDEAS FOR WRITING

Guided Writing

Write an extended definition of a term that you feel is critical to the understanding of race, gender, or class in American culture today. For example, "feminist," "multicultural," and "pluralistic" are in frequent use to label political and social attitudes. Create a definition of one of these words or a similar word within a particular field with which you are familiar, such as feminism in education or pluralism among employees at IBM.

1. Begin with a short anecdote from personal experience to introduce your interest in the word.
2. Create a clear understanding with your reader of your background and beliefs so that your perspective on the cultural value of the word is defined.
3. Use negation to extend your definition; show at least one thing that the word is *not*.
4. Use description and narration to extend the definition with personal experience or other stories.
5. Use a chronological structure to show how your definition of the word developed over a period of time.
6. Don't shy away from making the essay subjective—that is, from interjecting your own opinions.
7. Conclude by explaining whether you think the word you defined is useful in today's society or whether it has become overused.

More Writing Projects

1. In your journal, write your own definition of the word "self-esteem."
2. Select a word that you feel is crucial to your own self-definition. Write an extended definition in one paragraph in which you tell what the word means and why you chose it.
3. Write an extended definition of a term that describes a current, serious social issue—for example, homelessness, unemployment, neo-Nazism, substance abuse.

SUMMING UP: CHAPTER 7

1. In her essay on fun in this chapter, Suzanne Britt Jordan defines a term we all understand but might have difficulty explaining. One way she approaches this definition is through negation—that is, explaining what fun *is not*. Write an essay that defines by negation a similar, understood but difficult-to-explain term—for example "privacy," "the blues," "class," "happiness," or "success."
2. Working with another class member, make a comparative analysis of the Jordan and Scott pieces. Give consideration to theme, subject matter, tone, and language. Then decide how both essays would help a visitor to the United States understand something

about American culture. After you have discussed your findings, write your own essay on how the Jordan and Scott selections help to define American culture.

3. Both Gloria Naylor and Richard Rodriguez define words that relate to color and to values placed on color within an ethnic community. Think of a word that has troubled you or been used against you in your early life. It might be a word you associate, for example, with ethnicity, economic status, or personal appearance. Write an essay in which you define this word, considering both how the people who aimed it meant it to be interpreted and how an outsider might define it.

4. Gloria Naylor argues that a word is defined by "consensus." That is, a community agrees among its members on how the word will be used, despite outside definitions. On your campus find examples of current words, defined by "consensus" in the college community, whose meanings would be surprising to outsiders like your parents.

5. Look back over the titles of all the essays in this chapter and previous chapters of this book. Choose one term from any title (for example, "All-American Girl," "Survival," "Salvation," "Night Walker," "Complexion") and write an essay defining that term *subjectively* (from a personal viewpoint).

CHAPTER 8

Classification

WHAT IS CLASSIFICATION?

Classification is the arrangement of information into groups or categories in order to make clear the relations among members of the group. In a supermarket, the soups are together in one aisle, the frozen foods in another. In a record, tape, and disc store, all the jazz is in one section while the rap music is in a separate section. You wouldn't expect to find a can of tomato soup next to the butter pecan ice cream any more than you'd look for a tape of George Gershwin's *An American in Paris* in the same section as a tape by Ice-T.

Writers need to classify, because it helps them present a mass of material by means of some orderly system. Related bits of information seem clearer when presented together as parts of a group. Unlike writing narrative, for example, developing classification requires a different level of analysis and planning. The writer not only is presenting a single topic or event, but is placing the subject into a complex network of relations. In a narrative, we can tell the story of a single event from start to finish, such as the time we saw a Van Gogh painting in an art museum. In classification, we have to think beyond the personal experience to try to place that Van Gogh painting in a wider context. Where does Van Gogh "fit" in the history of painting? Why is he different from other painters? How does his style relate to other work of the same period? In pursuing these questions, we seek not only to *record* our experience in looking at the painting but to *understand* it more fully.

Classification, then, begins by thinking about a body of material and trying to break it down into distinct parts, or categories. Called *division* or *analysis,* this first task helps split an idea or object into usable components. Then, some of the parts can serve as categories into which the writer can fit individual pieces that share some common qualities.

For example, if the writer wanted to *analyze* the Van Gogh painting, she might begin with the large subject of painting. Then she could *divide,* or break the subject down, into two groups.

traditional painting
modern painting

Then, she could further *divide* the types of modern painting:

impressionist
postimpressionist
fauvist
art nouveau
cubist
art deco
abstract expressionist
op art
minimalist art

The purpose is to determine what the parts of the whole are. If we know what the components of *modern painting* are, then we can place or locate the Van Gogh painting in relation to other paintings. We would know whether it belonged in the soup aisle or the freezer section, so to speak. In this case, we would decide that it is *not* traditional painting, so that we would separate it from that group. We would place it in the modern group. Now we know which aisle it belongs in. But is it tomato or chicken soup? Now we relate it to the other modern types of painting, and place it in the postimpressionist group. Our decision is based on an analysis of the painter's use of color, his style, and the ways he differs from painters in the other groups.

Our analysis does not mean that the Van Gogh has nothing in common with traditional painting. Van Gogh, for instance, shares an interest in landscape and self-portraits with Rembrandt. But the bright, bold colors of his *Starry Night* are so dramatically different from the somber colors of the older Dutch painter's *Nightwatch* that we are inclined to emphasize their *division*. We could, for instance, set up a supermarket on the basis of what color the food labels were: all the red labels in one aisle, all the yellow labels together. But such a system would make it much harder to find what we wanted unless we were experts in package design. Similarly, our classification of painting is based on the most sensible method of division.

HOW DO WE READ CLASSIFICATION?

Reading classification involves the following steps:

- Identify what the author is classifying. Find the thesis to determine what the purpose or basis of the classification is.
- Make an outline of the essay. Find the divisions and the classifications into which the author has sorted the subject.
- Determine whether the categories are clearly defined. Do they overlap?
- Be alert for stereotypes. Has the author used them in order to build the groups? If so, see if the groups are oversimplified and thus unreliable.
- Identify the intended audience. How do we know who the audience is?

In this chapter, Judith Viorst classifies friends into eight groups, and even numbers them to make it is easy to follow her divisions. E. B. White analyzes three New Yorks, first separating its various strands for a close look at the city, but then weaving them back together to create the "whole" city he loved so much. Mary Mebane uses personal experience with prejudice directed at African Americans to explain the categories into which people are placed, and analyzes the impact of such grouping. James T. Baker brings together a variety of writing techniques to analyze the world of education with some humor. Each writer has a different purpose for classification, but each uses the same basic system of organization.

HOW DO WE WRITE CLASSIFICATION?

These four essayists should provide you with enough examples of how to classify to make your writing task easy. Classification resembles outlining. Whether the subject is personal, technical, simple, complex, or abstract, the writer can organize material into categories, and can move carefully from one category to another in developing an essay.

Select your topic and begin to divide it into categories. Try drawing a tree with branches or use a model from a biology book that shows the division of life into genus, species, phyla, and so on. Or make lists. Think about how your library classifies books. Arranging books by the color of the covers might look attractive, but it would presume that all library users already knew what a book looked like before they came to the library. Instead, libraries divide books by type. They generally begin with two large groups: fiction and nonfiction. With these categories, they create small ones: English fiction, Mexican fiction, Australian fiction. Within nonfiction, they divide books into history, religion, geography, mathematics, and so on. In this way, a reader can find a book based on need, and not prior knowledge. Keeping the library in mind, make a list of categories for your topic.

Make an outline and arrange the groups to avoid overlap from one group to the next.

Decide on a system of classification. Don't force objects into arbitrary slots, though. Don't ignore differences that violate your categories. Try to create a legitimate system that avoids stereotyping or oversimplification. Don't, like Mary Mebane's teachers, classify invalidly: all light-skinned students are smarter than all "black black" students. Be sure your categories are legitimate.

Write a thesis that identifies the purpose of your system of classification. Think of the ways in which your system can broaden a reader's understanding of the subject rather than narrow it.

Sample thesis statement:

At least three groups of immigrants reach the United States today—political refugees seeking asylum, economic refugees looking for a better life, and religious dissidents looking for freedom to practice their chosen beliefs.

Writing and Revising the Draft

Write a rough draft. Be sure that you explain the categories and give examples for each one.

For each category, use definition, description, illustration, or narrative to help the reader see the distinct nature of the division you have created. Use transitions between each category or group.

Proofread for correctness. Make a final copy.

Revise your first draft, making certain that you eliminate any extreme overlapping in your categories. Remember that each category must be fully and equally developed.

Friends, Good Friends—And Such Good Friends

Judith Viorst

In this essay Judith Viorst, who writes for numerous popular magazines, examines types of friends in her life. Her pattern of development is easy to follow, because she tends to stay on one level in the process of classification. As you read this essay, try to keep in mind the similarities and distinctions that Viorst makes among types of friends, as well as the principles of classification that she uses.

Words to Watch

nonchalant (par. 3)   showing an easy unconcern or disinterest

endodontist (par. 14)   a dentist specializing in diseases of dental pulp and root canals

sibling (par. 16)   brother or sister

dormant (par. 19)   as if asleep; inactive

self-revelation (par. 22)   self-discovery; self-disclosure

calibrated (par. 29)   measured; fixed; checked carefully

1   Women are friends, I once would have said, when they totally love and support and trust each other, and bare to each other the secrets of their souls, and run—no questions asked—to help each other, and tell harsh truths to each other (no, you can't wear that dress unless you lose ten pounds first) when harsh truths must be told.

2   Women are friends, I once would have said, when they share the same affection for Ingmar Bergman, plus train rides, cats, warm rain, charades, Camus, and hate with equal ardor Newark and Brussels sprouts and Lawrence Welk and camping.

3   In other words, I once would have said that a friend is a friend all the way, but now I believe that's a narrow point of view. For the friendships I have and the friendships I see are conducted at many levels of intensity, serve many different functions, meet different needs and range from those as all-the-way as

the friendship of the soul sisters mentioned above to that of the most nonchalant and casual playmates.

Consider these varieties of friendship: 4

1. Convenience friends. These are the women with whom,   5 if our paths weren't crossing all the time, we'd have no particular reason to be friends: a next-door neighbor, a woman in our car pool, the mother of one of our children's closest friends or maybe some mommy with whom we serve juice and cookies each week at the Glenwood Co-op Nursery.

Convenience friends are convenient indeed. They'll lend us   6 their cups and silverware for a party. They'll drive our kids to soccer when we're sick. They'll take us to pick up our car when we need a lift to the garage. They'll even take our cats when we go on vacation. As we will for them.

But we don't, with convenience friends, ever come too   7 close or tell too much; we maintain our public face and emotional distance. "Which means,"says Elaine, "that I'll talk about being overweight but not about being depressed. Which means I'll admit being mad but not blind with rage. Which means I might say that we're pinched this month but never that I'm worried sick over money."

But which doesn't mean that there isn't sufficient value to be   8 found in these friendships of mutual aid, in convenience friends.

2. Special-interest friends. These friendships aren't inti-   9 mate, and they needn't involve kids or silverware or cats. Their value lies in some interest jointly shared. And so we may have an office friend or a yoga friend or a tennis friend or a friend from the Women's Democratic Club.

"I've got one woman friend," says Joyce, "who likes, as I   10 do, to take psychology courses. Which makes it nice for me— and nice for her. It's fun to go with someone you know and it's fun to discuss what you've learned, driving back from the classes." And for the most part, she says, that's all they discuss.

"I'd say that what we're doing is *doing* together, not being   11 together," Suzanne says of her Tuesday-doubles friends. "It's mainly a tennis relationship, but we play together well. And I guess we all need to have a couple of playmates."

I agree.   12

My playmate is a shopping friend, a woman of marvelous   13 taste, a woman who knows exactly *where* to buy *what,* and furthermore is a woman who always knows beyond a doubt what one ought to be buying. I don't have the time to keep up with what's new in eyeshadow, hemlines and shoes and whether the smock look is in or finished already. But since (oh, shame!) I care a lot about eyeshadow, hemlines and shoes, and since I don't *want* to wear smocks if the smock look is finished, I'm very glad to have a shopping friend.

14   3. Historical friends. We all have a friend who knew us when . . . maybe way back in Miss Meltzer's second grade, when our family lived in that three-room flat in Brooklyn, when our dad was out of work for seven months, when our brother Allie got in that fight where they had to call the police, when our sister married the endodontist from Yonkers and when, the morning after we lost our virginity, she was the first, the only, friend we told.

15   The years have gone by and we've gone separate ways and we've little in common now, but we're still an intimate part of each other's past. And so whenever we go to Detroit we always go to visit this friend of our girlhood. Who knows how we looked before our teeth were straightened. Who knows how we talked before our voice got unBrooklyned. Who knows what we ate before we learned about artichokes. And who, by her presence, puts us in touch with an earlier part of ourself, a part of ourself it's important never to lose.

16   "What this friend means to me and what I mean to her," says Grace, "is having a sister without sibling rivalry. We know the texture of each other's lives. She remembers my grandmother's cabbage soup. I remember the way her uncle played the piano. There's simply no other friend who remembers those things."

17   4. Crossroads friends. Like historical friends, our crossroads friends are important for *what was*—for the friendship we shared at a crucial, now past, time of life. A time, perhaps, when we roomed in college together; or worked as eager young singles in the Big City together; or went together, as my friend Elizabeth and I did through pregnancy, birth and that scary first year of new motherhood.

18   Crossroads friends forge powerful links, links strong enough to endure with not much more contact than once-a-year letters at Christmas. And out of respect for those crossroads

years, for those dramas and dreams we once shared, we will always be friends.

5. Cross-generational friends. Historical friends and crossroads friends seem to maintain a special kind of intimacy—dormant but always ready to be revived—and though we may rarely meet, whenever we do connect, it's personal and intense. Another kind of intimacy exists in the friendships that form across generations in what one woman calls her daughter-mother and her mother-daughter relationships. [19]

Evelyn's friend is her mother's age—"but I share so much more than I ever could with my mother"—a woman she talks to of music, of books and of life. "What I get from her is the benefit of her experience. What she gets—and enjoys—from me is a youthful perspective. It's a pleasure for both of us." [20]

I have in my own life a precious friend, a woman of 65 who has lived very hard, who is wise, who listens well; who has been where I am and can help me understand it; and who represents not only an ultimate ideal mother to me but also the person I'd like to be when I grow up. [21]

In our daughter role we tend to do more than our share of self-revelation; in our mother role we tend to receive what's revealed. It's another kind of pleasure—playing wise mother to a questing younger person. It's another very lovely kind of friendship. [22]

6. Part-of-a-couple friends. Some of the women we call our friends we never see alone—we see them as part of a couple at couples' parties. And though we share interests in many things and respect each other's views, we aren't moved to deepen the relationship. Whatever the reason, a lack of time or—and this is more likely—a lack of chemistry, our friendship remains in the context of a group. But the fact that our feeling on seeing each other is always, "I'm *so* glad she's here" and the fact that we spend half the evening talking together says that this too, in its own way, counts as a friendship. [23]

(Other part-of-a-couple friends are the friends that came with the marriage, and some of these are friends we could live without. But sometimes, alas, she married our husband's best friend; and sometimes, alas, she *is* our husband's best friend. And so we find ourself dealing with her, somewhat against our will, in a spirit of what I'll call *reluctant* friendship.) [24]

25   7. Men who are friends. I wanted to write just of women friends, but the women I've talked to won't let me—they say I must mention man-woman friendships too. For these friendships can be just as close and as dear as those that we form with women. Listen to Lucy's description of one such friendship:

26   "We've found we have things to talk about that are different from what he talks about with my husband and different from what I talk about with his wife. So sometimes we call on the phone or meet for lunch. There are similar intellectual interests—we always pass on to each other the books that we love—but there's also something tender and caring too."

27   In a couple of crises, Lucy says, "he offered himself, for talking and for helping. And when someone died in his family he wanted me there. The sexual, flirty part of our friendship is very small, but *some*—just enough to make it fun and different." She thinks—and I agree—that the sexual part, though small, is always *some,* is always there when a man and a woman are friends.

28   It's only in the past few years that I've made friends with men, in the sense of a friendship that's *mine,* not just part of two couples. And achieving with them the ease and the trust I've found with women friends has value indeed. Under the dryer at home last week, putting on mascara and rouge, I comfortably sat and talked with a fellow named Peter. Peter, I finally decided, could handle the shock of me minus mascara under the dryer. Because we care for each other. Because we're friends.

29   8. There are medium friends, and pretty good friends, and very good friends indeed, and these friendships are defined by their level of intimacy. And what we'll reveal at each of these levels of intimacy is calibrated with care. We might tell a medium friend, for example, that yesterday we had a fight with our husband. And we might tell a pretty good friend that this fight with our husband made us so mad that we slept on the couch. And we might tell a very good friend that the reason we got so mad in that fight that we slept on the couch had something to do with that girl who works in his office. But it's only to our very best friends that we're willing to tell all, to tell what's going on with that girl in his office.

30   The best of friends, I still believe, totally love and support and trust each other, and bare to each other the secrets of their souls, and run—no questions asked—to help each other, and tell harsh truths to each other when they must be told.

But we needn't agree about everything (only 12-year-old ³¹ girl friends agree about *everything*) to tolerate each other's point of view. To accept without judgment. To give and to take without ever keeping score. And to *be* there, as I am for them and as they are for me, to comfort our sorrows, to celebrate our joys.

BUILDING VOCABULARY

1. Find *antonyms* (words that mean the opposite of given words) for the following entries:
   a. harsh (par. 1)
   b. mutual (par. 8)
   c. crucial (par. 17)
   d. intimacy (par. 29)
   e. tolerate (par. 31)
2. The *derivation* of a word—how it originated and where it came from—can make you more aware of meanings. Your dictionary normally lists abbreviations (for instance, L. for Latin, Fr. for French) for word origins, and sometimes explains fully the way a word came into use. Look up the following words to determine their origins:
   a. psychology (par. 10)
   b. historical (par. 14)
   c. sibling (par. 16)
   d. Christmas (par. 18)
   e. sexual (par. 27)

UNDERSTANDING THE WRITER'S IDEAS

1. What is Viorst's definition of friendship in the first two paragraphs? Does she accept this definition? Why or why not?
2. Name and describe in your own words the types of friends that Viorst mentions in her essay.
3. In what way are "convenience friends" and "special-interest friends" alike? How are "historical friends" and "crossroads friends" alike?
4. What does Viorst mean when she writes, "In our daughter role we tend to do more than our share of self-revelation; in our mother role we tend to receive what's revealed" (par. 22)?

5. How do part-of-a-couple friends who came with the marriage differ from primary part-of-a-couple friends?
6. Does Viorst think that men can be friends for women? Why or why not? What complicates such friendships?
7. For Viorst, who are the best friends?

UNDERSTANDING THE WRITER'S TECHNIQUES

1. Which paragraphs make up the introduction in this essay? How does Viorst organize these paragraphs? Where does she place her thesis sentence?
2. How does the thesis sentence reveal the principles of classification (the questions Viorst asks to produce the various categories) that the author employs in the essay?
3. Does Viorst seem to emphasize each of her categories equally? Is she effective in handling each category? Why or why not? Do you think that men belong in the article as a category? For what reasons?
4. Analyze the importance of illustration in this essay. From what sources does Viorst tend to draw her examples?
5. How do definition and comparison and contrast operate in the essay? Cite specific examples of these techniques.
6. The level of language in this essay tends to be informal at times, reflecting patterns that are as close to conversation as to formal writing. Identify some sentences that seem to resemble informal speech. Why does Viorst try to achieve a conversational style?
7. Which main group in the essay is further broken down into categories?
8. Analyze Viorst's conclusion. How many paragraphs are involved? What strategies does she use? How does she achieve balanced sentence structure (parallelism) in her last lines?

EXPLORING THE WRITER'S IDEAS

1. Do you accept all of Viorst's categories of friendship? Which categories seem the most meaningful to you?
2. Try to think of people you know who fit into the various categories established by Viorst. Can you think of people who might

exist in more than one category? How do you explain this fact? What are the dangers in trying to stereotype people in terms of categories, roles, backgrounds, or functions?

3. Viorst maintains that you can define friends in terms of functions and needs (see paragraph 3 and paragraphs 29 to 31). Would you agree? Why or why not? What principle or principles do you use to classify friends? In fact, *do* you classify friends? For what reasons?

IDEAS FOR WRITING

Guided Writing

Using the classification method, write an essay on a specific group of individuals—for instance, types of friends, types of enemies, types of students, types of teachers, types of politicians, types of dates.

1. Establish your subject in the first paragraph. Also indicate to the reader the principle(s) of classification that you plan to use. (For guidelines look again at the second sentence in paragraph 3 of Viorst's essay.)

2. Start the body of the essay with a single short sentence that introduces categories, as Viorst does in paragraph 4. In the body, use numbers and category headings ("Convenience friends" . . . "Special-interest friends") to separate groups.

3. Try to achieve a balance in the presentation of information on each category. Define each type and provide appropriate examples.

4. If helpful, use comparison and contrast to indicate from time to time the similarities and differences among groups. Try to avoid too much overlapping of groups, since this is harmful to the classification process.

5. Employ the personal "I" and other conversational techniques to achieve an informal style.

6. Return to your principle(s) of classification and amplify this feature in your conclusion. If you want, make a value judgment, as Viorst does, about which type of person in your classification scheme is the most significant.

More Writing Projects

1. As journal practice, classify varieties of show business comedians, singers, talk-show hosts, star athletes, or the like.
2. In a paragraph, use division and (or) classification to explain the various roles that you must play as a friend.
3. Ask each student in your class to explain what he or she means by the term "friendship." List all responses and then divide the list into at least three categories. Using your notes, write a classification essay reporting your findings.

The Three New Yorks

E. B. White

E. B. White, whose frequently used book *The Elements of Style* is well known to college composition students, here classifies "The Three New Yorks." Although the selection is an excerpt from his book *Here Is New York* (1949), the descriptive illustrations remain remarkably fresh after more than forty years. Look closely at the way White clearly defines his categories of classification, then skillfully blends them to create a vivid sense of the whole city.

Words to Watch

locusts (par. 1)   migratory grasshoppers that travel in swarms, stripping vegetation as they pass over the land

disposition (par. 1)   temperament; way of acting

deportment (par. 1)   the way in which a person carries himself or herself

tidal (par. 1)   coming in wavelike motions

continuity (par. 1)   uninterrupted flow of events

slum (par. 1)   a highly congested residential area marked by unsanitary buildings, poverty, and social disorder

indignity (par. 1)   humiliating treatment

vitality (par. 2)   lively and animated character

gloaming (par. 2)   a poetic term for "twilight"

ramparts (par. 2)   high, broad structures guarding a building

negligently (par. 2)   nonchalantly; neglectfully

loiterer (par. 2)   a person who hangs around aimlessly

spewing (par. 2)   coming in a flood or gush

rover (par. 2)   wanderer; roamer

There are roughly three New Yorks. There is, first, the New York 1 of the man or woman who was born here, who takes the city for granted and accepts its size and its turbulence as natural and inevitable. Second, there is the New York of the commuter—the city that is devoured by locusts each day and spat out each night. Third, there is the New York of the person who was born somewhere else and came to New York in quest of something. Of these three trembling cities the greatest is the last—the city of final destination, the city that is a goal. It is this third city that accounts for New York's high- strung disposition, its poetical deportment, its dedication to the arts, and its incomparable achievements. Commuters give the city its tidal restlessness; natives give it solidity and continuity; but the settlers give it passion. And whether it is a farmer arriving from Italy to set up a small grocery store in a slum, or a young girl arriving from a small town in Mississippi to escape the indignity of being observed by her neighbors, or a boy arriving from the Corn Belt with a manuscript in his suitcase and a pain in his heart, it makes no difference; each embraces New York with the intense excitement of first love, each absorbs New York with the fresh eyes of an adventurer, each generates heat and light to dwarf the Consolidated Edison Company.

2   The commuter is the queerest bird of all. The suburb he inhabits has no essential vitality of its own and is a mere roost where he comes at day's end to go to sleep. Except in rare cases, the man who lives in Mamaroneck or Little Neck or Teaneck, and works in New York, discovers nothing much about the city except the time of arrival and departure of trains and buses, and the path to a quick lunch. He is deskbound, and has never, idly roaming in the gloaming, stumbled suddenly on Belvedere Tower in the Park, seen the ramparts rise sheer from the water of the pond, and the boys along the shore fishing for minnows, girls stretched out negligently on the shelves of the rocks; he has never come suddenly on anything at all in New York as a loiterer, because he has had no time between trains. He has fished in Manhattan's wallet and dug out coins, but has never listened to Manhattan's breathing, never awakened to its morning, never dropped off to sleep in its night. About 400,000 men and women come charging onto the Island each week-day morning, out of the mouths of tubes and tunnels. Not many among them have ever spent a drowsy afternoon in the great rustling oaken silence of the reading room of the Public Library, with the book elevator (like an old water wheel) spewing out books onto the trays. They tend their furnaces in Westchester and in Jersey, but have never seen the furnaces of the Bowery, the fires that burn in oil drums on zero winter nights. They may work in the financial district downtown and never

see the extravagant plantings of Rockefeller Center—the daf-
fodils and grape hyacinths and birches of the flags trimmed to
the wind on a fine morning in spring. Or they may work in a
midtown office and may let a whole year swing round without
sighting Governor's Island from the sea wall. The commuter
dies with tremendous mileage to his credit, but he is no rover.
His entrances and exits are more devious than those in a
prairie-dog village; and he calmly plays bridge while his train
is buried in the mud at the bottom of the East River. The Long
Island Rail Road alone carried forty million commuters last
year; but many of them were the same fellow retracing his
steps.

    The terrain of New York is such that a resident sometimes ₃
travels farther, in the end, than a commuter. The journey of the
composer Irving Berlin from Cherry Street in the lower East Side
to an apartment uptown was through an alley and was only three
or four miles in length; but it was like going three times around
the world.

BUILDING VOCABULARY

1. Underline the numerous references in this essay to buildings,
   people, and areas in and around New York City and identify
   them. If necessary, consult a guidebook, map, or history of New
   York City for help.
2. Write *synonyms* (words that mean the same) for each of these
   words in the essay. Use a dictionary if necessary.
   a. turbulence (par. 1)
   b. inevitable (par. 1)
   c. quest (par. 1)
   d. high-strung (par. 1)
   e. incomparable (par. 1)
   f essential (par. 2)
   g. deskbound (par. 2)
   h. drowsy (par. 2)
   i. extravagant (par. 2)
   j. devious (par. 2)

UNDERSTANDING THE WRITER'S IDEAS

1. What are the three New Yorks?
2. What single-word designation does E. B. White assign to each of the three types of New Yorkers? Match up each of the three New Yorks you identified in the first question with each of the three types of New Yorkers.
3. For what reasons do people born elsewhere come to New York to live? What three illustrations of such people does White describe? What is the young girl's indignity? What is the occupation or hope of the boy from the Corn Belt? Why might he have "a pain in his heart"?
4. What does each type of New Yorker give to the city?
5. What is White's attitude toward the suburbs? What key phrases reveal this attitude?
6. What are some of the things commuters miss about New York by dashing in and out of the city? What does White ironically suggest will be the commuter's final fate?
7. Are we to take literally White's conclusion that "many of them are the same fellow retracing his steps"? Why or why not?
8. Explain the sentence "The terrain of New York is such that a resident sometimes travels farther, in the end, than a commuter." Be aware that White is using language figuratively.
9. The author tells of composer Irving Berlin's journey through an alley. He is referring to "Tin Pan Alley." Identify this place.

UNDERSTANDING THE WRITER'S TECHNIQUES

1. In this essay what is the thesis? Where is it? Is it developed fully?
2. What is the purpose of classification in this essay? What is the basis of the classification White uses? What key words at the beginning of paragraph 1 direct your attention to each category discussed? How do these key words contrast in tone with the descriptions in the first few sentences? What sort of rhythm is established?
3. White vividly *personifies* (see Glossary) New York City in paragraph 1. List and explain the effects of these personifications. Where else does he personify?

4. Refer to your answers to question 2 in the Building Vocabulary section. Are the literal meanings of those words appropriate to White's three types of New Yorkers? Defend your answer. Figuratively, what does each term make you think of? How do the figurative meanings enhance the essay?
5. How does White use *illustration* in this essay? Where does he use it most effectively?
6. What is the function of *negation* (see page 222) in the first part of paragraph 2? What is the *implied contrast* in this paragraph?
7. How is White's attitude toward New York reflected in the *tone* (see Glossary) of this essay?
8. White makes widespread use of *metaphor* (see Glossary) in this essay. How does his use of metaphor affect the tone of the essay? State in your own words the meaning of each of the following metaphors:
   a. . . . the city that is devoured by locusts each day and spat out each night (par. 1)
   b. The commuter is the queerest bird of all. (par. 2)
   c. a mere roost (par. 2)
   d. idly roaming in the gloaming (par. 2)
   e. He has fished in Manhattan's wallet and dug out coins, but he has never listened to Manhattan's breathing. (par. 2)
   f. the great rustling oaken silence (par. 2)
9. Among all the metaphors, White uses just one simile (see Glossary). What is it? What is the effect of placing it where he did?

EXPLORING THE WRITER'S IDEAS

1. At the beginning of the essay, E. B. White states that New York's "turbulence" is considered "natural and inevitable" by its native residents. But such a condition is true for any large city. If you live in a large city, or if you have ever visited one, what are some examples of its turbulence? Do you think it is always a good idea to accept the disorder of the place where you live? How can such acceptance be a positive attitude? How can it be negative? How do you deal with disruptions in your environment?
2. White writes of "a young girl arriving from a small town in Mississippi to escape the indignity of being observed by her neigh-

bors." Tell in your own words what might cause her indignity. How can neighbors bring about such a condition?

3. Some people feel that the anonymity of a big city like New York makes it easier just to "be yourself" without having to worry about what others might say. Others feel such anonymity creates a terrible feeling of impersonality. Discuss the advantages and disadvantages of each attitude.

4. Do you agree that the suburbs have "no essential vitality"? Explain your response by referring to suburbs you have visited, have read about, or have inhabited.

5. White claims that those who choose to leave their homes and who come to live in New York give the place a special vitality. Do you know any people who chose to leave their places of birth to live in a large city like New York? Why did they move? How have things gone for them since they began living in the city? Have you noticed any changes? For what reasons do people leave one place to live in another? When have you moved from place to place? Why?

IDEAS FOR WRITING

Guided Writing

Organize a classification essay around the city or town in which you live.

1. Begin with a simple direct thesis statement that tells the reader how many categories of classification you will consider.

2. Briefly outline the different categories. Indicate each with a key organizational word or phrase.

3. Indicate which category is the most important. Tell why.

4. Develop this category with at least three vivid illustrations.

5. Define one of the categories through both negation and an implied contrast to another category.

6. Use figurative language (metaphors, similes, personification) throughout your essay.

7. Use specific name or place references.

8. End your essay with a brief factual narrative that gives the reader a feel for your town or city.

More Writing Projects

1. Use classification in a journal entry to capture at least three ways of viewing your college.
2. Write a classification paragraph on the suburbs or the country.
3. Select a cultural group and classify in an essay various characteristics common to that group. Be careful to avoid stereotyping.

The Scheme of Color

Mary Mebane

In this celebration of the beauty of black-skinned women, Mary Mebane classifies African-American attitudes toward color. Using examples from her days as a college freshman, the author classifies her schoolmates and their families according to social class and, within that group, by skin color. Her categories illustrate the complex and usually unspoken rules she learned through observation of her college community and later her friends and colleagues. Although her examples lead us to the conclusion that racism ran deep within the community, Mebane also suggests that the social categories ironically created a group of highly skilled black women who moved into an integrated workplace in the 1970s. The post-1945 generation, she concludes, has recognized the limitations of this classification system while their parents remain encumbered by its limitations.

Words to Watch

pinnacle (par. 1)   peak; summit

recourse (par. 2)   turning to for help

affirmative (par. 2)   positive; supportive

fluke (par. 3)   accident; mistake

commiserating (par. 7)   sharing unhappiness

stymied (par. 11)   blocked

indoctrinated (par. 15)   taught to accept without questioning

zealous (par. 16)   devoted to strongly

doggedly (par. 17)   stubbornly

staunch (par. 20)   very firm

fervent (par. 20)   passionate

1   During my first week of classes as a freshman, I was stopped one day in the hall by the chairman's wife, who was indistinguishable in color from a white woman. She wanted to see me, she said.

2   This woman had no official position on the faculty, except that she was an instructor in English; nevertheless, her summons had to be obeyed. In the segregated world there were (and remain) gross abuses of authority because those at the pinnacle, and even their spouses, felt that the people "under" them had no

recourse except to submit—and they were right, except that sometimes a black who got sick and tired of it would go to the whites and complain. This course of action was severely condemned by the blacks, but an interesting thing happened—such action always got positive results. Power was thought of in negative terms: I can deny someone something, I can strike at someone who can't strike back, I can ride someone down; that proves I am powerful. The concept of power as a force for good, for affirmative response to people or situations, was not in evidence.

When I went to her office, she greeted me with a big smile. 3 "You know," she said, "you made the highest mark on the verbal part of the examination." She was referring to the examination that the entire freshman class took upon entering the college. I looked at her but I didn't feel warmth, for in spite of her smile her eyes and tone of voice were saying, "How could this black-skinned girl score higher on the verbal than some of the students who've had more advantages than she? It must be some sort of fluke. Let me talk to her." I felt it, but I managed to smile my thanks and back off. For here at North Carolina College at Durham, as it had been since the beginning, social class and color were the primary criteria used in determining status on the campus.

First came the children of doctors, lawyers, and college 4 teachers. Next came the children of public-school teachers, businessmen, and anybody else who had access to more money than the poor black working class. After that came the bulk of the student population, the children of the working class, most of whom were the first in their families to go beyond high school. The attitude toward them was: You're here because we need the numbers, but in all other things defer to your betters.

The faculty assumed that light-skinned students were more 5 intelligent, and they were always a bit nonplussed when a dark-skinned student did well, especially if she was a girl. They had reason to be appalled when they discovered that I planned to do not only well but better than my light-skinned peers.

I don't know whether African men recently transported to 6 the New World considered themselves handsome or, more important, whether they considered African women beautiful in comparison with Native American Indian women or immigrant European women. It is a question that I have never heard raised or seen research on. If African men considered African women beautiful, just when their shift in interest away from black black women occurred might prove to be an interesting topic for researchers. But one thing I know for sure: by the twentieth century, really black skin on a woman was considered ugly in this country. This was particularly true among those who were exposed to college.

7   Hazel, who was light brown, used to say to me, "You are *dark,* but not *too* dark." The saved commiserating with the damned. I had the feeling that if nature had painted one more brushstroke on me, I'd have had to kill myself.

8   Black skin was to be disguised at all costs. Since a black face is rather hard to disguise, many women took refuge in ludicrous makeup. Mrs. Burry, one of my teachers in elementary school, used white face powder. But she neglected to powder her neck and arms, and even the black on her face gleamed through the white, giving her an eerie appearance. But she did the best she could.

9   I observed all through elementary and high school that for various entertainments the girls were placed on the stage in order of color. And very black ones didn't get into the front row. If they were past caramel-brown, to the back row they would go. And nobody questioned the justice of these decisions—neither the students nor the teachers.

10   One of the teachers at Wildwood School, who was from the Deep South and was just as black as she could be, had been a strict enforcer of these standards. That was another irony—that someone who had been judged outside the realm of beauty herself because of her skin tones should have adopted them so wholeheartedly and applied them herself without question.

11   One girl stymied that teacher, though. Ruby, a black cherry of a girl, not only got off the back row but off the front row as well, to stand alone at stage center. She could outsing, outdance, and outdeclaim everyone else, and talent proved triumphant over pigmentation. But the May Queen and her Court (and in high school, Miss Wildwood) were always chosen from among the lighter ones.

12   When I was a freshman in high school, it became clear that a light-skinned sophomore girl named Rose was going to get the "best girl scholar" prize for the next three years, and there was

nothing I could do about it, even though I knew I was the better. Rose was caramel-colored and had shoulder-length hair. She was highly favored by the science and math teacher, who figured the averages. I wasn't. There was only one prize. Therefore, Rose would get it until she graduated. I was one year behind her, and I would not get it until after she graduated.

To be held in such low esteem was painful. It was difficult 13 not to feel that I had been cheated out of the medal, which I felt that, in a fair competition, I perhaps would have won. Being unable to protest or do anything about it was a traumatic experience for me. From then on I instinctively tended to avoid the college-exposed dark-skinned male, knowing that when he looked at me he saw himself and, most of the time, his mother and sister as well, and since he had rejected his blackness, he had rejected theirs and mine.

Oddly enough, the lighter-skinned black male did not seem 14 to feel so much prejudice toward the black black woman. It was no accident, I felt, that Mr. Harrison, the eighth-grade teacher, who was reddish-yellow himself, once protested to the science and math teacher about the fact that he always assigned sweeping duties to Doris and Ruby Lee, two black black girls. Mr. Harrison said to them one day, right in the other teacher's presence, "You must be some bad girls. Every day I come down here ya'll are sweeping." The science and math teacher got the point and didn't ask them to sweep anymore.

Uneducated black males, too, sometimes related very well 15 to the black black woman. They had been less firmly indoctrinated by the white society around them and were more securely rooted in their own culture.

Because of the stigma attached to having dark skin, a black 16 black woman had to do many things to find a place for herself. One possibility was to attach herself to a light-skinned woman, hoping that some of the magic would rub off on her. A second was to make herself sexually available, hoping to attract a mate. Third, she could resign herself to a more chaste life-style—either (for the professional woman) teaching and work in established churches or (for the uneducated woman) domestic work and zealous service in the Holy and Sanctified churches.

Even as a young girl, Lucy had chosen the first route. Lucy 17 was short, skinny, short-haired, and black black, and thus unacceptable. So she made her choice. She selected Patricia, the light-est-skinned girl in the school, as her friend, and followed her around. Patricia and her friends barely tolerated Lucy, but Lucy smiled and doggedly hung on, hoping that some who noticed Patricia might notice her, too. Though I felt shame for her behavior, even then I understood.

18 As is often the case of the victim agreeing with and adopt-ing the attitudes of the oppressor, so I have seen it with black black women. I have seen them adopt the oppressor's attitude that they are nothing but "sex machines," and their supposedly superior sexual performance becomes their sole reason for being and for esteeming themselves. Such women learn early that in order to make themselves attractive to men they have somehow to shift the emphasis from physical beauty to some other area— usually sexual performance. Their constant talk is of their desir-ability and their ability to gratify a man sexually.

19 I knew two such women well—both of them black black. To hear their endless talk of sexual conquests was very sad. I have never seen the category that these women fall into described anywhere. It is not that of promiscuity or nymphomania. It is the category of total self-rejection: "Since I am black, I am ugly, I am nobody. I will perform on the level that they have assigned to me." Such women are the pitiful results of what not only white America but also, and more important, black America has done to them.

20 Some, not taking the sexuality route but still accepting black society's view of their worthlessness, swing all the way across to in-tense religiosity. Some are staunch, fervent workers in the more tra-ditional Southern churches—Baptist and Methodist—and others are leaders and ministers in the lower-status, more evangelical Ho-liness sects.

21 Another avenue open to the black black woman is excel-lence in a career. Since in the South the field most accessible to such women is education, a great many of them prepared to be-come teachers. But here, too, the black black woman had prob-lems. Grades weren't given to her lightly in school, nor were pro-motions on the job. Consequently, she had to prepare especially well. She had to pass examinations with flying colors or be left be-hind; she knew that she would receive no special consideration. She had to be overqualified for a job because otherwise she didn't stand a chance of getting it—and she was competing only with

other blacks. She had to have something to back her up: not charm, not personality—but training.

The black black woman's training would pay off in the 22 1970s. With the arrival of integration the black black woman would find, paradoxically enough, that her skin color in an integrated situation was not the handicap it had been in an all-black situation. But it wasn't until the middle and late 1960s, when the post-1945 generation of black males arrived on college campuses, that I noticed any change in the situation at all. *He* wore an afro and *she* wore an afro, and sometimes the only way you could tell them apart was when his afro was taller than hers. Black had become beautiful, and the really black girl was often selected as queen of various campus activities. It was then that the dread I felt at dealing with the college-educated black male began to ease. Even now, though, when I have occasion to engage in any type of transaction with a college-educated black man, I gauge his age. If I guess he was born after 1945, I feel confident that the transaction will turn out all right. If he probably was born before 1945, my stomach tightens, I find myself taking shallow breaths, and I try to state my business and escape as soon as possible.

BUILDING VOCABULARY

1. Mebane uses adjectives to establish the color differences that are critical to her classification. Locate descriptions of skin color that she uses to separate her women in categories.
2. Using a thesaurus, find a synonym for each of the words below:
   a. nonplussed
   b. doggedly
   c. staunch
   d. fervent
   e. recourse
   f. status
   g. ludicrous
   h. eerie
   i. stymied
   j. pigmentation
   k. traumatic
   l. indoctrinated
   m. oppressor

n. evangelical
o. paradoxically
p. transaction

UNDERSTANDING THE WRITER'S IDEAS

1. According to Mebane, what is the chief basis upon which black women were classified in her college? Does she think this system was valid? What evidence is there in the essay to support your answer?
2. What differences in attitudes between men and women does the author observe toward skin color? Why does she imply that this is so?
3. Who do the faculty assume are the more intelligent students? Why? How do they demonstrate their attitudes?
4. Who is more likely to defend "black black" women: other black women on the faculty, white teachers, or black men? How do you know?
5. What is the conflict between Rose and the author? How is it resolved? How does the author feel about this conflict?
6. What does the author say happens to women who feel they have been categorized as "unacceptable" because of their skin color? Why does talk of sexual conquests make the author "sad" (par. 19)?
7. Why do some women "swing all the way across to intense religiosity" (par. 20)? What does the author mean by this classification of women?
8. In paragraph 22, the author refers to "the middle and late 1960s" as a period of change for black women. What political and social events is she alluding to in this paragraph? In what ways does she argue that men and women born after 1945 classify women differently from earlier generations?

UNDERSTANDING THE WRITER'S TECHNIQUES

1. What is the thesis of the essay? Where is it located?
2. Create an outline of the classification system Mebane says existed in her college. Consider color and gender in your list. List the names of students who illustrate each category.

3. How would you characterize the *tone* (see Glossary) of Mebane's essay? Find several examples from the essay to support your answer.

4. Who seems to be the intended audience for Mebane's essay? Is she speaking largely to black or white readers? to men or women? Support your answer with references to the essay.

5. How does the repetition of color words, like "black black," help to establish the author's system of classification? How do phrases like "a black cherry of a girl" in paragraph 11 suggest that Mebane disputes the validity of the system of classification used in the college.

6. Look closely at the transitional devices the author uses. Make a list of at least ten words or phrases used in the essay.

7. Why does the writer repeat phrases like "black black"?

8. Where does the author use *irony* (see Glossary) as a device?

9. How effective is the use of first-person point of view in this essay? Would the essay have been more effective if the author had chosen to use third person? Explain.

10. What is the author's purpose in identifying this system of classifying black women? How do you know?

11. How are the first paragraph and the last paragraph connected? Consider the author's relationship to authority in each paragraph.

EXPLORING THE WRITER'S IDEAS

1. Through her examples of the classification of black women on the basis of skin color, the author argues that blacks rather than whites generate causes of oppression. Does she defend her position adequately? How does her classification of skin color compare with that of Rodriguez in "Complexion" (pages 248–251)?

2. What motives does the author suggest are behind this classification of women by "social class and color"? What can you *infer* are the causes?

3. Mebane wrote this essay in 1981. Would she find a different situation if she entered college today? Explain.

4. What is the value of this classification system to college outsiders? How is it different for insiders? Does the system attempt to cover *all* members of the college community or does it generalize?

IDEAS FOR WRITING

Guided Writing

Write a classification of students in your college that divides them into at least three categories. Consider this opening:

Students at _____ College fall into three categories: the _____, the _____ and the _____.

1. Begin with a generalization about how administrators at your school view students, or how a new freshman might see the student body. Decide on a tone: humorous, serious, ironic, informative.
2. Create three categories and give each group a distinctive name.
3. Devote at least two paragraphs to each category. Arrange your essay in order of ascending importance of categories.
4. Use specific examples of students to illustrate each type.
5. Use transitional devices between each paragraph.
6. At the end of the essay, evaluate the classification system. Is it accurate or is it based on stereotypes?

More Writing Projects

1. For a journal entry, characterize three students you know according to their clothing. Draw conclusions about their academic potential on the basis of their wardrobe. Be inventive!
2. The next time you go to the movies, look closely at the actresses. Then write a paragraph classifying women according to Hollywood categories: ingenue, femme fatale, oppressed spouse, mysterious foreigner, and so on.
3. In an essay using classification, write about different categories of prejudice that exist in American society. You might consider prejudice against AIDS sufferers, against new immigrants, against the elderly when they apply for jobs, and so forth. Use personal experience, or material from your reading.

How Do We Find the Student in a World of Academic Gymnasts and Worker Ants?

James T. Baker

As you look around your classrooms, school cafeteria, lecture halls, or gymnasium, perhaps you will recognize representatives of the types of students that James Baker classifies in this witty, wry essay. The author enhances his unique categories by using description, definition, and colloquial language, which help make his deliberate stereotypes come alive.

Words to Watch

musings (par. 3)   dreamy, abstract thoughts

sabbatical (par. 3)   a paid leave from a job earned after a certain period of time

malaise (par. 3)   uneasiness; feelings of restlessness

impaired (par. 3)   made less effective

clones (par. 4)   exact biological replicas, asexually produced

recuperate (par. 5)   to undergo recovery from an illness

esoteric (par. 7)   understood by a limited group with special knowledge

primeval (par. 7)   primitive; relating to the earliest ages

mundane (par. 8)   ordinary

jaded (par. 20)   exhausted; bored by something from overexposure to it

Anatole France once wrote that "the whole art of teaching is only 1 the art of awakening the natural curiosity of young minds." I fully agree, except I have to wonder if, by using the word "only," he thought that the art of awakening such natural curiosity was an easy job. For me, it never has been—sometimes exciting, always challenging, but definitely not easy.

Robert M. Hutchins used to say that a good education pre- 2 pares students to go on educating themselves throughout their lives. A fine definition, to be sure, but it has at times made me doubt that my own students, who seem only too eager to graduate so they can lay down their books forever, are receiving a good education.

3   But then maybe these are merely the pessimistic musings of someone suffering from battle fatigue. I have almost qualified for my second sabbatical leave, and I am scratching a severe case of the seven-year itch. About the only power my malaise has not impaired is my eye for spotting certain "types" of students. In fact, as the rest of me declines, my eye seems to grow more acute.

4   Has anyone else noticed that the very same students people college classrooms year after year? Has anyone else found the same bodies, faces, personalities returning semester after semester? Forgive me for violating my students' individual "personhoods," but reality makes it so tempting to see them as types. Doubtless you will recognize at least some of them. They have twins, or perhaps clones, on your campus, too.

5   There is the eternal Good Time Charlie (or Charlene), who makes every party on and off the campus, who by November of his freshman year has worked his face into a case of terminal acne, who misses every set of examinations because of "mono," who finally burns himself out physically and mentally by the age of 19 and drops out to go home and recuperate, and who returns at 20 after a long talk with Dad to major in accounting.

6   There is the Young General Patton, the one who comes to college on an R.O.T.C. scholarship and for a year twirls his rifle at basketball games while loudly sniffing out pinko professors, who at midpoint takes a sudden but predictable, radical swing from far right to far left, who grows a beard and moves in with a girl who refuses to shave her legs, who then makes the just as predictable, radical swing back to the right and ends up preaching fundamentalist sermons on the steps of the student union while the Good Time Charlies and Charlenes jeer.

7   There is the Egghead, the campus intellectual who shakes up his fellow students—and even a professor or two—with references to esoteric formulas and obscure Bulgarian poets, who is recognized by friend and foe alike as a promising young academic, someday to be a professional scholar, who disappears every summer for six weeks ostensibly to search for primeval human remains in Colorado caves, and who at 37 is shot dead by Arab terrorists while on a mission for the C.I.A.

8   There is the Performer—the music or theater major, the rock or folk singer—who spends all of his or her time working up an act, who gives barely a nod to mundane subjects like histo-

ry, sociology, or physics, who dreams only of the day he or she will be on stage full time, praised by critics, cheered by audiences, who ends up either pregnant or responsible for a pregnancy and at 30 is either an insurance salesman or a housewife with a very lush garden.

There is the Jock, of course—the every-afternoon intramural champ, smelling of liniment and Brut, with bulging calves and a blue-eyed twinkle, the subject of untold numbers of female fantasies, the walking personification of he-manism—who upon graduation is granted managerial rank by a California bank because of his golden tan and low golf score, who is seen five years later buying the drinks at a San Francisco gay bar.   9

There is the Academic Gymnast—the guy or gal who sees college as an obstacle course, as so many stumbling blocks in the way of a great career or a perfect marriage—who strains every moment to finish and be done with "this place" forever, who toward the end of the junior year begins to slow down, to grow quieter and less eager to leave, who attends summer school, but never quite finishes those last six hours, who never leaves "this place," and who at 40 is still working at the campus laundry, still here, still a student.   10

There is the Medal Hound, the student who comes to college not to learn or expand any intellectual horizons but simply to win honors—medals, cups, plates, ribbons, scrolls—who is here because this is the best place to win the most the fastest, who plasticizes and mounts on his wall every certificate of excellence he wins, who at 39 will be a colonel in the U.S. Army and at 55 Secretary of something or other in a conservative Administration in Washington.   11

There is the Worker Ant, the student (loosely rendered) who takes 21 hours a semester and works 49 hours a week at the local car wash, who sleeps only on Sundays and during classes, who will somehow graduate on time and be the owner of his own vending-machine company at 30 and be dead of a heart attack at 40, and who will be remembered for the words chiseled on his tombstone: 12

All This Was Accomplished Without Ever Having So Much as Darkened The Door Of A Library   13

There is the Lost Soul, the sad kid who is in college only because teachers, parents, and society at large said so, who hasn't a career in mind or a dream to follow, who hasn't a clue, who heads home every Friday afternoon to spend the weekend cruising the local Dairee-Freeze, who at 50 will have done all his   14 teachers, parents, and society said to do, still without a career in mind or a dream to follow or a clue.

15   There is also the Saved Soul—the young woman who has received, through the ministry of one Gospel freak or another, a Holy Calling to save the world, or at least some special part of it—who majors in Russian studies so that she can be caught smuggling Bibles into the Soviet Union and be sent to Siberia where she can preach to souls imprisoned by the Agents of Satan in the Gulag Archipelago.

16   Then, finally, there is the Happy Child, who comes to college to find a husband or wife—and finds one—and there is the Determined Child, who comes to get a degree—and gets one.

17   Enough said.

18   All of which, I suppose, should make me throw up my hands in despair and say that education, like youth and love, is wasted on the young. Not quite.

19   For there does come along, on occasion, that one of a hundred or so who is maybe at first a bit lost, certainly puzzled; who may well start out a Good Timer, an Egghead, a Performer, a Jock, a Medal Hound, a Gymnast, a Worker Ant; who may indeed have trouble settling on a major, who will be distressed by what sometimes passes for education, who might even be a temporary dropout; but who has a vital capacity for growth and is able to fall in love with learning, who acquires a taste for intellectual pleasure, who becomes in the finest sense of the word a Student.

20   This is the one who keeps the most jaded of us going back to class after class, and he or she must be oh-so-carefully cultivated. He or she must be artfully awakened, given the tools needed to continue learning for a lifetime, and let grow at whatever pace and in whatever direction nature dictates.

21   For I try always to remember that this student is me, my continuing self, my immortality. This person is my only hope that my own search for Truth will continue after me, on and on, forever.

BUILDING VOCABULARY

1. Explain these *colloquialisms* (see Glossary) in Baker's essay:
   a. I am scratching a severe case of the seven-year itch (par. 3)
   b. someone suffering from battle fatigue (par. 3)

   c. worked his face into a case of terminal acne (par. 5)

   d. burns himself out physically and mentally (par. 5)

   e. loudly sniffing out pinko professors (par. 6)

   f. working up an act (par. 8)

   g. gives barely a nod (par. 8)

   h. the walking personification of he-manism (par. 9)

   i. to spend the weekend cruising the local Dairee-Freeze (par. 14)

   j. he or she must be oh-so-carefully cultivated (par. 20)

2. Identify these references:

   a. R.O.T.C. (par. 6)

   b. C.I.A. (par. 7)

   c. Brut (par. 9)

   d. Dairee-Freeze (par. 14)

   e. Gospel freak (par. 15)

   f. Agents of Satan (par. 15)

   g. Gulag Archipelago (par. 15)

UNDERSTANDING THE WRITER'S IDEAS

1. In common language, describe the various categories of college students that Baker names.

2. Who is Anatole France? What process is described in the quotation from him? Why does Baker cite it at the beginning of the essay? What is his attitude toward France's idea?

3. For how long has Baker been teaching? What is his attitude toward his work?

4. About what age do you think Baker is? Why? Explain the meaning of the sentence: "In fact, as the rest of me declines, my eye seems to grow more acute" (par. 3).

5. Choose three of Baker's categories and paraphrase each description and meaning in a serious way.

6. What does Baker feel, overall, is the contemporary college student's attitude toward studying and receiving an education? How does it differ from Baker's own attitude toward these things?

7. Although Baker's classification may seem a bit pessimistic, he refuses to "throw up . . . [his] hands in despair" (par. 18). Why?

8. Describe the characteristics that are embodied in the category of *Student*. To whom does Baker compare the "true" Student? Why?

UNDERSTANDING THE WRITER'S TECHNIQUES

1. What is Baker's thesis in this essay? Does he state it directly or not? What, in your own words, is his purpose?
2. In this essay Baker deliberately creates, rather than avoids, stereotypes. He does so to establish exaggerated representatives of types. Why?

    For paragraphs 5 to 16, prepare a paragraph-by-paragraph outline of the main groups of students classified. For each, include the following information:

    a. type represented by the stereotype
    b. motivation of type for being a student
    c. main activity as a student
    d. condition in which the type ends up

3. This article was published in *The Chronicle of Higher Education,* a weekly newspaper for college and university educators and administrators. How do you think this audience influenced Baker's analysis of types of students? His tone and language?
4. What is Baker's tone in the essay? Give specific examples. In general, how would you characterize his attitude toward the contemporary college student? Why? Does his attitude or tone undergo any shifts in the essay? Explain.
5. Why does Baker use the term "personhoods" in paragraph 4? What attitude, about what subject, does he convey in his use of that word?
6. Why does the author capitalize the names he gives to the various categories of students? Why does he capitalize the word "Truth" in the last sentence?
7. How does Baker use definition in this essay? What purpose does it serve?
8. How does Baker use description to enhance his analysis in this essay?
9. In this essay, what is the role of *process analysis?* (Process analysis, discussed in the next chapter, is telling how something is done or proceeds; see pages 296–297.) Look especially at Baker's descriptions of each type of student. How does process analysis figure into the title of the essay?

10. What is the purpose of the one-sentence paragraph 13? Why does Baker set it aside from paragraph 12, since it is a logical conclusion to that paragraph? Why does he use a two-word sentence as the complete paragraph 17? In what ways do these words signal the beginning of the essay's conclusion?

EXPLORING THE WRITER'S IDEAS

1. Do you think Baker's classifications in this essay are fair? Are they representative of the whole spectrum of students? How closely do they mirror the student population at your school? The article was written in 1982: How well have Baker's classifications held up to the present conditions?
2. Into which category (or categories) would you place yourself? Why?
3. Based on your reaction to and understanding of this article, would you like to have Baker as your professor? Why or why not?

IDEAS FOR WRITING

Guided Writing

Write a classification of at least three "types" in a situation with which you are familiar, other than school—a certain job, social event, sport, or some such situation.

1. Begin your essay with a reference, direct or indirect, to what some well-known writer or expert said about this situation.
2. Identify your role in relation to the situation described.
3. Write about your attitude toward the particular situation and why you are less than thrilled about it at present.
4. Make sure you involve the reader as someone who would be familiar with the situation and activities described.
5. Divide your essay into exaggerated or stereotyped categories which you feel represent almost the complete range of types in these situations. In your categorization, be sure to include motivations, activities, and results for each type.
6. Use description to make your categories vivid.

7. Use satire and a bit of gentle cynicism as part of your description.
8. Select a lively title.
9. In the conclusion, identify another type that you consider the "purest" or "most truthful" representative of persons in this situation. Either by comparison with yourself or by some other means, explain why you like this type best.

More Writing Projects

1. In your journal, write your own classification of three college "types." Your entry can be serious or humorous.
2. In a 250-word paragraph, classify types of college dates.
3. Look in current magazines for advertisements directed at men or women, or both. Write an essay in which you classify current advertisements according to some logical scheme. Limit your essay to three to five categories.

SUMMING UP: CHAPTER 8

1. Write an essay that classifies the readings in this book by a method other than *exposition* (detailed explanation). As you discuss each category, be sure to give examples that explain why particular readings fall into that classification.
2. Reread Judith Viorst's "Friends, Good Friends—And Such Good Friends" in this chapter. Then, write down the names of several of your closest friends. Keep a journal for one week in which you list what you did, how you felt, and what you talked about with each of these friends. Write an essay that classifies these friends into three categories. Use entries from your journal to support your method of classification.
3. With the class divided into four groups, assemble a guide to the city, town, or neighborhood surrounding your campus. Each group should be responsible for one category of information: types of people; types of places; types of entertainment; types of services; and so on. Be sure that each category is covered in detail; you may refer to E. B. White's essay "The Three New Yorks" as a model. After each group has completed its work, choose someone to present findings to the class. Now write your own guide to the areas based on the classifications discussed.

4. Although both Viorst's and Mebane's essays are classifications, they also present new ways of looking at a group of people. Viorst has an underlying message about how to choose friends, while Mebane has a warning about how not to see color. Write a classification essay entitled "What to Avoid When _____." Fill in the blank with an activity that would involve a decision-making process on the part of the reader.

5. Many of the essays in this book deal with crucial experiences in the various authors' lives. Among others, Hughes, Wong, and Atwood tell us of coming-of-age experiences; Selzer writes of his special insights into human nature; and Ehrlich and Thomas describe their relationships to the world of nature. Try writing an essay that classifies the personal essays that you have read in this anthology.

CHAPTER 9

Process Analysis

WHAT IS PROCESS ANALYSIS?

Process analysis explains to a reader how something is done, how something works, or how something occurs. Like classification, it is a form of analysis, or taking apart a process in order better to understand how it functions. This kind of writing is often called *expository* because it *exposes* or shows us information. If you use cookbooks, you are encountering process analysis each time you read a recipe. If you are setting up a new VCR, you may wish the writer of the manual were more adept at writing process analysis when you find the steps hard to follow. "How to" writing can therefore give the reader steps for carrying out a process. The writer might also analyze the steps someone took already in completing a process, such as explaining how Harriet Tubman organized the Underground Railroad or how women won the right to vote.

Planning a good process analysis requires the writer to include all the essential steps. Be sure you have all the tools or ingredients needed. Arrange the steps in the correct sequence. Like all good writing, a good process essay requires a thesis to tell the reader the *significance* of the process. The writer can tell the reader how to do something, but also should inform the reader about the usefulness or importance of the endeavor.

In this chapter, Russell Baker tells us, tongue in cheek, how to carve a turkey. Humorist Garrison Keillor explains how to write a personal letter. Grace Lichtenstein analyzes how one popular brand of beer made itself a household word. And, from Ernest

Hemingway, we learn how to make our next experience of sleeping a success. As you read these processes, watch how each writer uses the same technique to achieve a different result.

HOW DO WE READ PROCESS ANALYSIS?

Identify what process the writer is going to analyze. As you read, make a quick outline of the steps the writer introduces.

Watch the use of transitions as the writer moves from one step to the next.

Assess the audience that the writer has aimed at. Is the writer addressing innocents or experts? If the writer's purpose was to explain how to prepare beef stew, he would give different directions to a college freshman who has never cooked before than he would give to a cooking class at the Culinary Institute of America, where everyone was familiar with the fundamentals of cooking. Ask yourself, then: Is there enough information in the analysis? too much?

How does the writer try to make the piece lively? Does it sound as dry as a technical manual, or is there an engaging tone?

HOW DO WE WRITE PROCESS ANALYSIS?

Decide to analyze a process with which you are very familiar. Unless you can do it well yourself, you won't be able to instruct or inform your readers.

Process begins with a good shopping list. Once you have your topic, make lists of ingredients or tools.

Arrange the essential steps in logical order. Don't assume your reader already knows how to do the process. As you know from those incomprehensible VCR instructions, the reader should be given *every* step.

List the steps to *avoid* when carrying out the procedure.

If possible, actually try out the process, using your list as a guide, if you are presenting a method for a tangible product, like making an omelet. Or imagine that you are explaining the procedure over the telephone.

If your topic is abstract, like telling someone how to become an American citizen, read it aloud to a willing listener to see if he or she can follow the steps clearly.

Use *definition* to explain terms the reader may not know,

especially if you are presenting a technical process. At the same time, avoid jargon. Make the language as plain as possible.

Describe the appearance of the product or *compare* an unfamiliar item with a familiar one.

Be sure to think about your audience. Link the audience to the purpose of the process.

Formulate a thesis statement that tells what the process is, and why it is a good process to know.

Sample thesis statement:

Buying and renovating an old car is a time-consuming process, but the results are worthwhile.

Writing and Revising the Draft

Write a rough draft. Turn your list into an essay by developing the steps into sentences, using your thesis to add significance and coherence to the process you are presenting. Don't just list; analyze the procedure as you go along. Keep in mind the techniques of writers like Russell Baker, who doesn't just carve a turkey, but creates an entire dinner scene by the way he selects lively verbs and uses *hyperbole* (see Glossary) to raise his process analysis beyond the ordinary.

Add transitions when necessary to alert the reader that a new step is coming. The most common transition words help a reader to follow steps: first, second, third; first, next, after, last.

Proofread, revise, and create a final draft.

Slice of Life
Russell Baker

Russell Baker is well-known for his columns in *The New York Times,* in which he satirizes contemporary society, writing about trends in food and style, as well as the rigors of surviving in ordinary life. In "Slice of Life," he humorously describes the process of carving a turkey for a holiday dinner, demonstrating how even the most familiar task can lend itself to detailed and appealing analysis.

Words to Watch

sutures (par. 2)   stitches
skewered (par. 4)   secured with a long pin
chassis (par. 10)   body; frame
stampede (par. 15)   run

How to carve a turkey:

Assemble the following tools—carving knife, stone for 1 sharpening carving knife, hot water, soap, wash cloth, two bath towels, barbells, meat cleaver.

If the house lacks a meat cleaver, an ax may be substituted. 2 If it is, add bandages, sutures and iodine to above list.

Begin by moving the turkey from roasting pan to a suitable 3 carving area. This is done by inserting the carving knife into the posterior stuffed area of the turkey and the knife-sharpening stone into the stuffed area under the neck.

Thus skewered, the turkey may be lifted out of the hot 4 grease with relative safety. Should the turkey drop to the floor, however, remove the knife and stone, roll the turkey gingerly into the two bath towels, wrap them several times around it and lift the encased fowl to the carving place.

You are now ready to begin carving. Sharpen the knife on 5 the stone and insert it where the thigh joins the torso. If you do this correctly, which is improbable, the knife will almost immediately encounter a barrier of bone and gristle.

This may very well be the joint. It could, however, be your 6 thumb. If not, execute a vigorous sawing motion until satisfied that the knife has been defeated.

7   Withdraw the knife and ask someone nearby, in as testy a manner as possible, why the knives at your house are not kept in better carving condition.

8   Exercise the biceps and forearms by lifting barbells until they are strong enough for you to tackle the leg joint with bare hands.

9   Wrapping one hand firmly around the thigh, seize the turkey's torso in the other and scream. Run cold water over hands to relieve pain of burns.

10   Now, take a bath towel in each hand and repeat the above maneuver. The entire leg should snap away from the chassis with a distinct crack, and the rest of the turkey, obedient to Newton's law about equal and opposite reactions, should roll in the opposite direction, which means that if you are carving at the table the turkey will probably come to rest in someone's lap.

11   Get the turkey out of the lap with as little fuss as possible, and concentrate on the leg. Use the meat cleaver to sever the sinewy leather which binds the thigh to the drumstick.

12   If using the alternate, ax method, this operation should be performed on a cement walk outside the house in order to preserve the table.

13   Repeat the above operation on the turkey's uncarved side. You now have two thighs and two drumsticks. Using the wash cloth, soap and hot water, bathe thoroughly and, if possible, go to a movie.

14   Otherwise, look each person in the eye and say, "I don't suppose anyone wants white meat."

15   If compelled to carve the breast anyhow, sharpen the knife on the stone again with sufficient awkwardness to tip over the gravy bowl on the person who started the stampede for white meat.

16   While everyone is rushing about to mop the gravy off her slacks, hack at the turkey breast until it starts crumbling off the carcass in ugly chunks.

17   The alternative method for carving white meat is to visit around the neighborhood until you find someone who has a good carving knife and borrow it, if you find one, which is unlikely.

18   This method enables you to watch the football game on neighbors' television sets and also creates the possibility that somebody back at your table will grow tired of waiting and do the carving herself.

In this case, upon returning home, cast a pained stare upon 19
the mound of chopped white meat that has been hacked out by
the family carving knife and refuse to do any more carving that
day. No one who cares about the artistry of carving can be expected to work upon the mutilations of amateurs, and it would be
a betrayal of the carver's art to do so.

BUILDING VOCABULARY

1. One of Baker's most effective techniques in creating humor is to
select adjectives and verbs that not only illustrate the process he
is analyzing, but exaggerate the steps and the results. *Hyperbole*
in writing is the use of extreme exaggeration either to make a
particular point or to achieve a special effect. In paragraph 2, for
instance, Baker includes among the tools needed for carving a
turkey a meat cleaver or an ax. He describes the necessary
strength involved in removing a drumstick when he advises the
carver to "seize the turkey's torso in the other [hand] and scream"
(par. 8). Reread the essay, and select at least ten verbs or description words that use hyperbole, and then write synonyms for them.

UNDERSTANDING THE WRITER'S IDEAS

1. What does Baker reveal about the situation in which he is carving the turkey while he outlines the steps in the process? Give
examples.
2. What is the tone of the essay? What is the author's purpose in
satirizing the process of turkey carving? What does the tone
imply about the author's attitudes toward chores like turkey carving that conventionally fall to men at holiday dinners?
3. Who is the "you" the author is addressing?

UNDERSTANDING THE WRITER'S TECHNIQUES

1. Where is the thesis? What is unusual about how Baker sets up his
main idea?
2. Look at a cookbook page that gives instructions on how to carve

a turkey. How does the language in the cookbook differ from Baker's language? In what ways is Baker's process similar to that in the cookbook? Could you actually carve a turkey using the cookbook directions? using Baker's directions?

3. Why does Baker use so many short paragraphs? How would the effect of the essay change if it were written in longer paragraphs?

4. How would you characterize the tone of the essay? Look up the definitions of *irony, cynicism,* and *sarcasm.* Which term do you think most closely describes Baker's tone? Does his tone fit the subject matter? Explain.

    Go back to your list of hyperbolic words from Building Vocabulary and note for each whether you think it is intended to be ironic, cynical, or sarcastic.

5. Think about the title of the essay. What does this *metaphor* (see Glossary) suggest the essay is about besides turkey carving?

6. How does Baker use narration in this essay? description? illustration?

7. Which sentence alerts us that this is a process analysis essay? Write an outline of the process steps discussed.

8. Writing teachers often tell their students: "Show. Don't tell." In other words, use gestures and actions to characterize someone or make a point rather than just give the reader an explanation. How does Baker use "showing" rather than "telling" in this essay? Give five examples.

9. What does the final paragraph reveal about the author's attitude toward "the carver's art"?

EXPLORING THE WRITER'S IDEAS

1. Great satirists like Jonathan Swift, who wrote political and moral satire in *Gulliver's Travels* (1729), and Mark Twain, who wrote dozens of satirical tales of nineteenth-century American life, felt that satire was a technique for calling attention to weakness or flaws in the society in which they lived. In what way might Baker share this purpose?

2. Do you think Baker has written this essay from personal experience? Why do you think so?

3. Through his process analysis, Baker implies that holiday dinners

are not always the cheerful events pictured on greeting cards. In what ways have your experiences of holiday dinners been like Baker's, where nothing goes according to plan and even the simplest chores are disasters?

4. Turkey carving as Baker analyzes it is a ritual. Rituals are actions we repeat periodically that have symbolic value for us. What changes in society in recent years have made rituals often seem outdated or inappropriate?

5. What personal or family rituals are important to you? Has your attitude toward them changed in recent years?

IDEAS FOR WRITING

Guided Writing

Write an essay in which you explain how to do something that is generally thought of as a simple activity. Use process analysis to show that the activity may look simple, but is in reality a mine field of potential embarrassment. You could analyze changing a flat tire for the first time, for instance, or trying to assemble a Christmas present for a child.

1. Decide on a tone for your essay. Use some hyperbole, irony, or sarcasm.

2. Prepare a direct thesis statement.

3. Make a list of the tools needed for this process, and include it in the introduction.

4. Use the body of the essay to give instructions on the process and to describe the dangers hidden behind the apparently simple activity. Include the reactions of others who may observe you carrying out the process, for instance.

5. Give excuses for why the process won't work, assigning blame to others rather than yourself.

6. Conclude with a solution that will get you out of doing this process in the future.

More Writing Projects

1. In your journal, write about the process you recently used to deal with an extremely embarrassing moment. Make sure you tell what led up to the moment and what happened during and after the incident.

2. Write a paragraph about the process you use when you're out with one person and meet someone else whose name you don't remember.

3. Write a process analysis essay telling how to get satisfaction when you've bought a defective product or gotten bad service in a store.

How to Write a Personal Letter
Garrison Keillor

Garrison Keillor is well known for his creation of the mythical town of Lake Wobegon, Minnesota. For years, he delighted radio audiences with stories of the town's goings-on as host of the program A Prairie Home Companion. Leaving Home: Lake Wobegon Stories, published in 1987, made these tales available in print. In this essay, Keillor maintains his folksy, whimsical tone to tell us how to "Take it easy" when faced with a task that many of us find alternately guilt-inspiring and immobilizing—writing a personal letter! Keillor blends step-by-step technical advice with emotional reassurance to guide us through the process.

Words to Watch

immortal (par. 2)   eternal; undying

sincere (par. 2)   truthful; faithful

vague (par. 3)   unclear; uncertain

anonymity (par. 4)   the condition of being unknown or nameless

obligatory (par. 6)   required

sensuous (par. 8)   voluptuous; sexy

episode (par. 12)   occasion; circumstance

sibling (par. 12)   brother or sister

1   We shy persons need to write a letter now and then, or else we'll dry up and blow away. It's true. And I speak as one who loves to reach for the phone and talk. The telephone is to shyness what Hawaii is to February, it's a way out of the woods. *And yet:* a letter is better.

2   Such a sweet gift—a piece of handmade writing, in an envelope that is not a bill, sitting in our friend's path when she trudges home from a long day spent among wahoos and savages, a day our words will help repair. They don't need to be immortal, just sincere. She can read them twice and again tomorrow: *You're someone I care about, Corinne, and think of often, and every time I do, you make me smile.*

3   We need to write, otherwise nobody will know who we are.

They will have only a vague impression of us as A Nice Person, because, frankly, we don't shine at conversation, we lack the confidence to thrust our faces forward and say, "Hi, I'm Heather Hooten, let me tell you about my week." Mostly we say "Uh-huh" and "Oh really." People smile and look over our shoulder, looking for someone else to talk to.

4   So a shy person sits down and writes a letter. To be known by another person—to meet and talk freely on the page—to be close despite distance. To escape from anonymity and be our own sweet selves and express the music of our souls.

5   We want our dear Aunt Eleanor to know that we have fallen in love, that we quit our job, that we're moving to New York, and we want to say a few things that might not get said in casual conversation: *Thank you for what you've meant to me. I am very happy right now.*

6   The first step in writing letters is to get over the guilt of *not* writing. You don't "owe" anybody a letter. Letters are a gift. The burning shame you feel when you see unanswered mail makes it harder to pick up a pen and makes for a cheerless letter when you finally do. *I feel bad about not writing, but I've been so busy,* etc. Skip this. Few letters are obligatory, and they are *Thanks for the wonderful gift* and *I am terribly sorry to hear about George's death.* Write these promptly if you want to keep your friends. Don't worry about the others, except love letters, of course. When your true love writes *Dear Light of My Life, Joy of My Heart,* some response is called for.

7   Some of the best letters are tossed off in a burst of inspiration, so keep your writing stuff in one place where you can sit down for a few minutes and—*Dear Roy, I am in the middle of an essay but thought I'd drop you a line. Hi to your sweetie too*—dash off a note to a pal. Envelopes, stamps, address book, everything in a drawer so you can write fast when the pen is hot.

8   A blank white 8" × 11" sheet can look as big as Montana if the pen's not so hot—try a smaller page and write boldly. Get a pen that makes a sensuous line, get a comfortable typewriter, a friendly word processor—whichever feels easy to the hand.

9   Sit for a few minutes with the blank sheet of paper in front of you, and let your friend come to mind. Remember the last time you saw each other and how your friend looked and what you

said and what perhaps was unsaid between you; when your friend becomes real to you, start to write.

Write the salutation—*Dear You*—and take a deep breath and 10 plunge in. A simple declarative sentence will do, followed by another and another. As if you were talking to us. Don't think about grammar, don't think about style, just give us your news. Where did you go, who did you see, what did they say, what do you think?

If you don't know where to begin, start with the present: 11 *I'm sitting at the kitchen table on a rainy Saturday morning. Everyone is gone and the house is quiet.* Let the letter drift along. The toughest letter to crank out is one that is meant to impress, as we all know from writing job applications; if it's hard work to slip off a letter to a friend, maybe you're trying too hard to be terrific. A letter is only a report to someone who already likes you for reasons other than your brilliance. Take it easy.

Don't worry about form. It's not a term paper. When you 12 come to the end of one episode, just start a new paragraph. You can go from a few lines about the sad state of rock 'n' roll to the fight with your mother to your fond memories of Mexico to the kitchen sink and what's in it. The more you write, the easier it gets, and when you have a True True Friend to write to, a soul sibling, then it's like driving a car; you just press on the gas.

Don't tear up the page and start over when you write a bad 13 line—try to write your way out of it. Make mistakes and plunge on. Let the letter cook along and let yourself be bold. Outrage, confusion, love—whatever is in your mind, let it find a way to the page. Writing is a means of discovery, always, and when you come to the end and write *Yours ever* or *Hugs and Kisses,* you'll know something you didn't when you wrote *Dear Pal.*

Probably your friend will put your letter away, and it'll be 14 read again a few years from now—and it will improve with age.

And forty years from now, your friend's grandkids will dig it 15 out of the attic and read it, a sweet and precious relic of the ancient Eighties that gives them a sudden clear glimpse of the world we old-timers knew. You will have then created an object of art. Your simple lines about where you went, who you saw, what they said, will speak to those children and they will feel in their hearts the humanity of our times.

You can't pick up a phone and call the future and tell them 16 about our times. You have to pick up a piece of paper.

BUILDING VOCABULARY

1. Throughout the essay, Keillor uses numerous *idioms* that are fairly *colloquial* (see Glossary); that is, they are informal conversational expressions. For each excerpt below, rewrite the *whole* sentence, replacing just the italicized idiomatic expression with your own words.

   a. Some of the best letters are *tossed off* in a burst of inspiration. (par. 7)

   b. *dash off* a note to a pal (par. 7)

   c. take a deep breath and *plunge in* (par. 10)

   d. Let the letter *drift along* (par. 11)

   e. The toughest letter to *crank out* is the one that is meant to impress (par. 11)

   f. if it's hard work to *slip off* a letter to a friend (par. 11)

   g. Don't *tear up* the page and *start over* (par. 13)

   h. Make mistakes and *plunge on* (par. 13)

   i. Let the letter *cook along* (par. 13)

   j. You can't *pick up* a phone and call the future (par. 16)

2. Write sentences for any five of the words in the Words to Watch section (page 305).

UNDERSTANDING THE WRITER'S IDEAS

1. Explain in your own words why, according to Keillor, people need to write letters.

2. An *analogy* (see Glossary) is a figurative comparison that illustrates an idea by relating subjects from different categories. Explain Keillor's statement "The telephone is to shyness what Hawaii is to February" (par. 1). What does he mean by "it's a way out of the woods"?

3. In what ways is a letter "a small gift"? Why does it not "need to be immortal, just sincere"?

4. Who are "wahoos and savages" (par. 2)?

5. Who is "A Nice Person" (par. 3)? Why is the phrase capitalized?

6. Throughout the essay, Keillor uses direct address and specific names. Who are "Corinne" (par. 2) and "Aunt Eleanor" (par. 5)?

Find and list other names. Who are these people? Why does he use their names?

7. In paragraph 5, Keillor suggests that we might not say "Thank you for what you've meant to me. I am very happy right now" in casual conversation, but we could in a letter. Why might this be true? What other comparisons does he make between letter writing and conversation? What is his general feeling about the similarities or differences between the two activities?

8. What types of letters are obligatory? How does Keillor suggest we handle them? Why?

9. Explain the meaning of the following:

   a. the pen is hot (par. 7)
   b. A blank 8" × 11" sheet can look as big as Montana if the pen's not so hot (par. 8)
   c. Get a pen that makes a sensuous line (par. 8)

10. Why does Keillor make the following suggestion: "Don't think about grammar, don't think about style" (par. 10)?

11. In general, does Keillor think personal letter writing need be a very serious endeavor? Support your response with specific references to the essay.

12. Explain the "message" of paragraph 15 in your own words. Explain the "message" of paragraph 16.

UNDERSTANDING THE WRITER'S TECHNIQUES

1. Is there a single *thesis statement* in this essay? Explain.

2. Which paragraphs constitute the introduction, body, and conclusion of this essay? What *transitions* does Keillor use between the sections? Are they effective?

3. In process analysis, it is important to tailor the depth and range of your explanations to your audience. For what *audience* (see Glossary) do you think Keillor wrote this essay? Does he highlight any one particular group? How do his language and *tone* (see Glossary) reflect his audience?

4. A process analysis often provides a step-by-step explanation of

how to do something. Try to write a step-by-step outline of Keillor's *procedure* for writing personal letters. Would this procedure be easy to follow for someone who had trouble writing letters? Explain.

5. In the first five paragraphs of this essay, Keillor uses the first-person plural pronoun form ("we, our, us") instead of the more common first-person singular ("I, me") or second person ("you"). Why does he do this? To whom is he referring? What clues in the text lead you to believe this? What is the effect of using this particular *point of view?* Where does he shift the point of view? To what? How does this change affect the essay?

6. Evaluate the author's use of infinitive verb constructions in paragraph 4 ("to be known"; "to meet"; "to escape"). What tone is created by these constructions?

7. How would you describe the *level of diction* (see Glossary) in this essay? Is the diction appropriate to the subject? To the intended audience?

8. How does Keillor use *definition* in paragraphs 11 and 13?

9. Where does Keillor use *classification* in this essay?

10. Throughout the essay, Keillor uses italics. Identify each use, then explain its particular purpose.

11. Discuss in what ways Keillor uses *negation* (see page 222) in this essay.

12. Reread your answer to question 12 in the Understanding the Writer's Ideas section. What is the tone of paragraph 15? How does it differ from the rest of the essay? Is it appropriate to the message of that paragraph? What is the tone of paragraph 16? How does the tone change between paragraphs 15 and 16? Do you feel this transition is smooth? Explain.

EXPLORING THE WRITER'S IDEAS

1. How closely does Keillor's essay relate to your own letter-writing experiences? Do you enjoy letter writing? Why or why not? When do you feel most inspired to write a letter? What special procedure, if any, do you follow?

2. In this essay, Keillor offers various suggestions on how to approach letter writing from both a technical and an emotional standpoint. Look back over the essays in Chapter 1, "On Writ-

ing." Which of the four writers in this chapter do you think Garrison Keillor is most in tune with concerning his ideas about the *writing process* (not just letter writing)? Explain your answer with specific references to the essays.

3. Look over some old letters or postcards. How does it make you feel to read them? Are your impressions of the writer and (or) subject different now than they were when you first received the card or letter? Why?

4. In general, do you prefer face-to-face conversations, telephone conversations, or letter writing? In what *specific instances* would you prefer each means of communication? Which method do you find most effective?

IDEAS FOR WRITING

Guided Writing

Write an essay in which you explain how to call someone for a first date.

1. Begin the essay by explaining how this is an activity that we all share in at one time or another. Do this by:
   a Using the first-person plural point of view
   b Explaining why it is a difficult process in general
2. Explain what is pleasurable about the process despite its difficulties.
3. Compare calling for a first date to a similar but easier process, and use that process in an imaginative analogy.
4. Throughout your essay, use italics to highlight special examples of what to say or do to make the process go more smoothly.
5. Write a step-by-step process analysis. Begin with how to overcome normal fear and trepidation.
6. Maintain a lighthearted, personal, conversational tone throughout. Use colloquialisms to help create this tone.
7. Reassure your reader by explaining what he or she does *not* have to do or say during this process.
8. In your conclusion, shift to a somewhat more serious tone to discuss the possible outcome of the call. Explain the effects of making the call.

More Writing Projects

1. What guidelines do you follow when you write a letter? What characteristics do you think a letter should have? Respond to these questions in your journal.
2. Write a paragraph directed to a friend explaining how he or she can get the most out of an upcoming special event: a party, a reunion, a concert, a wedding, a football game, and so forth.
3. Write a personal letter. Keep Keillor's essay next to you as you write this letter. Reread each paragraph closely and follow his process step by step.

Coors Beer

Grace Lichtenstein

Process analysis often deals with mechanical or technical procedures. In this short selection by Grace Lichtenstein, who is a correspondent for *The New York Times,* the author examines a mechanical process—the brewing of beer. As you read this piece, look for the methods that the author uses to make this technical process interesting and understandable to the general reader.

Words to Watch

palate (par. 1)   taste or sense of taste

mystique (par. 2)   special, almost mysterious attitudes and feelings surrounding a person, place, or thing

Spartan (par. 3)   simple and severe

rancid (par. 3)   not fresh; having a bad smell

permeate (par. 3)   to spread through everything

nondescript (par. 3)   lacking any recognizable character or quality

cellulose (par. 4)   the main substance in woody parts of plants, used in many manufacturing processes

Coors is a light-bodied beer, meaning it is brewed with less malt, 1 fewer hops and more rice than beers with a tangy taste. Compared with Heineken's or other more full-bodied foreign beers, Coors does seem almost flavorless and it is this quality that could account for its popularity among young people just starting to get acquainted with the pleasures of beer drinking. A few locals scoff at Coors, calling it "Colorado Kool-Aid." But the fact is that, according to Ernest Pyler, "if you conducted a blindfold test of the four leading beers, the chances of picking our Coors would be minimal." Indeed, one national newspaper conducted an informal test among eight beer drinkers, finding that only three could correctly identify Coors. My own admittedly uneducated palate detects no difference between Coors and Schaefer. In short, the difference between Coors and any other decent beer could be 1,800 miles. Maybe, if Paul Newman suddenly switched to Schaefer, Denverites would pay $15 a case for it.

There is one aspect to the Coors mystique that does have 2

measurable validity. Company officials make much of the fact that Coors has good mountain water and the most expensive brewing process in the country. Several elements are unusual, though not unique.

3   Thousands of visitors have learned about the process on guided tours through the antiseptic, Spartan plant. (For out-of-towners, the tour is often a pilgrimage—but for local students of the Colorado School of Mines, it's usually more in the line of a quick belt before classes. The tour lasts 30 minutes, at the end of which visitors are invited to quaff to their heart's content in the hospitality lounge. "I've come here 50 times," boasted one student as he polished off a glass at 11:30 one morning in the lounge.) Situated in the center of town, between two high, flat mesas in the foothills of the Rockies, the plant dominates the community just as the somewhat rancid smell of malt seems to permeate the air; one-fourth of the town's families are said to owe their jobs to the factory's operations. Anyone expecting to see in Golden the foaming white waterfall amid mountain pines that is pictured on every yellow can of Coors will be disappointed. The water used in the brewing comes from nondescript wells hidden in concrete blockhouses. The brewery now puts out about 12 million barrels of beer a year, but construction sites throughout the grounds bear witness to the company's hopes for doubling that capacity by 1984.

4   Like other beers, Coors is produced from barley. Most of the big Midwestern brewers use barley grown in North Dakota and Minnesota. Coors is the single American brewer to use a Moravian strain, grown under company supervision, on farms in Colorado, Idaho, Wyoming and Montana. At the brewery, the barley is turned into malt by being soaked in water—which must be biologically pure and of a known mineral content—for several days, causing it to sprout and producing a chemical change—breaking down starch into sugar. The malt is toasted, a process that halts the sprouting and determines the color and sweetness (the more the roasting, the darker, more bitter the beer). It is ground into flour and brewed, with more pure water, in huge copper-domed kettles until it is the consistency of oatmeal. Rice and refined starch are added to make mash; solids are strained out, leaving an amber liquid malt extract, which is boiled with hops—the dried cones from the hop vine which add to the bitterness, or tang. The hops are

strained, yeast is added, turning the sugar to alcohol, and the beer is aged in huge red vats at near-freezing temperatures for almost two months, during which the second fermentation takes place and the liquid becomes carbonated, or bubbly. (Many breweries chemically age their beer to speed up production; Coors people say only naturally aged brew can be called a true "lager.") Next, the beer is filtered through cellulose filters to remove bacteria, and finally is pumped into cans, bottles or kegs for shipping.

The most unusual aspect of the Coors process is that the beer is not pasteurized, as all but a half-dozen of the 90 or so American beers are. In the pasteurization process, bottles or cans of beer are passed through a heating unit and then cooled. This destroys the yeast in the brew which could cause spoilage, if the cans or bottles or barrels are unrefrigerated for any long period. However, pasteurization also changes the flavor of beer. Coors stopped pasteurizing its product 18 years ago because it decided that "heat is an enemy of beer," according to a company spokesman.   5

Unpasteurized beer must be kept under constant refrigeration. Thus, Coors does not warehouse any of its finished product, as many other brewers do, but ships everything out cold, immediately. In effect, my tour guide, a young management trainee wearing a beer-can tie clip, explained as we wandered through the packaging area, watching workers in surgical masks feed aluminum lids into machines that sealed cans whirling by on conveyor belts, the six-pack you buy in a store contains not only a very fresh beer but also a beer that could be considered draft, since it has been kept cold from vat to home refrigerator.   6

BUILDING VOCABULARY

1. For the italicized word in each example in Column A below select a definition from Column B.

Column A
1. locals *scoff* (par. 1)
2. *informal* test (par. 1)
3. measurable *validity* (par. 2)
4. the *antiseptic* Spartan plant (par. 3)
5. to *quaff* to their heart's content (par. 3)
6. flat *mesas* (par. 3)
7. construction *sites* (par. 3)
8. a Moravian *strain* (par. 4)
9. the *consistency* of oatmeal (par. 4)
10. liquid malt *extract* (par. 4)

Column B
a. drink heartily
b. locations
c. thickness
d. not according to fixed rules
e. a line of certain species
f. a concentrated form of something
g. soundness
h. make fun of
i. free from infection
j. hills

2. Use five of the italicized words in the first exercise in sentences of your own.

UNDERSTANDING THE WRITER'S IDEAS

1. What is a "light-bodied" beer?
2. What does the author mean when she states, "In short, the difference between Coors and any other decent beer could be 1,800 miles"?
3. What *is* special about Coors beer?
4. Why do college students like to visit the Coors plant?
5. Describe the setting of the Coors brewery. How does it contrast with the picture on the Coors can?
6. Explain in your own words the process by which Coors is produced.
7. Why is the pasteurization process important to the final flavor of any beer?
8. Why can Coors almost be considered a draft beer?

UNDERSTANDING THE WRITER'S TECHNIQUES

1. What is the writer's thesis? Is it stated or implied?
2. How do comparison and contrast operate in the first paragraph? Does the author also use definition in this paragraph? Where? For what purpose?
3. What is the function of paragraph 2? What is the purpose of paragraph 3? How does the author develop paragraph 3?
4. Analyze the devices used for *transition* (see Glossary) between paragraphs 2 and 3.
5. Which paragraphs analyze the process of brewing Coors? Make a list of the steps on a sheet of paper. Is the process clear and complete? Does the author use process analysis simply to inform? Does she also provide commentary? Where?
6. Where does the author introduce personal or subjective elements into this essay? Why, at these points, does she provide personal rather than technical details?

EXPLORING THE WRITER'S IDEAS

1. Suppose that three unidentified brands of beer, cola, or cigarettes were placed before you. Would you be able to identify them by taste? What is the importance of "mystique" (or image) or "brand loyalty" to a product's success?
2. Can you think of other products that have a mystique associated with them? What are they, and what accounts for the mystique?
3. Would the fact that Paul Newman drinks Coors affect people's attitudes toward the brand? Why do manufacturers attempt to have certain celebrities associated with their products? Why should consumers be influenced by these associations?
4. Based on this essay, what are some ways to make a technical analysis of process interesting to the reader?

IDEAS FOR WRITING

Guided Writing

Explain how to make or to assemble a particular item or product. For example, you might want to explain how to prepare a certain dish; how to assemble a piece of equipment; how to produce something in a factory. You might want to follow Lichtenstein's example: Explain how a popular drink is made.

1. Start by introducing the reader to your "perfect product," indicating how it is possible to achieve high-quality results in its preparation.
2. Use as examples of the quality of the product, positive statements made by other individuals. These may be the ideas of friends, relatives, or experts.
3. Explain the "mystique," if there is one, surrounding the product.
4. After arousing reader interest sufficiently, describe the actual process involved, concentrating on all important details in the sequence.
5. In your last paragraph, try to capture the taste, look, or feel of the final product.

More Writing Projects

1. Many television commercials aim at selling beer to viewers. In your journal reflect on these commercials. What do they reveal about the manufacturers? the viewers? American society in general?
2. Set up an actual testing situation in your class. Have various members test three types of a particular item, such as chocolate, diet soda, or a kitchen cleanser. Then write a paragraph report describing either the process involved in the testing or the process by which results were obtained.
3. Consult an encyclopedia or other reference book to learn about the making of some product—steel, automobiles, plywood, and so forth. Then explain this process in your own words.

Camping Out
Ernest Hemingway

In this essay by Ernest Hemingway (1899–1961), the author uses the pattern of process analysis to order his materials on the art of camping. Hemingway wrote this piece for the *Toronto Star* in the early 1920s, before he gained worldwide recognition as a major American writer. In it, we see his lifelong interest in the outdoors and in his desire to do things well.

Words to Watch

relief map (par. 2)   a map that shows by lines and colors the various heights and forms of the land

Caucasus (par. 2)   a mountain range in southeastern Europe

proprietary (par. 7)   held under patent or trademark

rhapsodize (par. 9)   to speak enthusiastically

browse bed (par. 9)   a portable cot

tyro (par. 11)   an amateur; a beginner in learning something

dyspepsia (par. 13)   indigestion

mulligan (par. 18)   a stew made from odds and ends of meats and vegetables

Thousands of people will go into the bush this summer to cut the 1 high cost of living. A man who gets his two weeks' salary while he is on vacation should be able to put those two weeks in fishing and camping and be able to save one week's salary clear. He ought to be able to sleep comfortably every night, to eat well every day and to return to the city rested and in good condition.

But if he goes into the woods with a frying pan, an igno- 2 rance of black flies and mosquitoes, and a great and abiding lack of knowledge about cookery the chances are that his return will be very different. He will come back with enough mosquito bites to make the back of his neck look like a relief map of the Caucasus. His digestion will be wrecked after a valiant battle to assimilate half-cooked or charred grub. And he won't have had a decent night's sleep while he has been gone.

He will solemnly raise his right hand and inform you that 3 he has joined the grand army of never-agains. The call of the wild may be all right, but it's a dog's life. He's heard the call of the tame with both ears. Waiter, bring him an order of milk toast.

4   In the first place he overlooked the insects. Black flies, no-see-ums, deer flies, gnats and mosquitoes were instituted by the devil to force people to live in cities where he could get at them better. If it weren't for them everybody would live in the bush and he would be out of work. It was a rather successful invention.

5   But there are lots of dopes that will counteract the pests. The simplest perhaps is oil of citronella. Two bits' worth of this purchased at any pharmacist's will be enough to last for two weeks in the worst fly and mosquito-ridden country.

6   Rub a little on the back of your neck, your forehead and your wrists before you start fishing, and the blacks and skeeters will shun you. The odor of citronella is not offensive to people. It smells like gun oil. But the bugs do hate it.

7   Oil of pennyroyal and eucalyptol are also much hated by mosquitoes, and with citronella they form the basis for many proprietary preparations. But it is cheaper and better to buy the straight citronella. Put a little on the mosquito netting that covers the front of your pup tent or canoe tent at night, and you won't be bothered.

8   To be really rested and get any benefit out of a vacation a man must get a good night's sleep every night. The first requisite for this is to have plenty of cover. It is twice as cold as you expect it will be in the bush four nights out of five, and a good plan is to take just double the bedding that you think you will need. An old quilt that you can wrap up in is as warm as two blankets.

9   Nearly all outdoor writers rhapsodize over the browse bed. It is all right for the man who knows how to make one and has plenty of time. But in a succession of one-night camps on a canoe trip all you need is level ground for your tent floor and you will sleep all right if you have plenty of covers under you. Take twice as much cover as you think that you will need, and then put two-thirds of it under you. You will sleep warm and get your rest.

10   When it is clear weather you don't need to pitch your tent if you are only stopping for the night. Drive four stakes at the head of your made-up bed and drape your mosquito bar over that, then you can sleep like a log and laugh at the mosquitoes.

11   Outside of insects and bum sleeping the rock that wrecks

most camping trips is cooking. The average tyro's idea of cooking is to fry everything and fry it good and plenty. Now, a frying pan is a most necessary thing to any trip, but you also need the old stew kettle and the folding reflector baker.

A pan of fried trout can't be bettered and they don't cost 12 any more than ever. But there is a good and bad way of frying them.

The beginner puts his trout and his bacon in and over a 13 brightly burning fire the bacon curls up and dries into a dry tasteless cinder and the trout is burned outside while it is still raw inside. He eats them and it is all right if he is only out for the day and going home to a good meal at night. But if he is going to face more trout and bacon the next morning and other equally well-cooked dishes for the remainder of two weeks he is on the pathway to nervous dyspepsia.

The proper way is to cook over coals. Have several cans of 14 Crisco or Cotosuet or one of the vegetable shortenings along that are as good as lard and excellent for all kinds of shortening. Put the bacon in and when it is about half cooked lay the trout in the hot grease, dipping them in corn meal first. Then put the bacon on top of the trout and it will baste them as it slowly cooks.

The coffee can be boiling at the same time and in a smaller 15 skillet pancakes being made that are satisfying the other campers while they are waiting for the trout.

With the prepared pancake flours you take a cupful of pan- 16 cake flour and add a cup of water. Mix the water and flour and as soon as the lumps are out it is ready for cooking. Have the skillet hot and keep it well greased. Drop the batter in and as soon as it is done on one side loosen it in the skillet and flip it over. Apple butter, syrup or cinnamon and sugar go well with the cakes.

While the crowd have taken the edge from their appetites 17 with flapjacks the trout have been cooked and they and the bacon are ready to serve. The trout are crisp outside and firm and pink inside and the bacon is well done—but not too done. If there is anything better than that combination the writer has yet to taste it in a lifetime devoted largely and studiously to eating.

The stew kettle will cook you dried apricots when they have 18 resumed their predried plumpness after a night of soaking, it will serve to concoct a mulligan in, and it will cook macaroni. When you are not using it, it should be boiling water for the dishes.

19   In the baker, mere man comes into his own, for he can make a pie that to his bush appetite will have it all over the product that mother used to make, like a tent. Men have always believed that there was something mysterious and difficult about making a pie. Here is a great secret. There is nothing to it. We've been kidded for years. Any man of average office intelligence can make at least as good a pie as his wife.

20   All there is to a pie is a cup and a half of flour, one-half teaspoonful of salt, one-half cup of lard and cold water. That will make pie crust that will bring tears of joy into your camping partner's eyes.

21   Mix the salt with the flour, work the lard into the flour, make it up into a good workmanlike dough with cold water. Spread some flour on the back of a box or something flat, and pat the dough around a while. Then roll it out with whatever kind of round bottle you prefer. Put a little more lard on the surface of the sheet of dough and then slosh a little flour on and roll it up and then roll it out again with the bottle.

22   Cut out a piece of the rolled out dough big enough to line a pie tin. I like the kind with holes in the bottom. Then put in your dried apples that have soaked all night and been sweetened, or your apricots, or your blueberries, and then take another sheet of the dough and drape it gracefully over the top, soldering it down at the edges with your fingers. Cut a couple of slits in the top dough sheet and prick it a few times with a fork in an artistic manner.

23   Put it in the baker with a good slow fire for forty-five minutes and then take it out and if your pals are Frenchmen they will kiss you. The penalty for knowing how to cook is that the others will make you do all the cooking.

24   It is all right to talk about roughing it in the woods. But the real woodsman is the man who can be really comfortable in the bush.

BUILDING VOCABULARY

1. For each word below write your own definition, based on how the word is used in the selection. Check back to the appropriate paragraph in the essay for more help, if necessary.

a. abiding (par. 2)
b. assimilate (par. 2)
c. valiant (par. 2)
d. charred (par. 2)
e. solemnly (par. 3)
f. requisite (par. 8)
g. succession (par. 9)
h. studiously (par. 17)
i. concoct (par. 18)
j. soldering (par. 22)

UNDERSTANDING THE WRITER'S IDEAS

1. What is Hemingway's main purpose in this essay? Does he simply want to explain how to set up camp and how to cook outdoors?
2. What, according to the writer, are the two possible results of camping out on your vacation?
3. Why is oil of citronella the one insecticide that Hemingway recommends over all others?
4. Is it always necessary to pitch a tent when camping out? What are alternatives to it? How can you sleep warmly and comfortably?
5. Explain the author's process for cooking trout. Also explain his process for baking a pie.
6. Is it enough for Hemingway simply to enjoy "roughing it" while camping out?

UNDERSTANDING THE WRITER'S TECHNIQUES

1. Does the author have a stated thesis? Explain.
2. Identify those paragraphs in the essay that involve process analysis, and explain how Hemingway develops his subject in each.
3. What is the main writing pattern in paragraphs 1 and 2? How does this method serve as an organizing principle throughout the essay?
4. How would you characterize the author's style of writing? Is it appropriate to a newspaper audience? Is it more apt for professional fishermen?

5. In what way does Hemingway employ classification in this essay?
6. Analyze the tone of Hemingway's essay.
7. The concluding paragraph is short. Is it effective, nevertheless, and why? How does it reinforce the opening paragraph?

EXPLORING THE WRITER'S IDEAS

1. Camping out was popular in the 1920s, as it is in the 1990s. What are some of the reasons that it remains so attractive today?
2. Hemingway's essay describes many basic strategies for successful camping. He does not rely on "gadgets" or modern inventions to make camping easier. Do such gadgets make camping more fun today than it might have been in the 1920s?
3. The author suggests that there is a right way and a wrong way to do things. Does it matter if you perform a recreational activity right as long as you enjoy doing it? Why?

IDEAS FOR WRITING

Guided Writing

Write an essay on how to do something wrong, and how to do it right—going on vacation, looking for a job, fishing, or whatever.

1. Reexamine the author's first three paragraphs and imitate his method of introducing the right and wrong ways about the subject, and the possible results.
2. Adopt a simple, informal, "chatty" style. Feel free to use a few well-placed clichés and other forms of spoken English. Use several similes.
3. Divide your subject into useful categories. Just as Hemingway treated insects, sleeping, and cooking, try to cover the main aspects of your subject.
4. Explain the process involved for each aspect of your subject. Make certain that you compare and contrast the right and wrong ways of your activity.
5. Write a short, crisp conclusion that reinforces your longer introduction.

More Writing Projects

1. How do you explain the fascination that camping out holds for many people? Reflect on this question in your journal.
2. In a paragraph describe how to get to your favorite vacation spot, and what to do when you get there.
3. If you have ever camped out, write a process paper explaining one important feature of setting up camp.

SUMMING UP: CHAPTER 9

1. Divide the class into groups and choose one Guided Writing essay per group using the Keillor, Baker, or Hemingway selection. Collaboratively discuss, evaluate, correct, edit, and rewrite the Guided Writing process essay. By consensus, establish grades for the original and the revised essay. Present your findings to the class.
2. On the basis of your experience reading the four essays in the section, write about the *types* of processes the authors deal with (you may want to read the introduction to the previous chapter on classification) and *how* they manage these processes. Clarify the main steps that you consider to be important in the writing of any process analysis.
3. Grace Lichtenstein in her essay reveals the brewing process behind the "Coors mystique." Everyone has a favorite food. For this exercise, contribute a recipe for your favorite food to be included in a class cookbook. In addition to describing step by step the process for preparing the food, you should also tell something about the tradition behind the food, special occasions for eating it, the first time you ate it, and so forth. In other words, establish your own "mystique" for it.
4. Three of the essays in this chapter tell us how to do things that can have direct and immediate effects on our lives—writing letters, carving a turkey, camping—while the fourth illuminates a process that produces a product that may also directly affect our lives—beer. Try to write an essay that describes a process with much less immediate effect.
5. Interview a classmate about something that he or she does very well. Make sure the questions you ask don't omit any important

steps or materials used in the process. Take careful notes during the interview, then try to replicate the process on your own. If there were any difficulties in accomplishing the process, reinterview your classmate. After you are satisfied that no steps or materials were left out, write up the procedure in such a way that someone else could easily follow it.

CHAPTER 10

Cause-and-Effect Analysis

WHAT IS CAUSE-AND-EFFECT ANALYSIS?

Cause-and-effect analysis answers the basic human question: *Why?* Why do events occur, like hurricanes or the election of a new president? Why does one student do better in math than another? In addition, this form of analysis looks at the *expected* consequences of a chain of happenings. If we raise the minimum wage, what will the likely consequences be?

Basically, cause-and-effect analysis (also called causal analysis) looks for *causes* or conditions, and suggests or examines *results* or consequences (the effects).

Like most of the writing strategies you have been studying, causal analysis parallels a kind of thinking we do in everyday life. If you are a student who has returned to school after being away for several years, someone might ask you why you decided to come back. In answering, you would give causes: You needed a better job to support your children; you wanted to learn a new skill; your intellectual curiosity drove you back; and so on. These would be *causes*. Once you were attending school, a classmate might ask you what changes coming back to school have made in your life. You might consider the pride your children feel in your achievement, or the fact that you have less time to prepare meals, or that you sleep only four hours a night. Those are the *consequences* or results of your decision. In a few years' time, after graduation, the effects might be very different: A better job or a

327

scholarship to graduate school might be one of the long-term results.

Thinking about causes can go beyond everyday life to help
us understand social and political change: What were the causes
of the American Civil War? What were the consequences for the
nation? What caused the Great Depression? Why were women
denied the vote until 1920? Why did so many Irish immigrants
come to America around 1900, and what were the consequences
for the growth of American industry?

In looking at such large questions, you will realize that
there are different kinds of causes. First, there is the *immediate*
cause that gives rise to a situation. This is the cause (or causes)
most directly related, the one closest at hand. But as you can see
from the historical questions in the previous paragraph, we also
need to go beyond the immediate cause to the *ultimate* cause, the
basic conditions that stimulated the more obvious or immediate
ones.

For example, although we might identify the immediate
cause of the Los Angeles riots of 1992 as the Rodney King trial,
the ultimate causes for racial unrest grow from the social and
economic conditions of the poor in America. To find the "real"
causes, we have to think critically, to examine the situation
deeply.

Often, a writer has to consider many causes and rank them
in order of importance. Depending on the length of the essay, a
writer may have to select from among many causes. If a small
town begins to lose businesses to a large mall, the chamber of
commerce may ask why businesses and customers prefer the
mall to shopping in town. Convenience, parking, competitive
pricing, and entertainment may be identified as causes. Since the
town cannot solve all these problems at once, it may focus on
one, and try to lure shoppers back downtown by building a larger
municipal parking lot. The result, perhaps, will be that shoppers
will return to Main Street.

One difficulty in working with causal analysis is that we
cannot always prove that a cause or an effect is absolute. We
can only do our best to offer as much evidence as possible to
help the reader see the relation we wish to establish. Therefore,
we have to support our causes and effects with specific details
and evidence drawn from personal experience, from statistics, or

from experts' statements in newspapers or books. A writer can interview people, for instance, and collect data about local shopping habits or visit the library to read articles on the Los Angeles riots.

In the essays in this chapter, you will find a variety of uses for causal analysis. Anne Roiphe looks at the causes for the failure of half the marriages in America. Linda Bird Francke analyzes the difficult question of abortion when her political convictions cause her to think one way, but her personal experience leads in another direction. Robert Ragaini analyzes the reasons that a seemingly simple incident of neighborhood noise challenged his sense of manhood. Finally, Susan Jacoby combines both process analysis and narrative with causal analysis techniques to examine the reasons women opt out of courses in math and science. As you read each piece, keep in mind the kinds of causes the writers present and the ways in which they add support to their analysis.

HOW DO WE READ CAUSAL ANALYSIS?

Reading causal analysis requires us to ask ourselves these questions:

- What are the writer's topic and the main cause? Make an outline of the causes as you read.
- Are immediate causes or ultimate causes presented? How do you know?
- Does the author show the consequences of the event?
- How does the author develop the analysis? Identify the writing strategies used: narrative, description, illustration, process analysis, and so on. Which is most effective in supporting the causal analysis and why?
- What is the tone of the essay?

HOW DO WE WRITE CAUSAL ANALYSIS?

Select a topic you can manage. If you try to find the causes of psychological depression, you may need to study a great deal of Freud before you can write the essay. If, on the other hand, you decide to write about causes of suicide among college freshmen, you would narrow the scope of the essay and thus control it more easily.

Write a working thesis that tells the cause and effect you are analyzing. Why is it important?

Sample thesis statement:

Many causes lie behind Americans' return to healthier eating habits, but the most important are fear of disease, desire to lose weight, and curiosity about new types of food.

Make a list of the major causes and under each cause, add at least one specific example to support it.

Plan whether you want to concentrate on either causes or effects, or on a balance of the two.

Be sure that you have included all the necessary links in the chain of reasoning that you began in the thesis.

Avoid oversimplification.

Include both major and minor causes and effects.

Writing and Revising the Draft

Write an introduction that presents the thesis and your statement of the significance of the thesis.

Use transitions as you move from one cause to the next.

Use narrative, description, process analysis, and other techniques to support your causes.

Conclude by reminding your reader of the importance of understanding this chain of events.

Proofread your draft carefully. Ask a classmate to read it to see if your causes seem logical.

Make corrections and prepare a final copy.

Why Marriages Fail

Anne Roiphe

Anne Roiphe is the author of the well-known novel about relationships, *Up the Sandbox!*, which was later made into a popular film. In this essay, notice how she presents a series of interconnected reasons for the currently high divorce rate.

Words to Watch

obsolete (par. 1)   out-of-date; no longer in use

perils (par. 2)   dangers

infertility (par. 2)   the lack of ability to have children

turbulent (par. 2)   very chaotic or uneasy

stupefying (par. 2)   bewildering

obese (par. 3)   very fat, overweight

entrapment (par. 4)   the act of trapping, sometimes by devious methods

yearning (par. 4)   a strong desire

euphoric (par. 7)   characterized by a feeling of well-being

proverbial (par. 13)   relating to a proverb or accepted truth

infidelity (par. 13)   sexual unfaithfulness

These days so many marriages end in divorce that our most sacred vows no longer ring with truth. "Happily ever after" and "Till death do us part" are expressions that seem on the way to becoming obsolete. Why has it become so hard for couples to stay together? What goes wrong? What has happened to us that close to one-half of all marriages are destined for the divorce courts? How could we have created a society in which 42 percent of our children will grow up in single-parent homes? If statistics could only measure loneliness, regret, pain, loss of self-confidence and fear of the future, the numbers would be beyond quantifying.

Even though each broken marriage is unique, we can still find the common perils, the common causes for marital despair. Each marriage has crisis points and each marriage tests endurance, the capacity for both intimacy and change. Outside pressures such as job loss, illness, infertility, trouble with a child, care of aging parents and all the other plagues of life hit marriage the way hurricanes blast our shores. Some marriages survive these storms and others don't. Marriages fail, however, not simply because of the outside weather but because the inner climate becomes too hot or too cold, too turbulent or too stupefying.

3   When we look at how we choose our partners and what expectations exist at the tender beginnings of romance, some of the reasons for disaster become quite clear. We all select with unconscious accuracy a mate who will recreate with us the emotional patterns of our first homes. Dr. Carl A. Whitaker, a marital therapist and emeritus professor of psychiatry at the University of Wisconsin, explains, "From early childhood on, each of us carried models for marriage, femininity, masculinity, motherhood, fatherhood and all the other family roles." Each of us falls in love with a mate who has qualities of our parents, who will help us rediscover both the psychological happiness and miseries of our past lives. We may think we have found a man unlike Dad, but then he turns to drink or drugs, or loses his job over and over again or sits silently in front of the T.V. just the way Dad did. A man may choose a woman who doesn't like kids just like his mother or who gambles away the family savings just like his mother. Or he may choose a slender wife who seems unlike his obese mother but then turns out to have other addictions that destroy their mutual happiness.

4   A man and a woman bring to their marriage bed a blended concoction of conscious and unconscious memories of their parents' lives together. The human way is to compulsively repeat and recreate the patterns of the past. Sigmund Freud so well described the unhappy design that many of us get trapped in: the unmet needs of childhood, the angry feelings left over from frustrations of long ago, the limits of trust and the recurrence of old fears. Once an individual senses this entrapment, there may follow a yearning to escape, and the result could be a broken, splintered marriage.

5   Of course people can overcome the habits and attitudes that developed in childhood. We all have hidden strengths and amazing capacities for growth and creative change. Change, however, requires work—observing your part in a rotten pattern, bringing difficulties out into the open—and work runs counter to the basic

myth of marriage: "When I wed this person all my problems will be over. I will have achieved success and I will become the center of life for this other person and this person will be my center, and we will mean everything to each other forever." This myth, which every marriage relies on, is soon exposed. The coming of children, the pulls and tugs of their demands on affection and time, place a considerable strain on that basic myth of meaning everything to each other, of merging together and solving all of life's problems.

Concern and tension about money take each partner away 6 from the other. Obligations to demanding parents or still-depended-upon parents create further strain. Couples today must also deal with all the cultural changes brought on in recent years by the women's movement and the sexual revolution. The altering of roles and the shifting of responsibilities have been extremely trying for many marriages.

These and other realities of life erode the visions of marital 7 bliss the way sandstorms eat at rock and the ocean nibbles away at the dunes. Those euphoric, grand feelings that accompany romantic love are really self-delusions, self-hypnotic dreams that enable us to forge a relationship. Real life, failure at work, disappointments, exhaustion, bad smells, bad colds and hard times all puncture the dream and leave us stranded with our mate, with our childhood patterns pushing us this way and that, with our unfulfilled expectations.

The struggle to survive in marriage requires adaptability, 8 flexibility, genuine love and kindness and an imagination strong enough to feel what the other is feeling. Many marriages fall apart because either partner cannot imagine what the other wants or cannot communicate what he or she needs or feels. Anger builds until it erupts into a volcanic burst that buries the marriage in ash.

It is not hard to see, therefore, how essential communica- 9 tion is for a good marriage. A man and a woman must be able to tell each other how they feel and why they feel the way they do; otherwise they will impose on each other roles and actions that lead to further unhappiness. In some cases, the communication patterns of childhood—of not talking, of talking too much, of not listening, of distrust and anger, of withdrawal—spill into the marriage and prevent a healthy exchange of thoughts and feelings. The answer is to set up new patterns of communication and intimacy.

10   At the same time, however, we must see each other as individuals. "To achieve a balance between separateness and closeness is one of the major psychological tasks of all human beings at every stage of life," says Dr. Stuart Bartle, a psychiatrist at the New York University Medical Center.

11   If we sense from our mate a need for too much intimacy, we tend to push him or her away, fearing that we may lose our identities in the merging of marriage. One partner may suffocate the other partner in a childlike dependency.

12   A good marriage means growing as a couple but also growing as individuals. This isn't easy. Richard gives up his interest in carpentry because his wife, Helen, is jealous of the time he spends away from her. Karen quits her choir group because her husband dislikes the friends she makes there. Each pair clings to each other and are angry with each other as life closes in on them. This kind of marital balance is easily thrown as one or the other pulls away and divorce follows.

13   Sometimes people pretend that a new partner will solve the old problems. Most often extramarital sex destroys a marriage because it allows an artificial split between the good and the bad—the good is projected on the new partner and the bad is dumped on the head of the old. Dishonesty, hiding and cheating create walls between men and women. Infidelity is just a symptom of trouble. It is a symbolic complaint, a weapon of revenge, as well as an unraveler of closeness. Infidelity is often that proverbial last straw that sinks the camel to the ground.

14   All right—marriage has always been difficult. Why then are we seeing so many divorces at this time? Yes, our modern social fabric is thin, and yes the permissiveness of society has created unrealistic expectations and thrown the family into chaos. But divorce is so common because people today are unwilling to exercise the self-discipline that marriage requires. They expect easy joy, like the entertainment on TV, the thrill of a good party.

15   Marriage takes some kind of sacrifice, not dreadful self-sacrifice of the soul, but some level of compromise. Some of one's fantasies, some of one's legitimate desires have to be given up for the value of the marriage itself. "While all marital partners feel shackled at times, it is they who really choose to make the

marital ties into confining chains or supporting bonds," says Dr. Whitaker. Marriage requires sexual, financial and emotional discipline. A man and a woman cannot follow every impulse, cannot allow themselves to stop growing or changing.

Divorce is not an evil act. Sometimes it provides salvation **16** for people who have grown hopelessly apart or were frozen in patterns of pain or mutual unhappiness. Divorce can be, despite its initial devastation, like the first cut of the surgeon's knife, a step toward new health and a good life. On the other hand, if the partners can stay past the breaking up of the romantic myths into the development of real love and intimacy, they have achieved a work as amazing as the greatest cathedrals of the world. Marriages that do not fail but improve, that persist despite imperfections, are not only rare these days but offer a wondrous shelter in which the face of our mutual humanity can safely show itself.

BUILDING VOCABULARY

1. Roiphe loads her essay with some very common expressions to make the discussion more easily understandable to the reader. Below is a list of ten such expressions. Use each in a sentence of your own.
   a. ring with truth (par. 1)
   b. crisis points (par. 2)
   c. tender beginnings (par. 3)
   d. mutual happiness (par. 3)
   e. marriage bed (par. 4)
   f. hidden strengths (par. 5)
   g. marital bliss (par. 7)
   h. healthy exchange (par. 9)
   i. childlike dependency (par. 11)
   j. social fabric (par. 14)
2. Locate and explain five terms that the author draws from psychology

UNDERSTANDING THE WRITER'S IDEAS

1. What are the "sacred vows" the author mentions in paragraph 1? Identify the source of the expressions "happily ever after" and "till death do us part." What does she mean when she says that these expresions "seem on the way to becoming obsolete"?
2. What is a "single-parent home"?
3. How does Roiphe define "endurance" in a marriage? What does she mean by "outside pressures" in paragraph 2? What are some of these pressures? Does Roiphe feel they are the primary causes for marriages failing? Why?
4. According to the essay, how do we choose husbands and wives? What is the meaning of "our first home" in paragraph 3? According to Roiphe, for what reasons is the way we choose mates a possible cause for marriages failing?
5. What is the "basic myth" of marriage? How does it create a possibly bad marriage?
6. How have the women's movement and the sexual revolution created strains on modern marriages?
7. Explain what the writer means by "Real life, failure at work, disappointments, exhaustion, bad smells, bad colds, and hard times" in paragraph 7. How do they affect marriages?
8. What is the role of communication between husband and wife in a marriage? What are the results of poor communication? What solutions to this problem does Roiphe suggest?
9. What two types of "growth" does Roiphe suggest as necessary to a good marriage? Who are Richard, Helen, and Karen, named in paragraph 12?
10. According to Roiphe, what is the common cause of extramarital sexual affairs? What are her projected results of infidelity?
11. What does Roiphe identify as the primary cause of divorce? What does she propose as a solution to this problem?
12. According to the last paragraph, do you think Roiphe is in favor of each divorce? Why? In this paragraph, she presents both the positive and negative effects of divorce. What are the positive effects? the negative effects?

UNDERSTANDING THE WRITER'S TECHNIQUES

1. Where does the author place her thesis?

2. How does the title almost predict for the reader that the writer's main technique of development will be cause-and-effect analysis?

3. One strategy for developing an introductory paragraph is to ask a question. What is the purpose of the questions that the author asks in the opening paragraph? What is the relationship among the questions? How do the questions themselves dictate a cause-and-effect pattern of development? How do they immediately involve the reader in the topic?

4. In which paragraph does Roiphe list the immediate or common causes of marital failure? Why is this placement effective?

5. The use of clear *topic sentences* for each paragraph can often be an important technique in writing a clear causal analysis because topic sentences usually identify main causes for the effect under discussion. Identify the topic sentences for paragraphs 3, 4, and 6. What causes for marriage failure does each identify?

6. What causal chain of behavior does Roiphe build in paragraphs 8 to 13?

7. Why does Roiphe begin paragraph 14 with the words "All right"? Whom is she addressing? How does this address compare with the technique used in her introduction?

8. What two authorities does Roiphe quote in this essay? How are their citations useful? How are they identified? In what ways do their identifications add to their credibility as sources of opinions or information on Roiphe's topic?

9. Where does Roiphe use statistics in this essay? Why is it especially important to the development of the article?

10. Roiphe makes use of *definition* (see pages 220–222) in a number of places in this essay. What are her definitions of the following?
    a. "work" in a marriage (par. 5)
    b. "A good marriage" (par. 12)
    c. "divorce" (par. 16)
    d. "marriages that do not fail but improve" (par. 16)
    Locate other places where she uses definition.

11. In some essays, the introduction and conclusion are each simply the first and last paragraphs. In this essay, the writer uses more

than one paragraph for each. Which paragraphs make up her introduction? Which make up the conclusion? Why might she have structured her introduction and conclusion in this way? How does the structure affect the essay?

12. You have learned that two of the most common types of comparisons used by writers to enliven their essays are *similes* and *metaphors.* Look up the definition of these terms in the Glossary to refresh your memory. In addition, writers may use *extended metaphors.* This technique relies upon a number of metaphoric comparisons which revolve around a main idea rather than a single comparison. Roiphe uses comparisons in a number of paragraphs in this essay. In each of the following cases identify and explain the comparisons indicated:

   a. extended metaphor (par. 2)
   b. metaphor (par. 7)
   c. metaphor (par. 8)
   d. metaphor (par. 9)
   e. simile (par. 14)
   f. metaphor (par. 15)
   g. similes, metaphors (par. 16)

How does Roiphe's frequent use of metaphors and similes affect the tone of the essay?

13. Why does Roiphe end her essay with references to successful marriages? Would you consider that as being off the topic? Why or why not?

EXPLORING THE WRITER'S IDEAS

1. Roiphe discusses quite a few causes for marriages failing. Discuss with the class some additional causes. Why are they also important?

2. Paragraph 6 states, "Couples today must also deal with all the cultural changes brought on in recent years by the women's movement and the sexual revolution." Identify these two social phenomena. Among the people you know, have these cultural changes affected their marriages? How? If you are not married, and plan to marry, do you feel that the changes will present any foreseeable problems? If you are not married, and do not plan to marry, have they influenced your decision in any ways? What other effects have these two movements had in American society? Do you think these influences have been positive or negative? Why?

3. If you are married or in a close relationship, how did you choose your mate? If you are not married or in a relationship, what qualities would you look for in a mate? Why?

4. In paragraphs 6 and 7, Roiphe mentions "realities of life" that destroy romantic notions of "marital bliss." What other realities can you add to her list?

5. Paragraph 15 discusses the idea of self-sacrifice in marriage. Roiphe writes, "Some of one's fantasies, some of one's legitimate desires have to be given up for the value of the marriage itself." However, some people insist that for a marriage to survive, each partner must maintain complete integrity, that is, must not be forced into major sacrifices of values or life-styles. What is your opinion of these two opposing viewpoints?

6. Judy Brady in "I Want a Wife" (pages 000–000) provides some insights into marriage that complement Roiphe's. How does Brady's position compare with Roiphe's?

IDEAS FOR WRITING

Guided Writing

Using cause-and-effect analysis, write an essay in which you explain *why marriages succeed.*

1. Limit your topic sufficiently so that you can concentrate your discussion on closely interrelated cause-and-effect patterns.

2. In the introduction, involve your reader with a series of pertinent questions.

3. Identify what many people think are common or immediate causes of successful marriages; then show how other causes are perhaps even more important.

4. In the course of your essay, cite at least one relevant statistic that will add extra importance to your topic.

5. Try to use at least one quotation from a reputable authority. Consult your library for books and articles that deal with marriage. Be sure to include full identification of your source.

6. Use clear topic sentences in each paragraph as you present analyses of the various causes for successful marriages.

7. Make use of metaphors, similes, and extended metaphors.
8. In your essay, offer necessary definitions of terms that are especially important to your topic. Try for at least one definition by negation.
9. Write a conclusion in which you make some commentary upon divorce. Make your comment as an outgrowth of your discussion of a successful marriage.

More Writing Projects

1. What is the "ideal marriage"? In your journal, speculate on those qualities that you think would make a perfect marriage. Share observations with others in the class.
2. In a paragraph, explain some of your reasons for ending a relationship (a marriage, a close friendship, a relationship with a girlfriend or boyfriend).
3. Write an essay in which you explain the effects of divorce on the lives of the couple involved. Here, do not concern yourself with causes; look only at the results of the failed marriage.

The Ambivalence of Abortion
Linda Bird Francke

In this autobiographical narrative, author Linda Bird Francke tells about her mixed feelings toward the issue of abortion. Although she has strong political convictions on the subject, her ambivalence surfaces when she must confront abortion personally. Notice how she blends descriptive details with personal insights to explain the reasons for her uncertainty.

Words to Watch

dwell (par. 1)   keep attention directed on something

heralded (par. 1)   announced in a joyous manner

rationalize (par. 2)   to justify one's behavior (especially to oneself)

freelance (par. 3)   working without long-range contractual agreements

cycled (par. 5)   moved through a complete series of operations or steps

common denominator (par. 10)   similar traits or themes

rhetoric (par. 13)   ways of speaking or writing effectively

fetus (par. 13)   an unborn child still in the mother's womb

neurotic (par. 14)   emotionally unstable

vaccinated (par. 14)   injected with a harmless virus to produce immunity to a disease

inoculated (par. 14)   treated with a serum or antibody to prevent disease

uterus (par. 16)   the womb; the place within the mother where the fetus develops

sensation (par. 18)   feeling

Novocain (par. 18)   a drug used to numb the feeling of pain

quivered (par. 18)   shook

We were sitting in a bar on Lexington Avenue when I told my husband I was pregnant. It is not a memory I like to dwell on. Instead of the champagne and hope which had heralded the impending births of the first, second and third child, the news of this one was greeted with shocked silence and Scotch. "Jesus," my husband kept saying to himself, stirring the ice cubes around and around. "Oh, Jesus." 1

Oh, how we tried to rationalize it that night as the starting 2 time for the movie came and went. My husband talked about his plans for a career change in the next year, to stem the staleness that fourteen years with the same investment-banking firm had brought him. A new baby would preclude that option.

3   The timing wasn't right for me either. Having juggled pregnancies and child care with what freelance jobs I could fit in between feedings, I had just taken on a full-time job. A new baby would put me right back in the nursery just when our youngest child was finally school age. It was time for *us,* we tried to rationalize. There just wasn't room in our lives now for another baby. We both agreed. And agreed. And agreed.

4   How very considerate they are at the Women's Services, known formally as the Center for Reproductive and Sexual Health. Yes, indeed, I could have an abortion that very Saturday morning and be out in time to drive to the country that afternoon. Bring a first morning urine specimen, a sanitary belt and napkins, a money order or $125 cash—and a friend.

5   My friend turned out to be my husband, standing awkwardly and ill at ease as men always do in places that are exclusively for women, as I checked in at nine A.M. Other men hovered around just as anxiously, knowing they had to be there, wishing they weren't. No one spoke to each other. When I would be cycled out of there four hours later, the same men would be slumped in their same seats, locked downcast in their cells of embarrassment.

6   The Saturday morning women's group was more dispirited than the men in the waiting room. There were around fifteen of us, a mixture of races, ages and backgrounds. Three didn't speak English at all and a fourth, a pregnant Puerto Rican girl around eighteen, translated for them.

7   There were six black women and a hodgepodge of whites, among them a T-shirted teenager who kept leaving the room to throw up and a puzzled middle-aged woman from Queens with three grown children.

8   "What form of birth control were you using?" the volunteer asked each one of us. The answer was inevitably "none." She then went on to describe the various forms of birth control available at the clinic, and offered them to each of us.

9   The youngest Puerto Rican girl was asked through the interpreter which she'd like to use: the loop, diaphragm, or pill. She

shook her head "no" three times. "You don't want to come back here again, do you?" the volunteer pressed. The girl's head was so low her chin rested on her breastbone. "*Sí*," she whispered.

We had been there two hours by that time, filling out endless forms, giving blood and urine, receiving lectures. But unlike any other group of women I've been in, we didn't talk. Our common denominator, the one which usually floods across language and economic barriers into familiarity, today was one of shame. We were losing life that day, not giving it.

The group kept getting cut back to smaller, more workable units, and finally I was put in a small waiting room with just two other women. We changed into paper bathrobes and paper slippers, and we rustled whenever we moved. One of the women in my room was shivering and an aide brought her a blanket.

"What's the matter?" the aide asked her. "I'm scared," the woman said. "How much will it hurt?" The aide smiled. "Oh, nothing worse than a couple of bad cramps," she said. "This afternoon you'll be dancing a jig."

I began to panic. Suddenly the rhetoric, the abortion marches I'd walked in, the telegrams sent to Albany to counteract the Friends of the Fetus, the Zero Population Growth buttons I'd worn, peeled away, and I was all alone with my microscopic baby. There were just the two of us there, and soon, because it was more convenient for me and my husband, there would be one again.

How could it be that I, who am so neurotic about life that I step over bugs rather than on them, who spend hours planting flowers and vegetables in the spring even though we rent out the house and never see them, who make sure the children are vaccinated and inoculated and filled with vitamin C, could so arbitrarily decide that this life shouldn't be?

"It's not a life," my husband had argued, more to convince himself than me. "It's a bunch of cells smaller than my fingernail."

But any woman who has had children knows that certain feeling in her taut, swollen breasts, and the slight but constant ache in her uterus that signals the arrival of a life. Though I would march myself into blisters for a woman's right to exercise the option of motherhood, I discovered there in the waiting room that I was not the modern woman I thought I was.

17   When my name was called, my body felt so heavy the nurse had to help me into the examining room. I waited for my husband to burst through the door and yell "stop," but of course he didn't. I concentrated on three black spots in the acoustic ceiling until they grew in size to the shape of saucers, while the doctor swabbed my insides with antiseptic.

18   "You're going to feel a burning sensation now," he said, injecting Novocain into the neck of the womb. The pain was swift and severe, and I twisted to get away from him. He was hurting my baby, I reasoned, and the black saucers quivered in the air. "Stop," I cried. "Please stop." He shook his head, busy with his equipment. "It's too late to stop now," he said. "It'll just take a few more seconds."

19   What good sports we women are. And how obedient. Physically the pain passed even before the hum of the machine signaled that the vacuuming of my uterus was completed, my baby sucked up like ashes after a cocktail party. Ten minutes start to finish. And I was back on the arm of the nurse.

20   There were twelve beds in the recovery room. Each one had a gaily flowered draw sheet and a soft green or blue thermal blanket. It was all very feminine. Lying on these beds for an hour or more were the shocked victims of their sex, their full wombs now stripped clean, their futures less encumbered.

21   It was very quiet in that room. The only voice was that of the nurse, locating the new women who had just come in so she could monitor their blood pressure, and checking out the recovered women who were free to leave.

22   Juice was being passed about, and I found myself sipping a Dixie cup of Hawaiian Punch. An older woman with tightly curled bleached hair was just getting up from the next bed. "That was no goddamn snap," she said, resting before putting on her miniskirt and high white boots. Other women came and went, some walking out as dazed as they had entered, others with a bounce that signaled they were going right back to Bloomingdale's.

23   Finally then, it was time for me to leave. I checked out, making an appointment to return in two weeks for an IUD insertion. My husband was slumped in the waiting room, clutching a single yellow rose wrapped in a wet paper towel and stuffed into a Baggie.

We didn't talk the whole way home, but just held hands 24
very tightly. At home there were more yellow roses and a tray in
bed for me and the children's curiosity to divert.

It had certainly been a successful operation. I didn't bleed 25
at all for two days just as they had predicted, and then I bled only
moderately for another four days. Within a week my breasts had
subsided and the tenderness vanished, and my body felt mine
again instead of the eggshell it becomes when it's protecting
someone else.

My husband and I are back to planning our summer vaca- 26
tion and his career switch.

And it certainly does make more sense not to be having a 27
baby right now—we say that to each other all the time. But I
have this ghost now. A very little ghost that only appears when
I'm seeing something beautiful, like the full moon on the ocean
last weekend. And the baby waves at me. And I wave at the
baby. "Of course, we have room," I cry to the ghost. "Of
course, we do."

BUILDING VOCABULARY

1. Develop definitions of your own for the italicized words by relying
   on context clues, that is, clues from surrounding words and sentences. Then check your definition against a dictionary definition.
   a. "My husband talked about his plans for a career change in the
      next year, *to stem* the staleness that fourteen years with the
      same investment-banking firm had brought him. A new baby
      would *preclude* that *option*." (par. 2)
   b. "Though I would march myself into blisters for a woman's
      right to *exercise* the *option* of motherhood, I discovered there
      in the waiting room that I was not the modern woman I
      thought I was." (par. 16)
   c. "The pain was *swift* and *severe,* and I twisted to get away from
      him." (par. 18)
   d. "Lying on these beds for an hour or more were the shocked
      victims of their sex, their full wombs now stripped clean, their
      futures less *encumbered*." (par. 20)
   e. "It had certainly been a successful operation. I didn't bleed at

all for two days just as they had predicted, and then I bled only *moderately* for another four days." (par. 25)

2. For each italicized word in Column A, write the correct *synonym* (a word of similar meaning) from Column B. Look up unfamiliar words in a dictionary.

Column A	*Column B*
1. *impending* birth (par. 1	a. decreased
2. *hovered* around (par. 5)	b. complying
3. locked *downcast* (par. 5)	c. confused
4. more *dispirited* (par. 6)	d. lingered
5. *puzzled* middle-aged woman (par. 7)	e. about to happen
	f. tight
6. *inevitably* "none" (par. 8)	g. distract
	h. dejected
7. *taut*, swollen breasts (par. 16)	i. unavoidable
	j. discouraged
8. how *obedient* (par. 19)	
9. curiosity to *divert* (par. 24)	
10. had *subsided* (par. 25)	

UNDERSTANDING THE WRITER'S IDEAS

1. What is the setting in which Francke breaks the news to her husband that she is pregnant? How does he receive the news?
2. What reasons does her husband give for not wanting another child? Why does Francke feel it is a bad time for herself as well?
3. What is the attitude of the men waiting at the abortion clinic? Explain.
4. Why is there a women's group meeting before Francke actually gets her abortion? Are all the women pretty much alike at this meeting? How so? What is Francke's attitude toward these other women? Give specific examples to support your answer.
5. What common reason do all the women in the group share for being pregnant?
6. In the past, what was the author's viewpoint concerning women's rights to have abortions? What specific examples does

she give to illustrate this point of view? Do you assume that she still holds this opinion? Why?

7. What examples does Francke give to illustrate that she supports life? Are they convincing?

8. Explain what the author means by the statement "Though I would march myself into blisters for a woman's right to exercise the option of motherhood, I discovered there in the waiting room that I was not the modern woman I thought I was" (par. 16).

9. When she is in the examining room, what does the author do to deal with her anxieties about the abortion?

10. Explain what the woman means when she says to Francke, "That was no goddamn snap."

11. How does Francke know the operation has been successful?

UNDERSTANDING THE WRITER'S TECHNIQUES

1. What is Francke's thesis?

2. What rhetorical strategy does the word "ambivalence" in the title suggest? How does Francke use that strategy in the very first paragraph? Where does she use it elsewhere in the essay?

3. Does Francke successfully explain the ambivalence named in the title? Why or why not?

4. Which does this analysis concentrate on more—causes, effects, or a combination of the two? What evidence can you offer to support your answer? What specifically is the relationship between cause and effect in paragraphs 6 to 10? Analyze the pattern of cause and effect in paragraphs 19 to 22.

5. What is the use of narration in this essay? What is the narrative *point of view* (see Glossary) in this selection? How is it used to enhance the essay?

6. What would you say is the overall tone of the selection? The author uses repetition in this essay to help set that tone. How does the repetition in "We both agreed. And agreed. And agreed" (par. 3) contribute to it?

7. *Paradox* is a special variety of *irony* (see Glossary) in which there is a clear contradiction in a situation. A paradox is a statement or attitude which, on the surface, seems unlikely, and yet,

on analysis, can indeed be true. For example, it is paradoxical that the author should have such ambivalent feelings about abortion while she is sitting in an abortion clinic. Why is that situation considered paradoxical? What other paradoxes do you find in this essay?

8. What is the function of description in this essay? Select passages in which you feel the descriptions are especially vivid. How is description used by the author to characterize the women mentioned in paragraph 22? Are the women stereotyped in this description? Explain.

9. Only toward the last part of the essay does Francke use any metaphors or similes—some of them quite startling. Identify the metaphors or similes in paragraph 19, paragraph 25, and paragraph 27. Why do you think she saved this figurative language for the end?

10. Analyze the last paragraph. What causes and effects discussed throughout the essay are echoed here? What new ones are suggested? Compare the effect of the statement "Of course, we have room" with the statement in paragraph 3, "There just wasn't room. . . ." How does this repetition affect the conclusion?

11. Writers who write about highly charged emotional issues must take special care to avoid *sentimentality*—the excessive display of emotion (see Glossary). Has Francke been successful in avoiding it everywhere in the essay? How has she used concrete descriptions to avoid being sentimental? Does the conclusion strike you as being excessively emotional or does it strike you simply as a dramatic but effective closing? Explain your responses.

EXPLORING THE WRITER'S IDEAS

1. When this article was originally published in 1976, it appeared under the *pseudonym* (a fictitious name) "Jane Doe." What reason might Linda Francke have had for not using her real name? Why do you think that a few years later she admitted to the authorship of the article? In general, what do you think about a writer publishing his or her work under an assumed name? Explain. What historical examples can you offer for the use of pseudonyms?

2. Francke describes some very intimate personal emotions and experiences in her attempt to explain what causes her ambivalence toward abortion. On the basis of the material presented, do you think she is justified in feeling ambivalent? Do you feel she should have been more definite one way or the other? Why?

3. In her description of the Saturday morning women's group (pars. 6 to 10), Francke shows that the women present were of all types— "a mixture of races, ages, and backgrounds." This suggests, of course, that abortion is a subject affecting all women. Does it, in fact, affect all women equally? Explain your answer.

4. In paragraph 5, the author describes her husband as "standing awkwardly and ill at ease as men always do in places that are exclusively for women." What sorts of places are exclusively for persons of one sex? Discuss how you felt and acted if you were ever in a place which was really more for persons of the opposite sex.

5. Much controversy about abortion revolves around modern definitions of life and death. Some people argue that life begins at conception; others argue that life begins at birth. With which group do you agree? Why? How has modern science complicated our concepts of life and death?

6. Abortion and antiabortion forces have increased their attacks against each other dramatically in recent years. How does Francke's essay crystallize both sides of the complex, emotionally charged issue?

IDEAS FOR WRITING

Guided Writing

Select an important issue facing society, an issue with which you have had personal experience and about which you have mixed feelings. After you fill in the blank, write an essay titled "Two Sides of _____. " In your essay explore the reasons for your ambivalence. You can select from a wide range of social, moral, health, or education topics. For example, you might want to consider ambivalence toward interracial dating or marriages, a compulsory draft, legalization of drugs, cigarette smoking, a liberal arts education—but feel free to select any issue that is especially important to you.

1. Write the essay as a first-person narrative. Begin with an incident when you first clearly realized the ambivalent nature of the issue, and explain why or how this particular incident focused your attention on the subject.
2. Tell about how and for what reasons you came to a decision to take a certain action despite your mixed feelings. What rationalizations did you or others use to help you feel you were doing the right thing?
3. Narrate in detail the sequence of events that followed your decision. Make the narrative come to life with concrete sensory detail. As you tell your story, analyze the various causes and effects of your decision and actions.
4. Discuss how the same event you experienced affects others. Explain how the causes and effects of the action are different or similar for you and for others.
5. Explain how you felt immediately before, during, and after the crucial experience.
6. In your conclusion, express your deepest feelings about the consequences of your decision and experiences. Use similes, metaphors, and an echo of your original attempts to rationalize your ambivalence.

More Writing Projects

1. In your journal reflect on the issue of abortion. Analyze your reasons for your attitudes.
2. Write a brief paragraph in which you explain the causes and (or) effects of a political standpoint you feel very strongly about.
3. In an essay of analysis, propose the effects on children if elementary schools throughout the country had compulsory sex education programs.

A Question of Manhood
Robert Ragaini

Robert Ragaini uses first-person narrative to explore the causes and effects of his changing reactions to noisy neighbors. Starting with this common problem, the author goes on to analyze the shifting definitions of appropriate male conduct. He realizes that he is no longer a schoolyard good guy surrounded by bullies but, whether he likes it or not, a grownup in a world where rationality wins over physical force.

Words to Watch

jolted (par. 1)   disturbed

raucous (par. 1)   harsh; rough-sounding

unrestrained (par. 2)   not held back

pugnacious (par. 1)   in a mood to fight

quash (par. 3)   step on; hold down

boisterous (par. 4)   violent and turbulent

surreptitious (par. 8)   secret; concealed

blatant (par. 10)   obvious

coercions (par. 10)   forced measures

blustered (par. 11)   spoke noisily and violently

insidious (par. 14)   cheating; sneaky

remnant (par. 15)   scrap; fragment

I was jolted out of my sleep one morning last summer by the 1
sounds of shouting male voices and loud rock music. At first I assumed that the noise was coming from the tiny, one-man police station next door where kids with nothing to do sometimes gather, but this music was more raucous, the voices more pugnacious than those usually heard in the quiet family summer community where I have rented for the last four seasons.

Most often the earliest sounds are of children calling to 2
each other or their parents, shrill and happy, impatient to get at the day, not a bad thing to hear at 8 or 8:30. This was different. It was 6:30. With a flick of a switch the silence had been broken by a radio at high volume and unrestrained yelling and laughter. As I

became more awake, I realized that the din was coming from the house to the right of mine. I was surprised because, although this was a new rental and I didn't know my neighbors, the previous weekend the house had been occupied by a middle-aged couple who hadn't made a sound.

3   I lay awake deciding—or not deciding—what to do. My first impulse was to storm over indignantly and issue a lecture on consideration and manners, to shame the noisemakers into apologetic silence. It didn't take long to quash that impulse.

4   Then I considered reasoning with them. I would explain that I was trying to sleep and ask them to keep the noise down. Certainly they would respond to a reasonable request presented in a reasonable manner. At that moment the boisterous, cheerful voices were replaced by a single, angry one. It said, "Well, I've been living here for nine years and I make more money than you, you S.O.B." After that statement of manly defiance, the radio was turned off and the conversation level subsided, and I went back to sleep.

5   A couple of hours later, at breakfast, I heard familiar voices and looked out to see five men in their 20s, each with a bottle of beer in his hand, walking past my house to the one next door. Soon they were on the deck, drinking and roughhousing until all but one got on bicycles and rode off, leaving the fifth man asleep in a chair.

6   A friend dropped by that afternoon, and I told her what had happened. I explained that I believed there was nothing to gain by confronting them directly. They were interested only in themselves, would not listen to reason, were the kind who would enjoy intimidating me physically, and I would be left helpless and in a rage. She said that I had done the sensible thing by doing nothing, and we agreed that in the event of a recurrence I would call the police and let them handle it.

7   Then, having resolved the problem in a mature, adult fashion, I said something that made no sense to her at all. I told her I felt like a coward.

8   When I was young, there was a story that all boys knew. It went something like this. On his way home from school, a boy is attacked by the neighborhood bully. He runs crying to his mother who comforts him and cleans his wounds, but when his father comes home, the boy is told he must fight back like a man. Then

begins a period of   surreptitious training in self-defense, a
process which culminates with the ignominious and glorious defeat of the bully.

That was the myth, and, as every boy knows, it's a bare- 9
faced lie. In real life, the bully kills you.

But the truth is not important. What counts is that at some 10
time and in some way a boy is told to be a man, and he simply
doesn't know how. Whether it's as blatant as being given boxing
gloves for Christmas, as I was, or being pushed to play unwanted
games, or urged to try one more time, or any of the thousand coercions, all he knows is that somehow he has failed and he hasn't
even taken the test.

There are two ways a boy can go at this critical moment in 11
his life. He can become fearful and quit, get out of the game, or
begin to create his own little swagger and try to start winning. In
my case, I combined the two. Deep inside I was scared to death,
and I knew it well, but I was big and a pretty fair mimic, and I
developed an image that got me by. When physically confronted,
I blustered and posed and did my imitation of tough and usually
bluffed my way through. When that didn't work, I "chickened
out" and suffered the torments of the damned.

As I grew older, the rules were modified, but the game re- 12
mained the same. Being a man was still about winning, and
when, in my early 20s, I dropped out of the race, it was a rejection of all that I was "supposed" to be. Later, when I became am-
bitious, it was acceptance of the very same things, and in each
case I measured myself against the definition of manhood that I
had carried since I was 3 or 4 or 5.

Though the game was not of my devising, when I chose to 13
play, I did it well and accumulated the trophies that come with
success. But the catch was that for a real man there is never
enough. There's always a bigger prize, a greater challenge, a
tougher test, and to stop winning is to lose.

Now all of us know that this is ridiculous—crazy, in fact— 14
and no one need be so great a fool as to step into such a self-
destructive trap. But I'm not talking about what makes sense. I'm
talking about feelings, particularly the insidious feeling that is a
part of every American male no matter how sane or intelligent or
gentle or wise. The feeling deep in the pit of his stomach that
says, "I'm not a man."

15   That is how I felt when I didn't go next door and challenge those guys and force them to stop disturbing me. It didn't matter that it wouldn't have worked or that it didn't make sense or that there were other, more rational approaches. All that was head stuff, no match for the gnawing feeling, that remnant from my childhood, that once again I had failed the test.

BUILDING VOCABULARY

1. Ragaini uses language to re-create for his audience the unsocial behavior of his next-door neighbors. He uses action verbs like "jolted" (par. 1) to make his response to the noise vivid. Reread the essay and make a list of at least five other action verbs or descriptive adjectives the author uses in this way.

2. *Colloquial language* (see Glossary) is the language used in most conversation and in some informal writing. Ragaini uses some colloquial words to capture the characteristics of his neighbors. In paragraph 4, he imagines a conversation in which his neighbor responds to his complaints by saying, ". . . and I make more money than you, you S.O.B." Find the standard English equivalents for these colloquial phrases:
   a. S.O.B.
   b. quash the impulse (par. 3)
   c. roughhousing (par. 5)
   d. "chickened out" (par. 11)
   e. head stuff (par. 15)
   f. those guys (par. 15)

UNDERSTANDING THE WRITER'S IDEAS

1. How does the title of the essay reflect the writer's basic point?

2. Ragaini uses the cause-and-effect essay to explore his reactions to the incident with which he begins the essay. While he knows that he has done the right thing, he is haunted by "The feeling deep in the pit of his stomach that says 'I'm not a man.' " He uses the word "myth" to try to identify the cause of his conflicted feelings. What does the author mean by a "myth" in paragraph 9?

Who is responsible for creating myths? What is the danger of myths like the one about manhood that the author is describing?
3. Where is the writer living when the incident with the neighbors occurs? How long has he lived there?
4. Does the writer go next door to confront his neighbors? Explain his motives.
5. What does the writer mean when he says in paragraph 10 that "the truth is not important." What is more important than truth? Does the writer agree with this system of values himself?
6. What does Ragaini imply is happening to the definition of "manhood" among American men? How do they feel about this development?
7. How does Ragaini's definition of manhood differ from the definition he assumes is held by his neighbors?

UNDERSTANDING THE WRITER'S TECHNIQUES

1. Where is the thesis of the essay? How do you know?
2. Ragaini uses first-person narrative. What other techniques does he use to develop his analysis?
3. Ragaini plans his essay around two stories. One is the incident with noisy neighbors. The other is the story of his growing up and learning values about manhood. How does he use transitions to shift from one story to the other? Identify the transitional phrases. How does the last paragraph bring the two stories together?
4. Make an outline that lists the causes the author assigns to his decision not to confront his neighbors. Which is most important? Which is least important?
5. What would you say is Ragaini's overall attitude to the idea of manhood? Does he maintain this attitude throughout the essay? If not, where does it change? Why?
6. Ragaini uses both specifics and broad generalizations to develop his thesis. Make a list of specifics and a list of generalizations he uses. Which are most important in supporting the thesis? Why?

EXPLORING THE WRITER'S IDEAS

1. Ragaini uses a single, relatively unimportant incident to develop a cause-and-effect analysis of a deeply rooted American idea: manhood. How effective is he in explaining the reasons that this incident led him to his analysis?
2. Why does the author discuss "manhood" with a woman friend? How does her reaction differ from his? Can a woman understand the conflict the author feels in the same way a male friend might? Explain.
3. Why do you think Ragaini chose to *write* about his ideas rather than just talk about them with a friend? In what way is the *process* of writing different from the process of thinking aloud in conversation about an idea?

IDEAS FOR WRITING

Guided Writing

Write an essay in which you analyze your behavior in a situation where you felt conflict about how to act.

1. Begin the essay by telling what incident triggered your thinking. Use lots of active verbs and adjectives to bring the experience to life for the reader.
2. Describe two (or more) courses of action you could take. Use dialogue to illustrate what might happen if you took one action, and then use a second piece of dialogue to show the alternative action you could take.
3. Tell which course of action you chose. Analyze the reasons you made the decision you did. List at least three reasons or causes and explain each one.
4. Answer critics who would say you should have behaved in a different way.
5. Conclude by revealing how you felt after the event. Did you do the right thing? Why or why not?

More Writing Projects

1. In your journal, write about why you recently did something you really didn't want to do. Then try to explain why you did it.
2. Write a paragraph in which you explain the effects of a decision you made that you regret making.
3. In an essay, show the effects on men and women of holding on to prescribed ideas about "manhood" and "womanhood."

When Bright Girls Decide That Math Is "a Waste of Time"

Susan Jacoby

In this article, Susan Jacoby explains how cultural expectations and societal stereotyping are overshadowed by women's own decisions to keep themselves away from scientific and technological studies. Notice how she uses narrative and process analysis to reinforce the causes and effects she is exploring here.

Words to Watch

sanguine (par. 3)   cheerful, hopeful

vulnerable (par. 6)   open to attack or suggestion

syndrome (par. 7)   a group of symptoms that characterize a condition

akin to (par. 7)   similar to

phobia (par. 7)   an excessive fear of something

constitute (par. 7)   to make up; compose

epitomize (par. 8)   to be a prime example of

prone (par. 15)   disposed to; susceptible

accede to (par. 16)   give in to

1   Susannah, a 16-year-old who has always been an A student in every subject from algebra to English, recently informed her parents that she intended to drop physics and calculus in her senior year of high school and replace them with a drama seminar and a work-study program. She expects a major in art or history in college, she explained, and "any more science or math will just be a waste of my time."

2   Her parents were neither concerned by nor opposed to her decision. "Fine, dear," they said. Their daughter is, after all, an outstanding student. What does it matter if, at age 16, she has taken a step that may limit her understanding of both machines and the natural world for the rest of her life?

3   This kind of decision, in which girls turn away from studies that would give them a sure footing in the world of science and technology, is a self-inflicted female disability that is, regrettably,

almost as common today as it was when I was in high school. If Susannah had announced that she had decided to stop taking English in her senior year, her mother and father would have been horrified. I also think they would have been a good deal less sanguine about her decision if she were a boy.

In saying that scientific and mathematical ignorance is a 4 self-inflicted female wound, I do not, obviously, mean that cultural expectations play no role in the process. But the world does not conspire to deprive modern women of access to science as it did in the 1930's, when Rosalyn S. Yalow, the Nobel Prize-winning physicist, graduated from Hunter College and was advised to go to work as a secretary because no graduate school would admit her to its physics department. The current generation of adolescent girls—and their parents, bred on old expectations about women's interests—are active conspirators in limiting their own intellectual development.

It is true that the proportion of young women in science- 5 related graduate and professional schools, most notably medical schools, has increased significantly in the past decade. It is also true that so few women were studying advanced science and mathematics before the early 1970's that the percentage increase in female enrollment does not yet translate into large numbers of women actually working in science.

The real problem is that so many girls eliminate themselves 6 from any serious possibility of studying science as a result of decisions made during the vulnerable period of midadolescence, when they are most likely to be influenced—on both conscious and subconscious levels—by the traditional belief that math and science are "masculine" subjects.

During the teen-age years the well-documented phenome- 7 non of "math anxiety" strikes girls who never had any problem handling numbers during earlier schooling. Some men, too, experience this syndrome—a form of panic, akin to a phobia, at any task involving numbers—but women constitute the overwhelming majority of sufferers. The onset of acute math anxiety during the teen-age years is, as Stalin was fond of saying, "not by accident."

In adolescence girls begin to fear that they will be unattrac- 8 tive to boys if they are typed as "brains." Science and math epitomize unfeminine braininess in a way that, say, foreign languages do not. High-school girls who pursue an advanced interest in science and math (unless they are students at special institutions like the Bronx High School of Science where everyone is a brain) usually find that they are greatly outnumbered by boys in their classes. They are, therefore, intruding on male turf at a time when their sexual confidence, as well as that of the boys, is most fragile.

9   A 1981 assessment of female achievement in mathematics, based on research conducted under a National Institute for Education grant, found significant differences in the mathematical achievements of 9th and 12th graders. At age 13 girls were equal to or slightly better than boys in tests involving algebra, problem solving and spatial ability; four years later the boys had outstripped the girls.

10   It is not mysterious that some very bright high-school girls suddenly decide that math is "too hard" and "a waste of time." In my experience, self-sabotage of mathematical and scientific ability is often a conscious process. I remember deliberately pretending to be puzzled by geometry problems in my sophomore year in high school. A male teacher called me in after class and said, in a baffled tone, "I don't see how you can be having so much trouble when you got straight A's last year in my algebra class."

11   The decision to avoid advanced biology, chemistry, physics and calculus in high school automatically restricts academic and professional choices that ought to be wide open to anyone beginning college. At all coeducational universities women are overwhelmingly concentrated in the fine arts, social sciences and traditionally female departments like education. Courses leading to degrees in science- and technology-related fields are filled mainly by men.

12   In my generation, the practical consequences of mathematical and scientific illiteracy are visible in the large number of special programs to help professional women overcome the anxiety they feel when they are promoted into jobs that require them to handle statistics.

13   The consequences of this syndrome should not, however, be viewed in narrowly professional terms. Competence in science and math does not mean one is going to become a scientist or mathematician any more than competence in writing English means one is going to become a professional writer. Scientific

and mathematical illiteracy—which has been cited in several recent critiques by panels studying American education from kindergarten through college—produces an incalculably impoverished vision of human experience.

Scientific illiteracy is not, of course, the exclusive province 14 of women. In certain intellectual circles it has become fashionable to proclaim a willed, aggressive ignorance about science and technology. Some female writers specialize in ominous, uninformed diatribes against genetic research as a plot to remove control of childbearing from women, while some well-known men of letters proudly announce that they understand absolutely nothing about computers, or, for that matter, about electricity. This lack of understanding is nothing in which women or men ought to take pride.

Failure to comprehend either computers or chromosomes 15 leads to a terrible sense of helplessness, because the profound impact of science on everyday life is evident even to those who insist they don't, won't, can't understand why the changes are taking place. At this stage of history women are more prone to such feelings of helplessness than men because the culture judges their ignorance less harshly and because women themselves acquiesce in that indulgence.

Since there is ample evidence of such feelings in adoles- 16 cence, it is up to parents to see that their daughters do not accede to the old stereotypes about "masculine" and "feminine" knowledge. Unless we want our daughters to share our intellectual handicaps, we had better tell them no, they can't stop taking mathematics and science at the ripe old age of 16.

BUILDING VOCABULARY

1. Use a dictionary to look up any unfamiliar words in the phrases below from Jacoby's essay. Then, write a short explanation of each expression.
   a. sure footing (par. 3)
   b. cultural expectations (par. 4)
   c. overwhelming majority (par. 7)
   d. male turf (par. 8)

   e. spatial ability (par. 9)
   f. the exclusive province (par. 14)
   g. ominous, uninformed diatribes (par. 14)
   h. acquiesce in that indulgence (par. 15)
   i. ample evidence (par. 16)
   j. our intellectual handicaps (par. 16)
2. Explain the *connotations* (see Glossary) that the following words have for you. Use each word correctly in a sentence of your own.
   a. disability (par. 3)
   b. conspire (par. 4)
   c. adolescent (par. 4)
   d. vulnerable (par. 6)
   e. acute (par. 8)

UNDERSTANDING THE WRITER'S IDEAS

1. What condition is Jacoby trying to analyze? Is the main *effect* analyzed in this cause-and-effect analysis? On what primary cause does she blame women's "scientific and mathematical ignorance"? What exactly does she mean by that term? How is society to blame? What is the "process" mentioned in paragraph 4? What point does the example of Rosalyn S. Yalow illustrate?

2. Why does Jacoby think that the greater proportion of women students now in science and medical graduate and professional schools does not really mean that there are many women working in these areas?

3. According to Jacoby, when do most girls decide not to study the sciences? Why does this happen?

4. What is "math anxiety"? Who suffers more from it—boys or girls? Why? What does the author mean by "brains" (par. 8)?

5. Who was Joseph Stalin (par. 7)?

6. What subjects does Jacoby identify as "feminine"? Which are "unfeminine"?

7. According to the research evidence discussed in paragraph 9, how do the math abilities of girls and boys change between ninth and tenth grades? What does Jacoby say is the *cause* for this change? What are the *results?*

8. Explain what Jacoby means by the expression "self-inflicted female wound" (par. 4) and "self-sabotage" (par. 10). How are these expressions similar? How are they different?

9. What is the difference between what men and women study at coeducational universities?

10. What does Jacoby mean by "mathematical and scientific illiteracy" (par. 12)? Do only women suffer from this syndrome? According to Jacoby, why does it lead to "an incalculably impoverished vision of human experience"? What does she mean by this phrase? What examples of scientific illiteracy does Jacoby offer?

11. Why does the author think women feel more helpless than men do about scientific changes?

12. What suggestion does Jacoby offer in her conclusion?

UNDERSTANDING THE WRITER'S TECHNIQUES

1. What is the thesis statement of this essay? Why is it placed where it is? Find another statement before it that expresses a similar cause-and-effect relation. How are the two different?

2. Which paragraphs make up the introductory section of this essay? What cause-and-effect relation does Jacoby establish and how does she present it? How does Jacoby use narration in her introduction? How does she use illustration?

3. Both sentences of paragraph 5 begin with the phrase "It is true," yet the sentences contradict each other. How and why does the author set up this contradiction? What is the effect on Jacoby's analysis of beginning paragraph 6 with the words "The real problem is . . . "?

4. How does she use *process analysis* (see pages 296–297) from paragraph 6 to paragraph 8?

5. Where does the author use definition in this essay?

6. Trace the cause-and-effect developments in paragraphs 7 and 8.

7. In paragraph 9, Jacoby mentions a study conducted under "a National Institute for Education grant." How does the evidence she presents support her position in the essay?

8. What is the effect of the phrase "in my experience" in paragraph 10? What expository technique does she use there?

9. Trace the cause-and-effect patterns in paragraphs 11 through 13.

Be sure to show the interrelation between the causes and the effects (that is, how can the effect of something also be the cause of something else?)

10. How is the first sentence of paragraph 15 ("Failure to comprehend. . . .") a good example in itself of cause-and-effect development?

11. Why does Jacoby use quotation marks around the words "masculine" and "feminine" in the phrase " 'masculine' and 'feminine' knowledge" (par. 16)?

12. What is the overall tone of this essay? At three points, Jacoby switches tone and uses *irony* (see Glossary). Explain the irony in the following sentences:

    a. "What does it matter if, at age 16, she has taken a step that may limit her understanding of both machines and the natural world for the rest of her life?" (par. 2)

    b. "The onset of acute math anxiety during the teen-age years is, as Stalin was fond of saying, 'not by accident.' " (par. 7)

    c. "Unless we want our daughters to share our intellectual handicaps, we had better tell them no, they can't stop taking mathematics and science at the ripe old age of 16." (par. 16)

    Compare the irony in paragraph 16 with that in paragraph 2. How is the impact the same or different?

13. Who do you think is the intended audience for this essay? Cite evidence for your answer.

14. Jacoby uses a variety of transitional devices to connect smoothly the ideas expressed in the various paragraphs of this essay. Look especially at paragraphs 1 to 4. How does the writer achieve coherence between paragraphs? What transitional elements do you find in the opening sentences of each of those paragraphs? What other transitions do you find throughout the essay?

EXPLORING THE WRITER'S IDEAS

1. One of the underlying suggestions in this essay is that society has long considered there to be "masculine" and "feminine" subjects to study. What is your opinion on this issue? Do you feel that any subjects are particularly more suited to men or women? Which?

Why? Are there any other school activities that you feel are exclusively masculine or feminine? Why? Are there any jobs that are more suited to men or women?

2. In paragraph 4, Jacoby mentions the "old expectations about women's interests." What do you think these expectations are? What do you consider *new* expectations for women?

3. A *stereotype* is an opinion of a category of people that is unoriginal and often based on strong prejudices. For example, some prejudicial stereotypes include "All immigrants are lazy"; "All Republicans are rich"; "All women are terrible drivers." What other stereotypes do you know? Where do you think they originate?

4. The general implication of paragraph 8 is that people minimize their skills in order to be socially acceptable. In your experience, where have you seen this principle operating? Do you agree that people sometimes pretend to be unable to achieve something? What motivates them, do you think?

5. A recent study shows that among major nations in the world America's students—boys and girls—are the worst mathematics students. How do you account for the poor showing of Americans as mathematicians? How would you remedy this situation?

IDEAS FOR WRITING

Guided Writing

Select a job or profession that is usually male-dominated. Write a cause-and-effect analysis explaining how and why women both have been excluded from this profession *and* (or) have self-selected themselves from the job. (Some examples may include fire fighters, physicians, marines, bank executives, and carpenters.)

1. Begin with an anecdote to illustrate the condition that you are analyzing.

2. Present and analyze the partial causes of this condition that arise from society's expectations and norms.

3. State your main point clearly in a thesis statement.

4. Clearly identify what you consider "the real problem."

5. If you believe that women have deliberately excluded themselves, explain when and how the process of self-selection begins for women.

6. Analyze the consequences of this process of self-selection and give examples of the results of it.

7. Provide evidence that supports your analysis.

8. Link paragraphs with appropriate transitions.

9. In your conclusion offer a suggestion to change or improve this situation.

More Writing Projects

1. In your journal, make a list of everything that comes into your mind about the word "mathematics." Do not edit your writing. When you are finished, share your list with other people in the class. How do your impressions compare? contrast?

2. In a paragraph, analyze why you think boys and men exclude themselves from a certain field or profession—nursing, cooking, grammar-school teaching, and so on.

3. Margaret Mead, the famous anthropologist, once wrote, "Women in our society complain of the lack of stimulation, of the loneliness, of the dullness of staying at home." In an essay write a causal analysis of this situation.

SUMMING UP: CHAPTER 10

1. In her essay, Susan Jacoby analyzes a kind of "self-destructive behavior" on the part of many young women. Write an essay about a friend, relative, or someone else close to you who is doing something that you feel will have a very negative effect on him or her. Analyze *why* he or she is doing this and what effects, both short- and long-term, these actions are likely to have.

2. In this chapter, we hear female voices analyzing some of the experiences of women in American life today. Using their approaches to causal analysis, examine these experiences and the impact that they have had on your own thinking and activities. Clarify the connections between what you have read and how your sense of self has deepened or been sharpened.

3. Working in small groups, develop a questionnaire focusing on male and female roles in our society. After the questionnaire has been prepared, each group member should interview at least three people. When all the interviews have been completed, each group

should write a collective analysis of the results and present the analysis to the class.

4. In this chapter, both Roiphe and Francke deal with various aspects of married life. If you are currently married, write an essay analyzing why you did (or did not) want to get married. If you are unmarried, analyze why you do (or do not) plan to get married.

5. For the next week, keep a journal about something that is currently causing you to have mixed emotions. (Note: This should not be the same issue you've written about in the Guided Writing exercise following Linda Bird Francke's essay; it should be a *current* issue.) Try to write five reasons each day (or expand upon previous ones). At the end of the week, write an essay that analyzes how the issue is affecting your life or how you plan to deal with it in the future.

CHAPTER 11

Argumentation and Persuasion

WHAT ARE ARGUMENTATION AND PERSUASION?

When we use *argumentation*, we aim to convince someone to join our side of an issue. Often, we want the readers or listeners to change their views and adopt ours. We also use *persuasion* when we want a person to take action in a way that will advance our cause. In everyday life we hear the word "argument" used as a synonym for "fight." In writing, however, an argument is not a brawl but a kind of debate that requires subtle reasoning and careful use of the writers' tools you have learned so far. For this reason, we have put argumentation at the end of the writing course. In preparing your persuasive essay, you will be able to rehearse and refine the skills you have learned to this point.

The first step in arguing successfully is to state your position clearly. This means that a good thesis is crucial to your essay. For persuasive essays, the thesis is sometimes called a *major proposition*. This is an idea that can be debated or disputed, and the writer must take a definite side. Taking a strong position gives your essay its argumentative edge. Your readers must know what your position is, and must see that you have supported your main idea with convincing minor points. The weakest arguments are those in which the writer tries to take both sides, and as a result persuades no one. As you will see in the reading selections, writers often concede or yield a point to the opposition, but they do so only to strengthen the one side that they favor.

Writing arguments should make you even more aware of the need to think about audience. Since you already are convinced of the point you are presenting, your essay should focus on the people who will make up their minds on the basis of your evidence. Readers are not usually persuaded by assertion; you can't just tell them that something is true. You need to show them through well-organized support of main and minor points.

Evidence or support can come from many sources. Statistics, personal experience, historical events, news reports, and interviews can all serve to back up an argument. At the same time, a writer can use narrative, description, comparison and contrast, illustration, analysis, and definition to persuade.

Because we use argument in everyday life, we may think it is easy to argue in writing—but just the opposite is true. If we are arguing with someone in person, we can *see* our opponent's response, and quickly change our direction. In writing, we can only imagine the opponent and so must carefully prepare evidence for all possible responses. When we watch an argument on the evening news about abortion clinics, increasing the minimum wage, or accusations of sexual harassment, we often see only what media experts call "sound bites," tiny fragments of information. We may see just a slogan as a picket sign passes a camera. We may hear only a few sentences out of hours of testimony. We seldom see or hear the entire argument. When we turn to writing arguments ourselves, we need to remember to develop a complete and detailed and *rational* argument.

This does not mean that written arguments lack emotion. Rather, written argument channels that emotion into a powerful eloquence that can endure much longer than a shouting match.

In written arguments, the writer states the major proposition, or point he or she wants to make, and keeps it firmly in front of the reader. For example, a writer may want to argue that the U.S. government should grant amnesty to illegal aliens who have been in the country for at least two years. He may be writing to his member of Congress to persuade her to take action on a proposed bill. Once he knows his purpose and his audience, he is ready to plan an argument. Or the writer may want to convince readers that something is true—that single fathers make excellent parents, for example, or that wife abuse is an increasingly serious crime in our society.

Whatever the writer's topic, the keys to a good argument are

- A clear and effective major proposition
- A logical tone
- An abundance of evidence
- An avoidance of personal attacks

HOW DO WE READ ARGUMENTS?

Try to find out something about the background and credentials of the writer. In what way is he or she an expert on the topic?

Is the proposition presented in a rational and logical way? Is it credible?

Has the writer presented ample reliable evidence to back up the proposition? (If you look at the headlines on supermarket tabloid newspapers that try to persuade us that aliens have been keeping Elvis Presley alive on Mars, you will see why it is important to be able to evaluate a writer's evidence before accepting the proposition!)

Does the writer focus on the main idea, or does the essay distract us with unrelated information?

HOW DO WE WRITE ARGUMENTS?

State a clear major proposition, and stick to it.

Convince readers of the validity of your thesis by making an essay plan that introduces *minor propositions*. These are assertions that help clarify the reasons you offer to support your main idea.

Use *refutation*. This is a technique to anticipate what an opponent will say, and answer the objection ahead of time. Another technique is *concession*. You yield a small point to your opponent, but at the same time claim a larger point on your own side. Using these techniques makes your argument seem fairer. You acknowledge that there *are* at least two sides to the issue. Moreover, these devices help you make your own point more effectively.

Be aware of these pitfalls:

- Avoid personal attacks on your opponent, and don't let excessive appeals to emotion damage the tone of your argument.

- Avoid hasty generalization—that is, using main ideas without properly supporting them.
- Avoid drawing a conclusion that does not follow from the evidence in your argument.
- Avoid faulty analogies—that is, unequal comparisons.

Writing and Revising the Draft

Begin the rough draft. State your thesis boldly.

Back up all minor propositions with

statistics
facts
testimony from authorities
personal experience

Find a reliable listener and read your essay aloud. Encourage your listener to refute your points as strongly as possible.

Revise the essay, taking into account your listener's refutation. Find better support for your weakest points. Write a new draft.

Revise the essay carefully. Read it aloud again if possible. Prepare a final copy.

I Want a Wife
Judy Brady

Judy Brady, a wife and mother of two children, argues in this essay for a
wife of her own. Although her argument might seem strange, her position
will become apparent once you move into the essay. She presents many
points to support her position, so you want to keep in mind those you think
are the strongest.

Words to Watch

nurturant (par. 3)   giving affectionate care and attention

hors d'oeuvres (par. 6)   food served before the regular courses of the meal

monogamy (par. 8)   the habit of having only one mate; the practice of
    marrying only once during life

1   I belong to that classification of people known as wives. I am A
Wife. And, not altogether incidentally, I am a mother.

2   Not too long ago a male friend of mine appeared on the
scene fresh from a recent divorce. He had one child, who is, of
course, with his ex-wife. He is obviously looking for another
wife. As I thought about him while I was ironing one evening, it
suddenly occurred to me that I, too, would like to have a wife.
Why do I want a wife?

3   I would like to go back to school so that I can become eco-
nomically independent, support myself, and, if need be, support
those dependent upon me. I want a wife who will work and send
me to school. And while I am going to school I want a wife to
keep track of the children's doctor and dentist appointments. And
to keep track of mine, too. I want a wife to make sure my children eat properly and are kept clean. I want a wife who will wash
the children's clothes and keep them mended. I want a wife who
is a good nurturant attendant to my children, who arranges for
their schooling, makes sure that they have an adequate social life
with their peers, takes them to the park, the zoo, etc. I want a
wife who takes care of the children when they are sick, a wife
who arranges to be around when the children need special care,
because, of course, I cannot miss classes at school. My wife must

arrange to lose time at work and not lose the job. It may mean a small cut in my wife's income from time to time, but I guess I can tolerate that. Needless to say, my wife will arrange and pay for the care of the children while my wife is working.

I want a wife who will take care of *my* physical needs. I want a wife who will keep my house clean. A wife who will pick up after me. I want a wife who will keep my clothes clean, ironed, mended, replaced when need be, and who will see to it that my personal things are kept in their proper place so that I can find what I need the minute I need it. I want a wife who cooks the meals, a wife who is a *good* cook. I want a wife who will plan the menus, do the necessary grocery shopping, prepare the meals, serve them pleasantly, and then do the cleaning up while I do my studying. I want a wife who will care for me when I am sick and sympathize with my pain and loss of time from school. I want a wife to go along when our family takes a vacation so that someone can continue to care for me and my children when I need a rest and change of scene.

I want a wife who will not bother me with rambling complaints about a wife's duties. But I want a wife who will listen to me when I feel the need to explain a rather difficult point I have come across in my course of studies. And I want a wife who will type my papers for me when I have written them.

I want a wife who will take care of the details of my social life. When my wife and I are invited out by my friends, I want a wife who will take care of the babysitting arrangements. When I meet people at school that I like and want to entertain, I want a wife who will have the house clean, will prepare a special meal, serve it to me and my friends, and not interrupt when I talk about the things that interest me and my friends. I want a wife who will have arranged that the children are fed and ready for bed before my guests arrive so that the children do not bother us. I want a wife who takes care of the needs of my guests so that they feel comfortable, who makes sure that they have an ashtray, that they are passed the hors d'oeuvres, that they are offered a second helping of the food, that their wine glasses are replenished when necessary, that their coffee is served to them as they like it.

And I want a wife who knows that sometimes I need a night out by myself.

I want a wife who is sensitive to my sexual needs, a wife

who makes love passionately and eagerly when I feel like it, a wife who makes sure that I am satisfied. And, of course, I want a wife who will not demand sexual attention when I am not in the mood for it. I want a wife who assumes the complete responsibility for birth control, because I do not want more children. I want a wife who will remain sexually faithful to me so that I do not have to clutter up my intellectual life with jealousies. And I want a wife who understands that *my* sexual needs may entail more than strict adherence to monogamy. I must, after all, be able to relate to people as fully as possible.

9   If, by chance, I find another person more suitable as a wife than the wife I already have, I want the liberty to replace my present wife with another one. Naturally, I will expect a fresh, new life; my wife will take the children and be solely-responsible for them so that I am left free.

10   When I am through with school and have a job, I want my wife to quit working and remain at home so that my wife can more fully and completely take care of a wife's duties.

11   My God, who *wouldn't* want a wife?

BUILDING VOCABULARY

1. After checking a dictionary, write definitions of each of these words:
   a. attendant (par. 3)
   b. adequate (par. 3)
   c. peers (par. 3)
   d. tolerate (par. 3)
   e. rambling (par. 5)
   f. replenished (par. 6)
   g. adherence (par. 8)

2. Write an original sentence for each word above.

UNDERSTANDING THE WRITER'S IDEAS

1. What incident made Brady think about wanting a wife?
2. How would a wife help the writer achieve economic independence?

3. In what ways would a wife take care of the writer's children? Why would the writer like someone to assume those responsibilities?
4. What physical needs would Brady's "wife'" take care of?
5. How would a wife deal with the writer's social life? Her sex life?

UNDERSTANDING THE WRITER'S TECHNIQUES

1. In formal argumentation, we often call the writer's main point the *major* or *main proposition.* What is Brady's major proposition? Is it simply what she says in paragraph 2, or is the proposition more complex than that? State it in your own words.
2. What is the value of the question Brady asks in paragraph 2? Where else does she ask a question? What value does this other question have in its place in the essay? What impact does it have on the reader?
3. The points a writer offers to support the major proposition are called *minor propositions.* What minor propositions does Brady present to show why she wants a wife? In which instance do they serve as topic sentences within paragraphs? What details does she offer to illustrate those minor propositions?
4. What order has the writer chosen to arrange the minor propositions? Why has she chosen such an order? Do you think she builds from the least to the most important reasons for having a wife? What changes would you urge in the order of the minor propositions?
5. Most of the paragraphs here develop through illustration. Where has Brady used a simple listing of details? Why has she chosen that format?
6. Brady's style is obviously straightforward, her sentences for the most part simple and often brief. Why has she chosen such a style? What is the effect of the repetition of "I want" at the start of so many sentences? Why has Brady used several short paragraphs (5, 7, 9, 10, 11) in addition to longer ones?
7. What is the author's *tone* (see Glossary)? Point out the uses of *irony* (see Glossary) in the essay. How does irony contribute to Brady's main intent in this essay? How does the fact that Brady is a woman contribute to this sense of irony?

EXPLORING THE WRITER'S IDEAS

1. By claiming that she wants a wife, Brady is showing us all the duties and responsibilities of the woman in a contemporary household. Has Brady represented these duties fairly? Do husbands generally expect their wives to do all these things?

2. To what degree do wives today fit Brady's description? How could a wife avoid many of the responsibilities spelled out in the essay? How does the "modern husband" figure in the way many couples meet household responsibilities now?

3. Brady has characterized all the traditional and stereotyped roles usually assigned to wives. What "wifely responsibilities" has she left out?

4. Has Brady presented a balanced picture of the issues or is her argument one-sided? Support your opinion with specific references to the essay. Could the author have dealt effectively with opposing arguments? Why or why not? What might these opposing arguments be?

5. Answer the question in the last line of the essay.

6. Read the essays "Night Walker" by Brent Staples (pages 163–166) and "How Do We Find the Student in a World of Academic Gymnasts and Worker Ants" by James T. Baker (pages 287–290). Compare the use of stereotyping in these essays. How is it different from Brady's stereotypes?

IDEAS FOR WRITING

Guided Writing

Write an essay of 750 to 1,000 words titled, "I Want a Husband."

1. Write the essay from the point of view of a *man*. As Brady wrote as a woman who wanted a wife, you write this essay as a man who wants a husband.

2. Start your essay with a brief personal story as in paragraph 2 in "I Want a Wife."

3. Support your main point with a number of minor points. Expand each minor point with details that explain your premises.

4. Arrange your minor premises carefully so that you build to the most convincing point at the end.
5. Use a simple and straightforward style. Connect your points with transitions; use repetition as one transitional device.
6. Balance your longer paragraphs with occasional shorter ones.
7. End your essay with a crisp, one-sentence question of your own.

More Writing Projects

1. In your journal, copy any three sentences from Brady's essay that you find particularly provocative, challenging, strange, or unbelievable. Explain why you chose them.
2. Write a paragraph in which you argue *for* or *against* this issue: "A married woman belongs at home."
3. Write an essay in which you argue about whose role you think is harder to play effectively in today's society: the role of the mother or the role of the father.

Are the Homeless Crazy?

Jonathan Kozol

Jonathan Kozol is an educator and writer on social issues who, until recently, was perhaps best known for his book-length study *Why Children Fail*. In the past few years, he has turned his attention to America's ever-increasing problem of homelessness. In 1988, he published the book *Rachel and Her Children* on the subject, along with this essay, which derives from "Distancing the Homeless," published in the *Yale Review*. In this essay, Kozol effectively challenges the common idea that much of today's homelessness has resulted from the release of patients from mental hospitals in the 1970s. Instead, he presents a convincing argument that the "deinstitutionalizing" explanation is a self-serving myth, and that the reality is much simpler: Homelessness is caused by insufficient and overly expensive housing.

Words to Watch

deinstitutionalize (par. 1)   to let inmates out of hospitals, prisons, and so forth

conceding (par. 2)   acknowledging; admitting to

arson (par. 4)   the crime of deliberately setting a fire

subsidized (par. 5)   aided with public money

destitute (par. 6)   very poor

afflictions (par. 7)   ills; problems

stigma (par. 7)   a mark of shame or discredit

complacence (par. 7)   self-satisfaction

bulk (par. 10)   the main part

de facto (par. 11)   actually; in reality

resilience (par. 12)   ability to recover easily from misfortune

paranoids (par. 13)   psychotic people who believe everyone is persecuting them

vengeance (par. 14)   retribution; retaliation

1   It is commonly believed by many journalists and politicians that the homeless of America are, in large part, former patients of large mental hospitals who were deinstitutionalized in the 1970s—the consequence, it is sometimes said, of misguided lib-

eral opinion that favored the treatment of such persons in community-based centers. It is argued that this policy, and the subsequent failure of society to build such centers or to provide them in sufficient number, is the primary cause of homelessness in the United States.

Those who work among the homeless do not find that explanation satisfactory. While conceding that a certain number of the homeless are or have been mentally unwell, they believe that, in the case of most unsheltered people, the primary reason is economic rather than clinical. The cause of homelessness, they say with disarming logic, is the lack of homes and of income with which to rent or acquire them.

They point to the loss of traditional jobs in industry (2 million every year since 1980) and to the fact that half of those who are laid off end up in work that pays a poverty-level wage. They point out that since 1968 the number of children living in poverty has grown by 3 million, while welfare benefits to families with children have declined by 35 percent.

And they note, too, that these developments have occurred during a time in which the shortage of low-income housing has intensified as the gentrification of our major cities has accelerated. Half a million units of low-income housing are lost each year to condominium conversion as well as to arson, demolition, or abandonment. Between 1978 and 1980, median rents climbed 30 percent for people in the lowest income sector, driving many of these families into the streets. Since 1980, rents have risen at even faster rates.

Hard numbers, in this instance, would appear to be of greater help than psychiatric labels in telling us why so many people become homeless. Eight million American families now use half or more of their income to pay their rent or mortgage. At the same time, federal support for low-income housing dropped from $30 billion (1980) to $7.5 billion (1988). Under Presidents Ford and Carter, 500,000 subsidized private housing units were constructed. By President Reagan's second term, the number had dropped to 25,000.

In our rush to explain the homeless as a psychiatric problem even the words of medical practitioners who care for homeless people have been curiously ignored. A study published by the Massachusetts Medical Society, for instance, has noted that, with the exceptions of alcohol and drug use, the most frequent illnesses among a sample of the homeless population were trauma (31 percent), upper-respiratory disorders (28 percent), limb disorders (19 percent), mental illness (16 percent), skin diseases (15 percent), hypertension (14 percent), and neurological illnesses (12 percent). Why, we may ask, of all these calamities, does mental illness command so much political and press attention? The answer may be that the label of mental illness places the destitute outside the sphere of ordinary life. It personalizes an anguish that is public in its genesis; it individualizes a misery that is both general in cause and general in application.

7   There is another reason to assign labels to the destitute and single out mental illness from among their many afflictions. All these other problems—tuberculosis, asthma, scabies, diarrhea, bleeding gums, impacted teeth, etc.—bear no stigma, and mental illness does. It conveys a stigma in the United States. It conveys a stigma in the Soviet Union as well. In both nations the label is used, whether as a matter of deliberate policy or not, to isolate and treat as special cases those who, by deed or word or by sheer presence, represent a threat to national complacence. The two situations are obviously not identical, but they are enough alike to give Americans reason for concern.

8   The notion that the homeless are largely psychotics who belong in institutions, rather than victims of displacement at the hands of enterprising realtors, spares us from the need to offer realistic solutions to the deep and widening extremes of wealth and poverty in the United States. It also enables us to tell ourselves that the despair of homeless people bears no intimate connection to the privileged existence we enjoy—when, for example, we rent or purchase one of those restored town houses that once provided shelter for people now huddled in the street.

9   What is to be made, then, of the supposition that the homeless are primarily the former residents of mental hospitals, persons who were carelessly released during the 1970s? Many of them are, to be sure. Among the older men and women in the streets and shelters, as many as one-third (some believe as many as one-half) may be chronically disturbed, and a number of these people were deinstitutionalized during the 1970s. But to operate on that assumption in a city such as New York—where

nearly half the homeless are small children whose average age
is six—makes no sense. Their parents, with an average age of
twenty-seven, are not likely to have been hospitalized in the
1970s, either.

A frequently cited set of figures tells us that in 1955 the aver-   10
age daily census of non-federal psychiatric institutions was
677,000, and that by 1984 the number had dropped to 151,000.
But these people didn't go directly from a hospital room to the
street. The bulk of those who had been psychiatric patients and
were released from hospitals during the 1960s and early 1970s
had been living in low-income housing, many in skid-row hotels or boardinghouses. Such housing—commonly known as
SRO (single-room occupancy) units—was drastically diminished
by the gentrification of our cities that began in the early '70s. Almost 50 percent of SRO housing was replaced by luxury apart-
ments or office buildings between 1970 and 1980, and the remain-
ing units have been disappearing even more rapidly.

Even for those persons who are ill and were deinstitutional-   11
ized during the decades before 1980, the precipitating cause of
homelessness in 1987 is not illness but loss of housing. SRO
housing offered low-cost sanctuaries for the homeless, providing
a degree of safety and mutual support for those who lived within
them. They were a demeaning version of the community health
centers that society had promised; they were the de facto
"halfway houses" of the 1970s. For these people too—at most
half of the homeless single persons in America—the cause of
homelessness is lack of housing.

Even in those cases where mental instability is apparent,   12
homelessness itself is often the precipitating factor. For example,
many pregnant women without homes are denied prenatal care
because they constantly travel from one shelter to another. Many
are anemic. Many are denied essential dietary supplements by recent federal cuts. As a consequence, some of their children do
not live to see their second year of life. Do these mothers sometimes show signs of stress? Do they appear disorganized, depressed, disordered? Frequently. They are immobilized by pain,
traumatized by fear. So it is no surprise that when researchers
enter the scene to ask them how they "feel," the resulting reports
tell us that the homeless are emotionally unwell. The reports do
not tell us that we have *made* these people ill. They do not tell us

that illness is a natural response to intolerable conditions. Nor do they tell us of the strength and the resilience that so many of these people retain despite the miseries they must endure.

13   A writer in the *New York Times* describes a homeless woman standing on a traffic island in Manhattan. "She was evicted from her small room in the hotel just across the street," and she is determined to get revenge. Until she does, "nothing will move her from that spot. . . . Her argumentativeness and her angry fixation on revenge, along with the apparent absence of hallucinations, mark her as a paranoid." Most physicians, I imagine, would be more reserved in passing judgment with so little evidence, but this reporter makes his diagnosis without hesitation. "The paranoids of the street," he says, "are among the most difficult to help."

14   Perhaps so. But does it depend on who is offering the help? Is anyone offering to help this woman get back her home? Is it crazy to seek vengeance for being thrown into the street? The absence of anger, some psychiatrists believe, might indicate much greater illness.

15   "No one will be turned away," says the mayor of New York City, as hundreds of young mothers with their infants are turned from the doors of shelters season after season. That may sound to some like a denial of reality. "Now you're hearing all kinds of horror stories," says the President of the United States as he denies that anyone is cold or hungry or unhoused. On another occasion he says that the unsheltered "are homeless, you might say, by choice." That sounds every bit as self-deceiving.

16   The woman standing on the traffic island screaming for revenge until her room has been restored to her sounds relatively healthy by comparison. If 3 million homeless people did the same, and all at the same time, we might finally be forced to listen.

BUILDING VOCABULARY

1. Throughout this essay, Kozol uses medical and psychiatric *jargon* (see Glossary). List the medical or psychiatric terms or references that you find here. Then look up any five in the dictionary and write definitions for them.

2. Explain in your own words the meanings of the following phrases. Use clues from the surrounding text to help you understand.
   a. sufficient number (par. 1)
   b. primary cause (par. 1)
   c. poverty-level wage (par. 3)
   d. median rents (par. 4)
   e. low-income housing (par. 5)
   f. sheer presence (par. 7)
   g. intimate connection (par. 8)
   h. chronically disturbed (par. 9)
   i. skid-row hotels (par. 10)
   j. precipitating cause (par. 11)
   k. low-cost sanctuaries (par. 11)
   l. mutual support (par. 11)
   m. demeaning version (par. 11)
   n. natural response (par. 12)
   o. intolerable conditions (par. 12)
   p. angry fixation (par. 13)

UNDERSTANDING THE WRITER'S IDEAS

1. According to Kozol, who has suggested that the deinstitutionalizing of mental-hospital patients is the major cause of homelessness? Does he agree? If not, what does he identify as the major causes?
2. In the opening paragraph, what two groups does Kozol link together? Why? What relation between them does he suggest?
3. In New York City today, what percentage of the homeless are children? What is the average age of their parents? In the past twenty years, has the number of children living in poverty increased or decreased? What about welfare payments to families with children? How has this affected the homelessness situation?
4. What are "gentrification" and "condominium conversion" (par. 4)? How have they affected homelessness?
5. Explain the meaning of the statement: "Hard numbers, in this instance, would appear to be of greater help than psychiatric labels in telling us why so many people become homeless" (par. 5).
6. List in descending order the most common illnesses among the

homeless. From what does Kozol draw these statistics? What is
his conclusion about them?

7. In your own words, summarize why Kozol feels that journalists
and politicians concentrate so heavily on the problems of mental
illness among the homeless.

8. What are SROs? Explain how they figure in the homeless situation.

9. What is meant by the "press" (par. 6)? What are "halfway houses" (par. 11)?

10. What is Kozol's attitude toward former President Reagan? toward former New York City Mayor Ed Koch? Explain your answers with specific references to the beginning and ending of
the essay.

11. Summarize in your own words *The New York Times* story to
which Kozol refers. According to the *Times* reporter, why did
the homeless woman mentioned refuse to move from the traffic
island? Does Kozol agree with the reporter's interpretation? Explain.

12. In one sentence, state in your own words the opinion Kozol expresses in the last paragraph.

UNDERSTANDING THE WRITER'S TECHNIQUES

1. Which sentence states the *major proposition* of the essay?

2. Describe Kozol's argumentative purpose in this essay. Is it primarily to *convince* or to *persuade?* Explain.

3. In paragraph 1, the author uses a particular verbal construction
that he doesn't repeat elsewhere in the essay. He writes: "It is
commonly believed . . ."; "it is sometimes said . . ."; and "It
is argued. . . ." Why does he use the "it is" construction? What
effect does it have? How does he change that pattern in paragraph 2? Why?

4. In paragraph 2, Kozol uses the phrase "mentally unwell" instead of the more common "mentally ill," and he uses "unsheltered people" instead of "homeless people." Why does he use
these less-expected phrases? Does he use them again in the
essay? Why?

5. *Cynicism* adds an edge of pessimism or anger to a statement that
might otherwise be perceived as *irony* (see Glossary). In the sen-

tence, "The cause of homelessness, they say with disarming logic, is the lack of homes and of income with which to rent or acquire them" (par. 2), the clause set off by commas might be considered cynical. Why? Find and explain several other examples of cynicism in this essay. Are they effective? Are they justified?

6. Identify the *minor proposition* statements in this essay. How do they add *coherence* (see Glossary) to the essay?

7. How important is Kozol's use of *statistics* in this essay? Which are the most effective? Why?

8. What is the difference between *refutation* (see Glossary) and *negation* (see page 222)? Kozol uses refutation as a major technique in this essay. Analyze his use of refutation in paragraphs 1 and 2. List and discuss at least three other instances where he uses refutation. Where in the essay does he specifically use negation?

9. Evaluate Kozol's use of *cause-and-effect analysis* in paragraphs 1 through 6. In paragraph 12, how does Kozol revise the more commonly cited causal relationship between homelessness and mental illness?

10. Discuss Kozol's use of *comparison* in paragraph 7.

11. In what ways does he use *illustration?* How is his use of illustration in the last paragraph different from his other uses of it?

12. Characterize the overall *tone* of the essay. *How* does Kozol develop this tone? *Why* does he develop it?

13. Who is the intended *audience* for this essay? What is the *level of diction?* How are the two connected? What assumption about the audience is implied in the last sentence of paragraph 8?

14. Writers often use *rhetorical questions* in order to prompt the reader to pay special attention to an issue, but rhetorical questions are usually not meant to be answered. Evaluate Kozol's use of rhetorical questions in paragraph 12. What is the effect of the one-word answer, "Frequently"? Where else does he use rhetorical questions? What message does he attempt to convey with them?

15. Returning to the thesis in the course of an essay is often an effective technique to refocus the reader's attention before beginning a new analysis or a conclusion. Explain how Kozol uses this technique in paragraph 11 to make it a key turning point in the essay.

16. Although Kozol cites various studies and authorities, he makes little use of *direct quotations.* Why? Identify and analyze the

three instances where he *does* use direct quotations. How does it help to convey his attitude toward the material he's quoting?

17. Evaluate Kozol's conclusion. How does he establish an aura of unreality in paragraphs 15 and 16? Why does he do so? Does he effectively answer the title question? Explain.

EXPLORING THE WRITER'S IDEAS

1. In small groups, discuss your own experiences, both positive and negative, with homeless people.

2. If possible, conduct an interview with one or more homeless people. Try to find out:
   a. how they became homeless
   b. how long they've been homeless
   c. what they do to survive
   d. whether they feel there may be an end to their homelessness
   Write a report based on your interviews and share it with your classmates.

3. This essay is an excerpt from a much longer essay entitled "Distancing the Homeless," published in the *Yale Review*. How is the theme of that title expressed in this essay?

4. Kozol presents an impressive array of statistics. Working in small groups, compile as many other statistics about homelessness as possible. Each group should then draw a subjective conclusion from the data and be prepared to present and defend it to the class as a whole.

5. Read the following description of New York City's Bowery district:

> Walk under the El at night and all you feel is a sort of cold guilt. Touched for a dime, you try to drop the coin and not touch the hand, because the hand is dirty; you try to avoid the glance, because the glance accuses. This is not so much personal menace as universal— the cold menace of unresolved human suffering and poverty and the advanced stages of the disease alcoholism. On a summer night the drunks sleep in the open. The sidewalk is a free bed, and there are no lice. Pedestrians step along and over and around the still forms as though walking on a battlefield among the dead. In doorways, on the steps of the savings bank, the bums lie sleeping it off. Standing sentinel at each sleeper's head is the empty bottle from which he drained his release. Wedged in the crook of his arm is the paper bag containing his things.

This description is from E. B. White's 1949 essay "Here Is New York," the same essay from which the selection "The Three New Yorks" (pages 271–273) is drawn. It is but one small indication that the current problem of homelessness is nothing new. Try to find other examples, either written or visual, that indicate that homelessness is a long-standing social issue. (You may want to contact such organizations as the Coalition for the Homeless and the Salvation Army.)

In your own experience, how have the conditions of homelessness changed in your own environment over the past five years? The past one year?

IDEAS FOR WRITING

Guided Writing

Choose a controversial local issue about which you hold a strong opinion that is not the generally accepted one. (For example, you might write about a decision by the town council to build a new shopping mall on an old vacant lot; the limiting of public library hours in order to save money; a decision to open a halfway house in your neighborhood; and so forth.) Write an essay that will convince the reader of the validity of your stance on the issue.

1. Begin your essay with a discussion of the commonly held opinion on this issue. Use the verbal construction "it is" to help distance you from that opinion.
2. In the next section, strongly refute the commonly held opinion by stating your major proposition clearly and directly.
3. Develop your opinion by the use of comparative statistics.
4. While trying to remain as objective as possible, establish a slightly cynical edge to your tone.
5. If appropriate, include some jargon related to the issue.
6. Explain and refute the causal logic (cause-and-effect analysis) of the common opinion.
7. About midway through the essay, return to the thesis in a paragraph that serves as a "pivot" for your essay.
8. Link ideas, statistics, and opinions by means of well-placed minor proposition statements.
9. Continue to refute the common opinion by
   a. using rhetorical questions

b. citing and showing the invalidity of a recent media item on the issue

c. lightly ridiculing some of the "big names" associated with the common opinion on the issue

10. Conclude your essay with a somewhat unrealistic, exaggerated image that both reinforces your opinion and invokes the reader to reexamine the issue more closely.

More Writing Projects

1. In your journal write freely about this topic: the homeless. Do not edit your writing. Write nonstop for at least fifteen minutes. When you finish, exchange journal entries with another student in the class. How do your responses compare? contrast?

2. Do you think it is correct to give money to panhandlers? Write a paragraph in which you state and defend your opinion.

3. Write an essay in the form of a letter to your local chief executive (mayor, town supervisor, and so forth) in which you express your opinion about the local homeless situation. Include some specific measures that you feel need to be enacted. Draw freely on your journal entry in question 1 of this exercise.

Americans Work Too Hard

Juliet B. Schor

Juliet B. Schor teaches economics at Harvard University. Her recent book, *The Overworked American* (1991), argues that the philosophy of hard work clung to by both workers and employers leads not to greater wealth and productivity, but to exhaustion and inefficiency. Comparing American work practices with those in Europe, Schor attempts to persuade companies to increase vacation time if they want to compete in the global market.

Words to Watch

municipalities (par. 5)   cities
option (par. 5)   choice
induce (par. 6)   persuade
incentive (par. 6)   motivation
compensatory (par. 8)   made up for
mandatory (par. 8)   required
dearth (par. 10)   lack of

Americans suffer from an overdose of work. Regardless of who 1 they are or what they do, Americans spend more time at work than at any time since World War II.

In 1950, the U.S. had fewer working hours than any indus- 2 trialized country. Today, it exceeds every country but Japan, where industrial employees log 2,155 hours a year compared with 1,951 in the U.S. and 1,603 in the former West Germany.

Between 1969 and 1989, employed Americans added an 3 average of 138 hours to their yearly work schedules. The workweek has remained at about 40 hours, but people are working more weeks each year. Moreover, paid time off—holidays, vacations, sick leave —shrank by 15 percent in the 1980's.

As corporations have experienced stiffer competition and 4 slower growth in productivity, they have pressed employees to work longer. Cost-cutting layoffs in the 1980's reduced the professional and managerial ranks, leaving fewer people to get the job done. In lower-paid occupations, where wages have been reduced, workers have added hours in overtime or extra jobs to preserve their living standard. The Government estimates that more than seven million people hold a second job.

5   For the first time, large numbers of people say they want to cut back on working hours, even if it means earning less money. But most employers are unwilling to let them do so. The Government, which has stepped back from its traditional role as a regulator of work time, should take steps to make shorter work hours possible.

6   First, it should require employers to give employees the opportunity to trade income for time. Growth in productivity makes it possible to raise income or reduce working hours. Since World War II, we have "chosen" money over time; one reason is that companies give annual raises but rarely offer more free time. But California municipalities have offered this option successfully.

7   Second, standard hours should be required for all salaried jobs. Salaried workers often work 50 to 60 hours a week. When annual pay is fixed, an employer has a powerful motive to induce ever-longer hours of work, since each added hour is "free." This incentive would disappear if companies were obliged to set a standard work week for salaried jobs. Employees who worked beyond the standard would be entitled to paid time off.

8   Congress should legislate an annual four-week vacation regardless of a worker's length of service. Nearly all Western European workers get four- to six-week vacations. Americans struggle to hold on to their two weeks.

9   Other reforms are long overdue. Paid parental leave is necessary. Fringe benefits should be pro-rated by hours of work to give bosses reason not to overwork employees. Time-and-a-half pay for overtime should give way to compensatory time off, and mandatory overtime should be eliminated. Wages of adults who earn less than $10 an hour should be raised so they can avoid overwork.

10   Citing Japanese competition and other pressures, many employers would complain that they cannot afford such measures. But trading income for time is cost-free. And guaranteed vacations are likely to improve employees' performance: The fatigue and inefficiency resulting from long hours are a major reason why Japan's productivity remains lower than ours.

11   The growing scarcity of leisure, dearth of family time and

horrors of commuting all point to the need to resume an old but long-ignored discussion on the merits of the 30-hour or even the four-day work week.

BUILDING VOCABULARY

1. Examine the contexts in which the following italicized words are used in Schor's essay. Then try to write definitions for them. Check your definitions against the definitions in a dictionary.
   a. an *overdose* of work (par. 1)
   b. industrial employees *log* (par. 2)
   c. *stiffer* competition (par. 4)
   d. when annual pay is *fixed* (par. 7)
   e. long *overdue* (par. 9)
2. Use the following words in sentences of your own:
   a. industrialized (par. 2)
   b. competition (par. 4)
   c. productivity (par. 4)
   d. regulator (par. 5)
   e. legislate (par. 8)
3. Read paragraph 9 carefully. Then rewrite the paragraph in your own words. Keep the same ideas as Schor presents, but change the words, and even the sentence structure. Use a thesaurus to find synonyms.

UNDERSTANDING THE WRITER'S IDEAS

1. The author uses statistics in paragraphs 2 and 3 to begin her argument that Americans work more hours than workers in all other countries except Japan. In your words, write a sentence that summarizes what these statistics tell us, but do not use the numbers.
2. Why do American workers work so hard? What are the causes the author cites to explain her point?
3. In paragraph 5, Schor argues that workers are willing to trade money for time. Why does she believe that this would improve the workplace?

4. What is the difference between workers who are "salaried" (paragraph 7) and those who earn "wages" (paragraph 4)?
5. Why does the writer think that employers will try to refute her argument?
6. What is Schor's strongest argument in favor of giving workers longer holidays and limiting their weekly workload?

UNDERSTANDING THE WRITER'S TECHNIQUES

1. What is the thesis of the essay? Where is it placed? In your own words, what is Schor's *major proposition* in the essay? Where is it stated? Where is it repeated?
2. Why does the writer use statistics in paragraphs 2 and 3? Why does she place these statistics *before* she gives her argument?
3. At whom does Schor chiefly aim her argument? Whom is she trying to persuade to do what? How do you know? Who else would she want to influence?
4. Make an outline of the key points the writer makes to support her argument and note each transitional device she uses to shift from one point to the next. Which is her weakest point? Which is her strongest? How does she arrange them within the essay?
5. How does Schor try to anticipate her opponents' objections to her proposal? Where in the essay does she refute the opposition?
6. Where does the writer tell her readers how to solve the problem she raises?
7. What tone does Schor use throughout her argument? Give at least three examples to support your answer. Is this tone appropriate for the audience she wants to persuade? Why?

EXPLORING THE WRITER'S IDEAS

1. Many Americans grow up believing that there is no such thing as too much hard work. The American ethic condemns people who are seen as idle or lazy. What is Schor's response to this belief? Why does she think we need to change our system of values about work? Is her argument persuasive? Why?
2. How much is the minimum wage in your state? Figure out how

much money a worker earning that amount would make in a forty-hour week. Is this enough to maintain a standard of living above the poverty level? Use the library to research what the federal government considers "poverty level." Is this figure realistic? Explain.

3. Schor does not raise such issues as child care leave, provisions for health insurance in contracts, and the environmental quality of the workplace. How important are these and similar factors in computing how hard Americans work?

IDEAS FOR WRITING

Guided Writing

Write an argumentative essay in which you propose one major change in the American workplace that would improve the quality of workers' lives and raise productivity. You might persuade an employer to introduce a child care facility, to change to a four-day workweek, or to allow workers to use flex-time or job-share options.

1. Write a thesis statement and place it in the first paragraph. Use the introduction to explain why the lack of the change you propose is hurting American labor at present.

2. Use the library to find statistics to support your position. Find out how another country has solved this problem.

3. Anticipate your opponents' objections before you begin your key points.

4. Introduce your reasons, placing one in each body paragraph and using transitions to sequence the reasons. Start with the least important and build up to the most important.

5. Conclude by persuading your readers that *only* by using the steps you recommend will the American worker survive in the next century.

More Writing Projects

1. In your journal, describe an incident at work or in school where you saw a better way to do something and tried to persuade your

employer or teacher to adopt your method. Did the person take
your advice? Why?

2. Write a letter to the editor of your local paper in which you argue
   for or against a proposed civic project or proposed community
   program.

3. Write an argumentative essay that responds to one of these
   points:

   a. In America, women earn about eighty cents for every dollar a
      man earns.

   b. Illegal immigrants are frequently employed by American busi-
      ness because they work for less than minimum wage and en-
      dure substandard working conditions.

   c. Budget cutbacks in educational systems across the country
      mean that recent graduates are not equipped with the scientific
      and technological training they need to survive in the modern
      workplace.

America Needs Its Nerds

Leonid Fridman

Leonid Fridman studied mathematics at Harvard University and was in the doctoral program there. He claims with pride that he is a founding member of the Society of Nerds and Geeks. Fridman uses terms often thought of as negative to argue in favor of a change in America's values.

Words to Watch

derogatory (par. 1)   detracting; belittling
rampant (par. 3)   running wild
ostracized (par. 3)   banished; excluded
haunt (par. 6)   to be continually present
deride (par. 10)   to treat with mirthful contempt
debase (par. 10)   to lower in character, quality, or value

There is something very wrong with the system of values in a so- 1
ciety that has only derogatory terms like nerd and geek for the in-
tellectually curious and academically serious.

A geek, according to "Webster's New World Dictionary," 2
is a street performer who shocks the public by biting off heads of
live chickens. It is a telling fact about our language and our culture that someone dedicated to pursuit of knowledge is compared
to a freak biting the head off a live chicken.

Even at a prestigious academic institution like Harvard, 3
anti-intellectualism is rampant: Many students are ashamed to
admit, even to their friends, how much they study. Although
most students try to keep up their grades, there is but a minority
of undergraduates for whom pursuing knowledge is the top prior-
ity during their years at Harvard. Nerds are ostracized while athletes are idolized.

The same thing happens in U.S. elementary and high 4
schools. Children who prefer to read books rather than play football, prefer to build model airplanes rather than get wasted at parties with their classmates, become social outcasts. Ostracized for
their intelligence and refusal to conform to society's anti-

intellectual values, many are deprived of a chance to learn adequate social skills and acquire good communication tools.

5   Enough is enough.

6   Nerds and geeks must stop being ashamed of who they are. It is high time to face the persecutors who haunt the bright kid with thick glasses from kindergarten to the grave. For America's sake, the anti-intellectual values that pervade our society must be fought.

7   There are very few countries in the world where anti-intellectualism runs as high in popular culture as it does in the U.S. In most industrialized nations, not least of all our economic rivals in East Asia, a kid who studies hard is lauded and held up as an example to other students.

8   In many parts of the world, university professorships are the most prestigious and materially rewarding positions. But not in America, where average professional ballplayers are much more respected and better paid than faculty members of the best universities.

9   How can a country where typical parents are ashamed of their daughter studying mathematics instead of going dancing, or of their son reading Weber while his friends play baseball, be expected to compete in the technology race with Japan or remain a leading political and cultural force in Europe? How long can America remain a world-class power if we constantly emphasize social skills and physical prowess over academic achievement and intellectual ability?

10   Do we really expect to stay afloat largely by importing our scientists and intellectuals from abroad, as we have done for a major portion of this century, without making an effort to also cultivate a pro-intellectual culture at home? Even if we have the political will to spend substantially more money on education than we do now, do we think we can improve our schools if we deride our studious pupils and debase their impoverished teachers?

11   Our fault lies not so much with our economy or with our politics as within ourselves, our values and our image of a good life. America's culture has not adapted to the demands of our times, to the economic realities that demand a highly educated workforce and innovative intelligent leadership.

12   If we are to succeed as a society in the 21st century, we had

better shed our anti-intellectualism and imbue in our children the vision that a good life is impossible without stretching one's mind and pursuing knowledge to the full extent of one's abilities.

And until the words "nerd" and "geek" become terms of 13 approbation and not derision, we do not stand a chance.

BUILDING VOCABULARY

1. How does knowledge of prefixes, suffixes, or roots contribute to your understanding the meaning of the words below? Identify and explain the key word parts and provide definitions for the words themselves. Use a dictionary if you need one.
   a. prestigious (par. 3)
   b. anti-intellectualism (par. 3)
   c. undergraduates (par. 3)
   d. outcasts (par. 4)
   e. professorships (par. 8)
   f. world-class (par. 9)
   g. afloat (par. 10)
   h. pro-intellectual (par. 10)
   i. workforce (par. 11)
   j. leadership (par. 11)
2. Use context clues to determine meanings of the following words in italics. Then, choose the letter of the word or expression that most closely matches the meaning of the italicized word.
   1. face the *persecutors* (par. 6)
      a. those who relax
      b. those who support or defend
      c. those who oppress or annoy
      d. those who complain
   2. values that *pervade* our society (par. 6)
      a. are present throughout
      b. persecute
      c. weaken
      d. are important in
   3. *lauded* and held up as an example (par. 7)
      a. laughed at
      b. praised

    c. condemned

    d. ignored

  4. physical *prowess* (par. 9)

    a. weakness

    b. undeserved privilege

    c. attractiveness

    d. superior ability

  5. *cultivate* a pro-intellectual culture at home (par. 10)

    a. study in school

    b. develop by farming in

    c. trap

    d. promote the growth of

  6. their *impoverished* teachers (par. 10)

    a. hard-working

    b. poor

    c. long-suffering

    d. thoughtful

  7. *innovative* intelligent leadership (par. 11)

    a. bold and dramatic

    b. weak and tedious

    c. new and creative

    d. lost and hopeless

  8. *imbue* in our children (par. 12)

    a. inspire

    b. deny

    c. demonstrate

    d. avoid

  9. terms of *approbation*

    a. endearment

    b. weakness

    c. approval

    d. appreciation

 10. and not *derision* (par. 13)

    a. sorrow

    b. love

    c. support

    d. scorn

UNDERSTANDING THE WRITER'S IDEAS

1. What, according to Fridman, is the denotation of the word "geek"? In what way is the word metaphorical as we use it?
2. According to the writer, how are intellectuals viewed on American campuses? What about athletes? How is the situation similar in elementary and high schools?
3. What does Fridman see as a consequence of our making outcasts of schoolchildren who prefer to read or build models? In what societies does he think this situation is different?
4. What point does the writer make about professors and ball players?
5. What, according to Fridman, is the relation between our view of intellectuals and America's economic and political future?

UNDERSTANDING THE WRITER'S TECHNIQUES

1. What is the thesis of this essay? Would you consider it the major proposition? Why or why not? What sentence do you think best expresses the thesis? What would you point to as minor propositions?
2. How do the introduction and conclusion support each other in this essay?
3. How does Fridman use definition? comparison and contrast? causal analysis? In what ways do those strategies contribute to the argument?
4. What specific examples does Fridman provide to support his propositions?
5. What is the purpose of using the short fragment alone in paragraph 5? What other short paragraphs do you find? Why does Fridman use them?
6. Who is the audience for this piece? It was first published on the Op-Ed page of *The New York Times*. Does that surprise you? Why or why not?
7. What is the tone of this selection? Would you call it *serious, angry, relaxed, annoyed,* or *humorous?* Defend your choice.
8. Comment on the writer's vocabulary and word choice. Is the language well suited to the intent of the essay? What do the

slang words "nerd" and "geek" contribute here? In other instances would you say that the vocabulary was more difficult than necessary? Comment particularly on the appropriateness of words like "derogatory," "prestigious," "ostracized," "anti-intellectualism," and "approbation."

9. What transitional devices has the writer used to advantage here?

10. Comment on the strengths and weaknesses, if any, in the title. Why has Fridman chosen it instead of a title like "On Intellectualism" or "Opposing Anti-Intellectualism"?

UNDERSTANDING THE WRITER'S IDEAS

1. Do you agree that most students are ashamed to admit, even to their friends, how much they study? Why do you think this is so? How much do you study? Would you be reluctant to share your response with others in the class? Why or why not?

2. Do you agree with the statement, "For America's sake, the anti-intellectual values that pervade our society must be fought"? Why or why not? Has Fridman made the point satisfactorily that our future economy depends on our academic achievement and intellectual ability?

3. Fridman separates intellectuals and athletes. Must the two be split? Is it possible that both groups make important contributions to American society? Can any person represent the values inherent in both athletics and academics? Explain your position.

4. Fridman raises the issue of comparative worth in considering salaries for different jobs. Do you agree that athletes are paid much more than they are worth in our society? Are teachers paid less than they are worth? If so, how would you propose remedying the situation? Would you support government-set limits on how much people in certain job categories could earn?

5. The writer questions the value of accenting social skills over other skills that he feels are more important. What social skills do you think Fridman means? Do you see any value in emphasizing the development of social skills? Which social skills should we emphasize? Why?

IDEAS FOR WRITING

Guided Writing

Write an essay called "America Needs Its _____."
Fill in the blank with a word or term—preferably a slang or colloquial word—that names a group you feel has been ignored, overlooked, undervalued, or unsupported in our society. You might
want to use a word like "jocks," "loners," "kooks," "rednecks,"
"airheads," "losers," "showoffs," "boneheads," "con-artists." Or
choose a slang word of your own.

1. Write a short introduction to set the stage for your argument.
   Develop a major proposition and state it in a thesis sentence.
   Place your thesis strategically—either in the introduction or in
   some other key position in the essay. State minor propositions
   clearly.
2. Briefly define the term you've used to fill the blank in the title.
   Use a dictionary to develop your definition; then comment on it.
3. Develop a clear sense of who your audience is, and direct your
   argument to that group. Be sure that your word choice reflects
   your sense of audience.
4. Use specific examples to support your propositions.
5. Draw on other rhetorical strategies as needed—comparison,
   causal analysis, exemplification, and so forth.
6. Include one short paragraph—a fragment, perhaps, or a single
   sentence.
7. Develop a conclusion that logically extends your introduction
   and thesis.

More Writing Projects

1. In your journal make a list of everything that comes to mind
   when you think of the word "nerd." Don't edit your thoughts.
2. Using the journal entry above, write a one-paragraph argument
   for defining "nerd" as you have used the word. You may use a
   dictionary to get started, but essentially you should draw on your
   own perceptions to flesh out your definition and argument. To
   support your point provide examples where necessary.
3. Write an essay in which you argue *against* the need for a particular group. You might want to call your essay "America Does Not

Need Its _____." (Fill in the blank with a slang word, such as one of those mentioned at the beginning of the Guided Writing section.)

SUMMING UP: CHAPTER 11

1. Keep a journal in which you record your thoughts on, and observations of, homelessness in your part of the country. Try to gather specific data from reading, television viewing, or observation. Ask such questions as:

   How many are male? female?

   How many are children?

   How many are elderly?

   How many appear to be mentally ill?

   What symptoms or signs do they exhibit?

   Use the data, along with your observations, to present your position on homelessness in a letter to the editor of your campus or local newspaper.
2. Invite a local expert to class to speak on a current controversial issue. Write an essay of support for, or opposition to, the speaker's opinions.
3. Justify the inclusion of the essays by Kozol, Schor, Brady, and Fridman under the category "Argumentation and Persuasion." Treat the major issues that they raise, their positions on these issues, their minor propositions and use of evidence, and the tone of their language. Finally, establish the degree to which you are persuaded by these arguments.
4. Exchange with a classmate essays you've each written for a Guided Writing exercise in this chapter. Even if you agree with your partner's opinion, write a strongly worded response opposing it. Be sure you touch on the same, or similar, major and minor propositions.
5. Fill in the blanks in the following essay topic as you please, and use it as the major proposition for a well-developed argumentation-persuasion paper. Draw on the expository writing skills you have studied throughout the book.

   "I am very concerned about _____, and I believe it's necessary to _____."

CHAPTER 12

Prose for
Further Reading

An American Childhood

Annie Dillard

When everything else has gone from my brain—the President's name, the state capitals, the neighborhoods where I lived, and then my own name and what it was on earth I sought, and then at length the faces of my friends, and finally the faces of my family—when all this has dissolved, what will be left, I believe, is topology: the dreaming memory of land as it lay this way and that.

I will see the city poured rolling down the mountain valleys like slag, and see the city lights sprinkled and curved around the hills' curves, rows of bonfires winding. At sunset a red light like housefires shines from the narrow hillside windows; the houses' bricks burn like glowing coals.

The three wide rivers divide and cool the mountains. Calm old bridges span the banks and link the hills. The Allegheny River flows in brawling from the north, from near the shore of Lake Erie, and from Lake Chautauqua in New York and eastward. The Monongahela River flows in shallow and slow from the south, from West Virginia. The Allegheny and the Monongahela meet and form the westward-wending Ohio.

Where the two rivers join lies an acute point of flat land from which rises the city. The tall buildings rise lighted to their tips. Their lights illumine other buildings' clean sides, and illumine the narrow city canyons below, where people move, and shine reflected red and white at night from the black waters.

When the shining city, too, fades, I will see only those forested mountains and hills, and the way the rivers lie flat and moving among them, and the way the low land lies wooded among them, and the blunt mountains rise in darkness from the rivers' banks, steep from the rugged south and rolling from the north, and from farther, from the inclined eastward plateau where the high ridges begin to run so long north and south unbroken that to get around them you practically have to navigate Cape Horn.

In those first days, people said, a squirrel could run the long length of Pennsylvania without ever touching the ground. In those first days, the woods were white oak and chestnut, hickory, maple, sycamore, walnut, wild ash, wild plum, and white pine. The pine grew on the ridgetops where the mountains' lumpy spines stuck up and their skin was thinnest.

The wilderness was uncanny, unknown. Benjamin Franklin had already invented his stove in Philadelphia by 1753, and Thomas Jefferson was a schoolboy in Virginia; French soldiers had been living in forts along Lake Erie for two generations. But west of the Alleghenies in western Pennsylvania, there was not even a settlement, not even a cabin. No Indians lived there, or even near there.

Wild grapevines tangled the treetops and shut out the sun. Few songbirds lived in the deep woods. Bright Carolina parakeets—red, green, and yellow—nested in the dark forest. There were ravens then, too. Woodpeckers rattled the big trees' trunks, ruffed grouse whirred their tail feathers in the fall, and every long once in a while a nervous gang of empty-headed turkeys came hustling and kicking through the leaves—but no one heard any of this, no one at all.

In 1753, young George Washington surveyed for the English this point of land where rivers met. To see the forest-blurred lay of the land, he rode his horse to a ridgetop and climbed a tree. He judged it would make a good spot for a fort. And an English fort it became, and a depot for Indian traders to the Ohio country, and later a French fort and way station to New Orleans.

But it would be another ten years before any settlers lived there on that land where the rivers met, lived to draw in the flowery scent of June rhododendrons with every breath. It would be another ten years before, for the first time on earth, tall men and women lay exhausted in their cabins, sleeping in the sweetness, worn out from planting corn.

Shaved Heads and Pop-Tarts

Jeannine Stein

Almost every night at 10, you'll find heavy-metal rock 'n' rollers with long hair, pierced noses, tattoos, biker boots and leather jackets cruising the aisles of the Hollywood Ralphs on Sunset.

It's not how you'd envision a rocker's natural habitat, but even headbangers have to eat. Sure, any 7-Eleven will do when you have a craving for beef jerky and Junior Mints, but metalheads do not live by preserved meat and candy alone.

So in Hollywood, the grocery store of choice has been dubbed Rock 'N' Roll Ralphs. It's a hulking structure on the east end of the strip, near Poinsettia, a few minutes' drive to rock clubs like Gazzari's, the Roxy and Coconut Teaszer.

At the clubs, the long hair, tatts and motorcycles belong. Seeing those same people at Ralphs is a case of when worlds collide, a surrealistic blend of shaved heads, Pop-Tarts and Muzak, where baskets contain generic corn flakes and Metal Edge magazine and punkers share space with more mainstream types.

On a Thursday night in the liquor aisle, a woman hoists a large bottle of whiskey and hands it to her male companion. She is barely in her 20s. She wears Kabuki-ish makeup, her face whited out and accented with bright pink lipstick and eye shadow; she has a small hoop in her pierced eyebrow. She wears a black and white polka-dot floppy hat, an old T-shirt, pink and black horizontal striped tights and pink bouclé bike shorts. The man with her is yin to her yang—middle aged, dressed in brown trousers and a plaid shirt. They disappear down the aisle.

Two young guys stand in front of the deli counter. One keeps combing his hand through his dark Pre-Raphaelite hair. They stare and stare at the selection of luncheon meats for several minutes before Mr. Hair says, "Uhhhhh . . . so d'you like pickle loaf?"

Two more rockers, one with long bleached blond hair, the other with long blue-black hair, lope on gangly legs to the bread aisle, where they pick up a few loaves, squeeze and then abandon the bread. They take two cookies from the bakery pantry and eat them.

A tall, skinny guy with a skull and crossbones T-shirt and black baseball cap with "Suicidal Tendencies" stitched on it rushes over to the frozen food section clutching a coupon. He looks furtively up and down the case until he finds a box of Nestle's Crunch ice cream bars, grabs it, then picks up four six-packs of Coke and heads for the express line.

In the household aisle, a young woman with hair dyed to match her purple mini-skirt methodically eats California rolls and contemplates extension cords.

Meanwhile, a touching scene is unfolding by the cat food. A man with chunky silver rings and biker boots crouches down and takes about 10 minutes to decide between the 9-Lives chicken and cheese and the tuna for his pampered pet.

It's fair to say that most rockers who shop here aren't stocking up for the long haul. They come for the essentials, what it's going to take to get them through the night. The most frequently purchased items appear to be:

- Beer (usually 12-can packs in the cardboard carrying case)
- Water (gallon jugs)
- Luncheon meats
- Chips (tortilla, potato)
- Canned chili and soup
- Dried pasta
- Hamburger and hot dog buns
- Steak
- Pet food

Female rockers tend to make healthier choices, going for yogurt, fresh fruit, tuna and low-cholesterol margarine.

Even the wildest clubbies appear somehow tamed in this benign world of the grocery store. While they may spend every night in clubs, banging heads to Metallica, Megadeth and L7, here they're entranced by the Zen-like calm.

Maybe it's the flatness of the fluorescent lights, or the Muzak. It's hard to get jumpy when a syrupy rendition of the already syrupy "Garden Party" plays over the loudspeakers, or when the Video Recipe of the Week offers tips on how to cook a pork tenderloin. ("Sprinkle with parsley and serve!")

It's an atmosphere that's conducive to spending quantity time vacillating between hamburger dill chips and zesty bread-and-butter pickles. Faces go slack and eyes glaze over as the staggering number of choices renders people passive. Conversations rarely consist of anything more substantial than "Should we get the low-salt chips?"

If Black English Isn't a Language, Then Tell Me, What Is?

James Baldwin

The argument concerning the use, or the status, or the reality, of black English is rooted in American history and has absolutely nothing to do with the question the argument supposes itself to be posing. The argument has nothing to do with language itself but with the *role* of language. Language, incontestably, reveals the speaker. Language, also, far more dubiously, is meant to define the other—and, in this case, the other is refusing to be defined by a language that has never been able to recognize him.

People evolve a language in order to describe and thus control their circumstances, or in order not to be submerged by a reality that they cannot articulate. (And, if they cannot articulate it, they *are* submerged.) A Frenchman living in Paris speaks a subtly and crucially different language from that of the man living in Marseilles; neither sounds very much like a man living in Quebec; and they would all have great difficulty in apprehending what the man from Guadeloupe, or Martinique, is saying, to say nothing of the man from Senegal—although the "common" language of all these areas is French. But each has paid, and is paying, a different price for this "common" language, in which, as it turns out, they are not saying, and cannot be saying, the same things: They each have very different realities to articulate or control.

What joins all languages, and all men, is the necessity to confront life, in order, not inconceivably, to outwit death: The price for this is the acceptance, and achievement, of one's temporal identity. So that, for example, though it is not taught in the schools (and this has the potential of becoming a political issue) the south of France still clings to its ancient and musical Provençal, which resists being described as a "dialect." And much of the tension in the Basque countries, and in Wales, is due to the Basque and Welsh determination not to allow their languages to be destroyed. This determination also feeds the flames in Ireland for among the many indignities the Irish have been forced to undergo at English hands is the English contempt for their language.

It goes without saying, then, that language is also a political instrument, means, and proof of power. It is the most vivid and crucial key to identity: It reveals the private identity, and connects one with, or divorces one from, the larger public, or communal identity. There have been, and are, times, and places, when to speak a certain language could be dangerous, even fatal. Or, one may speak the same language, but in such a way that one's antecedents are revealed, or (one hopes) hidden. This is true in France, and is absolutely true in England: The range (and reign) of accents on that damp little island make England coherent for the English and totally incomprehensible for everyone else. To open your mouth in England is (if I may use black English) to "put your business in the street": You have confessed your parents, your youth, your school, your salary, your self-esteem, and, alas, your future.

Now, I do not know what white Americans would sound like if there had never been any black people in the United States, but they would not sound the way they sound. *Jazz,* for example, is a very specific sexual term, as in *jazz me, baby,* but white people purified it into the Jazz Age. *Sock it to me,* which means, roughly, the same thing, has been adopted by Nathaniel Hawthorne's descendants with no qualms or hesitations at all, along with *let it all hang out* and *right on! Beat to his socks,* which was once the black's most total and despairing image of poverty, was transformed into a thing called the Beat Generation, which phenomenon was, largely, composed of *uptight,* middle-class white people, imitating poverty, trying to *get down,* to get *with it,* doing their *thing,* doing their despairing best to be *funky,* which we, the blacks, never dreamed of doing—we *were* funky, baby, like *funk* was going out of style.

Now, no one can eat his cake, and have it, too, and it is late in the day to attempt to penalize black people for having created a language that permits the nation its only glimpse of reality, a language without which the nation would be even more *whipped* than it is.

I say that this present skirmish is rooted in American history, and it is. Black English is the creation of the black Diaspora. Blacks came to the United States chained to each other, but from different tribes: Neither could speak the other's language. If two black people, at that bitter hour of the world's history, had been able to speak to each other, the institution of chattel slavery could never have lasted as long as it did. Subsequently, the slave was given, under the eye, and the gun, of his master, Congo Square, and the Bible—or, in other words, and under these conditions, the slave began the formation of the black church, and it is within this unprecedented tabernacle that black English began to be formed. This was not, merely, as in the European example, the adoption of a foreign tongue, but an alchemy that transformed ancient elements into new language: *A language comes into existence by means of brutal necessity, and the rules of the language are dictated by what the language must convey.*

There was a moment, in time, and in this place, when my brother, or my mother, or my father, or my sister, had to convey to me, for example, the danger in which I was standing from the white man standing just behind me, and to convey this with a speed, and in a language, that the white man could not possibly understand, and that, indeed, he cannot understand, until today. He cannot afford to understand it. This understanding would reveal to him too much about himself, and smash that mirror before which he has been frozen for so long.

Now, if this passion, this skill, this (to quote Toni Morrison) "sheer intelligence," this incredible music, the mighty achievement of having brought a people utterly unknown to, or despised by "history"—to have brought this people to their present, troubled, troubling, and unassailable and unanswerable place—if this absolutely unprecedented journey does not indicate that black English is a language, I am curious to know what definition of language is to be trusted.

A people at the center of the Western world, and in the midst of so hostile a population, has not endured and transcended by means of what is patronizingly called a "dialect." We, the blacks, are in trouble, certainly, but we are not doomed, and we are not inarticulate because we are not compelled to defend a morality that we know to be a lie.

The brutal truth is that the bulk of the white people in America never had any interest in educating black people, except as this could serve white purposes. It is not the black child's language that is in question, it is not his language that is despised: It is his experience. A child cannot be taught by anyone who despises him, and a child cannot afford to be fooled. A child cannot be taught by anyone whose demand, essentially, is that the child repudiate his experience, and all that gives him sustenance, and enter a limbo in which he will no longer be black, and in which he knows that he can never become white. Black people have lost too many black children that way.

And, after all, finally, in a country with standards so untrustworthy, a country that makes heroes of so many criminal mediocrities, a country unable to face why so many of the nonwhite are in prison, or on the needle, or standing, futureless, in the streets—it may very well be that both the child, and his elder, have concluded that they have nothing whatever to learn from the people of a country that has managed to learn so little.

Women Are Just Better

Anna Quindlen

My favorite news story so far this year was the one saying that in
England scientists are working on a way to allow men to have
babies. I'd buy tickets to that. I'd be happy to stand next to any
man I know in one of those labor rooms the size of a Volkswagen
trunk and whisper "No, dear, you don't really need the Demerol;
just relax and do your second-stage breathing." It puts me in
mind of an old angry feminist slogan: "If men got pregnant, abortion would be a sacrament." I think this is specious. If men got
pregnant, there would be safe, reliable methods of birth control.
They'd be inexpensive, too.

I can almost hear some of you out there thinking that I do
not like men. This isn't true. I have been married for some years
to a man and I hope that someday our two sons will grow up to
be men. All three of my brothers are men, as is my father. Some
of my best friends are men. It is simply that I think women are
superior to men. There, I've said it. It is my dirty little secret.
We're not supposed to say it because in the old days men used to
say that women were superior. What they meant was that we
were too wonderful to enter courtrooms, enjoy sex, or worry our
minds about money. Obviously, this is not what I mean at all.

The other day a very wise friend of mine asked: "Have you
ever noticed that what passes as a terrific man would only be an
adequate woman?" A Roman candle went off in my head; she
was absolutely right. What I expect from my male friends is that
they are polite and clean. What I expect from my female friends
is unconditional love, the ability to finish my sentences when I
am sobbing, a complete and total willingness to pour their hearts
out to me, and the ability to tell me why the meat thermometer
isn't supposed to touch the bone.

The inherent superiority of women came to mind just the
other day when I was reading about sanitation workers. New
York City has finally hired women to pick up the garbage, which
makes sense to me, since, as I discovered, a good bit of being a
woman consists of picking up garbage. There was a story about
the hiring of these female sanitation workers, and I was struck by
the fact that I could have written that story without ever leaving

my living room—a reflection not upon the quality of the reporting but the predictability of the male sanitation workers' responses.

The story started by describing the event, and then the two
women, who were just your average working women trying to
make a buck and get by. There was something about all the ma-
neuvering that had to take place before they could be hired, and
then there were the obligatory quotes from male sanitation workers about how women were incapable of doing this job. They
were similar to quotes I have read over the years suggesting that
women are not fit to be rabbis, combat soldiers, astronauts, fire-
fighters, judges, ironworkers, and President of the United States.
Chief among them was a comment from one sanitation worker,
who said it just wasn't our kind of job, that women were cut out
to do dishes and men were cut out to do yard work.

As a woman who has done dishes, yard work, and tossed a
fair number of Hefty bags, I was peeved—more so because I
would fight for the right of any laid-off sanitation man to work,
for example, at the gift-wrap counter at Macy's, even though any
woman knows that men are hormonally incapable of wrapping
packages and tying bows.

I simply can't think of any jobs any more that women can't
do. Come to think of it, I can't think of any job women don't do.
I know lots of men who are full-time lawyers, doctors, editors
and the like. And I know lots of women who are full-time
lawyers and part-time interior decorators, pastry chefs, algebra
teachers, and garbage slingers. Women are the glue that holds our
day-to-day world together.

Maybe the sanitation workers who talk about the sex division of duties are talking about girls just like the girls that married dear old dad. Their day is done. Now lots of women know
that if they don't carry the garbage bag to the curb, it's not going
to get carried—either because they're single, or their husband is
working a second job, or he's staying at the office until midnight,
or he just left them.

I keep hearing that there's a new breed of men out there
who don't talk about helping a woman as though they're doing
you a favor and who do seriously consider leaving the office if a
child comes down with a fever at school, rather than assuming
that you will leave yours. But from what I've seen, there aren't
enough of these men to qualify as a breed, only as a subgroup.

This all sounds angry; it is. After a lifetime spent with winds of sexual change buffeting me this way and that, it still makes me angry to read the same dumb quotes with the same dumb stereotypes that I was reading when I was eighteen. It makes me angry to realize that after so much change, very little is different. It makes me angry to think that these two female sanitation workers will spend their days doing a job most of their co-workers think they can't handle, and then they will go home and do another job most of their co-workers don't want.

The Ugly Tourist

Jamaica Kincaid

The thing you have always suspected about yourself the minute you become a tourist is true: a tourist is an ugly human being. You are not an ugly person all the time; you are not an ugly person ordinarily; you are not an ugly person day to day. From day to day, you are a nice person. From day to day, all the people who are supposed to love you on the whole do. From day to day as you walk down a busy street in the large and modern and prosperous city in which you work and live, dismayed, puzzled (a cliché, but only a cliché can explain you) at how alone you feel in this crowd, how awful it is to go unnoticed, how awful it is to go unloved, even as you are surrounded by more people than you could possibly get to know in a lifetime that lasted for millennia, and then out of the corner of your eye you see someone looking at you and absolute pleasure is written all over that person's face, and then you realize that you are not as revolting a presence as you think you are (for that look just told you so). And so, ordinarily, you are a nice person, an attractive person, a person capable of drawing to yourself the affection of other people (people just like you), a person at home in your own skin (sort of; I mean, in a way; I mean, your dismay and puzzlement are natural to you, because people like you just seem to be like that, and so many of the things people like you find admirable about yourselves—the things you think about, the things you think really define you— seem rooted in these feelings): a person at home in your own house (and all its nice house things), with its nice back yard (and its nice back-yard things), at home on your street, your church, in community activities, your job, at home with your family, your relatives, your friends—you are a whole person. But one day, when you are sitting somewhere, alone in that crowd, and that awful feeling of displacedness comes over you, and really, as an ordinary person you are not well equipped to look too far inward and set yourself aright, because being ordinary is already so taxing, and being ordinary takes all you have out of you, and though the words "I must get away" do not actually pass across your lips, you make a leap from being that nice blob just sitting like a boob in your amniotic sac of the modern experience to being a

person visiting heaps of death and ruin and feeling alive and inspired at the sight of it; to being a person lying on some faraway
beach, your stilled body stinking and glistening in the sand, looking like something first forgotten, then remembered, then not important enough to go back for; to being a person marveling at the
harmony (ordinarily, what you would say is the backwardness)
and the union these other people (and they are other people) have
with nature. And you look at the things they can do with a piece
of ordinary cloth, the things they fashion out of cheap, vulgarly
coloured (to you) twine, the way they squat down over a hole
they have made in the ground, the hole itself is something to
marvel at, and since you are being an ugly person this ugly but
joyful thought will swell inside you: their ancestors were not
clever in the way yours were and not ruthless in the way yours
were, for then would it not be you who would be in harmony
with nature and backwards in that charming way? An ugly thing,
that is what you are when you become a tourist, an ugly, empty
thing, a stupid thing, a piece of rubbish pausing here and there to
gaze at this and taste that, and it will never occur to you that the
people who inhabit the place in which you have just paused cannot stand you, that behind their closed doors they laugh at your
strangeness (you do not look the way they look); the physical
sight of you does not please them; you have bad manners (it is
their custom to eat their food with their hands; you try eating
their way, you look silly; you try eating the way you always eat,
you look silly); but they do not like the way you speak (you have
an accent); they collapse helpless from laughter, mimicking the
way they imagine you must look as you carry out some everyday
bodily function. They do not like you. *They do not like me!* That
thought never actually occurs to you. Still, you feel a little uneasy. Still, you feel a little foolish. Still, you feel a little out of
place. But the banality of your own life is very real to you; it
drove you to this extreme, spending your days and your nights in
the company of people who despise you, people you do not like
really, people you would not want to have as your actual neigh-
bour. And so you must devote yourself to puzzling out how much
of what you are told is really, really true (Is ground-up bottle
glass in peanut sauce really a delicacy around here, or will it do
just what you think ground-up bottle glass will do? Is this rare,
multicoloured, snout-mouthed fish really an aphrodisiac, or will

it cause you to fall asleep permanently?). Oh, the hard work all of this is, and is it any wonder, then, that on your return home you feel the need of a long rest, so that you can recover from your life as a tourist?

That the native does not like the tourist is not hard to explain. For every native of every place is a potential tourist, and every tourist is a native of somewhere. Every native everywhere lives a life of overwhelming and crushing banality and boredom and desperation and depression, and every deed, good and bad, is an attempt to forget this. Every native would like to find a way out, every native would like a rest, every native would like a tour. But some natives—most natives in the world—cannot go anywhere. They are too poor. They are too poor to escape the reality of their lives; and they are too poor to live properly in the place where they live, which is the very place you, the tourist, want to go—so when the natives see you, the tourist, they envy you, they envy your ability to leave your own banality and boredom, they envy your ability to turn their own banality and boredom into a source of pleasure for yourself.

Daddy Tucked the Blanket

Randall Williams

About the time I turned 16, my folks began to wonder why I didn't stay home any more. I always had an excuse for them, but what I didn't say was that I had found my freedom and I was getting out.

I went through four years of high school in semirural Alabama and became active in clubs and sports; I made a lot of friends and became a regular guy, if you know what I mean. But one thing was irregular about me: I managed those four years without ever having a friend visit at my house.

I was ashamed of where I lived. I had been ashamed of where I lived. I had been ashamed for as long as I had been conscious of class.

We had a big family. There were several of us sleeping in one room, but that's not so bad if you get along, and we always did. As you get older, though, it gets worse.

Being poor is a humiliating experience for a young person trying hard to be accepted. Even now—several years removed—it is hard to talk about. And I resent the weakness of these words to make you feel what it was really like.

We lived in a lot of old houses. We moved a lot because we were always looking for something just a little better than what we had. You have to understand that my folks worked harder than most people. My mother was always at home, but for her that was a full-time job—and no fun, either. But my father worked his head off from the time I can remember in construction and shops. It was hard, physical work.

I tell you this to show that we weren't shiftless. No matter how much money Daddy made, we never made much progress up the social ladder. I got out thanks to a college scholarship and because I was a little more articulate than the average.

I have seen my Daddy wrap copper wire through the soles of his boots to keep them together in the wintertime. He couldn't buy new boots because he had used the money for food and shoes for us. We lived like hell, but we went to school well-clothed and with a full stomach.

It really is hell to live in a house that was in bad shape 10 years before you moved in. And a big family puts a lot of wear and tear on a new house, too, so you can imagine how one goes downhill if it is teetering when you move in. But we lived in houses that were sweltering in summer and freezing in winter. I woke up every morning for a year and a half with plaster on my face where it had fallen out of the ceiling during the night.

This wasn't during the Depression; this was in the late 60's and early 70's.

When we boys got old enough to learn trades in school, we would try to fix up the old houses we lived in. But have you ever tried to paint a wall that crumbled when the roller went across it? And bright paint emphasized holes in the wall. You end up more frustrated than when you began, especially when you know that at best you might come up with only enough money to improve one of the six rooms in the house. And we might move out soon after, anyway.

The same goes for keeping a house like that clean. If you have a house full of kids and the house is deteriorating, you'll never keep it clean. Daddy used to yell at Mama about that, but she couldn't do anything. I think Daddy knew it inside, but he had to have an outlet for his rage somewhere, and at least yelling isn't as bad as hitting, which they never did to each other.

But you have a kitchen which has no counter space and no hot water, and you will have dirty dishes stacked up. That sounds like an excuse, but try it. You'll go mad from the sheer sense of futility. It's the same thing in a house with no closets. You can't keep clothes clean and rooms in order if they have to be stacked up with things.

Living in a bad house is generally worse on girls. For one thing, they traditionally help their mother with the housework. We boys could get outside and work in the field or cut wood or even play ball and forget about the living conditions. The sky was still pretty.

But the girls got the pressure, and as they got older it became worse. Would they accept dates knowing they had to "receive" the young man in a dirty hallway with broken windows, peeling wallpaper and a cracked ceiling? You have to live it to understand it, but it creates a shame which drives the soul of a young person inward.

I'm thankful none of us ever blamed our parents for this, because it would have crippled our relationships. As it worked out, only the relationship between our parents was damaged. And I think the harshness which they expressed to each other was just an outlet to get rid of their anger at the trap their lives were in. It ruined their marriage because they had no one to yell at but each other. I knew other families where the kids got the abuse, but we were too much loved for that.

Once I was about 16 and Mama and Daddy had a particularly violent argument about the washing machine, which had broken down. Daddy was on the back porch—that's where the only water faucet was—trying to fix it and Mama had a washtub out there washing school clothes for the next day and they were screaming at each other.

Later that night everyone was in bed and I heard Daddy get up from the couch where he was reading. I looked out from my bed across the hall into their room. He was standing right over Mama and she was already asleep. He pulled the blanket up and tucked it around her shoulders and just stood there and tears were dropping off his cheek and I thought I could faintly hear them splashing against the linoleum rug.

Now they're divorced.

I had courses in college where housing was discussed, but the sociologist never put enough emphasis on the impact living in substandard housing has on a person's psyche. Especially children's.

Small children have a hard time understanding poverty. They want the same things children from more affluent families have. They want the same things they see advertised on television, and they don't understand why they can't have them.

Other children can be incredibly cruel. I was in elementary school in Georgia—and this is interesting because it is the only thing I remember about that particular school—when I was about eight or nine.

After Christmas vacation had ended, my teacher made each student describe all his or her Christmas presents. I became more and more uncomfortable as the privilege passed around the room toward me. Other children were reciting the names of the dolls they had been given, the kinds of bicycles and the grandeur of their games and toys. Some had lists which seemed to go on and on for hours.

It took me only a few seconds to tell the class that I had gotten for Christmas a belt and a pair of gloves. And then I was laughed at—because I cried—by a roomful of children and a teacher. I never forgave them, and that night I made my mother cry when I told her about it.

In retrospect, I am grateful for that moment, but I remember wanting to die at the time.

He Rocked, I Reeled

Tama Janowitz

In high school, I took a remedial English class—maybe it wasn't remedial, exactly, but without my knowing it, I had signed up for some kind of English class for juvenile delinquents.

Well, it wasn't supposed to be a class for juvenile delinquents, but somehow everybody but me knew that that was who it was for; maybe it was listed in the course catalog as being for those students in the commercial program, the general program, whatever it was called to distinguish it from the academic precollege preparation program.

But anyway, on the first day I figured out who this course was directed at: The students were surly and wore leather jackets, and the girls all had shag hair-dos as opposed to straight and ironed, which was how the "nice" girls wore their hair.

Knowing me, I must have signed up for that class because it indicated that no work would be involved. And I was prepared for the worst, because somehow, having moved and switched schools so many times, I had been stuck in juvenile delinquent classes before.

The juvenile delinquent classes generally meant angry teachers and angry students who never read the books assigned and never spoke in class, which was no wonder because the teacher was generally contemptuous and sneering.

But this class ended up being different; the main thing was that the teacher, Mr. Paul Steele, didn't seem to know he was teaching students who weren't supposed to be able to learn. He assigned the books—by Sherwood Anderson, by Hemingway, by Melville—and somehow by the due date everyone had read them and was willing to talk about them.

Mr. Steele was a little distracted, a little dreamy, and most excellent. It was one of the few times up until that age I had a teacher who spoke to me—and the rest of the class—with the honesty of one adult talking to others, without pretense or condescension; there was no wrong or right, just discussion.

In college, I had another great course—in geology, a subject for which I had no interest. Once again, I had signed up for something that looked easy, a "gut" course to fulfill the science requirement.

But this guy—I believe his name was Professor Sand, an apt name for a geology teacher—was so excited and in love with rocks, with everything pertaining to the formation of the earth, that to this day rocks and everything pertaining to the formation of the earth still get me excited.

Oolitic limestone, feldspar, gypsum, iron pyrite, Manhattan schist—the names were like descriptions of food, almost edible, and as around that time I was starting to become interested in writing, the enthusiasm that the teacher had for the subject was transferred to me into an enthusiasm for language.

And the names of the different periods—the Jurassic, the Pre-Cambrian—even though I can't remember much about them, the words still hold mystery and richness.

At the end of the semester, there was a field trip up to the Catskills, to put into practice some of the techniques discussed in class. We were taken to a fossil bed of trilobites where, due to the particular condition of the sedimentary bed, only the trilobite bodies had been preserved over the millennia.

After a few minutes of listening to the professor's explanation, I bent over and picked up a piece of rock with a small lump sticking out of it and took it over to him.

To me, all I had found was a rock with a lump; but Professor Sand was totally amazed—I was the only one ever to find a fossilized trilobite complete with head.

Really, at that point there was little to stop me from becoming a geologist except for the fact that I knew I could never do anything involving numbers, weights or measurements, which I suspected would at some point have some bearing on the subject.

I remember another teacher, in graduate school, Francine du Plessix Gray, who taught a course called Religion and Literature—another subject in which I had no interest. But the way she spoke was so beautiful, in an accent slightly French-tinged. And because she was so interested in her topic, the students became interested, and her seminars were alive and full of argument.

Of course, I had many other fine teachers along the way, but the ones who stand out in my mind were those who were most enthusiastic about what they were teaching.

Many subjects in which I initially thought I was interested were totally destroyed for me by the teacher's dry, aloof, pompous, disengaged way of speaking.

But when the teacher was as excited about the topic—as if he or she was still a little kid, rushing in from the yard to tell a story—that was when the subject became alive for me.

Is It Really That Wacky?

Pico Iyer

Yes, yes, we've heard all the jokes: we know that "spacy" and "flaky" seem almost to have been invented for California and that in the dictionary *California* is a virtual synonym for "far out." Ever since gold was first found flowing in its rivers, the Shangri-La La of the West has been the object of as many gibes as fantasies: just over a century ago, Rudyard Kipling was already pronouncing that "San Francisco is a mad city, inhabited for the most part by perfectly insane people" (others might say "insanely perfect"); and more than 40 years ago, S.J. Perelman was barreling down the yellow brick road to L.A., the "mighty citadel which had given the world the double feature, the duplexburger, the motel, the hamfurter, and the shirt worn outside the pants." Yes, we know, all too well, that "going to California" is tantamount, for many people, to going to seed.

And yes, much of the image does fit. Returning to California recently, I picked up a copy of the San Francisco *Chronicle* and read about people attending a funeral in pinks and turquoises and singing along to Bette Midler ("Dress for a Brazilian party!" the invitation—from the deceased—read); about a missing cat identifiable by "a rhinestone collar w/name and electronic cat door opener"; about women from Los Angeles hiring migrant workers to wait in line for them to buy watches shaped like cucumbers or bacon and eggs. On Hollywood Boulevard I saw a HISTORIC LANDMARK sign outside the site of "The First Custom T-Shirt Shop in California," flyers on the wall promoting a group call Venal Opulance and, in a store across the street, "Confucius X-Rated Mini-Condom Fortune Cookies." No wonder, I thought, that when I tell people I live in California—worse, that I choose to live in California—they look at me as if I had decided not to get serious or grow up; as if I had seceded from reality.

Part of the reason for all this, no doubt, is circumstance. For one thing, California wears its contradictions, its clashing hearts, on its sleeve: even its deepest passions are advertised on bumper sticker, T shirt and vanity plate. California is America without apologies or inhibitions, pleased to have found itself here and unembarrassed about its pleasure. So too, society in California is less a society than a congregation of subcultures, many of them with a membership of one: every man's home is his castle in the air here.

In addition, California's image has been fashioned largely by interlopers from the East, who tend to look on it as a kind of recumbent dumb blond, so beautiful that it cannot possibly have any other virtues. Thus the California of the imagination is an unlikely compound of Evelyn Waugh's Forest Lawn, Orson Welles' Hearst Castle, every screenwriter's Locustland and Johnny Carson's "beautiful downtown Burbank." Nice house, as they say, but nobody's at home.

By now the notion of California as a wigged-out free-for-all has become a legend, and as self-sustaining as every other myth. If I had read about vegetable-shaped watches in the Des Moines *Register*, I would have taken it as a reflection not on Iowa but humanity; but California has been associated with flakiness for so long that it is only the flaky things we see as Californian. There are five pet cemeteries in California registered with the International Association of Pet Cemeteries (vs. eight in New York State), but it is the canine mortuaries in L.A. that everybody mentions.

When California is ahead of the world, it seems outlandish; yet when its trends become commonplace, no one thinks of them as Californian. Large-scale recycling, health clubs, postmodern enchiladas all were essentially Californian fads until they became essential to half the countries in the world. And many people do not recall that such everyday, down-to-earth innovations as the bank credit card, the 30-year mortgage and the car loan were all, as David Rieff, in a new book about Los Angeles, points out, more or less developed by that great California institution the Bank of America.

And as the California myth gains circulation, it attracts precisely the kind of people who come here to sustain it: many of the newcomers to the "end of America" are Flat Earthers, Free Speechers or latter-day sinners drawn by the lure of a place where unorthodoxy is said to be the norm. Frank Lloyd Wright once said that all the loose nuts in America would end up in Los Angeles because of the continental tilt. Aldous Huxley suggested that the world resembled a head on its side, with the superrational Old World occupying a different sphere from the vacant, dreamy spaces of the collective subconscious of the West. California, he was implying, is the name we give our hopes and highest fantasies: an antiworld of sorts, governed by an antireality principle and driven by an antigravitational push. That is why he, like Thomas Pynchon and Ursula Le Guin and a hundred others, set his Utopia in California: with its deserts and rich farmland and a valley (if not a sea) named after death, California has impressed many as a kind of modern Holy Land.

California, in short, doesn't stand to reason (doesn't even lie down to reason). "The drive-in restaurant has valet parking," notes P. J. O'Rourke, and "practically everyone runs and jogs. Then he gets in the car to go next door." There's no beach at North Beach, he might have added, and *Sunset Boulevard* was shot on Wilshire. William Faulkner was arrested for walking here, and teenagers look older than their parents. "The tolerant Pacific air," in Auden's words, "makes logic seem so silly." And that air of unreality is only quickened by the fact that California is the illusion maker of the world: "Everyman's Eden" has made a living almost out of living up to other people's expectations.

What tends to get forgotten in all this is that the aerospace industry is centered in Southern California. The source of the state's wealth is that least dreamy and most realpolitik-bound of industries, defense. Yes, the late Gene Roddenberry may have dreamed up *Star Trek* here, but he drew upon his experience in the Los Angeles police department. For every quaint, picture-book San Francisco floating in the air there is an Oakland across the bay, gritty, industrial and real; for every Zen-minded "Governor Moonbeam" there is a hardheaded Richard Nixon; for every real estate office in the shape of a Sphinx there is a man behind the desk counting dollars.

The town in which I live, the pretty, sunlit, red-roofed Mediterranean-style resort of Santa Barbara, is typical. The town prides itself on being the birthplace of hot tubs and the site of the first Egg McMuffin. There is little or no industry here, and everyone seems to be working, full time, on his lifestyle. Thus people from Melbourne to Marseilles tune into the *Santa Barbara* soap opera, and in the Kansai region of Japan, women in SANTA BARBARA sweatshirts crowd into the Santa Barbara ice-cream parlor. Yet there is a theoretical-physics institute here, and there used to

be a think tank peopled by refugees from the University of
Chicago.

Besides, it is in the nature of bright sunlight to cast long
shadows: when Santa Barbara has hit the headlines recently, it
has been because of an eight-year drought so severe that even
showers were limited; a fire that destroyed 600 houses (including
mine); and one of the country's most poisonous homeless battles.
AIDS to the north, gang wars to the south; droughts interrupted by
floods; mudslides down the coast that left 91 dead in 1969; earth-
quakes that bring in their wake bubonic plague (contracted by
160 people as a result of San Francisco's 1906 earthquake): California, as Christopher Isherwood saw, "is a tragic country—like
Palestine, like every Promised Land."

Not long ago in Garden Grove, just two miles south of Dis-
ney-land, where Vietnamese *dentistas* (SE HABLA ESPAÑOL, say
their windows) bump against halal (Islam's equivalent to kosher)
grocery stores in Spanish-style malls, I paid a visit to the Crystal
Cathedral. On first encounter the area seems a vision of the ca-
cophonous dystopia of the future in which a hundred California
dreams collide and each one drowns the others out. Yet beneath
the surface there is a kind of commonness, a shared belief in all
of them that the future can be custom-made. This faith is implicit
in the immigrants' assumptions—they have voted with their feet
in coming here—and it is made explicit, for longtime residents,
by the Rev. Robert Schuller, who fills his sprawling Crystal
Cathedral with hymns to "Possibility Thinking."

Schuller's great distinction, perhaps, is not just that he was
a pioneer of the drive-in church (and his sermons are still broad-
cast, via a wide-screen TV, to overflow parishioners in the parking lot outside), nor that he has managed to erect a glittering
monument to his "Be-Happy Attitudes," but rather that he has
gathered a huge nationwide following out of preaching what is in
effect Californianism. For if you look at his books *(Your Future
Is Your Friend, Success Is Never Ending, Failure Is Never Final)*,
and if you walk around his church, as airy and futuristic and free
of Christian iconography, almost, as a Hyatt Regency hotel, you
can see that the heart of his scripture is simple optimism, on the
surface scarcely different from that espoused by New Age gurus
across the state (in the Bodhi Tree bookstore, *Create Your Own
Future* tapes are on sale, made by a Stanford professor).

Faced by such unlikelihoods, one begins to see that California is still, in a sense, what America used to be: a spiritual refuge, a utopian experiment, a place plastic enough, in every sense, to shape itself to every group of newcomers. It is a state set in the future tense (and the optative mood), a place in a perpetual state of becoming. Of course it's strange: it is precisely the shape of things to come, as unexpected as tomorrow. Of course it's unsettled: it's making itself up as it goes along.

"Ever Et Raw Meat?" and Other Weird Questions

Stephen King

It seems to me that, in the minds of readers, writers actually exist to serve two purposes, and the more important may not be the writing of books and stories. The primary function of writers, it seems, is to answer readers' questions. These fall into three categories. The third is the one that fascinates me most, but I'll identify the other two first.

The One-of-a-Kind Questions: Each day's mail brings a few of these. Often they reflect the writer's field of interest—history, horror, romance, the American West, outer space, big business. The only thing they have in common is their uniqueness. Novelists are frequently asked where they get their ideas (see category No. 2), but writers must wonder where this relentless curiosity, these really strange questions, come from.

There was, for instance, the young woman who wrote to me from a penal institution in Minnesota. She informed me she was a kleptomaniac. She further informed me that I was her favorite writer, and she had stolen every one of my books she could get her hands on. "But after I stole *Different Seasons* from the library and read it, I felt moved to send it back," she wrote. "Do you think this means you wrote this one the best?" After due consideration, I decided that reform on the part of the reader has nothing to do with artistic merit. I came close to writing back to find out if she had stolen *Misery* yet but decided I ought to just keep my mouth shut.

From Bill V. in North Carolina: "I see you have a beard. Are you morbid of razors?"

From Carol K. in Hawaii: "Will you soon write of pimples or some other facial blemish?"

From Don G., no address (and a blurry postmark): "Why do you keep up this disgusting mother worship when anyone with any sense knows a MAN has no use to his mother once he is weened?"

From Raymond R. in Mississippi: "Ever et raw meat?" (It's the laconic ones like this that really get me.)

I have been asked if I beat my children and/or my wife. I

have been asked to parties in places I have never been and hope never to go. I was once asked to give away the bride at a wedding, and one young woman sent me an ounce of pot, with the attached question: "This is where I get my inspiration—where do you get yours?" Actually, mine usually comes in envelopes—the kind through which you can view your name and address printed by a computer—that arrive at the end of every month.

My favorite question of this type, from Anchorage, asked simply: "How could you write such a why?" Unsigned. If E. E. Cummings were still alive, I'd try to find out if he'd moved to the Big North.

The Old Standards: These are the questions writers dream of answering when they are collecting rejection *slips, and the ones they tire of quickest once they start* to publish. In other words, they are the questions that come up without fail in every dull interview the writer has ever given or will ever give. I'll enumerate a few of them:

Where do you get your ideas? (I get mine in Utica.)

How do you get an agent? (Sell your soul to the Devil.)

Do you have to know somebody to get published? (Yes; in fact, it helps to grovel, toady and be willing to perform twisted acts of sexual depravity at a moment's notice, and in public if necessary.)

How do you start a novel? (I usually start by writing the number 1 in the upper right-hand corner of a clean sheet of paper.)

How do you write best sellers? (Same way you get an agent.)

How do you sell your book to the movies? (Tell them they don't want it.)

What time of day do you write? (It doesn't matter; if I don't keep busy enough, the time inevitably comes.)

Do you ever run out of ideas? (Does a bear defecate in the woods?)

Who is your favorite writer? (Anyone who writes stories I would have written had I thought of them first.)

There are others, but they're pretty boring, so let us march on.

The Real Weirdies: Here I am, bopping down the street, on my morning walk, when some guy pulls over in his pickup truck or just happens to walk by and says, "Hi, Steve! Writing any good books lately?" I have an answer for this; I've developed it over the years out of pure necessity. I say, "I'm taking some time off." I say that even if I'm working like mad, thundering down homestretch on a book. The reason *why* I say this is because no other answer seems to fit. Believe me, I know. In the course of the trial and error that has finally resulted in "I'm taking some time off," I have discarded about 500 other answers.

Having an answer for "You writing any good books late-ly?" is a good thing, but I'd be lying if I said it solves the prob-lem of *what the question means.* It is this inability on my part to make sense of this odd query, which reminds me of that Zen rid-dle—"Why is a mouse when it runs?"—that leaves me feeling mentally shaken and impotent. You see, it isn't just *one* question; it is a *bundle* of questions, cunningly wrapped up in one package. It's like that old favorite, "Are you still beating your wife?"

If I answer in the affirmative, it means I may have writ-ten—how many books? two? four?—(all of them good) in the last—how long? Well, how long is "lately"? It could mean I wrote maybe three good books just last week, or maybe two *on this very walk up to Bangor International Airport and back!* On the other hand, if I say no, what does *that* mean? I wrote three or four *bad* books in the last "lately" (surely "lately" can be no longer than a month, six weeks at the outside)?

Or here I am, signing books at the Betts' Bookstore or B. Dalton's in the local consumer factory (nicknamed "the mall"). This is something I do twice a year, and it serves much the same purpose as those little bundles of twigs religious people in the Middle Ages used to braid into whips and flagellate themselves with. During the course of this exercise in madness and self-ab-negation, at least a dozen people will approach the little coffee table where I sit behind a barrier of books and ask brightly, "Don't you wish you had a rubber stamp?"

I have an answer to this one, too, an answer that has been developed over the years in a trial-and-error method similar to "I'm taking some time off." The answer to the rubber-stamp question is: "No, I don't mind."

Never mind if I really do or don't (this time it's my own motivations I want to skip over, you'll notice); the question is, Why does such an illogical query occur to so many people? My signature is actually stamped on the covers of several of my books, but people seem just as eager to get these signed as those that aren't so stamped. Would these questioners stand in line for the privilege of watching me slam a rubber stamp down on the title page of "The Shining" or "Pet Sematary"? I don't think they would.

If you still don't sense something peculiar in these questions, this one might help convince you. I'm sitting in the cafe around the corner from my house, grabbing a little lunch by myself and reading a book (reading at the table is one of the few bad habits acquired in my youth that I have nobly resisted giving up) until a customer or maybe even a waitress sidles up and asks, "How come you're not reading one of your own books?"

This hasn't happened just once, or even occasionally; it happens *a lot.* The computer-generated answer to this question usually gains a chuckle, although it is nothing but the pure, logical and apparent truth. "I know how they all come out," I say. End of exchange. Back to lunch, with only a pause to wonder why people assume you want to read what you wrote, rewrote, read again following the obligatory editorial conference and yet again during the process of correcting the mistakes that a good copy editor always prods, screaming, from their hiding places (I once heard a crime writer suggest that God could have used a copy editor, and while I find the notion slightly blasphemous, I tend to agree).

And then people sometimes ask in that chatty, let's-strike-up-a-conversation way people have, "How long does it take you to write a book?" Perfectly reasonable question—at least until you try to answer it and discover there *is* no answer. This time the computer-generated answer is a total falsehood, but it at least serves the purpose of advancing the conversation to some more discussable topic. "Usually about nine months," I say, "the same length of time it takes to make a baby." This satisfies everyone but me. I know that nine months is just an average, and probably a completely fictional one at that. It ignores *The Running Man* (published under the name Richard Bachman), which was written in four days during a snowy February vacation when I was teaching high school. It also ignores *It* and my latest, *The Tommy-knockers. It* is over 1,000 pages long and took four years to write.

The Tommyknockers is 400 pages shorter but took five years to write.

Do I mind these questions? Yes . . . and no. Anyone minds questions that have no real answers and thus expose the fellow being questioned to be not a real doctor but a sort of witch doctor. But no one—at least no one with a modicum of simple human kindness—resents questions from people who honestly want answers. And now and then someone will ask a really interesting question, like, Do you write in the nude? The answer—not generated by computer—is: I don't think I ever have, but if it works, I'm willing to try it.

Wolf Rhythms

Barry Lopez

Imagine a wolf moving though the northern woods. The movement, over a trail he has traversed many times before, is distinctive, unlike that of a cougar or a bear, yet he appears, if you are watching, sometimes catlike or bearlike. It is purposeful, deliberate movement. Occasionally the rhythm is broken by the wolf's pause to inspect a scent mark, or a move off the trail to paw among stones where a year before he had cached meat.

The movement down the trail would seem relentless if it did not appear so effortless. The wolf's body, from neck to hips, appears to float over the long, almost spindly legs and the flicker of wrists, a bicycling drift through the trees, reminiscent of the movement of water or of shadows.

The wolf is three years old. A male. He is of the subspecies *occidentalis,* and the trees he is moving among are spruce and subalpine fir on the eastern slope of the Rockies in northern Canada. He is light gray; that is, there are more blond and white hairs mixed with gray in the saddle of fur that covers his shoulders and extends down his spine than there are black and brown. But there are silver and even red hairs mixed in.

It is early September, an easy time of year, and he has not seen the other wolves in his pack for three or four days. He has heard no howls, but he knows the others are about, in ones and twos like himself. It is not a time of year for much howling. It is an easy time. The weather is pleasant. Moose are fat. Suddenly the wolf stops in mid-stride. A moment, then his feet slowly come alongside each other. He is staring into the grass. His ears are rammed forward, stiff. His back arches and he rears up and pounces like a cat. A deer mouse is pinned between his forepaws. Eaten. The wolf drifts on. He approaches a trail crossing, an undistinguished crossroads. His movement is now slower and he sniffs the air as though aware of a possibility for scents. He sniffs a scent post, a scrawny blueberry bush in use for years, and goes on.

The wolf weighs ninety-four pounds and stands thirty inches at the shoulder. His feet are enormous, leaving prints in the mud along a creek (where he pauses to hunt crayfish but not with much interest) more than five inches long by just over four wide.

He has two fractured ribs, broken by a moose a year before. They are healed now, but a sharp eye would notice the irregularity. The skin on his right hip is scarred, from a fight with another wolf in a neighboring pack when he was a yearling. He has not had anything but a few mice and a piece of arctic char in three days, but he is not hungry. He is traveling. The char was a day old, left on rocks along the river by bears.

The wolf is tied by subtle threads to the woods he moves through. His fur carries seeds that will fall off, effectively dispersed, along the trail some miles from where they first caught in his fur. And miles distant is a raven perched on the ribs of a caribou the wolf helped kill ten days ago, pecking like a chicken at the decaying scraps of meat. A smart snowshoe hare that eluded the wolf and left him exhausted when he was a pup has been dead a year now, food for an owl. The den in which he was born one April evening was home to porcupines last winter.

It is now late in the afternoon. The wolf has stopped traveling, has lain down to sleep on cool earth beneath a rock outcropping. Mosquitoes rest on his ears. His ears flicker. He begins to waken. He rolls on his back and lies motionless with his front legs pointed toward the sky but folded like wilted flowers, his back legs splayed, and his nose and tail curved toward each other on one side of his body. After a few moments he flops on his side, rises, stretches, and moves a few feet to inspect—minutely, delicately— a crevice in the rock outcropping and finds or doesn't find what draws him there. And then he ascends the rock face, bounding and balancing momentarily before bounding again, appearing slightly unsure of the process—but committed. A few minutes later he bolts suddenly into the woods, achieving full speed, almost forty miles per hour, for forty or fifty yards before he begins to skid, to lunge at a lodgepole pine cone. He trots away with it, his head erect, tail erect, his hips slightly to one side and out of line with his shoulders, as though hindquarters were impatient with forequarters, the cone inert in his mouth. He carries it for a hundred feet before dropping it by the trail. He sniffs it. He goes on.

The underfur next to his skin has begun to thicken with the coming of fall. In the months to follow it will become so dense between his shoulders it will be almost impossible to work a finger down to his skin. In seven months he will weigh less: eighty-nine pounds. He will have tried unsuccessfully to mate with another wolf in the pack. He will have helped kill four moose and thirteen caribou. He will have fallen through ice into a creek at twenty-two below zero but not frozen. He will have fought other wolves.

He moves along now at the edge of a clearing. The wind coming down valley surrounds him with a river of odors, as if he were a migrating salmon. He can smell ptarmigan and deer droppings. He can smell willow and spruce and the fading sweetness of fireweed. Above, he sees a hawk circling, and farther south, lower on the horizon, a flock of sharp-tailed sparrows going east. He senses through his pads with each step the dryness of the moss beneath his feet, and the ridges of old tracks, some his own. He hears the sound his feet make. He hears the occasional movement of deer mice and voles. Summer food.

Toward dusk he is standing by a creek, lapping the cool water, when a wolf howls—a long wail that quickly reaches pitch and then tapers, with several harmonics, long moments to a tremolo. He recognizes his sister. He waits a few moments, then, throwing his head back and closing his eyes, he howls. The howl is shorter and it changes pitch twice in the beginning, very quickly. There is no answer.

The female is a mile away and she trots off obliquely through the trees. The other wolf stands listening, laps water again, then he too departs, moving quickly, quietly through the trees, away from the trail he had been on. In a few minutes the two wolves meet. They approach each other briskly, almost formally, tails erect and moving somewhat as deer move. When they come together they make high squeaking noises and encircle each other, rubbing and pushing, poking their noses into each other's neck fur, backing away to stretch, chasing each other for a few steps, then standing quietly together, one putting a head over the other's back. And then they are gone, down a vague trail, the female first. After a few hundred yards they begin, simultaneously, to wag their tails.

In the days that follow, they will meet another wolf from the pack, a second female, younger by a year, and the three of them will kill a caribou. They will travel together ten or twenty miles a day, through the country where they live, eating and sleeping, birthing, playing with sticks, chasing ravens, growing old, barking at bears, scent-marking trails, killing moose, and staring at the way water in a creek breaks around their legs and flows on.

Living with My VCR

Nora Ephron

When all this started, two Christmases ago, I did not have a video-cassette recorder. What I had was a position on video-cassette recorders. I was against them. It seemed to me that the fundamental idea of the VCR—which is that if you go out and miss what's on television, you can always watch it later—flew in the face of almost the only thing I truly believed—which is that the whole point of going out is to miss what's on television. Let's face it: Part of being a grown-up is that every day you have to choose between going out at night or staying home, and it is one of life's unhappy truths that there is not enough time to do both.

Finally, though, I broke down, but not entirely. I did not buy a video-cassette recorder. I rented one. And I didn't rent one for myself—I myself intended to stand firm and hold to my only principle. I rented one for my children. For $29 a month, I would tape "The Wizard of Oz" and "Mary Poppins" and "Born Free," and my children would be able to watch them from time to time. In six months, when my rental contract expired, I would re-evaluate.

For quite a while, I taped for my children. Of course I had to subscribe to Home Box Office and Cinemax in addition to my normal cable service, for $19 more a month—but for the children. I taped "Oliver" and "Annie" and "My Fair Lady" for the children. And then I stopped taping for the children—who don't watch much television, in any case—and started to tape for myself.

I now tape for myself all the time. I tape when I am out, I tape when I am at home and doing other things, and I tape when I am asleep. At this very moment, as I am typing, I am taping. The entire length of my bedroom bookshelf has been turned over to video cassettes, mostly of movies; they are numbered and indexed and stacked in order in a household where absolutely nothing else is. Occasionally I find myself browsing through publications like Video Review and worrying whether I shouldn't switch to chrome-based videotape or have my heads cleaned or upgrade to a machine that does six or seven things at once and can be set to tape six or seven months in advance. No doubt I will soon find myself shopping at some Video Village for racks and storage systems especially made for what is known as "the serious collector."

How this happened, how I became a compulsive videotaper, is a mystery to me, because my position on video-cassette recorders is very much the same as the one I started with. I am still against them. Now, though, I am against them for different reasons: Now I hate them out of knowledge rather than ignorance. The other technological breakthroughs that have made their way into my life after my initial pigheaded opposition to them—like the electric typewriter and the Cuisinart—have all settled peacefully into my home. I never think about them except when I'm using them, and when I'm using them I take them for granted. They do exactly what I want them to do. I put the slicing disk into the Cuisinart, and damned if the thing doesn't slice things up just the way it's supposed to. But there's no taking a VCR for granted. It squats there, next to the television, ready to rebuke any fool who expects something of it.

A child can operate a VCR, of course. Only a few maneuvers are required to tape something, and only a few more are required to tape something while you are out. You must set the time to the correct time you wish the recording to begin and end. You must punch the channel selector. You must insert a videotape. And, on my set, you must switch the "on" button to "time record." Theoretically, you can then go out and have a high old time, knowing that even if you waste the evening, your video-cassette recorder will not.

Sometimes things work out. Sometimes I return home, rewind the tape, and discover that the machine has recorded exactly what I'd hoped it would. But more often than not, what is on the tape is not at all what I'd intended; in fact, the moments leading up to the revelation of what is actually on my video cassettes are without doubt the most suspenseful of my humdrum existence. As I rewind the tape, I have no idea what, if anything, will be on it; as I press the "play" button, I have not a clue as to what in particular has gone wrong. All I ever know for certain is that something has.

Usually it's my fault. I admit it. I have mis-set the timer or channel selector or misread the newspaper listing. I have knelt at the foot of my machine and methodically, carefully, painstakingly set it—and set it wrong. This is extremely upsetting to me—I am normally quite competent when it comes to machines—but I can live with it. What is far more disturbing are the times when what has gone wrong is not my fault at all but the fault of outside forces over which I have no control whatsoever. The program listing in the newspaper lists the channel incorrectly. The cable guide inaccurately lists the length of the movie, lopping off the last 10 minutes. The evening's schedule of television programming is thrown off by an athletic event. The educational station is having a fund-raiser.

You would be amazed at how often outside forces affect a video-cassette recorder, and I think I am safe in saying that video-cassette recorders are the only household appliances that outside forces are even relevant to. As a result, my video-cassette library is a raggedy collection of near misses: "The Thin Man" without the opening; "King Kong" without the ending; a football game instead of "Murder, She Wrote"; dozens of PBS auctions and fund-raisers instead of dozens of episodes of "Masterpiece Theater." All told, my success rate at videotaping is even lower than my success rate at buying clothes I turn out to like as much as I did in the store; the machine provides more opportunities per week to make mistakes than anything else in my life.

Every summer and at Christmastime, I re-evaluate my six-month rental contract. I have three options: I can buy the video-cassette recorder, which I would never do because I hate it so much; I can cancel the contract and turn in the machine, which I would never do because I am so addicted to videotaping; or I can go on renting. I go on renting. In two years I have spent enough money renting to buy two video-cassette recorders at the discount electronics place in the neighborhood, but I don't care. Renting is my way of deluding myself that I have some power over my VCR; it's my way of believing that I can still some day reject the machine in an ultimate way (by sending it back)—or else forgive it (by buying it)—for all the times it has rejected me.

In the meantime, I have my pathetic but ever-expanding collection of cassettes. "Why don't you just rent the movies?" a friend said to me recently, after I finished complaining about the fact that my tape of "The Maltese Falcon" now has a segment of "Little House on the Prairie" in the middle of it. Rent them?

What a bizarre suggestion. Then I would have to watch them. And I don't watch my videotapes. I don't have time. I would virtually have to watch my videotapes for the next two years just to catch up with what my VCR has recorded so far; and in any event, even if I did have time, the VCR would be taping and would therefore be unavailable for use in viewing.

So I merely accumulate video cassettes. I haven't accumulated anything this mindlessly since my days in college, when I was obsessed with filling my bookshelf, it didn't matter with what; what mattered was that I believed that if I had a lot of books, it would say something about my intelligence and taste. On some level, I suppose I believe that if I have a lot of video cassettes, it will say something—not about my intelligence or taste, but about my intentions. I intend to live long enough to have time to watch my videotapes. Any way you look at it, that means forever.

To the Victor Belongs the Language
Rita Mae Brown

Language is the road map of culture. It tells you where its people come from and where they are going. A study of the English language reveals a dramatic history and astonishing versatility. It is the language of survivors, of conquerors, of laughter.

A word is more like a pendulum than a fixed entity. It can sweep by your ear and through its very sound suggest hidden meanings, preconscious associations. Listen to these words: "blood," "tranquil," "democracy." Besides their literal meanings, they carry associations that are cultural as well as personal.

One word can illustrate this idea of meaning in flux: "revolution." The word enters English in the 14th century from the Latin via French. (At least that's when it was first written; it may have been spoken earlier.) "Revolution" means a turning around; that was how it was used. Most often "revolution" was applied to astronomy to describe a planet revolving in space. The word carried no political meaning.

"Rebellion" was the loaded political word. It too comes from Latin (as does about 60 percent of our word pool), and it means a renewal of war. In the 14th century "rebellion" was used to indicate a resistance to lawful authority. This can yield amusing results. Whichever side won called the losers rebels—they, the winners, being the repositories of virtue and more gunpowder. This meaning lingers today. The Confederate fighters are called rebels. Since the North won that war, it can be dismissed as a rebellion and not called a revolution. Whoever wins the war redefines the language.

"Revolution" did not acquire a political meaning in English until at least the 16th century. Its meaning—a circular movement—was still tied to its origin but had spilled over into politics. It could now mean a turnaround in power. This is more complicated than you might think.

The 16th century, vibrant, cruel, progressive, held as a persistent popular image the wheel of fortune—an image familiar to anyone who has played with a tarot deck. Human beings dangle on a giant wheel. Some are on the bottom turning upward, some are on the top, and some are hurtling toward the ground. It's as good an image as any for the sudden twists and turns of Fate, Life or the Human Condition. This idea was so dominant at the time that the word "revolution" absorbed its meaning. Instead of a card or a complicated explanation of the wheel of fortune, that one word captured the concept. It's a concept we would do well to remember.

Politically, "rebellion" was still the more potent word. Cromwell's seizure of state power in the mid-17th century came to be called the Great Rebellion, because Charles II followed Cromwell in the restoration of monarchy. Cromwell didn't call his own actions rebellious. In 1689 when William and Mary took over the throne of England, the event was tagged the Glorious Revolution. "Revolution" is benign here and politically inferior in intensity to "rebellion."

By 1796 a shift occurred and "revolution" had come to mean the subversion or overthrow of tyrants. Rebellion, specifically, was a subversion of the laws. Revolution was personal. So we had the American Revolution, which dumped George III out of the colonies, and the French Revolution, which gave us the murder of Louis XVI and the spectacle of a nation devouring itself. If you're a Marxist you can recast that to mean one class destroying another. At any rate, the French Revolution was a bloodbath and "revolution" began to get a bad name as far as monarchists were concerned. By that time, "revolution" was developing into the word we know today—not just the overthrow of a tyrant but action based on the belief in a new principle. Revolution became a political idea, not just a political act.

The Russian Revolution, the Chinese Revolution, the Cuban Revolution—by now "revolution" is the powerful word, not "rebellion." In the late 1960's and early 1970's young Americans used the word "revolution" indiscriminately. True, they wanted political power, they were opposed to tyrants and believed in a new political principle (or an old one, depending on your outlook) called participatory democracy. However, that period of unrest, with its attendant creativity, did not produce a revolution. The word quickly became corrupted until by the 80's "revolution" was a word used to sell running shoes.

Whither goest thou, Revolution?

GLOSSARY

Abstract and concrete are ways of describing important qualities of language. Abstract words are not associated with real, material objects that are related directly to the five senses. Such words as "love," "wisdom," "patriotism," and "power" are abstract because they refer to ideas rather than to things. Concrete language, on the other hand, names things that can be perceived by the five senses. Words like "table," "smoke," "lemon," and "halfback" are concrete. Generally you should not be too abstract in writing. It is best to employ concrete words naming things that can be seen, touched, smelled, heard, or tasted in order to support your more abstract ideas.

Allusion is a reference to some literary, biographical, or historical event. It is a "figure of speech" (a fresh, useful comparison) used to illuminate an idea. For instance, if you want to state that a certain national ruler is insane, you might refer to him as a "Nero"—an allusion to the emperor who burned Rome.

Alternating method in comparison and contrast involves a point-by-point treatment of the two subjects that you have selected to discuss. Assume that you have chosen five points to examine in a comparison of the Volkswagen "Jetta" (subject A) and the Honda "Accord" (subject B): cost, comfort, gas mileage, road handling, and frequency of repair. In applying the alternating method, you would begin by discussing cost in relation to A + B; then comfort in relation to A + B; and so on. The alternating method permits you to isolate points for a balanced discussion.

Ambiguity means uncertainty. A writer is ambiguous when using a word, phrase, or sentence that is not clear. Ambiguity usually results in misunderstanding, and should be avoided in essay writing. Always strive for clarity in your compositions.

Analogy is a form of figurative comparison that uses a clear illustration to explain a difficult idea or function. It is unlike a formal comparison in that its subjects of comparison are from different categories or areas. For example, an analogy likening "division of labor" to the activity of bees in a hive makes the first concept more concrete by showing it to the reader through the figurative comparison with the bees.

Antonym is a word that is opposite in meaning to that of another word: "hot" is an antonym of "cold"; "fat" is an antonym of "thin"; "large" is an antonym of "small."

Argumentation is a type of writing in which you offer reasons in favor of or against something. (See Chapter 11, pp. 368–371.)

Audience refers to the writer's intended readership. Many essays (including most in this book) are designed for a general audience, but a writer may also try to reach a special group. For example, William Zinsser in his essay "Simplicity" (p. 32) might expect to appeal more to potential writers than to the general reading public. Similarly, Linda Bird Francke's "The Ambivalence of Abortion" (p. 341) might have special relevance for young married women, and Elizabeth Wong's "The Struggle to Be an All-American Girl" (p. 119) could mean something particularly special to young Chinese-Americans. The intended audience affects many of the writer's choices, including level of diction, range of allusions, types of figurative language, and so on.

Block method in comparison and contrast involves the presentation of all information about the first subject (A), followed by all information about the second subject (B). Thus, using the objects of comparison explained in the discussion of the "alternating method" (see p. 445), you would for the block method first present all five points about the Volkswagen. Then you would present all five points about the Honda. When using the block method, remember to present the same points for each subject, and to provide an effective transition in moving from subject A to subject B.

Causal analysis is a form of writing that examines causes and effects of events or conditions as they relate to a specific subject (see Chapter 10, pp. 327–330).

Characterization is the description of people. As a particular type of description in an essay, characterization attempts to capture as vividly as possible the features, qualities, traits, speech, actions, and personality of individuals.

Chronological order is the arrangement of events in the order that they happened. You might use chronological order to trace the history of the Vietnam War, to explain a scientific process, or to present the biography of a close relative or friend. When you order an essay by chronology, you are moving from one step to the next in time.

Classification is a pattern of writing in which the author divides a subject into categories and then groups elements in each of those categories according to their relation to each other (see Chapter 8, pp. 257–261).

Clichés are expressions that were once fresh and vivid, but have become tired and worn from overuse. "I'm so hungry that I could eat a horse" is a typical cliché. People use clichés in conversation, but writers generally should avoid them.

Closings or "conclusions" are endings for your essay. Without a closing, your essay is incomplete, leaving the reader with the feeling that something important has been left out. There are numerous closing possibilities available to writers: summarizing main points in the essay; restating the main idea; using an effective quotation to bring the essay to an end; offering the reader the climax to a series of events; returning to the conclusion and echoing it; offering a solution to a problem; emphasizing the topic's significance; or setting a new frame of reference by generalizing from the main thesis. Whatever type of closing you use, make certain that it ends the essay in a firm and emphatic way.

Coherence is a quality in effective writing that results from the careful ordering of each sentence in a paragraph, and each paragraph in the essay. If an essay is coherent, each part will grow naturally and logically from those parts that come before it. Coherence depends on the writer's ability to organize materials in a logical way, and to order segments so that the reader is carried along easily from start to finish. The main devices used in achieving coherence are transitions, which help to connect one thought with another.

Colloquial language is language used in conversation and in certain types of informal writing, but rarely in essays, business writing, or research papers. There is nothing wrong with colloquialisms like "gross," "scam," or "rap" when used in conversational settings. However, they are often unacceptable in essay writing—except when used sparingly for special effects.

Comparison/contrast is a pattern of essay writing treating similarities and differences between two subjects. (See Chapter 6, pp. 188–191.)

Composition is a term used for an essay or for any piece of writing that reveals a careful plan.

Conclusion (See *Closings*)

Concrete (See *Abstract and concrete*)

Connotation/denotation are terms specifying the way a word has meaning. Connotation refers to the "shades of meaning" that a word might have because of various emotional associations it calls up for writers and readers alike. Words like "American," "physician," "mother," "pig," and "San Francisco" have strong connotative overtones to them. With denotation, however, we are concerned not with the suggestive meaning of a word but with its exact, literal meaning. Denotation refers to the "dictionary definition" of a word—its exact meaning. Writers must understand the connotative and denotative value of words, and must control the shades of meaning that many words possess.

Context clues are hints provided about the meaning of a word by another word or words, or by the sentence or sentences coming before or after it. Thus in the sentence, "Mr. Rome, a true *raconteur*, told a story that thrilled the guests," we should be able to guess at the meaning of the italicized word by the context clues coming both before and after it. (A "raconteur" is a person who tells good stories.)

Definition is a method of explaining a word so that the reader knows what you mean by it. (See Chapter 7, pp. 220–224.)

Derivation is how a word originated and where it came from. Knowing the origin of a word can make you more aware of its meaning, and more able to use it effectively in writing. Your dictionary normally lists abbreviations (for example, O.E. for Old English, G. for Greek) for word origins and sometimes explains fully how they came about.

Description is a type of writing that uses details of sight, color, sound, smell, and touch to create a word picture and to explain or illustrate an idea. (See Chapter 3, pp. 81–84.)

Dialogue is the exact duplication in writing of something people say to each other. Dialogue is the reproduction of speech or conversation; it can add concreteness and vividness to an essay, and can also help to reveal character. When using dialogue, writers must be careful to use correct punctuation. Moreover, to use dialogue effectively in essay writing, you must develop an ear for the way other people talk, and an ability to create it accurately.

Diction refers to the writer's choice or use of words. Good diction reflects the topic of the writing. Baldwin's diction, for example, can be rather formal, despite his purpose of expressing deeply felt emotions. Malcolm X's diction is more varied, including subtle descriptions in standard diction and conversational sarcasms. Levels of diction refer both to the purpose of the essay and to the writer's audience. Skillful choice of the level of diction keeps the reader intimately involved with the topic.

Division is that aspect of classification (see Chapter 8, pp. 257–261) in which the writer divides some large subject into categories. For example, you might divide "fish" into saltwater and freshwater fish; or "sports" into team and individual sports. Division helps writers to split large and potentially complicated subjects into parts for orderly presentation and discussion.

Effect is a term used in causal analysis (see Chapter 10, pp. 327–330) to indicate the outcome or expected result of a chain of happenings. When dealing with the analysis of effects, writers should determine whether they want to work with immediate or final effects, or both. Thus, a writer analyzing the effects of an accidental nuclear explosion might choose to analyze effects immediately after the blast, as well as effects that still linger.

Emphasis suggests the placement of the most important ideas in key positions in the essay. Writers can emphasize ideas simply by placing important ones at the beginning or at the end of the paragraph or essay. But several other techniques help writers to emphasize important ideas: (1) key words and ideas can be stressed by repetition; (2) ideas can be presented in climactic order, by building from lesser ideas at the beginning to the main idea at the end; (3) figurative language (for instance, a vivid simile) can call attention to a main idea; (4) the relative proportion of detail offered to support an idea can emphasize its importance; (5) comparison and contrast of an idea with other ideas can emphasize its importance; and (6) mechanical devices like underlining, capitalizing, and using exclamation points (all of which should be used sparingly) can stress significance.

Essay is the name given to a short prose work on a limited topic. Essays take many forms, ranging from a familiar narrative account of an event in your life to explanatory, argumentative, or critical investigations of a subject. Normally, in one way or the other, an essay will convey the writer's personal ideas about the subject.

Euphemism is the use of a word or phrase simply because it seems less distasteful or less offensive than another word. For instance, "mortician" is a euphemism for "undertaker"; "sanitation worker" for "garbage collector."

Fable is a narrative with a moral (see Chapter 4, pp. 114–118). The story from which the writer draws the moral can be either true or imaginary. When writing a fable, a writer must clearly present the moral to be derived from the narrative, as Rachel Carson does in "A Fable for Tomorrow."

Figurative language, as opposed to "*literal,*" is a special approach to writing that departs from what is typically a concrete, straightforward style. It involves a vivid, imaginative comparison that goes beyond plain or ordinary statements. For instance, instead of saying that "Joan is wonderful," you could write that "Joan is like a summer's rose" (a *simile*); "Joan's hair is wheat, pale and soft and yellow" (a *metaphor*); "Joan is my Helen of Troy" (an *allusion*); or use a number of other comparative approaches. Note that Joan is not a rose, her hair is not wheat, nor is she some other person named Helen.

Figurative language is not logical; instead, it requires an ability on the part of the writer to create an imaginative comparison in order to make an idea more striking.

Flashback is a narrative technique in which the writer begins at some point in the action and then moves into the past in order to provide necessary background information. Flashback adds variety to the narrative method, enabling writers to approach a story not only in terms of straight chronology, but in terms of a back-and-forth movement. However, it is at best a very difficult technique and should be used with great care.

General/specific words are necessary in writing, although it is wise to keep your vocabulary as specific as possible. General words refer to broad categories and groups, while specific words capture with more force and clarity the nature of a term. The distinction between general and specific language is always a matter of degree. "A woman walked down the street" is more general than "Mrs. Walker walked down Fifth Avenue," while "Mrs. Webster, elegantly dressed in a muslin suit, strolled down Fifth Avenue" is more specific than the first two examples. Our ability to use specific language depends on the extent of our vocabulary. The more words we know, the more specific we can be in choosing words.

Hyperbole is obvious and intentional exaggeration.

Illustration is the use of several examples to support an idea (see Chapter 5, pp. 150–153).

Imagery is clear, vivid description that appeals to our sense of sight, smell, touch, sound, or taste. Much imagery exists for its own sake, adding descriptive flavor to an essay, as when Richard Selzer in "The Discus Thrower" writes, "I unwrap the bandages from the stumps, and begin to cut away the black scabs and the dead, glazed fat with scissors and forceps. A shard of white bone comes loose." However, imagery can also add meaning to an essay. For example, in Francke's essay, the pattern of imagery connected with the setting and procedure of her abortion alerts the reader to the importance of that event in the author's life. Again, when Orwell writes at the start of "A Hanging," "It was in Burma, a sodden morning of the rains. A sickly light, like yellow tinfoil, was slanting over the high walls into the jail yard," we see that the author uses imagery to prepare us for the sombre and terrifying event to follow. Writers can use imagery to contribute to any type of wording, or they can rely on it to structure an entire essay. It is always difficult to invent fresh, vivid description, but it is an effort that writers must make if they wish to improve the quality of their prose.

Introductions are the beginning or openings of essays. Introductions should perform a number of functions. They should alert the reader to the subject, set the limits of the essay, and indicate what the *thesis* (or main idea) will be. Moreover, they should arouse the reader's interest in the subject, so that the reader will want to continue reading into the essay. There are several devices available to writers that will aid in the development of sound introductions.

1. Simply state the subject and establish the thesis. See the essay by E. B. White (p. 271).
2. Open with a clear, vivid description of a setting that will become important as your essay advances. Save your thesis for a later stage, but indicate what your subject is. See the essay by Ehrlich (p. 105).
3. Ask a question or a series of questions, which you might answer in the introduction or in another part of the essay. See the Jordan essay (p. 233).
4. Tell an anecdote (a short, self-contained story of an entertaining nature) that serves to illuminate your subject. See the Staples essay (p. 163).
5. Use comparison or contrast to frame your subject and to present the thesis. See the Goodman essay (p. 204).
6. Establish a definitional context for your subject. See the Scott essay (p. 225).
7. Begin by stating your personal attitude toward a controversial issue. See the Baldwin essay (p. 409).

These are only some of the devices that appear in the introductions to essays in this text. Writers can also ask questions, give definitions, or provide personal accounts—there are many techniques that can be used to develop introductions. The important thing to remember is that you *need* an introduction to an essay. It can be a single sentence or a much longer paragraph, but it must accomplish its purpose—to introduce readers to the subject, and to engage them so that they want to explore the essay further.

Irony is the use of language to suggest the opposite of what is stated. Writers use irony to reveal unpleasant or troublesome realities that exist in life, or to poke fun at human weaknesses and foolish attitudes. For instance, in "A Hanging," the men who are in charge of the execution engage in laughter and lighthearted conversation after the event. There is irony in the situation and in their speech because we sense that they are actually very tense—almost unnerved—by the hanging; their laughter is the opposite of what their true emotional state actually is. Many situations and conditions lend themselves to ironic treatment.

Jargon is the use of special words associated with a specific area of knowledge or a specific profession. It is similar to "shop talk" that members of a certain trade might know, but not necessarily people outside it. For example, in Bettelheim's essay there are several terms or applications of jargon relating to psychology, while the medical jargon in Kozol's essay helps him defend his opinion on a nonmedical subject. Use jargon sparingly in your writing, and be certain to define all specialized terms that you think your readers might not know.

Journalese is a level of writing associated with prose types normally found in newspapers and popular magazines. A typical newspaper article tends to present information factually or objectively; to use simple language and simple sentence structure; and to rely on relatively short paragraphs. It also stays close to the level of conversational English without becoming chatty or colloquial.

Metaphor is a type of figurative language in which an item from one category is compared briefly and imaginatively with an item from another area. Writers create metaphors to assign meaning to a word in an original way.

Narration is telling a story in order to illustrate an important idea (see Chapter 4, pp. 114–118).

Objective/subjective writing refers to the attitude that writers take toward their subject. When writers are objective, they try not to report their own personal feelings about their subject. They attempt to control, if not eliminate, their own attitude toward the topic. Thus in the essay by Roiphe (pp. 331–335), we learn about the underlying causes of divorce, but the writer doesn't try to convince us of the rightness or wrongness of it. Many essays, on the other hand, reveal the authors' personal attitudes and emotions. In Frisina's essay (pp. 65–67), the author's personal approach to the process of reading seems clear. She takes a highly subjective approach to the topic. Other essays, such as Kozol's (see pp. 378–382), blend the two approaches to help balance the author's expression of a strong opinion. For some kinds of college writing, such as business or laboratory reports, research papers, or literary analyses, it is best to be as objective as possible. But for many of the essays in composition courses, the subjective touch is fine.

Order is the manner in which you arrange information or materials in an essay. The most common ordering techniques are *chronological order* (involving time sequence); *spatial order* (involving the arrangement of descriptive details); *process order* (involving a step-by-step approach to an activity); *deductive order* (in which you offer a thesis and then the evidence to support it); and *inductive order* (in which you present evidence first and build toward the thesis). Some rhetorical patterns such as comparison and contrast, classification, and argumentation require other ordering techniques. Writers should select those ordering principles that permit them to present materials clearly.

Paradox is a statement that *seems* to be contradictory but actually contains an element of truth. Writers use it in order to call attention to their subject.

Parallelism is a variety of sentence structure in which there is "balance" or coordination in the presentation of elements. "I came, I saw, I conquered" is a good example of parallelism, presenting both pronouns and verbs in a coordinated manner. Parallelism can also be applied to several sentences and to entire paragraphs (see the Brady essay, pp. 372–374). It can be an effective way to emphasize ideas.

Personification is giving an object, thing, or idea lifelike or human qualities. For instance, Ray Bradbury personifies Halloween when he writes that it "didn't just stroll into our yards" (see p. 155). Like all forms of figurative writing, personification adds freshness to description, and makes ideas vivid by setting up striking comparisons.

Point of view is the angle from which a writer tells a story. Many personal or informal essays take the *first-person* (or "I") point of view, as the essays by Malcolm X, Saroyan, Moon, Hughes, Orwell, Didion, Miller, and others reveal. The first-person "I" point of view is natural and fitting for essays when the writer wants to speak in a familiar and intimate way to the reader. On the other hand, the *third-person* point of view ("he," "she," "it," "they") distances the reader somewhat from the writer. The third-person point of view is useful in essays where writers are not talking exclusively about themselves, but about other people, things, and events, as in the essays by Kozol, Carson, and White. Occasionally, the second-person ("you") point of view will appear in essays, notably in essays involving process analysis where the writer directs the reader to do something; part of Ernest Hemingway's essay (which also uses a third-person point of view) uses this strategy. Other point-of-view combinations are possible when a writer wants to achieve a special effect. For example, Fridman's and Keillor's essays combine *first-* and *second-person* points of view. The position that you take as a writer depends largely on the type of essay you write.

Prefix is one or more syllables attached to the front of another word in order to influence its meaning or to create a new word. A knowledge of prefixes and their meanings aids in establishing the meanings of words and in increasing the vocabulary that we use in writing. Common prefixes and their meanings include *bi-*(two), *ex-*(out, out of), *per-*(through), *pre-*(before), *re-*(again), *tele-*(distant), and *trans-* (across, beyond).

Process analysis is a pattern of writing that explains in a step-by-step way the methods for doing something or reaching a desired end (see Chapter 9, pp. 296–298).

Proposition is the main point in an argumentative essay. It is like a *thesis* except that it usually presents an idea that is debatable or can be disputed.

Purpose refers to what a writer hopes to accomplish in a piece of writing. For example, the purpose may be *to convince* the reader to adopt a certain viewpoint (as in Kincaid's essay "The Ugly Tourist," p. 416), *to explain* a process (as in Garrison Keillor's "How to Write a Personal Letter," p. 305), or to allow the reader *to feel a dominant impression* (as in Gretel Ehrlich's "A River's Route," p. 105). Purpose helps a writer to determine which expository technique will dominate the essay's form, as well as what kinds of supporting examples will be used. Purpose and *audience* are often closely related.

Refutation is a technique in argumentative writing where you recognize and deal effectively with the arguments of your opponents. Your own argument will be stronger if you can refute—prove false or wrong— all opposing arguments.

Root is the basic part of a word. It sometimes aids us in knowing what the larger word means. Thus if we know that the root *doc-* means "teach" we might be able to figure out a word like "doctrine." *Prefixes* and *suffixes* are attached to roots to create words.

Sarcasm is a sneering or taunting attitude in writing. It is designed to hurt by ridiculing or criticizing. Basically, sarcasm is a heavy-handed form of irony, as when an individual says, "Well, you're exactly on time, aren't you" to someone who is an hour late, and says it with a sharpness in the voice, designed to hurt. Writers should try to avoid sarcastic writing and to use more acceptable varieties of irony and satire to criticize their subject.

Satire is the humorous or critical treatment of a subject in order to expose the subject's vices, follies, stupidities, and so forth. Brady, for instance, satirizes stereotyped notions of wives, hoping to change these attitudes by revealing them as foolish. Satire is a better weapon than sarcasm in the hands of the writer because satire is used to correct, whereas sarcasm merely hurts.

Sentimentality is the excessive display of emotion in writing, whether it is intended or unintended. Because sentimentality can distort the true nature of a situation, writers should use it cautiously, or not at all. They should be especially careful when dealing with certain subjects, for example the death of a loved one, the remembrance of a mother or father, a ruined romance, the loss of something valued, that lend themselves to sentimental treatment. Only the best writers—like Thomas, Francke, Hughes, and others in this text—can avoid the sentimental traps rooted in their subjects.

Simile is an imaginative comparison using "like" or "as." When Orwell writes, "A sickly light, like yellow tinfoil, was slanting over the high walls into the jail yard," he uses a vivid simile in order to reinforce the dull description of the scene.

Slang is a level of language that uses racy and colorful expressions associated more often with speech than with writing. Slang expressions like "Mike's such a dude" or "She's a real fox" should not be used in essay writing, except when the writer is reproducing dialogue or striving for a special effect. Hughes is one writer in this collection who uses slang effectively to convey his message to the reader.

Suffix is a syllable or syllables appearing at the end of a word and influencing its meaning. As with prefixes and roots, you can build vocabulary and establish meanings by knowing about suffixes. Some typical suffixes are *-able* (capable of), *-al* (relating to), *-ic* (characteristic of), *-ion* (state of), *-er* (one who), which appear often in standard writing.

Symbol is something that exists in itself but also stands for something else. Thus the "stumps" in paragraph 20 of Selzer's essay "The Discus Thrower" are not just the patient's amputated legs, but they serve as symbols of the man's helplessness and immobility. As a type of figurative language, the symbol can be a strong feature in an essay, operating to add depth of meaning, and even to unify entire essays.

Synonym is a word that means roughly the same as another word. In practice, few words are exactly alike in meaning. Careful writers use synonyms to vary word choice, without ever moving too far from the shade of meaning intended.

Theme is the central idea in an essay; it is also often termed the *thesis.* Everything in an essay should support the theme in one way or another.

Thesis is the main idea in an essay. The *thesis sentence,* appearing early in the essay, and normally somewhere in the first paragraph, serves to convey the main idea to the reader in a clear way. It is always useful to state your central idea as soon as possible, and before you introduce other supporting ideas.

Title for an essay should be a short, simple indication of the contents of your essay. Titles like "The Ugly Tourist," "I Want a Wife," "The Ambivalence of Abortion," and "How to Write a Personal Letter" convey the central subjects of these essays in brief, effective ways. Others, such as "Survival" and "Night Walker," also convey the central idea, but more abstractly. Always provide titles for your essays.

Tone is the writer's attitude toward his or her subject or material. An essay writer's tone may be objective ("Arizona 87"), ironic ("I Want a Wife"), comic ("Slice of Life"), nostalgic ("Moon on a Silver Spoon"), or a reflection of numerous other attitudes. Tone is the "voice" that you give to an essay; every writer should strive to create a "personal voice" or tone that will be distinctive throughout any type of essay under development.

Transition is the linking of one idea to the next in order to achieve essay coherence (see *Coherence*). Transitions are words that connect these ideas. Among the most common techniques to achieve smooth transition are: (1) repeating a key word or phrase; (2) using a pronoun to refer back to a key word or phrase; (3) relying on traditional connectives like "thus," "for example," "moreover," "therefore," "however," "finally," "likewise," "afterward," and "in conclusion"; (4) using parallel structure (see *Parallelism*); and (5) creating a sentence or an entire paragraph that serves as a bridge from one part of your essay to the next. Transition is best achieved when the writer presents ideas and details carefully and in logical order. Try not to lose the reader by failing to provide for adequate transition from idea to idea.

Unity is that feature in an essay where all material relates to a central concept and contributes to the meaning of the whole. To achieve a unified effect in an essay, the writer must design an introduction and conclusion, maintain a consistent tone and point of view, develop middle paragraphs in a coherent manner, and always stick to the subject, never permitting unimportant elements to enter. Thus, unity involves a successful blending of all elements that go into the creation of a sound essay.

Vulgarisms are words that exist below conventional vocabulary, and are not accepted in polite conversation. Always avoid vulgarisms in your own writing, unless they serve an illustrative purpose.

Acknowledgments

McGraw-Hill wishes to thank the copyright owners for permission to reprint the following copyrighted works.

Margaret Atwood, "Survival," excerpt from *Survival: A Thematic Guide to Canadian Literature.* Reprinted with the permission of Stoddart Publishing Co. Limited, Toronto.

James T. Baker, "How Do We Find the Students in a World of Academic Gymnastics and Worker Ants?" in *Chronicle of Higher Education,* 1982. Reprinted by permission of the author.

Russell Baker, "Slice of Life" from *There's a Country in My Cellar.* Copyright © 1990 by Russell Baker. Reprinted by permission of Don Congdon Associates, Inc.

James Baldwin, "If Black English Isn't a Language, Then Tell Me What Is?" in *The New York Times,* July 29, 1979. Copyright © 1979 by The New York Times Company. Reprinted by permission.

Bruno Bettelheim, "Fairy Tales and Modern Stories" from *The Uses of Enchantment: The Meaning and Importance of Fairy Tales.* Copyright © 1975, 1976 by Bruno Bettelheim. Reprinted by permission of Alfred A. Knopf, Inc.

Ray Bradbury, "Tricks! Treats! Gangway!" in *Reader's Digest,* October 1975. Copyright © 1975 by Ray Bradbury. Reprinted by permission of Don Congdon Associates, Inc.

Judy Brady, "I Want a Wife" from *The First Ms. Reader.* Copyright © 1970 by Judy Brady. Reprinted by permission of Judy Brady.

Suzanne Britt, "Fun, Oh Boy, Fun. You Could Die from It." in *The New York Times,* December 23, 1979. Copyright © 1979 by The New York Times Company. Reprinted by permission.

Rita Mae Brown, "To the Victor Belongs the Language," excerpt from *Starting from Scratch: A Different Kind of Writer's Manual.* Copyright ©

1988 by Speakeasy Productions Inc. Used by permission of Bantam Books, a division of Bantam Doubleday Dell Publishing Group, Inc.

Rachel Carson, "A Fabel for Tomorrow" from *Silent Spring.* Copyright © 1962 by Rachel L. Carson, renewed 1990 by Roger Christie. Reprinted by permission of Houghton Mifflin Company.

Annie Dillard, "An American Childhood," excerpt from *An American Childhood.* Copyright © 1987 by Annie Dillard. Reprinted by permission of HarperCollins Publishers, Inc.

Michael Dorris, "The Minnie Mouse Kitchen" in *Parents,* December 1990. Copyright © 1990 by Gruner & Jahr USA Publishing. Reprinted by permission of *Parents* magazine.

Nora Ephron, "Living with My VCR," from *The New York Times Magazine,* December 23, 1984. Copyright © 1984 by Nora Ephron. Reprinted by permission of International Creative Management, Inc.

Gretel Ehrlich, "A River's Route," from 1989 Sierra Club Calendar. Copyright © 1989 by Gretel Ehrlich. Reprinted by permission of the author.

Linda Bird Francke, "The Ambivalence of Abortion," in *The New York Times,* May 14, 1976. Copyright © 1976 by The New York Times Company. Reprinted by permission.

Leonid Fridman, "America Needs Its Nerds," in *The New York Times,* January 11, 1990. Copyright © 1990 by The New York Times Company. Reprinted by permission.

Ellen Tashie Frisina, "See Spot Run: Teaching My Grandmother to Read." Reprinted by permission of Houghton Mifflin Company.

Ellen Goodman, "The Tapestry of Friendships," from *Close to Home.* Copyright © 1979 by The Washington Post Company. Reprinted by permission of Simon & Schuster, Inc.

Ernest Hemingway, "Camping Out," from *Ernest Hemingway Dateline: Toronto,* edited by William White. Copyright © 1985 by Mary Hemingway, John Hemingway, Patrick Hemingway, and Gregory Hemingway. This article first appeared in *The Toronto Star Weekly,* June 26, 1920. Reprinted with the permission of Charles Scribner's Sons, an imprint of Macmillan Publishing Company.

Langston Hughes, "Salvation," from *The Big Sea.* Copyright 1940 by Langston Hughes, renewed © 1968 by Arna Bontemps and George Houston Bass. Reprinted by permission of Hill and Wang, a division of Farrar, Straus and Giroux, Inc.

Pico Iyer, "Is It Really That Wacky?" from *Time,* November 18, 1991. Copyright © 1991 by Time, Inc. Reprinted by permission.

Susan Jacoby, "When Bright Girls Decide That Math Is 'a Waste of Time'," *The New York Times,* June 2, 1983. Copyright © 1983 by Susan Jacoby. Reprinted by permission of Georges Borchardt, Inc., for the author.

Robert Ragaini, "A Question of Manhood," in *Newsday,* March 29, 1987. Reprinted by permission of the author.

Richard Rodriguez, "Complexion," from *Hunger of Memory.* Copyright © 1982 by Richard Rodriguez. Reprinted by permission of David A. Godine, Publisher.

Anne Roiphe, "Why Marriages Fail," in *Family Weekly,* February 27, 1983. Copyright © 1983 by Anne Roiphe. Reprinted by permission of the author.

William Saroyan, "Why I Write," from *The William Saroyan Reader.* Copyright © 1990 by the William Saroyan Foundation. Reprinted by permission of the William Saroyan Foundation.

Juliet B. Schor, "Americans Work Too Hard" (1991). Reprinted by permission of the author.

Jack Denton Scott, "What's a Bagel?" in *Reader's Digest,* June 1988. Copyright © 1988 by The Reader's Digest Association, Inc. Reprinted by permission.

Richard Selzer, "The Discus Thrower," from *Confessions of a Knife.* Copyright © 1979 by Richard Selzer. Reprinted by permission of William Morrow & Company, Inc. Publishers.

Brent Staples, "Night Walker," originally published in *Ms.* Magazine as "Walk on By: A Black Man Ponders His Power to Alter Public Space." Reprinted by permission of the author.

Jeannine Stein, "Shaved Heads and Pop-Tarts," in *Los Angeles Times,* July 8, 1992. Reprinted by permission of the *Los Angeles Times.*

William Stafford, "Writing," From "A Way of Writing." Reprinted by permission from *Field: Contemporary Poetry and Poetics,* no. 2, Oberlin College Press.

Amy Tan, "Mother Tongue," in *The Threepenny Review.* Copyright © 1990 by Amy Tan. Reprinted by permission of the author and the Sandra Dijkstra Literary Agency.

Lewis Thomas, "Death in the Open," from *The Lives of a Cell.* Copyright © 1973 by the Massachusetts Medical Society. Originally published in the *New England Review of Medicine.* Reprinted by permission of Viking Penguin, a division of Penguin Books USA Inc.

Judith Viorst, "Friends, Good Friends—and Such Good Friends," originally appeared in *Redbook.* Copyright © 1977 by Judith Viorst. Reprinted by permission of Lescher & Lescher, Ltd.

Patricia Volk, "A Family of Firsts," in *The New York Times,* October 4, 1987. Copyright © 1987 by The New York Times Company. Reprinted by permission.

Alice Walker, "The Place Where I Was Born," from *Her Blue Body,* in *Essence,* June 1991, pp. 58–59. All rights reserved.